METHUEN'S MONOGRAPHS ON PHYSICAL SUBJECTS

General Editors:

B. L. WORSNOP, B.Sc., Ph.D.
G. K. T. CONN, M.A., Ph.D.

Elasticity, Fracture and Flow

Elasticity, Fracture and Flow

with Engineering and Geological Applications

J. C. JAEGER

*Professor of Geophysics
in the Australian National University*

METHUEN & CO LTD
and
SCIENCE PAPERBACKS

First published 1956
by Methuen & Co Ltd
11 New Fetter Lane, London EC4 P4EE
Second edition, 1962
Reprinted with corrections, 1964
Third edition, 1969

First published as a Science Paperback 1971

Printed in Great Britain by
Butler & Tanner Ltd, Frome and London

SBN 412 20890 3

Distributed in the U.S.A.
by Barnes & Noble Inc.

PREFACE

IN this monograph I have attempted to set out, in as elementary a form as possible, the basic mathematics of the theories of elasticity, plasticity, viscosity, and rheology, together with a discussion of the properties of the materials involved and the way in which they are idealized to form a basis for the mathematical theory. There are many mathematical text-books on these subjects, but they are largely devoted to methods for the solution of special problems, and, while the present book may be regarded as an introduction to these, it is also intended for the large class of readers such as engineers and geologists who are more interested in the detailed analysis of stress and strain, the properties of some of the materials they use, criteria for flow and fracture, and so on, and whose interest in the theory is rather in the assumptions involved in it and the way in which they affect the solutions than in the study of special problems.

The first chapter develops the analysis of stress and strain rather fully, giving, in particular, an account of Mohr's representations of stress and of finite homogeneous strain in three dimensions. In the second chapter, on the behaviour of materials, the stress-strain relations for elasticity (both for isotropic and simple anisotropic substances), viscosity, plasticity and some of the simpler rheological models are described. Criteria for fracture and yield, including Mohr's, Tresca's and von Mises's, are discussed in detail with some applications. In the third chapter the equations of motion and equilibrium are derived, and a number of special problems are solved. These have been chosen partly because of their practical importance and partly to illustrate the differences in behaviour between the various types of material discussed.

In the second edition of this monograph a new chapter was added to cover briefly the mathematical and experimental foundations of structural geology and the rapidly developing engineering subject of rock mechanics. In this, the discussion of the various criteria for fracture was greatly amplified and extended to porous media. A fuller treatment of stresses in the Earth's crust, faulting, and related matters was given. Also, because of their importance in rock mechanics and in the measurement of stress, a number of problems on the stresses and displacements around underground openings was solved and a brief introduction to the use of the complex variable in the treatment of such problems was given.

In this third edition, the treatment of rock mechanics in the fourth chapter has been extended in the light of modern developments. The main addition has been a fifth chapter dealing with the fundamentals of structural geology, most of the mathematical prologomena for which have been set out in the earlier chapters. This deals largely with the applications of the theory of finite homogeneous strain, the elementary theory of folding, and the orientation of particles in a deforming medium. This chapter has been written in collaboration with Dr N. Gay of the University of the Witwatersrand who has supplied the geological knowledge: my part has merely been that of stating it in a manner which conforms with the theory developed in the earlier parts of the book.

J. C. JAEGER

CANBERRA
January 1969

CONTENTS

CHAPTER I

STRESS AND STRAIN

1. INTRODUCTORY

THE mathematical theories of elasticity, viscosity, and plasticity all follow the same course.[1] Firstly, the notions of stress and strain are developed; secondly, a stress-strain relationship between these quantities or their derivatives is assumed which idealizes the behaviour of actual materials; and finally, using this relationship, equations of motion or equilibrium are set up which enable the state of stress or strain to be calculated when a body is subjected to prescribed forces.

In this chapter the analysis of stress and strain will be developed in detail. The analysis of stress is essentially a branch of statics which is concerned with the detailed description of the way in which the stress at a point of a body varies. In two dimensions this involves only elementary trigonometry, and the two-dimensional theory not only gives a useful insight into the general behaviour but also is applicable to many important problems: it is therefore given in detail in § 3. The three-dimensional theory is given in § 4, leading to Mohr's representation in § 5 which provides a simple geometrical construction for the stress across any plane.

The analysis of strain is essentially a branch of geometry which deals with the deformation of an assemblage of particles. For the development of the theory of elasticity only the case of infinitesimal strain is needed, and a conventional treatment of this is given in §§ 10, 11. This theory is formally very similar to that of stress and, as before, the two- and three-dimensional cases have been worked out independently.

[1] On elasticity, reference may be made to Timoshenko, *Theory of Elasticity* (McGraw-Hill, 1934); Southwell, *Theory of Elasticity* (Oxford, Ed. 2, 1941); Love, *Mathematical Theory of Elasticity* (Cambridge, Ed. 4, 1927): on viscosity, Lamb, *Hydrodynamics* (Cambridge, Ed. 4, 1916); Milne-Thomson, *Theoretical Hydrodynamics* (Macmillan, Ed. 2, 1949): on plasticity, Nadai, *Theory of Flow and Fracture of Solids* (McGraw-Hill, Ed. 2, 1950); Prager and Hodge, *Theory of Perfectly Plastic Solids* (Wiley, 1951); Hill, *Plasticity* (Oxford, 1950).

The assumptions involved in the theory of infinitesimal strain are so restrictive that many important details of the geometrical changes which take place during straining are obscured; also, some knowledge of finite strain is needed when, as in geology, large strains occur. For these reasons the theory of finite homogeneous strain is developed by the methods of coordinate geometry in two dimensions in § 7, and by Mohr's method in three dimensions in § 9.

2. STRESS. DEFINITIONS AND NOTATION

In order to specify the forces acting within a body we proceed as follows: at the point O in which we are interested we take a definite direction OP and a small flat surface of area δA perpendicular to OP and containing O, Fig. 1 (a). OP is called the normal to the surface δA, and the side of the surface in the direction OP will be called the 'positive side' and that in the opposite direction the 'negative side'.

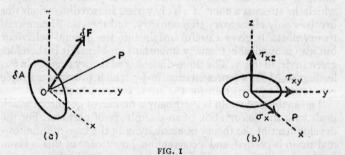

FIG. 1

At each point of the surface δA the material on one side of the surface exerts a definite force upon the material on the other side, so that conditions in the solid as a whole would be unaltered if a cut were made across the surface δA and these forces inserted. The resultant of all the forces exerted by the material on the positive side of δA upon the material on the other side will be a force δF (strictly, there will be a couple also, but, as the area δA is supposed to be infinitesimally small, this is negligible).

The limit of the ratio $\delta F/\delta A$ as δA tends to zero is called the *stress at the point O across the plane whose normal is in the direction OP*, so that, writing p_{OP} for this,

$$p_{OP} = \lim_{\delta A \to 0} \frac{\delta F}{\delta A}. \quad . \quad . \quad . \quad (1)$$

p_{OP} is a vector whose magnitude has the dimensions of force per unit area,[1] so that the situation is that, for every point O of the body and every direction through it, a vector p_{OP} exists such that if we take a small surface of area δA through O and normal to OP, the material on the positive side of the surface exerts a force $p_{OP}\,\delta A$ upon the material on the negative side, and, action and reaction being equal and opposite, the material on the negative side exerts a force $-p_{OP}\delta A$ upon that on the positive side.

It is usual in developing the mathematical theory of a subject to begin by setting up a rectangular coordinate system, so at the point O we take mutually perpendicular right-handed axes Ox, Oy, Oz. Suppose, now, that OP is taken in the direction Ox as in Fig. 1 (*b*) so that the area δA is in the yz-plane. The vector p_{Ox} can be resolved into components

$$\sigma_x, \quad \tau_{xy}, \quad \tau_{xz}, \quad . \quad . \quad . \quad (2)$$

in the directions Ox, Oy, Oz, respectively. The component σ_x, which is in the direction Ox and normal to the area δA, is called the *direct* or *normal* component of stress, while the components τ_{xy}, τ_{xz}, which are in the plane of the area δA, are called *transverse*, or *shear* stresses. This notation of σ for a normal stress and τ for a shear stress will always be used: in the latter the *first suffix denotes the direction of the normal* to the small area δA and the *second suffix the direction in which the component acts*; for normal stresses, only one suffix is needed since the direction of the component is the same as that of the normal to the surface. If the normal component of the stress across a surface is positive [2] it is called a tensile stress (it tends to pull the material on the positive

---

[1] Occasionally in geological and engineering literature the term stress is used in a general way and 'unit stress' for the force per unit area in the present sense. p_{OP} is sometimes called a *stress vector* or a *traction*.

[2] In many cases a conventional sign opposite to the one chosen here is used: that is, σ is reckoned positive when compressive. This is, perhaps, more convenient if the stresses considered are most frequently compressive as in geological work, but the present convention is the most natural in mathematics and the one more widely used.

side of the surface away from that on the negative side), and if it is negative it is called a compressive stress.

In the same way the stress at O across a plane whose normal is in the direction Oy will have components

$$\tau_{yx}, \sigma_y, \tau_{yz}, \quad . \quad\quad . \quad\quad . \quad\quad . \quad (3)$$

and that across a plane whose normal is in the direction Oz will have components

$$\tau_{zx}, \tau_{zy}, \sigma_z . \quad . \quad\quad . \quad\quad . \quad\quad . \quad (4)$$

The nine quantities (2) to (4), which are collected in (5), are called the *stress-components* or *components of stress* at the point O:

$$\left.\begin{matrix} \sigma_x & \tau_{xy} & \tau_{xz} \\ \tau_{yx} & \sigma_y & \tau_{yz} \\ \tau_{zx} & \tau_{zy} & \sigma_z \end{matrix}\right\} \quad . \quad\quad . \quad\quad . \quad (5)$$

It will be found in §§ 3, 4 that the stress across any plane through O can be expressed in terms of them so that they give a complete specification of the stress at the point (in fact, it will appear also that $\tau_{yz}=\tau_{zy}$, $\tau_{zx}=\tau_{xz}$, $\tau_{xy}=\tau_{yx}$, so that only six quantities are needed to specify the stress at a point).

For the complete specification of the stress in a body it is necessary to know the stress-components at each point of it.

It is unfortunate that several different notations are in use in the Theory of Elasticity: the one given above is that commonly used by Continental and American writers, in particular in the works of Timoshenko, Nadai, and Prager and Hodge referred to above. The most common English notation, that of Love and Southwell, uses X_x, Y_x, Z_x in place of (2) for the components of the vector p_{Ox}, and so on. Other commonly used symbols for these quantities are p_{xx}, p_{xy}, p_{xz}, and $\widehat{xx}$, $\widehat{xy}$, $\widehat{xz}$, etc., where the latter set consists of the suffixes of the former set with a distinguishing mark above.

The stress-components in (5) are in fact the components of a mathematical entity called a tensor, and tensor analysis is much used in developing the higher parts of the theory. The main change, from the present point of view, is that the notation x, y, z for the coordinates is replaced by x_1, x_2, x_3, so that they are specified by the numbers 1, 2, 3. The stress-components across a plane whose normal is in the direction of Ox are then written p_{11}, p_{12}, p_{13}, and the stress tensor is described, and used in the analysis, as p_{rs}, where values of r and s running from 1 to 3 give the various components.

3. STRESSES IN TWO DIMENSIONS

Many of the difficulties of the theory of elasticity are caused by the rather complicated three-dimensional geometry involved. Frequently, a clear understanding of the fundamental ideas can be obtained comparatively simply by studying the corresponding two-dimensional problem. Accordingly, we shall first develop the theory of stress in two dimensions, taking Ox, Oy of Fig. 2 in the plane of the paper and Oz perpendicular to it, and assuming that

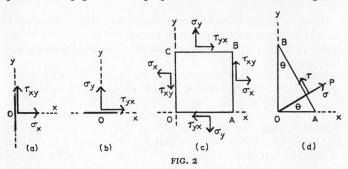

FIG. 2

all quantities are independent of z, so that it need never be considered at all.[1]

Then, as in Fig. 2 (a), the force per unit area at O exerted across the plane $x=0$ by the material on its right upon that on its left has components σ_x, τ_{xy}. Similarly, as in Fig. 2 (b), the force per unit area at O across the plane $y=0$, has components τ_{yx}, σ_y.

Next we have to consider the relations between these components. In doing this we assume that the solid is at rest and that all quantities vary slowly from point to point, so that the stress-components at a point a small distance a from O will be very nearly equal to those at O (in fact, they will differ from them by quantities of the order of magnitude of a, which we are assuming to be small).

[1] The theory of this section is applicable to several important situations in three dimensions; these will be discussed in § 14.

Now consider the forces on a very small square of material $OABCO$ whose side length $OA=OC=a$ is very small. The forces on the face AB (per unit length perpendicular to the plane of the paper) are $a\sigma_x$ and $a\tau_{xy}$, as shown in Fig. 2 (c). Those on the face CO, remembering that they are those exerted by the material to the left on the material to the right, are $-a\sigma_x$ and $-a\tau_{xy}$, and so on. Considering the equilibrium of the square as a whole, it appears that the forces are in equilibrium, but that there is a couple

$$a^2(\tau_{xy}-\tau_{yx})$$

tending to rotate the square to the left. Since the system is in equilibrium this couple must vanish so we must have

$$\tau_{xy}=\tau_{yx}. \qquad . \qquad . \qquad . \qquad . \qquad (1)$$

Thus, of the four stress-components with which we started, only three are independent. It is convenient to continue to use both τ_{xy} and τ_{yx} as they arise in different ways, remembering that they are equal.

Next we show that the stress across any plane through O whose normal OP is inclined at θ to Ox can be expressed in terms of σ_x, σ_y and τ_{xy}. To do this we calculate the normal and shear stresses σ and τ across a plane AB near to O: these will differ very little from those across a parallel plane through O. As shown by the arrow in Fig. 2 (d), τ is reckoned positive when it is directed towards the left of OP. Considering the equilibrium of the triangle OAB (or rather a prism of unit height on this as base), resolving in the direction of OP, writing a for the length AB, and remembering that to get the force across any face the stresses must be multiplied by the area of the face, we get

$$a\sigma=a\sin\theta(\tau_{yx}\cos\theta+\sigma_y\sin\theta)+a\cos\theta(\sigma_x\cos\theta+\tau_{xy}\sin\theta), \quad .(2)$$

and, resolving in the direction AB,

$$a\tau=a\sin\theta(-\tau_{yx}\sin\theta+\sigma_y\cos\theta)+a\cos\theta(-\sigma_x\sin\theta+\tau_{xy}\cos\theta). \quad (3)$$

Thus, remembering that $\tau_{xy}=\tau_{yx}$, (2) and (3) become

$$\sigma=\sigma_x\cos^2\theta+2\tau_{xy}\sin\theta\cos\theta+\sigma_y\sin^2\theta, \qquad . \qquad (4)$$

$$\tau=(\sigma_y-\sigma_x)\sin\theta\cos\theta+\tau_{xy}(\cos^2\theta-\sin^2\theta). \qquad . \qquad (5)$$

The calculation above is for the angle θ acute, but it is easy to show with a similar figure that it holds for all values of θ with the convention mentioned above, namely, that τ is measured positively in the direction to the left of the outward normal.

(4) and (5) may be used to give the stress-components $\sigma_{x'}$, $\sigma_{y'}$, $\tau_{x'y'}$ relative to axes Ox', Oy' rotated through θ from Ox and Oy. $\tau_{x'y'}$ is given by (5); and using (4) for angles θ and $\frac{1}{2}\pi+\theta$, respectively, gives

$$\sigma_{x'}=\sigma_x \cos^2\theta+2\tau_{xy}\sin\theta\cos\theta+\sigma_y\sin^2\theta, \qquad . \quad (6)$$

$$\sigma_{y'}=\sigma_x \sin^2\theta-2\tau_{xy}\sin\theta\cos\theta+\sigma_y\cos^2\theta. \qquad . \quad (7)$$

Adding (6) and (7) gives

$$\sigma_{x'}+\sigma_{y'}=\sigma_x+\sigma_y, \qquad . \qquad . \qquad . \quad (8)$$

that is, if the axes are rotated, this quantity $\sigma_x+\sigma_y$ remains unchanged or *invariant* though both σ_x and σ_y themselves change. Such invariants are of great importance in the development of the theory.

Equations (4) and (5) give a complete description of the way in which the stress at a point varies with direction: we now discuss this behaviour in detail and obtain some simple geometrical representations for it. Differentiating (4) gives

$$\frac{d\sigma}{d\theta}=2(\sigma_y-\sigma_x)\sin\theta\cos\theta+2\tau_{xy}(\cos^2\theta-\sin^2\theta) \qquad . \quad (9)$$

$$=2\tau. \qquad . \qquad . \qquad . \qquad . \qquad . \qquad . \quad (10)$$

It follows from (9) that the normal stress is a maximum or minimum (and also from (5) that the shear stress is zero) when θ is given by

$$\tan 2\theta=\frac{2\tau_{xy}}{\sigma_x-\sigma_y} \qquad . \qquad . \qquad . \quad (11)$$

Equation (11) defines two directions at right angles such that the normal stresses over them are the greatest and least at the point and the shear stresses over them are zero. These are called the *principal axes of stress* and the stresses over them are called the *principal stresses*. The notation σ_1 and σ_2 will always be used for the principal stresses, σ_1 being assumed to be the greatest (algebraically), and, as always, tensile stresses being reckoned positive. The effect of (11) is that, if the state of stress at a point is known, the directions of the principal axes and the values of the principal stresses can be found immediately. When these are known, it is much simpler to take the principal axes as axes of reference: thus, if we take these as new x and y axes, we have $\sigma_x=\sigma_1$, $\sigma_y=\sigma_2$, $\tau_{xy}=0$

in (4) and (5), and the normal and shear stresses across a plane whose normal is inclined at θ to the x-axis become

$$\sigma = \sigma_1 \cos^2 \theta + \sigma_2 \sin^2 \theta, \qquad . \qquad . \qquad . \quad (12)$$

$$= \tfrac{1}{2}(\sigma_1 + \sigma_2) + \tfrac{1}{2}(\sigma_1 - \sigma_2) \cos 2\theta, \qquad . \qquad . \quad (13)$$

$$\tau = -\tfrac{1}{2}(\sigma_1 - \sigma_2) \sin 2\theta. \qquad . \qquad . \quad (14)$$

The way in which σ and τ vary with θ is shown graphically in Fig. 3: it appears that τ has its greatest magnitude $\tfrac{1}{2}(\sigma_1 - \sigma_2)$ when θ is 45° or 135°.

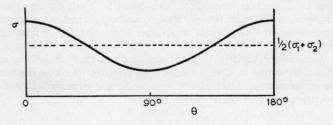

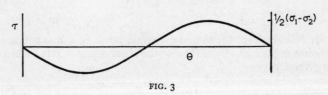

FIG. 3

Another representation which is of great theoretical importance is obtained by taking a line from the origin in the direction θ of the normal and choosing a point P on it whose distance r from the origin is

$$r = k\sigma^{-\frac{1}{2}}, \quad \text{so that} \quad \sigma = k^2/r^2, \qquad . \qquad . \quad (15)$$

where σ is the normal stress across the plane and k is a constant. Putting (15) in (12) gives

$$\sigma_1 r^2 \cos^2 \theta + \sigma_2 r^2 \sin^2 \theta = k^2,$$

so that, since $x = r \cos \theta$, $y = r \sin \theta$ are the coordinates of the point P, it lies on the conic

$$\sigma_1 x^2 + \sigma_2 y^2 = k^2. \qquad . \qquad . \quad (16)$$

This is called the *stress conic*: it is an ellipse if σ_1 and σ_2 have the same sign, and an hyperbola if they have opposite signs. The same conic, rotated through an angle given by (11), would have been found if we had discussed (4) in the same way, and the principal axes and principal stresses could have been found from it: this is, in fact, a common approach and one which can be used in three dimensions, cf. § 4. If σ becomes negative it must be replaced by $|\sigma|$ in (15) to get a real representation.

In the same way, using $\tau = k^2/r^2$ in (14), the shear stress can be represented by a point on the hyperbola

$$(\sigma_2 - \sigma_1)xy = k^2. \qquad . \qquad . \qquad . \qquad (17)$$

Yet another representation, *Mohr's circle diagram*, is the simplest and most useful of all.

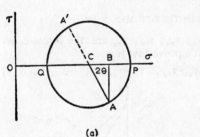

FIG. 4

Suppose that, as in Fig. 4 (a), we mark off lengths $OP = \sigma_1$ and $OQ = \sigma_2$ on a line and draw a circle on PQ as diameter with centre C. Then, if A is a point on the circle such that the angle PCA measured clockwise is 2θ and AB is perpendicular to PQ, it follows from (13) and (14) that $OB = \sigma$ and $AB = \tau$. That is, A represents the direct and shear stresses across the plane θ plotted on a (σ, τ) plane, and the circle of centre C is their locus as θ changes. This representation holds for all signs of σ_1 and σ_2 provided, as always, that $\sigma_1 > \sigma_2$: it also holds for all values of θ, in particular, A' gives the values of σ and τ for a plane perpendicular to that corresponding to A. It follows immediately from Fig. 4 (a) that the shear stress has its greatest magnitude when $\theta = 45°$ and $135°$.

This diagram may be used to give a simple construction for the principal stresses and axes if the quantities σ_x, σ_y, τ_{xy} are known.

The x- and y-axes, being at right angles, will correspond to two points such as A and A' in Fig. 4 (a), and a circle on AA' as diameter will give the circle of Fig. 4 (a). Thus, as in Fig. 4 (b), we plot the points E, (σ_x, τ_{xy}) and [1] $F(\sigma_y, -\tau_{xy})$ and draw a circle on EF as diameter. Then in Fig. 4 (b) OH and OG are the principal stresses and the angle EKH is twice the angle between the principal axes and the old x- and y-axes. Also the maximum value of the shear stress is seen to be

$$\tfrac{1}{2}[(\sigma_x-\sigma_y)^2+4\tau_{xy}{}^2]^{\frac{1}{2}}, \qquad . \qquad . \qquad (18)$$

and the principal stresses are

$$\tfrac{1}{2}(\sigma_x+\sigma_y)\pm\tfrac{1}{2}[(\sigma_x-\sigma_y)^2+4\tau_{xy}{}^2]^{\frac{1}{2}}, \qquad . \qquad . \qquad (19)$$

these could have been found by differentiating (5).

4. STRESSES IN THREE DIMENSIONS

Suppose that σ_x, σ_y, σ_z, τ_{yz}, τ_{zx}, τ_{xy} are the stress-components as defined in § 2. We prove first that

$$\tau_{xy}=\tau_{yx}, \quad \tau_{yz}=\tau_{zy}, \quad \tau_{zx}=\tau_{xz}. \qquad . \qquad . \qquad (1)$$

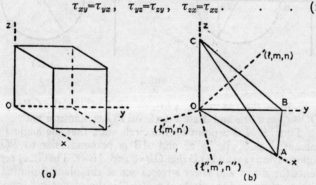

FIG. 5

To do this we consider the equilibrium of the small rectangular parallelepiped of Fig. 5 (a).

[1] The reason for the negative sign in $-\tau_{xy}$ is that our convention is that in (5) shear stress is measured positively in the direction to the left of the normal. For the y-axis, this is the negative x-direction, while τ_{yx} is measured in the positive x-direction.

Just as in § 3, the fact that the resultant couple about the z-axis must vanish gives $\tau_{xy} = \tau_{yx}$, and, similarly, the other two directions give the other two of equations (1). As in two dimensions, it is convenient to use both τ_{xy} (for the y-component of stress across the plane $x=0$) and τ_{yx} (in the sense of the x-component of stress across the plane $y=0$), remembering always that they are equal.

Next, we have to calculate the stress across a plane through O whose normal has direction cosines [1] (l, m, n) relative to the axes Ox, Oy, Oz. To do this we consider the equilibrium of the small tetrahedron $OABC$ whose face ABC is normal to the direction (l, m, n) and has area ω so that the areas of the faces OAB, OBC and OCA are $\omega n, \omega l, \omega m$, respectively. Suppose that p_x, p_y, p_z are the components of the stress across the face ABC in the directions of the axes Ox, Oy, Oz. Then, resolving in the direction Ox we get

$$\omega p_x = \omega l \sigma_x + \omega m \tau_{yx} + \omega n \tau_{zx},$$
$$p_x = l \sigma_x + m \tau_{yx} + n \tau_{zx} \quad . \quad . \quad . \quad . \quad (2)$$

And, similarly,

$$p_y = l \tau_{xy} + m \sigma_y + n \tau_{zy}, \quad . \quad . \quad . \quad . \quad (3)$$
$$p_z = l \tau_{xz} + m \tau_{yz} + n \sigma_z . \quad . \quad . \quad . \quad (4)$$

(2), (3) and (4) specify the stress across the plane whose normal has direction cosines (l, m, n), but they are not very directly related to this plane since they refer to the coordinate directions Ox, Oy, Oz. The most interesting quantities are the normal stress σ and the shear stress τ across the plane.

The normal stress follows immediately by resolving in the direction of the normal and using (2) to (4). This gives

$$\sigma = l p_x + m p_y + n p_z \quad . \quad . \quad . \quad . \quad . \quad (5)$$
$$= l(l\sigma_x + m\tau_{yx} + n\tau_{zx}) + m(l\tau_{xy} + m\sigma_y + n\tau_{zy}) + n(l\tau_{xz} + m\tau_{yz} + n\sigma_z)$$
$$= l^2\sigma_x + m^2\sigma_y + n^2\sigma_z + 2mn\tau_{yz} + 2nl\tau_{zx} + 2lm\tau_{xy} . \quad . \quad . \quad (6)$$

In the same way, the shear stress across the plane could be resolved into its components τ' in the direction (l', m', n') and τ''

[1] The direction cosines l, m, n of a line are the cosines of the angles it makes with the mutually perpendicular lines Ox, Oy, Oz. They are connected by the relation $l^2 + m^2 + n^2 = 1$. The angle ψ between lines of direction cosines (l, m, n) and (l', m', n') is given by $\cos \psi = ll' + mm' + nn'$. Cf. Bell, *Coordinate Geometry of Three Dimensions* (Macmillan, Ed. 2, 1912).

in the direction (l'', m'', n''), where (l', m', n') and (l'', m'', n'') are two perpendicular directions in the plane. Thus, resolving in the direction (l', m', n') gives

$$\tau' = l'p_x + m'p_y + n'p_z$$
$$= ll'\sigma_x + mm'\sigma_y + nn'\sigma_z + (mn' + m'n)\tau_{yz} + (nl' + n'l)\tau_{zx}$$
$$+ (lm' + l'm)\tau_{xy}, \quad . \quad (7)$$

with a similar formula for τ''. This, however, is not the simplest method of calculating the shear stress.

(6) and (7) may also be regarded as formulae for change of axes which give the stress-components for the new system of rectangular axes (l, m, n), (l', m', n'), (l'', m'', n'') in terms of those for the system $Oxyz$.

Returning to the normal stress (6) we proceed to find its maximum and minimum values. The analysis is similar to that of § 3, but is a little more complicated since two of l, m, n may vary independently, the third being related to them by

$$l^2 + m^2 + n^2 = 1. \quad . \quad . \quad . \quad (8)$$

Thus the conditions for σ to be stationary are

$$\frac{\partial \sigma}{\partial l} = 0, \quad \frac{\partial \sigma}{\partial m} = 0, \quad . \quad . \quad (9)$$

together with, by (8),

$$l + n\frac{\partial n}{\partial l} = 0, \quad m + n\frac{\partial n}{\partial m} = 0 \quad . \quad . \quad (10)$$

Using (6) and the values (2) to (4) of p_x, p_y, p_z, (9) become

$$p_x + p_z\frac{\partial n}{\partial l} = 0, \quad p_y + p_z\frac{\partial n}{\partial m} = 0. \quad . \quad . \quad (11)$$

Combining (10) and (11) gives

$$\frac{p_x}{l} = \frac{p_y}{m} = \frac{p_z}{n}. \quad . \quad . \quad . \quad (12)$$

Now p_x, p_y, p_z are the components of the stress across the plane (l, m, n), so (12) states that when the direction (l, m, n) is such that the normal stress is stationary, the components of the stress across this plane are in the direction (l, m, n), that is, that the stress across the plane is purely normal and so the shear stress in it is zero. If σ is the value of this normal stress, (12) may be written

$$p_x = l\sigma, \quad p_y = m\sigma, \quad p_z = n\sigma. \quad . \quad . \quad (13)$$

Using (2) to (4) in (13) gives

$$\left.\begin{array}{l} l(\sigma_x-\sigma)+m\tau_{yx}+n\tau_{zx}=0, \\ l\tau_{xy}+m(\sigma_y-\sigma)+n\tau_{zy}=0, \\ l\tau_{xz}+m\tau_{yz}+n(\sigma_z-\sigma)=0. \end{array}\right\} \quad . \quad . \quad . \quad (14)$$

The equations (14) are a set of three homogeneous linear equations for l, m, n. It is known from algebraical theory that they have a non-zero solution only if σ is a root of the equation

$$\begin{vmatrix} \sigma_x-\sigma & \tau_{yx} & \tau_{zx} \\ \tau_{xy} & \sigma_y-\sigma & \tau_{zy} \\ \tau_{xz} & \tau_{yz} & \sigma_z-\sigma \end{vmatrix}=0. \quad . \quad . \quad . \quad (15)$$

This is a cubic in σ, it has three (real) roots $\sigma_1, \sigma_2, \sigma_3$, and corresponding to each of these (14) gives a set of direction cosines $(l_1, m_1, n_1), (l_2, m_2, n_2), (l_3, m_3, n_3)$, respectively. These directions are, in fact, mutually perpendicular; this may be proved by multiplying equations (14) containing σ_1, l_1, m_1, n_1, by l_2, m_2, n_2, in order, adding, and then subtracting from the sum the expression formed by interchanging the suffixes 1 and 2 in it; this gives

$$(\sigma_1-\sigma_2)(l_1l_2+m_1m_2+n_1n_2)=0,$$

and so, if $\sigma_1 \neq \sigma_2$, the directions (l_1, m_1, n_1) and (l_2, m_2, n_2) are perpendicular.

The final conclusion is that there are three mutually perpendicular directions called the *principal axes of stress* in which the stress is purely normal and has values $\sigma_1, \sigma_2, \sigma_3$ which are called the *principal stresses*. We shall always use the convention $\sigma_1 > \sigma_2 > \sigma_3$, and, since the normal stress has been proved above to be stationary in the direction of the principal axes, it follows that σ_1 is (algebraically) the greatest, and σ_3 the least, normal stress at the point. If the six stress-components at the point are given numerically, it is possible by the above analysis to determine the principal axes and stresses; needless to say, it is rarely necessary to do this, and the importance of the present discussion is that it gives a complete picture of the way in which the normal stress varies.

The geometrical representation of § 3 may also be used. If we plot a point distant $k/\sqrt{\sigma}$ from the origin in the direction (l, m, n), its coordinates will be

$$x=lk/\sqrt{\sigma}, \quad y=mk/\sqrt{\sigma}, \quad z=nk/\sqrt{\sigma},$$

and putting these values in (6) it follows that the point lies on the quadric surface [1]

$$x^2\sigma_x+y^2\sigma_y+z^2\sigma_z+2yz\tau_{yz}+2zx\tau_{zx}+2xy\tau_{xy}=k^2. \qquad . \quad (16)$$

This surface is called the *stress quadric*. It is known from pure geometry that it has a set of three mutually perpendicular axes referred to which the terms of type yz, zx, xy in (16) disappear. These are the principal axes found above.

It should be mentioned that the determination of principal axes is unique only if none of σ_1, σ_2, σ_3 are equal. If they are all equal (hydrostatic pressure or tension), the stress quadric is a sphere and any set of mutually perpendicular axes may be taken as principal axes. If two of them are equal, there is rotational symmetry about the third axis.

If the determinant in (15) is expanded the equation may be written

$$\sigma^3-I_1\sigma^2-I_2\sigma-I_3=0, \qquad . \qquad . \qquad . \quad (17)$$

where

$$I_1=\sigma_x+\sigma_y+\sigma_z, \qquad . \qquad . \qquad . \quad (18)$$

$$I_2=-(\sigma_y\sigma_z+\sigma_z\sigma_x+\sigma_x\sigma_y)+\tau_{yz}{}^2+\tau_{zx}{}^2+\tau_{xy}{}^2, \qquad . \quad (19)$$

$$I_3=\sigma_x\sigma_y\sigma_z+2\tau_{yz}\tau_{zx}\tau_{xy}-\sigma_x\tau_{yz}{}^2-\sigma_y\tau_{zx}{}^2-\sigma_z\tau_{xy}{}^2. \qquad . \quad (20)$$

These quantities I_1, I_2, I_3 apparently depend upon the initial choice of the x-, y- and z-axes, but the roots of (17) which are the principal stresses are independent of this choice and so the coefficients I_1, I_2, I_3 must also be independent of it. Put in another way, the quantities I_1, I_2, I_3 must remain unchanged or *invariant* if the axes are changed. Thus, for example, since I_1 is unchanged by the change from the original axes to principal axes, we must have

$$\sigma_x+\sigma_y+\sigma_z=\sigma_1+\sigma_2+\sigma_3. \qquad . \qquad . \qquad . \quad (21)$$

Invariants always play an important part in the mathematical development of a theory: a quantity similar to I_2 will be found in § 27 to be fundamental in the theory of plasticity.

---

[1] The general surface of the second degree (i.e., that which is cut by any line in two points) is called a quadric surface. It may be an ellipsoid, a hyperboloid (of one or two sheets), a paraboloid, a cone, or a pair of planes according to the sign and nature of the coefficients. The process of reduction to principal axes is effectively that given above, cf. Bell, *loc. cit.* If σ in (6) becomes negative it is necessary to replace it by $|\sigma|$ to get a complete geometrical representation of its variation in this way.

In the same way, it follows from (18) and (19) that

$$\sigma_y\sigma_z+\sigma_z\sigma_x+\sigma_x\sigma_y-\tau_{yz}{}^2-\tau_{zx}{}^2-\tau_{xy}{}^2=\sigma_2\sigma_3+\sigma_3\sigma_1+\sigma_1\sigma_2 \,, \quad . \quad (22)$$

$$\sigma_x{}^2+\sigma_y{}^2+\sigma_z{}^2+2\tau_{yz}{}^2+2\tau_{zx}{}^2+2\tau_{xy}{}^2=\sigma_1{}^2+\sigma_2{}^2+\sigma_3{}^2. \quad . \quad (23)$$

The whole of the preceding discussion has been based on the normal stress for the excellent reasons that this is the easiest to discuss and that it leads directly to the principal axes. Having found

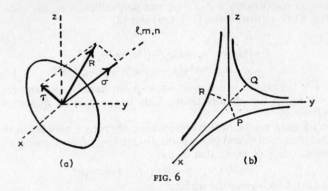

FIG. 6

these we may begin the subsequent discussion by taking the axes of reference to be principal axes.

Suppose, now, that Ox, Oy, Oz are the principal axes and σ_1, σ_2, σ_3 the associated principal stresses with, as usual, $\sigma_1>\sigma_2>\sigma_3$. Then by (2) to (4) the components (in the directions of the axes) of the stress across a plane whose normal is in the direction (l, m, n) are

$$p_x=l\sigma_1\,, \quad p_y=m\sigma_2\,, \quad p_z=n\sigma_3\,. \quad . \quad . \quad (24)$$

It follows, by (8), that

$$\frac{p_x{}^2}{\sigma_1{}^2}+\frac{p_y{}^2}{\sigma_2{}^2}+\frac{p_z{}^2}{\sigma_3{}^2}=1, \quad . \quad . \quad . \quad (25)$$

so that the components of the stress across any plane lie on an ellipsoid sometimes called the ellipsoid of stress.

The normal stress σ across the plane is by (6)

$$\sigma=l^2\sigma_1+m^2\sigma_2+n^2\sigma_3\,. \quad . \quad . \quad . \quad (26)$$

Also the magnitude R of the stress across the plane follows immediately from (24): it is

$$R=(p_x{}^2+p_y{}^2+p_z{}^2)^{\frac{1}{2}}$$
$$=(l^2\sigma_1{}^2+m^2\sigma_2{}^2+n^2\sigma_3{}^2)^{\frac{1}{2}}. \qquad . \quad . \quad (27)$$

The shear stress across the plane could be found from (7), but since we are chiefly interested in its magnitude τ it is a little simpler to calculate it by resolving the stress R across the plane into its components τ and σ in, and perpendicular to, the plane, Fig. 6 (a), so that, using (27), (26) and (8)

$$\tau^2=R^2-\sigma^2 \qquad . \qquad . \qquad . \qquad . \qquad . \qquad . \qquad (28)$$
$$=l^2\sigma_1{}^2+m^2\sigma_2{}^2+n^2\sigma_3{}^2-(l^2\sigma_1+m^2\sigma_2+n^2\sigma_3)^2$$
$$=(\sigma_1-\sigma_2)^2l^2m^2+(\sigma_2-\sigma_3)^2m^2n^2+(\sigma_3-\sigma_1)^2n^2l^2. \qquad (29)$$

For the case in which $\sigma_1=\sigma_2=\sigma_3=-p$, we have by (29) and (26) $\tau=0$, $\sigma=-p$ for all directions. This is the case of *hydrostatic pressure p*.

To get a geometrical representation of (29) we may (as in the case of normal stress) plot a point distant $k/\sqrt{\tau}$ from the origin in the direction (l, m, n), that is, put

$$x=kl/\sqrt{\tau}, \quad y=km/\sqrt{\tau}, \quad z=kn/\sqrt{\tau}$$

in (29), which gives the surface

$$(\sigma_1-\sigma_2)^2x^2y^2+(\sigma_2-\sigma_3)^2y^2z^2+(\sigma_3-\sigma_1)^2z^2x^2=k^4. \qquad . \qquad (30)$$

This is a fourth degree surface in place of the simple second-degree surface (16) for the normal stress. Its intersections with the planes $x=0$, $y=0$, $z=0$ are rectangular hyperbolae as in Fig. 6 (b). It may be remarked that the coefficients in (30) are always positive so that the type of the surface does not vary with the signs of σ_1, σ_2, σ_3 in the way that (16) does.

Because of the importance of shear in the failure of materials, it is obviously necessary to discuss the variation of τ with l, m, n in great detail. The first problem is to find when τ is a maximum. To do this we put $n^2=1-l^2-m^2$ in (29), which gives

$$\tau^2=l^2(\sigma_1{}^2-\sigma_3{}^2)+m^2(\sigma_2{}^2-\sigma_3{}^2)+\sigma_3{}^2-\{l^2(\sigma_1-\sigma_3)+m^2(\sigma_2-\sigma_3)+\sigma_3\}^2. \quad (31)$$

In this l and m may be varied independently, and the condition for τ to be stationary is

$$\frac{\partial \tau}{\partial l}=0, \quad \frac{\partial \tau}{\partial m}=0. . \qquad . \qquad . \qquad . \qquad (32)$$

Now, from (31)

$$\tau\frac{\partial\tau}{\partial l}=l(\sigma_1-\sigma_3)\{(\sigma_1+\sigma_3)-2[l^2(\sigma_1-\sigma_3)+m^2(\sigma_2-\sigma_3)+\sigma_3]\}, \qquad (33)$$

$$\tau\frac{\partial\tau}{\partial m}=m(\sigma_2-\sigma_3)\{(\sigma_2+\sigma_3)-2[l^2(\sigma_1-\sigma_3)+m^2(\sigma_2-\sigma_3)+\sigma_3]\}. \qquad (34)$$

To make both (33) and (34) vanish as required by (32), we may take $l=0$ so that (33) is satisfied, and, using this value in (34) we must have

$$1-2m^2=0$$

to make the second bracket in (34) vanish. Thus if

$$l=0, \quad m=2^{-\frac{1}{2}}, \quad n=2^{-\frac{1}{2}}, \qquad . \qquad . \qquad . \quad (35)$$

τ is stationary, and by (29) its value is $\frac{1}{2}(\sigma_2-\sigma_3)$.

Similarly, (33) and (34) can be satisfied by taking $m=0$ in (34), which leads to

$$l=2^{-\frac{1}{2}}, \quad m=0, \quad n=2^{-\frac{1}{2}}, \qquad . \qquad . \qquad . \quad (36)$$

with the value $\frac{1}{2}(\sigma_1-\sigma_3)$ of τ.

Finally, by an independent calculation, τ has a stationary value of $\frac{1}{2}(\sigma_1-\sigma_2)$ in the direction

$$l=2^{-\frac{1}{2}}, \quad m=2^{-\frac{1}{2}}, \quad n=0. \qquad . \qquad . \qquad . \quad (37)$$

These stationary values of the shear stress are called the principal shear stresses and are denoted by τ_1, τ_2, τ_3, so that

$$\tau_1=\tfrac{1}{2}(\sigma_2-\sigma_3), \quad \tau_2=\tfrac{1}{2}(\sigma_1-\sigma_3), \quad \tau_3=\tfrac{1}{2}(\sigma_1-\sigma_2). \qquad . \quad (38)$$

Since, by our convention, $\sigma_1>\sigma_2>\sigma_3$, the greatest of (38) is τ_2. Using (35), (36) and (37) in (26), it appears that the normal stresses corresponding to τ_1, τ_2, τ_3, are

$$\tfrac{1}{2}(\sigma_2+\sigma_3), \quad \tfrac{1}{2}(\sigma_3+\sigma_1), \quad \tfrac{1}{2}(\sigma_1+\sigma_2). \qquad . \qquad . \quad (39)$$

Finally, it follows from (35), (36) and (37) that the directions for which the shear stress is stationary bisect the angles between the principal axes, so that stationary values of the shear correspond to the points P, Q, R of Fig. 6 (b).

The most important result is that *the greatest shear stress is $\frac{1}{2}(\sigma_1-\sigma_3)$ and is across a plane whose normal bisects the angle between the directions of greatest and least principal stress.*

In § 5 the variation of both normal and shear stress will be discussed by an extension of the method of Mohr described in § 3.

The discussion above and that of § 5 only consider the magnitude of the shear stress; this is sufficient for many purposes. If, in addition, the direction of the shear stress is needed, it can be found from the fact that it lies in the plane of (l, m, n) and the resultant stress whose components are $l\sigma_1$, $m\sigma_2$, $n\sigma_3$ by (24). The direction cosines of the normal to this plane are proportional to

$$mn(\sigma_3-\sigma_2), \quad nl(\sigma_1-\sigma_3), \quad lm(\sigma_2-\sigma_1). \qquad . \qquad . \qquad (40)$$

The direction of the shear is the intersection of this plane with the plane (l, m, n), and thus its direction cosines are proportional to

$$\left.\begin{array}{c} l\{(\sigma_1-\sigma_3)n^2-(\sigma_2-\sigma_1)m^2\}, \quad m\{(\sigma_2-\sigma_1)l^2-(\sigma_3-\sigma_2)n^2\}, \\ n\{(\sigma_3-\sigma_2)m^2-(\sigma_1-\sigma_3)l^2\}. \end{array}\right\} \qquad . \qquad (41)$$

5. MOHR'S REPRESENTATION OF STRESS
IN THREE DIMENSIONS

In two dimensions Mohr's representation provided the most elegant representation of the variation of normal and shear stress with direction, and in three dimensions it proves to do so also.

We start with the equations § 4 (26) and § 4 (28) for the normal and shear stress across the plane whose normal has direction cosines l, m, n, namely

$$\sigma=l^2\sigma_1+m^2\sigma_2+n^2\sigma_3, \qquad . \qquad . \qquad . \qquad (1)$$

$$\tau^2=l^2\sigma_1^2+m^2\sigma_2^2+n^2\sigma_3^2-\sigma^2, \qquad . \qquad . \qquad (2)$$

where
$$l^2+m^2+n^2=1. \qquad . \qquad . \qquad . \qquad (3)$$

Solving (1) to (3) for l^2, m^2, n^2, gives

$$l^2=\frac{(\sigma_2-\sigma)(\sigma_3-\sigma)+\tau^2}{(\sigma_2-\sigma_1)(\sigma_3-\sigma_1)}, \qquad . \qquad . \qquad . \qquad (4)$$

$$m^2=\frac{(\sigma_3-\sigma)(\sigma_1-\sigma)+\tau^2}{(\sigma_3-\sigma_2)(\sigma_1-\sigma_2)}, \qquad . \qquad . \qquad . \qquad (5)$$

$$n^2=\frac{(\sigma_1-\sigma)(\sigma_2-\sigma)+\tau^2}{(\sigma_1-\sigma_3)(\sigma_2-\sigma_3)}. \qquad . \qquad . \qquad . \qquad (6)$$

Now suppose that one direction cosine, say n, is fixed; this implies that the normal to the plane considered makes a fixed angle $\cos^{-1}n$ with the z-axis. Then by (6), σ and τ for such a plane are related by

$$(\sigma_1-\sigma)(\sigma_2-\sigma)+\tau^2=n^2(\sigma_1-\sigma_3)(\sigma_2-\sigma_3),$$

or
$$\tau^2+\{\sigma-\tfrac{1}{2}(\sigma_1+\sigma_2)\}^2=\tfrac{1}{4}(\sigma_1-\sigma_2)^2+n^2(\sigma_1-\sigma_3)(\sigma_2-\sigma_3). \qquad . \qquad (7)$$

That is, plotted on the (σ, τ) plane, σ and τ lie on a circle whose centre is at $(\tfrac{1}{2}(\sigma_1+\sigma_2), 0)$ and whose radius is

$$\{\tfrac{1}{4}(\sigma_1-\sigma_2)^2+n^2(\sigma_1-\sigma_3)(\sigma_2-\sigma_3)\}^{\frac{1}{2}}. \qquad . \qquad . \qquad (8)$$

Plotting the points P, $(\sigma_1, 0)$; Q, $(\sigma_2, 0)$; R, $(\sigma_3, 0)$ in Fig. 7 (a), the centre is at A, and the radius varies from $AQ=\tfrac{1}{2}(\sigma_1-\sigma_2)$ for $n=0$ to $AR=\tfrac{1}{2}(\sigma_1+\sigma_2)-\sigma_3$ for $n=1$, a typical circle of this family being DEF.

In the same way taking l constant in (4) gives the family of circles

$$\tau^2 + \{\sigma - \tfrac{1}{2}(\sigma_2 + \sigma_3)\}^2 = \tfrac{1}{4}(\sigma_2 - \sigma_3)^2 + l^2(\sigma_2 - \sigma_1)(\sigma_3 - \sigma_1) \qquad . \quad (9)$$

with centres at the point B, $(\tfrac{1}{2}(\sigma_2 + \sigma_3),\ 0)$ and radii varying from BQ for $l=0$ to BP for $l=1$, a typical circle being GEH.

Finally, taking m constant in (5) gives the family

$$\tau^2 + \{\sigma - \tfrac{1}{2}(\sigma_1 + \sigma_3)\}^2 = \tfrac{1}{4}(\sigma_1 - \sigma_3)^2 + m^2(\sigma_3 - \sigma_2)(\sigma_1 - \sigma_2) \qquad . \quad (10)$$

with centres at the point C, $(\tfrac{1}{2}(\sigma_1 + \sigma_3),\ 0)$ and radii decreasing from CR for $m=0$ to CQ for $m=1$.

The way in which a point is fixed by its direction cosines may be seen from Fig. 7 (b) in which the points in which a line of direction cosines l, m, n meets an octant of a unit sphere are shown. The circle GEH on

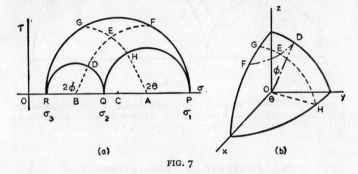

FIG. 7

the unit sphere (the intersection of a cone whose axis is Ox and the sphere) corresponds to the points $l=$const.; if $l=\cos\theta$ the point H in which it meets the xy-plane for which $n=0$ is such that the angle HOx is θ, $l=\cos\theta$, $m=\sin\theta$. Similarly the circle FED corresponds to $n=$const., and if the angle DOz is ϕ, OD is $l=0$, $n=\cos\phi$, $m=\sin\phi$.

Now the circles of centres B and A, Fig. 7 (a), are in fact the two-dimensional Mohr circles for the yz- and xy-planes, but for completeness we shall derive their properties again here. Considering the latter, the stresses corresponding to the point H of Fig. 7 (b) for which $l=\cos\theta$, $m=\sin\theta$, $n=0$, are by § 4 (26) and § 4 (29), respectively,

$$\sigma = \sigma_1\cos^2\theta + \sigma_2\sin^2\theta$$
$$= \tfrac{1}{2}(\sigma_1 + \sigma_2) + \tfrac{1}{2}(\sigma_1 - \sigma_2)\cos 2\theta,$$
$$\tau^2 = \tfrac{1}{4}(\sigma_1 - \sigma_2)^2\sin^2 2\theta.$$

Since the stress [1] at this point is known to be represented by H in Fig. 7 (a) it follows that the angle HAP is 2θ. In the same way it follows that the angle DBR is 2ϕ.

---

[1] Note that here τ is the magnitude of the shear stress. In the two-dimensional discussion of § 3 both sign and magnitude were treated.

This gives a simple, completely geometrical construction for the stress at the point E determined as in Fig. 7 (b) by $l = \cos \theta$, $n = \cos \phi$. Marking off the angles 2θ and 2ϕ as in Fig. 7 (a) gives the points H and D, and the

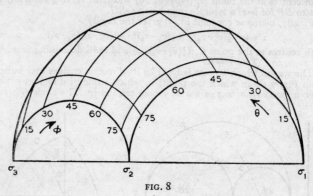

FIG. 8

intersection of circles through them, with centres B and A respectively, gives the required stress. A diagram with a family of such circles is shown in Fig. 8 in which the numbers on the curves are the values of ϕ and θ in degrees.

6. DISPLACEMENT AND STRAIN. INTRODUCTION

When a substance is distorted so that the relative configuration of a system of marked particles $O, P, Q, R, \ldots$ in it is changed in any way, it is said to be strained. The analysis of strain is essentially a branch of geometry which studies such changes of configuration.

Suppose that in Fig. 9 (a) the full lines represent the 'initial' or 'unstrained' position of the substance and the dotted lines the 'final' or 'strained' position, $O', P', Q', \ldots$ being the strained positions of the points $O, P, Q, \ldots$ The vector OO' is called the *displacement* of the point O, and, if the displacement is specified for every point of the substance, the state of strain is completely known.

The ultimate objectives of the theory of elasticity are problems such as the calculation of the displacements in a body which is subjected to known stresses. Before such problems can be discussed, it is necessary to study stress and strain and the relationship between them. Just as in the analysis of stress we assumed a knowledge of certain stresses at a point and then studied in detail the variation of stress with direction, so, in the analysis of strain, we assume that the displacements are known and are given by a formula, and we study in detail the nature of the strain and its variation with direction.

It should be remarked that strain as defined above is a change in *relative* configuration of the particles of the substance. Thus if the displacement corresponds to translation and rotation as a rigid body there is no strain. It is convenient, however, to allow displacements to be quite general, and, in the course of the analysis, to separate out the elements of translation and rotation. It should

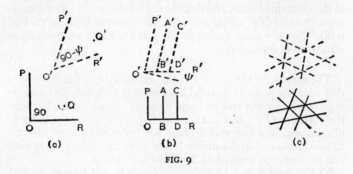

FIG. 9

be understood also that the displacements may have any magnitude; in the problems of elasticity which arise in engineering they are usually quite small, but in problems of plasticity and hydrodynamics to which much of the geometrical theory applies they can be indefinitely large.

The purpose of the analysis of strain is largely to introduce quantities which give a measure of the strain, and to discuss the way in which these vary in the neighbourhood of a point. There are two obvious measures of strain, firstly, the change in the length of a line, and secondly, the change in the angle between two lines or between a line and a plane: these give rise to the notions of extension and shear, respectively.

Suppose that l is the distance between two neighbouring points O and P in the unstrained state, and l' that between the corresponding points O' and P' in the strained state, then ε, the *extension* corresponding to the points O and P in the unstrained state, is defined by

$$\varepsilon = \frac{l' - l}{l}, \quad . \quad . \quad . \quad . \quad (1)$$

that is, it is the ratio of the change in length to the original length. This is not the only quantity of this type in use as a measure of the extensional strain, in fact in discussing finite strain it is more convenient to use the *quadratic elongation* λ defined by

$$\lambda = (l'/l)^2 = (1 + \varepsilon)^2. \quad . \quad . \quad (2)$$

Next, suppose that OP, OR are perpendicular directions at O in the unstrained state, and that the angle between the corresponding directions $O'P'$ and $O'R'$ in the strained state is $\frac{1}{2}\pi - \psi$, cf. Fig. 9 (a). Then the *shear strain* γ at the point O associated with these directions is defined as

$$\gamma = \tan \psi. \quad . \quad . \quad . \quad (3)$$

The reason for the name and the importance of the concept is that near the point O, parallel lines such as OP, BA, DC may be regarded as having slid or been 'sheared' across each other into the positions $O'P'$, $B'A'$, $D'C'$, etc., Fig. 9 (b). Similarly, in three dimensions, if a line and a plane are perpendicular in the unstrained state and in the strained state make an angle of $\frac{1}{2}\pi - \psi$ with one another, the amount of the shear is $\gamma = \tan \psi$.

The general theory [1] indicated above is in fact so complicated as to be almost useless for practical purposes. This is, essentially, because of the fact that straight lines in the unstrained state become curves on straining. There are two simplifying assumptions on which a workable theory is obtained:

(i) *Infinitesimal Strain.* Here it is assumed that at every point of the body the quantities ε and γ defined in (1) and (3) are so small that their squares and product are negligible. This is the normal assumption of the Theory of Elasticity.

[1] The general theory is developed in Love's *Mathematical Theory of Elasticity* (Cambridge, Ed. 4, 1927), also, using more advanced mathematical methods, in Murnaghan, *Finite Deformation of an Elastic Solid* (Wiley, 1951), and Green and Zerna, *Theoretical Elasticity* (Oxford, 1954). Fairly full and elementary discussions of homogeneous strain occur quite early in the literature, e.g. Thomson and Tait, *Treatise on Natural Philosophy*, Vol. 1, § 155 ff., Becker, 'Finite homogeneous strain', *Bull. Geol. Soc. Amer.*, **4** (1893), 13. See also Brace, *ibid.*, **72** (1961), 1059.

(ii) *Homogeneous Strain*. This is a special case of the general theory of finite strain which can be studied by elementary methods. A strain is called homogeneous if all straight lines remain straight lines after straining, and parallel straight lines remain parallel, though their direction may be altered. It follows by elementary geometry from this definition that similar and similarly situated figures at all points of the body are deformed in the same way, cf. Fig. 9 (*c*). This implies that the state of strain may be regarded as being the same all over the body. This is one reason for the name 'homogeneous'.

There are two reasons for studying homogeneous strain: firstly, it will be shown in §§ 10, 11 that in the general case there is a small region in which the strain is homogeneous surrounding any point, so that results proved for homogeneous strain apply in this region; secondly, while the strains occurring in engineering practice are usually infinitesimal, large strains do occur, occasionally in engineering and frequently in geology, and it is very desirable to have a detailed knowledge of their nature in a special case.

The theory of finite homogeneous strain is developed in §§ 7–9, and that of infinitesimal strain independently in §§ 10, 11. It is instructive to deduce results for the latter case from the former as in the derivation of § 10 (15).

7. THE GEOMETRY OF FINITE HOMOGENEOUS STRAIN IN TWO DIMENSIONS

A general account of the analysis of finite homogeneous strain in two dimensions [1] will be given in this section. This can be done by the methods of elementary co-ordinate geometry: this treatment has the advantage that any specific quantity can be calculated readily although the formulae are often rather clumsy.

The displacements of all points of a body can in principle always be represented by an algebraic formula which gives the final position of a point in terms of its initial position. If O is the initial position of a point which we choose as origin and O' is its final position, we may choose parallel rectangular axes Oxy and $O'x'y'$ through O and O' and the formula will relate the final position (x', y') of a particle to its initial position (x, y). To get the actual

---

[1] A discussion of the three-dimensional problems to which the two-dimensional theory applies is given in § 14.

displacement of the particle the translation of the origin from O to O' must be added.

It is almost obvious (and it will be proved formally in (10) below) that homogeneous strain as defined in § 6 corresponds to a linear relation between x', y' and x, y. Before considering the general case, the important special cases which often occur will be mentioned briefly.

(i) *Simple Extension along the x-axis*,

$$x'=kx, \quad y'=y, \qquad . \qquad . \qquad . \qquad (1)$$

if $k>1$ the strain is an extension, and if $0<k<1$, a contraction.

(ii) *Extension along both the x- and y-axes*,

$$x'=k_1x, \quad y'=k_2y, \qquad . \qquad . \qquad (2)$$

where k_1 and k_2 may have any positive values.

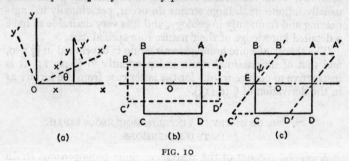

FIG. 10

(iii) *Pure Shear.* This is the special case of (ii) in which $k_1=k>1$, $k_2=k^{-1}$, so that

$$x'=kx, \quad y'=k^{-1}y. \qquad . \qquad . \qquad (3)$$

(iv) *Simple Shear.*

$$x'=x+2sy, \quad y'=y, \qquad . \qquad . \qquad (4)$$

where s is a constant (the factor 2 is inserted for analytical convenience).

(v) *Rotation through an Angle θ.* The formulae for finite rotation (which frequently occurs in combination with strain) may be written down from Fig. 10 (a). They are

$$x'=x\cos\theta+y\sin\theta, \quad y'=-x\sin\theta+y\cos\theta, \qquad . \qquad (5)$$
$$x=x'\cos\theta-y'\sin\theta, \quad y=x'\sin\theta+y'\cos\theta. \qquad . \qquad (6)$$

The way in which a square $ABCD$ with sides parallel to the axes is deformed by pure shear (3) and simple shear (4) is shown in Fig. 10 (b) and (c). It will appear later that these two important types are closely related: for the present we merely note that simple shear corresponds to a sliding of lines parallel to AB across one another without distorting them, so that the right angle BEO becomes the angle $B'EO$ of $\frac{1}{2}\pi - \psi$ where

$$\tan \psi = 2s,$$

and this is the shear strain γ as defined in § 6 (3).

The General Linear Transformation. (1) to (5) are all special cases of the formula

$$x' = ax + by, \quad y' = cx + dy, \quad . \quad . \quad . \quad (7)$$

where we shall assume $a > 0$, $d > 0$. Solving (7) for x and y gives

$$h^2 x = dx' - by', \quad h^2 y = -cx' + ay', \quad . \quad . \quad (8)$$

where

$$h^2 = ad - bc. \quad . \quad . \quad . \quad (9)$$

It will appear later that areas are increased by the strain in the ratio $h^2 : 1$, so it may be assumed that $h^2 > 0$. We shall now consider in detail the changes in configuration caused by the strain (7).

The Transformation of Straight Lines. The line

$$y = mx + c$$

in the unstrained state becomes by (8)

$$(a + bm)y' = (c + dm)x' + ch^2, \quad . \quad . \quad (10)$$

so that all straight lines remain straight lines after straining, and parallel straight lines remain parallel. Thus the formulae (7) fulfil all the conditions for homogeneous strain given in § 6 and, clearly, the linear transformation (7) is the most general transformation which does so.

Next, we consider the way in which the angle between two straight lines which are perpendicular in the unstrained state is altered by straining. As remarked in § 6, if this angle changes to $\frac{1}{2}\pi - \psi$, $\gamma = \tan \psi$ is the shear associated with these directions. Suppose that initially OA and OB are perpendicular lines which make angles θ and $\frac{1}{2}\pi + \theta$ with Ox, Fig. 11 (a), and that $O'A'$ and $O'B'$ are their final positions after straining which make angles θ' and $\frac{1}{2}\pi - \psi + \theta'$ with $O'x'$, Fig. 11 (b).

3

Writing $m=\tan\theta$, so that $\tan(\tfrac{1}{2}\pi+\theta)=-m^{-1}$, it follows from (10) that

$$\tan\theta'=\frac{c+dm}{a+bm}, \quad \tan(\theta'+\tfrac{1}{2}\pi-\psi)=\frac{c-dm^{-1}}{a-bm^{-1}}. \qquad (11)$$

Therefore, using (9),

$$\tan(\tfrac{1}{2}\pi-\psi)=\frac{h^2(m+m^{-1})}{b^2+d^2-a^2-c^2-(ab+cd)(m-m^{-1})}. \qquad (12)$$

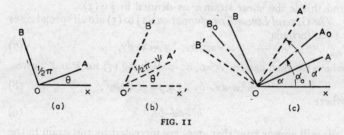

FIG. 11

Since $m=\tan\theta$ it follows that

$$2h^2\tan\psi=2(ab+cd)\cos 2\theta+(b^2+d^2-a^2-c^2)\sin 2\theta. \qquad (13)$$

Since $\gamma=\tan\psi$ this gives the way in which the shear γ varies with direction. It follows from (13) that OA' and OB' are perpendicular, $\psi=0$, only [1] if θ has the values α or $\alpha+\tfrac{1}{2}\pi$ where

$$\tan 2\alpha=\frac{2(ab+cd)}{a^2+c^2-b^2-d^2}. \qquad (14)$$

Thus there is only one pair of lines which are perpendicular before straining and which remain perpendicular after straining. The initial positions of these lines are called the *principal axes of strain*.

A result of great importance, which follows immediately by differentiating (13), is that ψ, and therefore the shear $\gamma=\tan\psi$, has its greatest magnitude when $\theta=\alpha\pm\tfrac{1}{4}\pi$, where α is given by (14), that is, for directions in the unstrained state which bisect the angles between the principal axes.

Except for the trivial case $a=d$, $b=-c$ for which $\psi=0$ for all θ. This corresponds to an extension which is the same for all directions combined with a rotation, cf. (5).

The angles α and $\alpha+\frac{1}{2}\pi$ which the principal axes make with Ox in the unstrained state have been found in (14). We also need the angles α' and $\alpha'+\frac{1}{2}\pi$ which their final positions make with $O'x'$. To find these put $\tan\theta'=\tan\alpha'=m'$, $\tan\alpha=m$, $\psi=0$, in (11) which become

$$bmm'+am'-dm-c=0, \qquad \cdot \qquad \cdot \qquad \cdot \qquad (15)$$

$$cmm'-dm'+am-b=0. \qquad \cdot \qquad \cdot \qquad \cdot \qquad (16)$$

Adding and subtracting (15) and (16) gives

$$\tan(\alpha'+\alpha)=\frac{m'+m}{1-mm'}=\frac{b+c}{a-d}, \qquad \cdot \qquad \cdot \qquad (17)$$

$$\tan(\alpha'-\alpha)=\frac{m'-m}{1+mm'}=\frac{c-b}{a+d}. \qquad \cdot \qquad \cdot \qquad (18)$$

It follows from (17) and (18) that

$$\tan 2\alpha'=\frac{2(ac+bd)}{a^2+b^2-c^2-d^2}. \qquad \cdot \qquad \cdot \qquad (19)$$

The angle $\alpha'-\alpha$ given by (18) is called the *rotation*; it is the angle between the principal axes and their final positions. If $b=c$ the rotation vanishes and the strain is called *irrotational*.

The Transformation of a Circle. So far the discussion has been confined to the changes in direction of straight lines: we next consider their changes in length. The simplest way of doing this is to study the deformation of the circle of unit radius in the unstrained state, namely,

$$x^2+y^2=1. \qquad \cdot \qquad \cdot \qquad \cdot \qquad (20)$$

By (8) this becomes the ellipse

$$\frac{c^2+d^2}{h^4}x'^2-\frac{2(ac+bd)}{h^4}x'y'+\frac{a^2+b^2}{h^4}y'^2=1. \qquad \cdot \qquad (21)$$

This is called the *strain ellipse* and is fundamental to the whole subject. It gives an immediate picture of the nature of the deformation. To find the proportional change of length ρ in any direction, put $x'=\rho\cos\theta'$, $y'=\rho\sin\theta'$ in (21) which gives

$$(c^2+d^2)\cos^2\theta'-2(ac+bd)\sin\theta'\cos\theta'+(a^2+b^2)\sin^2\theta'=h^4/\rho^2. \quad (22)$$

Differentiating (22) it appears that ρ has a stationary value when

$$(a^2+b^2-c^2-d^2)\sin 2\theta'-2(ac+bd)\cos 2\theta'=0,$$

that is, when θ' has values α' or $\alpha'+\frac{1}{2}\pi$, where α' is given by (19).

These directions are those of the axes of the strain ellipse (21), and it thus appears by (19) that they coincide with the final positions of the principal axes of strain.

To find the lengths of the axes of the strain ellipse (21), following the usual method of coordinate geometry, we consider its intersection with the circle of radius R,

$$\frac{x'^2}{R^2}+\frac{y'^2}{R^2}=1. \qquad \qquad . \qquad . \qquad (23)$$

Subtracting (21) and (23) gives

$$\left\{\frac{c^2+d^2}{h^4}-\frac{1}{R^2}\right\}x'^2-\frac{2(ac+bd)}{h^4}x'y'+\left\{\frac{a^2+b^2}{h^4}-\frac{1}{R^2}\right\}y'^2=0 \quad . \quad (24)$$

for the equation of the pair of straight lines through the origin and the points of intersection of the circle (23) and the ellipse (21). If (24) is a perfect square these lines coincide, that is, the circle touches the ellipse, and the condition for this is

$$\left\{\frac{c^2+d^2}{h^4}-\frac{1}{R^2}\right\}\left\{\frac{a^2+b^2}{h^4}-\frac{1}{R^2}\right\}-\frac{(ac+bd)^2}{h^8}=0,$$

or, using (9),

$$R^4-(a^2+b^2+c^2+d^2)R^2+h^4=0. \qquad . \qquad . \qquad (25)$$

The quadratic (25) gives two values for the radii of circles which touch the ellipse (21); these are the lengths of its major and minor axes. Writing A and B for these with $A \geqslant B$, (25) gives

$$A^2+B^2=a^2+b^2+c^2+d^2, \qquad . \qquad . \qquad (26)$$

$$AB=h^2. \qquad . \qquad . \qquad . \qquad (27)$$

It follows, again using (9), that,

$$(A+B)^2=(a+d)^2+(b-c)^2, \qquad . \qquad . \qquad (28)$$

$$(A-B)^2=(a-d)^2+(b+c)^2. \qquad . \qquad . \qquad (29)$$

The lengths A and B of the axes follow from (28) and (29). Since the area of the ellipse is πAB and that of the circle which was deformed into it was π, it follows from (27) that h^2 is the ratio of these two areas. The quantity (h^2-1) is called the *dilatation*; if it is zero the strain causes no change in area.

Now that the directions and lengths of the axes of the strain ellipse are known it is frequently convenient to use them as new axes of reference.

If x_1 and y_1 are coordinates relative to them, the equation of the strain ellipse is

$$\frac{x_1{}^2}{A^2}+\frac{y_1{}^2}{B^2}=1. \qquad \cdot \qquad \cdot \qquad \cdot \qquad (30)$$

Firstly, the lines whose lengths are unchanged by straining may be found. These are the lines through the origin and the intersection of (30) with the circle of unit radius $x_1{}^2+y_1{}^2=1$, that is, the lines

$$x_1{}^2\left(\frac{1}{A^2}-1\right)+y_1{}^2\left(\frac{1}{B^2}-1\right)=0. \qquad \cdot \qquad \cdot \qquad (31)$$

These are real only if $A>1>B$, and they make angles $\pm\delta'$ with the Ox_1 axis where

$$\tan\delta'=\frac{B(A^2-1)^{\frac{1}{2}}}{A(1-B^2)^{\frac{1}{2}}}. \qquad \cdot \qquad \cdot \qquad \cdot \qquad (32)$$

(32) gives the position of these lines in the strained state: their initial position is given by (38) below.

Secondly, the shear strain can be determined in the following way: in the unstrained state the radius vector to a point of the unit circle and the tangent to the circle at that point are perpendicular; if the radius vector to the corresponding point of the strain ellipse and the tangent at that point make an angle $\frac{1}{2}\pi-\psi$ the shear strain is $\gamma=\tan\psi$. To calculate this, suppose that (x_1, kx_1) is a point on the strain ellipse (30); the normal at this point makes an angle $\tan^{-1}(kA^2/B^2)$ with the x_1-axis and therefore

$$\gamma=\tan\psi=\frac{k(A^2-B^2)}{B^2+A^2k^2}. \qquad \cdot \qquad \cdot \qquad (33)$$

As k varies, γ given by (33) has a maximum when $k=\pm B/A$. That is, the angle ϕ' between the final position of the directions of maximum shear and the major axis of the strain ellipse is given by

$$\phi'=\pm\tan^{-1}(B/A). \qquad \cdot \qquad \cdot \qquad \cdot \qquad (34)$$

The initial positions of these directions have already been found to bisect the angles between the principal axes of strain.

The Reciprocal Strain Ellipse. In general, ellipses are transformed into ellipses, but there is one case of great importance. namely, the ellipse

$$(a^2+c^2)x^2+2(ab+cd)\,xy+(b^2+d^2)y^2=1 \qquad \cdot \qquad (35)$$

which is transformed into the circle $x'^2+y'^2=1$. This follows immediately from (7). (35) is called the reciprocal strain ellipse. The same type of analysis used in (21) to (29) shows that its axes are inclined to Ox at angles given by (14), that is, that they are the principal axes of strain. Also the lengths of its axes are

$$(1/B) \text{ and } (1/A), \qquad \cdot \qquad \cdot \qquad (36)$$

where A and B are given by (28) and (29), that is, they are the reciprocals of the lengths of the axes of the strain ellipse. If $AB=h^2=1$, the condition for no change in area by the strain, the two ellipses are equal.

The initial positions of the lines of unchanged length, whose final positions were found to be given by (32), follow in the same way from the intersection of the unit circle and the reciprocal strain ellipse: they are inclined at $\pm\delta$ to its major axis where

$$\tan \delta=[(1-B^2)/(A^2-1)]^{\frac{1}{2}}. \qquad . \qquad . \qquad . \quad (37)$$

If there is no rotation, the major axis of the reciprocal strain ellipse coincides with the minor axis of the strain ellipse. Such a strain is called a *pure strain*, and the analysis of this section shows that the most general homogeneous strain in two dimensions can be expressed as the combination of a pure strain and a rotation.

The Case of Steadily Increasing Strain. It is of some interest to consider what happens if the strain is increased steadily from zero to its final value (7). Since zero strain corresponds to $x=x'$, $y=y'$, steadily increasing strain may be represented by replacing a, b, c, d by $1+\mu(a-1)$, μb, μc, $1+\mu(d-1)$, respectively, where μ increases from 0 to 1. For infinitesimal strain, i.e., very small μ, (18) gives

$$\alpha'-\alpha=\tfrac{1}{2}\mu(c-b),$$

so that $\alpha' \longrightarrow \alpha$ and the rotation tends to zero as $\mu \longrightarrow 0$. If α_0 is the common value of α and α' as $\mu \longrightarrow 0$, (17) gives

$$\tan 2\alpha_0=\frac{b+c}{a-d}. \qquad . \qquad . \qquad . \quad (38)$$

This gives the position of the principal axes for infinitesimal strain. From (17) and (38)

$$\alpha_0=\tfrac{1}{2}(\alpha+\alpha'), \qquad . \qquad . \qquad . \quad (39)$$

so that the position of the principal axes for infinitesimal strain bisects the angle between the principal axes and their final position for any finite strain. The relation between these sets of axes is shown in Fig. 11 (c): as μ increases from 0 to 1, all lines in the angle A_0OA successively become principal axes.

The Quadratic Elongation. The results obtained above by considering the geometry of the strain ellipse and the reciprocal strain ellipse might also have been found by studying the change in length of a line initially inclined at θ to the x-axis. If r is the initial length of the line, so that $x=r\cos\theta$, $y=r\sin\theta$, the quadratic elongation λ, § 6 (2), is, by (7),

$$\lambda=(x'^2+y'^2)/r^2$$
$$=(a^2+c^2)\cos^2\theta+2(ab+cd)\sin\theta\cos\theta+(b^2+d^2)\sin^2\theta. \quad (40)$$

This may be discussed as before; for example, it follows on differentiating that λ has maximum and minimum values in the directions (14) of the principal axes.

A Numerical Example. Consider the case

$$a=2, \quad b=1, \quad c=0\cdot3, \quad d=0\cdot8.$$

By (17) and (18), $\alpha'+\alpha=47\cdot3°$, $\alpha'-\alpha=-14\cdot0°$, so that $\alpha=30\cdot7°$, $\alpha'=16\cdot6°$, also by (39) $\alpha°=23\cdot7°$. The rotation is $14°$ clockwise. By (9), $h^2=1\cdot3$ so that areas are increased in this ratio. (28) and (29) give $A=2\cdot33$, $B=0\cdot56$ for the axes of the strain ellipse. The axes of the reciprocal strain ellipse are

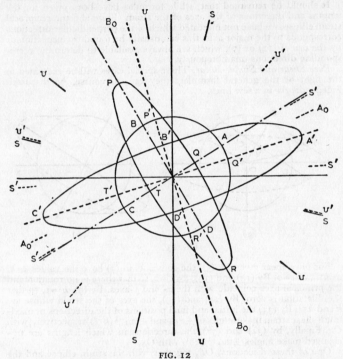

FIG. 12

$1/B=1\cdot79$ and $1/A=0\cdot43$. By (37) and (32) the lines of unchanged length initially make angles $\pm\delta=\pm21\cdot5°$ with the major axis of the reciprocal strain ellipse and in their final position make angles $\pm\delta'=31\cdot3°$ with the major axis of the strain ellipse. By (34) the final positions of the directions of maximum shear make angles $\pm\phi'=\pm13\cdot5°$ with the major axis of the strain ellipse, while their initial positions bisect the angles between the principal axes.

In Fig. 12 the principal axes OA, OB are shown together with their final positions OA', OB'. $A'B'C'D'$ is the strain ellipse and A, B, C, D on the unit circle are the initial positions of the points A', B', C', D'. $PQRT$ is the reciprocal strain ellipse and P', Q', R', T' are the points on the unit circle into which the points P, Q, R, T are strained. The initial and final directions OU, OU' of the lines of unchanged length, and OS, OS' of the directions of maximum shear strain are also shown, as well as the directions OA_0, OB_0 of the principal axes for infinitesimal strain.

It should be remarked that, while formulae have been given for the lengths and directions of the axes of the strain ellipse and the reciprocal strain ellipse, we have not indicated which of the perpendicular directions corresponds to the major axis: this can usually be found by inspection or by the use of (11) or (7), which are always available to determine corresponding directions unambiguously.

Pure Shear and Simple Shear. These special cases will be examined in the light of the general formulae: they can, of course, be discussed independently in a few lines.

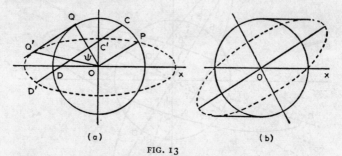

(a)   (b)

FIG. 13

For pure shear given by (3), the constants in (7) have the values $a=k$, $d=k^{-1}$, $b=c=0$. By (14) and (19), $\alpha=\alpha'=0$, so that there is no rotation and the principal axes coincide with the x- and y-axes. By (9), $h^2=1$, so that the dilatation is zero. By (28) and (29), the axes of the strain ellipse are k and k^{-1}. By (34) the initial and final positions of the directions of maximum shear strain make angles of $\pm\pi/4$ and $\pm\tan^{-1}(k^{-2})$, respectively, with Ox. Finally, by (32) and (37), the directions in which lengths are unchanged make angles $\pm\tan^{-1}(k^{-1})$ with Ox.

One of these directions, OP, together with the strain ellipse and the circle from which it has been deformed, is shown in Fig. 13 (a) to illustrate an important property of pure shear. Since all lines parallel to OP are unchanged in length, the chord $C'D'$ of the ellipse is equal in length to the chord CD of the circle, and the strain may be regarded as being produced by the sliding of chords of the circle parallel to OP (simple shear). The locus of the midpoints of these chords makes an angle $Q'Ox$ equal to $\pi-\tan^{-1}(k^{-3})$ with Ox, so that the shear strain $\tan\psi$ is given by

$$\tan\psi=\tan\left\{\tfrac{1}{2}\pi-\tan^{-1}(k^{-3})-\tan^{-1}(k^{-1})\right\}$$
$$=k-k^{-1}.$$

Thus a pure shear may be regarded as a simple shear referred to axes inclined at $\tan^{-1}(k^{-1})$ with Ox. The value of s in (4) is $\frac{1}{2}(k-k^{-1})$.

Considering next simple shear given by (4), we have $a=d=1$, $b=2s$, $c=0$. By (17) and (18), $\alpha+\alpha'=\frac{1}{2}\pi$, $\alpha-\alpha'=\tan^{-1}s$; thus the rotation is $-\tan^{-1}s$, the principal axes make angles $\frac{1}{2}\tan^{-1}s \pm\frac{1}{4}\pi$ with Ox, and their final positions make angles $\pm\frac{1}{4}\pi-\frac{1}{2}\tan^{-1}s$ with Ox. From (28) and (29), $A=\sqrt{(s^2+1)}+s$, $B=\sqrt{(s^2+1)}-s$. It follows that a simple shear corresponds exactly to a pure shear with $k=\sqrt{(s^2+1)}+s$ and the major axis of the strain ellipse inclined at $\frac{1}{4}\pi-\frac{1}{2}\tan^{-1}s=\tan^{-1}(k^{-1})$ with Ox. This is the result derived above by considering pure shear. The position of the strain ellipse is shown in Fig. 13 (b).

8. FINITE HOMOGENEOUS STRAIN IN
THREE DIMENSIONS

In this section the way in which the two-dimensional theory of § 7 is extended to three dimensions is indicated briefly. Actual quantitative calculations are best performed by Mohr's method discussed in the next section.

In three dimensions, the most general transformation from the unstrained position (x, y, z) to the strained position (x', y', z') will be

$$x'=a_1x+a_2y+a_3z, \qquad . \qquad . \qquad . \qquad (1)$$
$$y'=b_1x+b_2y+b_3z, \qquad . \qquad . \qquad . \qquad (2)$$
$$z'=c_1x+c_2y+c_3z. \qquad . \qquad . \qquad . \qquad (3)$$

It is found that in general there is only one set of three mutually perpendicular directions in the unstrained state (*the principal axes of strain*) which remain mutually perpendicular after straining. If the initial and final positions of this set are the same, the strain is *irrotational*; if not, they can be made to coincide by a finite rotation about some axis. A sphere of unit radius is deformed into the *strain ellipsoid* whose axes are the final positions of the principal axes; while the ellipsoid which deforms into a sphere of unit radius is the *reciprocal strain ellipsoid* and its axes are the principal axes of strain. The most general strain of this type can be expressed as a combination of a pure strain (which is specified by the shape of the strain ellipsoid) and the rotation which brings the principal axes of strain from their initial to their final positions. The ratio of the difference in volume between the strain ellipsoid and the sphere from which it was deformed to the volume of the sphere is the dilatation. If this vanishes the strain is sometimes called equivoluminal.

If A, B, C, where $A \geqslant B \geqslant C$, are the lengths of the axes of the strain ellipsoid, and x_1, y_1, z_1 are coordinates relative to these axes, its equation will be

$$\frac{x_1{}^2}{A^2} + \frac{y_1{}^2}{B^2} + \frac{z_1{}^2}{C^2} = 1, \qquad . \qquad . \qquad . \qquad . \qquad (4)$$

and the sphere from which it was deformed will be

$$x_1{}^2 + y_1{}^2 + z_1{}^2 = 1. \qquad . \qquad . \qquad . \qquad . \qquad (5)$$

The intersection of (4) and (5) gives the lines whose lengths are unchanged. Subtracting (4) and (5), it appears that these lines lie on the cone

$$x_1{}^2\left(\frac{1}{A^2} - 1\right) + y_1{}^2\left(\frac{1}{B^2} - 1\right) + z_1{}^2\left(\frac{1}{C^2} - 1\right) = 0 \qquad . \qquad . \qquad (6)$$

which is real only if $A > 1$ and $C < 1$. This is the analogue of the pair of lines of unchanged length of § 7 (31).

The intersection of (4) with a sphere of radius B (the intermediate axis of the strain ellipsoid) lies on the pair of planes through the origin

$$x_1{}^2\left(\frac{1}{A^2} - \frac{1}{B^2}\right) + z_1{}^2\left(\frac{1}{C^2} - \frac{1}{B^2}\right) = 0 \qquad . \qquad . \qquad . \qquad (7)$$

which are real and inclined to the x_1-axis at angles

$$\pm \tan^{-1}\left\{\frac{C(A^2 - B^2)^{\frac{1}{2}}}{A(B^2 - C^2)^{\frac{1}{2}}}\right\}. \qquad . \qquad . \qquad . \qquad (8)$$

These planes and all planes parallel to them cut the strain ellipsoid in circles called the *circular sections*. They are planes in which the lengths of all lines are increased in the same ratio, namely $B:1$. If $B = 1$ the cone (6) and the planes (7) are the same and the circular sections give the lines of unchanged length. If $B = 1$ and $C = 1/A$ so that the strain is equivoluminal, (8) becomes

$$\pm \tan^{-1}(1/A). \qquad . \qquad . \qquad . \qquad . \qquad (9)$$

The circular sections have been much discussed in connection with strain hypotheses of failure, cf. § 25.

9. MOHR'S REPRESENTATION OF FINITE HOMOGENEOUS STRAIN WITHOUT ROTATION

Consider the strain

$$x' = x(1 + \epsilon_1), \quad y' = y(1 + \epsilon_2), \quad z' = z(1 + \epsilon_3) \qquad . \qquad . \qquad (1)$$

which is the general pure strain in three dimensions with coordinates referred to the principal axes of strain. A complete representation of the variations of extension and shear in any direction may be obtained by the methods of Mohr which were developed in § 5 for the representation of stress.

If the length of a line OP is r in the unstrained state and is $OP' = r'$ in the strained state, we have as in § 6 (1)

$$\frac{r'}{r} = 1 + \epsilon, \qquad . \qquad . \qquad . \qquad . \qquad (2)$$

where ϵ is the extension corresponding to the initial direction OP. In calculating the lengths of the lines it is the squares of the lengths which appear, so that the natural quantity to consider is not r'/r but its square

$$\lambda = r'^2/r^2. \qquad \qquad \qquad (3)$$

This is called the *quadratic elongation*, and in dealing with finite strains it is always this which is studied.[1]

The quantities

$$\lambda_1 = (1+\epsilon_1)^2, \quad \lambda_2 = (1+\epsilon_2)^2, \quad \lambda_3 = (1+\epsilon_3)^2 \qquad \qquad (4)$$

are called the *principal quadratic elongations*.

If the direction cosines of OP are (l, m, n), so that $x = lr$, $y = mr$, $z = nr$, and so, by (1) and (4), $x'^2 = \lambda_1 x^2 = \lambda_1 l^2 r^2$, etc., we get

$$\lambda = r'^2/r^2 = \lambda_1 l^2 + \lambda_2 m^2 + \lambda_3 n^2. \qquad \qquad (5)$$

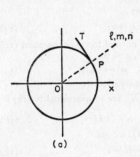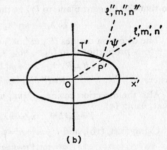

FIG. 14

This gives the quadratic elongation corresponding to any initial direction. Also from (1), the sphere

$$x^2 + y^2 + z^2 = 1 \qquad \qquad \qquad (6)$$

becomes the strain ellipsoid

$$\frac{x'^2}{\lambda_1} + \frac{y'^2}{\lambda_2} + \frac{z'^2}{\lambda_3} = 1, \qquad \qquad \qquad (7)$$

while the reciprocal strain ellipsoid

$$\lambda_1 x^2 + \lambda_2 y^2 + \lambda_3 z^2 = 1 \qquad \qquad \qquad (8)$$

becomes the sphere

$$x'^2 + y'^2 + z'^2 = 1. \qquad \qquad \qquad (9)$$

To find the shear corresponding to an initial direction (l, m, n), suppose that P and P' are corresponding points on the sphere (6) and the strain ellipsoid (7). Let T and T' be the tangent planes to the sphere and the ellipsoid at these points. We shall use the notation (l, m, n) for the

---

[1] In dealing with infinitesimal strain in §§ 10, 11, ϵ is assumed to be so small that ϵ^2 is negligible and so $\lambda = 1 + 2\epsilon$. λ is also closely related to the 'natural strain' defined in § 18.

direction cosines of the direction OP in the unstrained state, (l', m', n') for its direction cosines in the final state, and (l'', m'', n'') for the direction cosines of the normal to the tangent plane T', Fig. 14. All these directions are of physical importance and it is useful to be able to express quantities such as elongation and shear in terms of any of them. As in § 6 (3), the shear γ corresponding to the initial direction (l, m, n) is defined by

$$\gamma = \tan \psi, \qquad . \qquad . \qquad . \qquad . \qquad (10)$$

where ψ is the angle between the radius vector OP' and the normal to the plane T', so that

$$\cos \psi = l' \, l'' + m' \, m'' + n' \, n''. \qquad . \qquad . \qquad (11)$$

To evaluate this, we notice that the point P' is by (1)

$$l\lambda_1{}^{\frac{1}{2}}, \quad m\lambda_2{}^{\frac{1}{2}}, \quad n\lambda_3{}^{\frac{1}{2}}, \qquad . \qquad . \qquad . \qquad (12)$$

so that the tangent plane to (7) at this point is

$$lx'\lambda_1{}^{-\frac{1}{2}} + my'\lambda_2{}^{-\frac{1}{2}} + nz'\lambda_3{}^{-\frac{1}{2}} = 1. \qquad . \qquad . \qquad (13)$$

The direction cosines (l'', m'', n'') of the normal to (7) at the point (12) are thus proportional to $l\lambda_1{}^{-\frac{1}{2}}, m\lambda_2{}^{-\frac{1}{2}}, n\lambda_3{}^{-\frac{1}{2}}$, and so

$$l'' = l(\lambda_1 R)^{-\frac{1}{2}}, \quad m'' = m(\lambda_2 R)^{-\frac{1}{2}}, \quad n'' = n(\lambda_3 R)^{-\frac{1}{2}}, \qquad . \qquad (14)$$

where

$$R = (l^2/\lambda_1) + (m^2/\lambda_2) + (n^2/\lambda_3). \qquad . \qquad . \qquad (15)$$

Also the direction cosines (l', m', n') of OP' are proportional to (12) so that, using (5),

$$l' = l\lambda_1{}^{\frac{1}{2}}\lambda^{-\frac{1}{2}}, \quad m' = m\lambda_2{}^{\frac{1}{2}}\lambda^{-\frac{1}{2}}, \quad n' = n\lambda_3{}^{\frac{1}{2}}\lambda^{-\frac{1}{2}}. \qquad . \qquad (16)$$

Using (14), (16), and $l^2 + m^2 + n^2 = 1$ in (11), we get

$$\gamma^2 = \tan^2 \psi = \sec^2 \psi - 1 = R\lambda - 1. \qquad . \qquad . \qquad (17)$$

Multiplying out, we get finally,

$$\lambda_1\lambda_2\lambda_3\gamma^2 = \lambda_1(\lambda_2-\lambda_3)^2 m^2 n^2 + \lambda_2(\lambda_3-\lambda_1)^2 n^2 l^2 + \lambda_3(\lambda_1-\lambda_2)^2 l^2 m^2. \quad . \quad (18)$$

(5) and (18) give the quadratic elongation and shear corresponding to the initial direction (l, m, n) of OP.

Using (16) in $l^2 + m^2 + n^2 = 1$ gives

$$\frac{1}{\lambda} = \frac{l'^2}{\lambda_1} + \frac{m'^2}{\lambda_2} + \frac{n'^2}{\lambda_3}, \qquad . \qquad . \qquad . \qquad (19)$$

and using it in (18) gives

$$\frac{\gamma^2}{\lambda^2} = \left(\frac{1}{\lambda_2} - \frac{1}{\lambda_3}\right)^2 m'^2 n'^2 + \left(\frac{1}{\lambda_3} - \frac{1}{\lambda_1}\right)^2 n'^2 l'^2 + \left(\frac{1}{\lambda_1} - \frac{1}{\lambda_2}\right)^2 l'^2 m'^2. \qquad . \qquad (20)$$

These express λ and γ in terms of the direction cosines (l', m', n') of the line OP' in the strained state.

Finally, manipulation of a similar type gives for the formula for γ in terms of (l'', m'', n''), the direction cosines of the normal to T',

$$\gamma^2 = \frac{(\lambda_1-\lambda_2)^2 l''^2 m''^2 + (\lambda_2-\lambda_3)^2 m''^2 n''^2 + (\lambda_3-\lambda_1)^2 l''^2 m''^2}{(\lambda_1 l''^2 + \lambda_2 m''^2 + \lambda_3 n''^2)^2}. \qquad . \qquad (21)$$

Two very interesting representations of Mohr's type for the variation of λ and γ may now be found. The first of these is in terms of (l', m', n'). If we use the notation

$$\lambda' = \frac{1}{\lambda}, \quad \lambda'_1 = \frac{1}{\lambda_1}, \quad \lambda'_2 = \frac{1}{\lambda_2}, \quad \lambda'_3 = \frac{1}{\lambda_3}, \quad \gamma' = \frac{\gamma}{\lambda}, \quad . \quad . \quad (22)$$

in (19) and (20), these become

$$\lambda' = \lambda'_1 l'^2 + \lambda'_2 m'^2 + \lambda'_3 n'^2, \quad . \quad . \quad . \quad (23)$$

$$\gamma'^2 = (\lambda'_1 - \lambda'_2)^2 l'^2 m'^2 + (\lambda'_2 - \lambda'_3)^2 m'^2 n'^2 + (\lambda'_3 - \lambda'_1)^2 n'^2 l'^2. \quad . \quad (24)$$

These are identical in form with the equations § 4 (26) and (29) for normal and shear stress across a plane, so that λ' and γ' can be represented completely by Mohr's circle diagram. The whole of § 5 can be taken over *mutatis mutandis*.

Clearly the above, which involves circles only, is the geometrically simplest type of representation: it is possible, however, to get a similar representation of λ and γ in terms of (l, m, n) which involves ellipses. To do this, using (15) we write (17) in the form

$$\frac{l^2}{\lambda_1} + \frac{m^2}{\lambda_2} + \frac{n^2}{\lambda_3} = \frac{\gamma^2 + 1}{\lambda}, \quad . \quad . \quad . \quad (25)$$

and then, solving (25), (5), and $l^2 + m^2 + n^2 = 1$ for l^2, m^2, n^2, gives

$$l^2 = \frac{\lambda_1(\lambda - \lambda_2)(\lambda - \lambda_3) + \gamma^2 \lambda_1 \lambda_2 \lambda_3}{\lambda(\lambda_1 - \lambda_2)(\lambda_1 - \lambda_3)}, \quad . \quad . \quad (26)$$

$$m^2 = \frac{\lambda_2(\lambda - \lambda_1)(\lambda - \lambda_3) + \gamma^2 \lambda_1 \lambda_2 \lambda_3}{\lambda(\lambda_2 - \lambda_3)(\lambda_2 - \lambda_1)}, \quad . \quad . \quad (27)$$

$$n^2 = \frac{\lambda_3(\lambda - \lambda_1)(\lambda - \lambda_2) + \gamma^2 \lambda_1 \lambda_2 \lambda_3}{\lambda(\lambda_3 - \lambda_1)(\lambda_3 - \lambda_2)}. \quad . \quad . \quad (28)$$

If $n = 0$, (28) becomes

$$[\lambda - \tfrac{1}{2}(\lambda_1 + \lambda_2)]^2 + \lambda_1 \lambda_2 \gamma^2 = \tfrac{1}{4}(\lambda_1 - \lambda_2)^2, \quad . \quad . \quad (29)$$

which is an ellipse in the (λ, γ) plane with its centre at $(\tfrac{1}{2}(\lambda_1 + \lambda_2), 0)$, and λ- and γ-axes of $\tfrac{1}{2}(\lambda_1 - \lambda_2)$ and $\tfrac{1}{2}(\lambda_1 - \lambda_2)(\lambda_1 \lambda_2)^-$, respectively. If $\epsilon_1 > \epsilon_2 > \epsilon_3$ we have $\lambda_1 > \lambda_2 > \lambda_3$ and the curves corresponding to $l = 0, m = 0, n = 0$ are the ellipses shown in Fig. 15. In the same way other constant values of l, m, n lead also to ellipses.

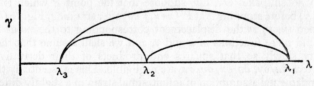

FIG. 15

For $m=0$, which by Fig. 15 gives the largest values of γ, we have, writing $l=\cos \alpha$, $n=\sin \alpha$ in (5) and (18),

$$\lambda=\lambda_1 \cos^2 \alpha+\lambda_3 \sin^2 \alpha, \quad . \quad \quad . \quad \quad . \quad \quad . \quad (30)$$

$$\gamma=\frac{\lambda_1-\lambda_3}{2(\lambda_1\lambda_3)^{\frac{1}{2}}} \sin 2\alpha. \quad . \quad \quad . \quad \quad . \quad (31)$$

It follows that the greatest shear occurs when $\alpha=\pi/4$, and so by (16) corresponds to a direction in the strained state making an angle

$$\tan^{-1} (\lambda_3/\lambda_1)^{\frac{1}{2}}$$

with the x-axis which is the direction of greatest extension. This is the result of § 7 (34).

10. INFINITESIMAL STRAIN IN TWO DIMENSIONS

In this section the theory of infinitesimal strain will be developed, and, in particular, the way in which extension and shear vary with direction in the neighbourhood of a point will be calculated subject to the assumptions stated in § 6, namely, that the squares and product of these quantities are negligible.

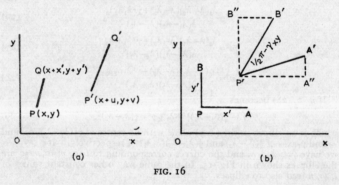

FIG. 16

Choosing axes Ox, Oy, suppose that the point P which is at (x, y) before straining is at P' $(x+u, y+v)$ after straining, Fig. 16 (a). Then (u, v) is the displacement corresponding to the point P. u and v are functions of x and y, and we shall assume that they vary slowly so that squares and products of their derivatives $\partial u/\partial x$, $\partial u/\partial y$, $\partial v/\partial x$, $\partial v/\partial y$, are negligible. This is essentially the fundamental assumption of infinitesimal strain in a slightly different form.

Now consider a point Q close to P whose coordinates are $(x+x', y+y')$, where x' and y' are so small that their squares and product are negligible compared with x' and y'. The displacement of Q will be $(u+u', v+v')$ where

$$u'=\frac{\partial u}{\partial x}x'+\frac{\partial u}{\partial y}y', \qquad \cdot \qquad \cdot \qquad \cdot \qquad (1)$$

$$v'=\frac{\partial v}{\partial x}x'+\frac{\partial v}{\partial y}y', \qquad \cdot \qquad \cdot \qquad \cdot \qquad (2)$$

by Taylor's theorem, neglecting terms in x'^2, $x'y'$, etc. It follows from (1) and (2) that the coordinates of Q relative to P, which are changed from (x', y') to $(x'+u', y'+v')$ by the strain, are linear functions of x' and y', and thus that the strain *in the immediate neighbourhood of any point P* is homogeneous in the sense of § 7 so that the whole of the theory of that section is applicable. It is more convenient, however, to develop the theory *ab initio* in a manner closely related to the theory of stress in § 3.

Introducing the fundamental notation

$$\varepsilon_x=\frac{\partial u}{\partial x}, \quad \varepsilon_y=\frac{\partial v}{\partial y}, \quad \gamma_{xy}=\gamma_{yx}=\frac{\partial u}{\partial y}+\frac{\partial v}{\partial x}, \qquad \cdot \qquad \cdot \qquad (3)$$

$$\omega=\tfrac{1}{2}\left(\frac{\partial v}{\partial x}-\frac{\partial u}{\partial y}\right), \qquad \cdot \qquad \cdot \qquad (4)$$

(1) and (2) become

$$u'=\varepsilon_x x'+\tfrac{1}{2}\gamma_{xy}y'-\omega y', \qquad \cdot \qquad \cdot \qquad \cdot \qquad (5)$$

$$v'=\tfrac{1}{2}\gamma_{xy}x'+\varepsilon_y y'+\omega x'. \qquad \cdot \qquad \cdot \qquad \cdot \qquad (6)$$

The terms $(-\omega y', \omega x')$ in (5) and (6) are just the components of the displacement of the point (x', y') due to rotation through a small angle ω, so that ω is called the *component of rotation*. If $\omega=0$ the strain is *irrotational*.

The quantities ε_x, ε_y, γ_{xy} are called the *components of strain*: to find their physical significance, consider the displacements of the points A and B in Fig. 16 (b) for which $y'=0$ and $x'=0$, respectively. By (5) and (6), A moves to the point A' such that $P'A''=(1+\varepsilon_x)x'$, $A'A''=(\omega+\tfrac{1}{2}\gamma_{xy})x'$, and B moves to the point B' such that $P'B''=(1+\varepsilon_y)y'$, $B'B''=y'(\tfrac{1}{2}\gamma_{xy}-\omega)$. It follows (since squares of ε_x, etc., are negligible) that ε_x is the extension of an element initially parallel to the x-axis, and ε_y that of one initially parallel to the y-axis. Also, the lines $P'A'$ and $P'B'$, which before strain were parallel to the x- and y-axes, are inclined at $\frac{1}{2}\gamma_{xy}+\omega$ and $\frac{1}{2}\gamma_{xy}-\omega$ to them, respectively, after strain: thus ω represents the angle through which they must be rotated to make them symmetrical with the x- and y-axes, and the angle between them is $\frac{1}{2}\pi-\gamma_{xy}$, corresponding to a shear of this amount as in § 6 (3).

The *three* components of strain have been derived by differentiation from the *two* components of displacement so it might be expected that they are not independent. In fact, there is a relation between their derivatives, namely,

$$\frac{\partial^2\varepsilon_x}{\partial y^2}+\frac{\partial^2\varepsilon_y}{\partial x^2}=\frac{\partial^2\gamma_{xy}}{\partial x\,\partial y}, \qquad . \qquad . \qquad (7)$$

which follows immediately from (3). This is called the *compatibility condition* for the components of strain.

Having defined the components of strain, we now proceed to express the extension of the element PQ in terms of them. Using (1) and (2) and neglecting squares and products of $\partial u/\partial x$, etc., we have

$$P'Q'^2=(x'+u')^2+(y'+v')^2$$

$$=\left\{\left(1+\frac{\partial u}{\partial x}\right)x'+\frac{\partial u}{\partial y}y'\right\}^2+\left\{\frac{\partial v}{\partial x}x'+\left(1+\frac{\partial v}{\partial y}\right)y'\right\}^2$$

$$=x'^2+y'^2+2\frac{\partial u}{\partial x}x'^2+2\left(\frac{\partial u}{\partial y}+\frac{\partial v}{\partial x}\right)x'y'+2\frac{\partial v}{\partial y}y'^2$$

$$=x'^2+y'^2+2\varepsilon_x x'^2+2\gamma_{xy}x'y'+2\varepsilon_y y'^2, \qquad . \qquad . \qquad (8)$$

using the notation (3). Now suppose that PQ is of length r and makes an angle θ with Ox so that

$$x'=r\cos\theta, \quad y'=r\sin\theta,$$

then by (8)

$$P'Q'^2=r^2\{1+2\varepsilon_x\cos^2\theta+2\gamma_{xy}\sin\theta\cos\theta+2\varepsilon_y\sin^2\theta\}, \quad . \quad (9)$$

and taking the square root, remembering that the squares of ε_x, etc., are negligible,

$$P'Q'=r\{1+\varepsilon_x\cos^2\theta+\gamma_{xy}\sin\theta\cos\theta+\varepsilon_y\sin^2\theta\}. \quad . \quad (10)$$

The extension ε, § 6 (1), of a line at P in the direction θ is thus

$$\varepsilon=\frac{P'Q'-r}{r}=\varepsilon_x\cos^2\theta+\gamma_{xy}\sin\theta\cos\theta+\varepsilon_y\sin^2\theta. \quad . \quad (11)$$

This is the fundamental result, analogous to § 3 (4) for the normal stress across a plane inclined to the axes, and the subsequent analysis differs only from that of § 3 in notation and in the unfortunate absence [1] of a factor 2 in the second term of (11).

The variation of ε with θ may be discussed as in § 3. ε is stationary when

$$0 = \frac{d\varepsilon}{d\theta} = (\varepsilon_y - \varepsilon_x)\sin 2\theta + \gamma_{xy}\cos 2\theta, \qquad . \qquad . \quad (12)$$

that is, when

$$\tan 2\theta = \frac{\gamma_{xy}}{\varepsilon_x - \varepsilon_y}. \qquad . \qquad . \quad (13)$$

The directions given by (13) are the unstrained directions for which greatest and least extension occurs, so that they are the axes of the reciprocal strain ellipse defined in § 7. They are called, as before, the *principal axes of strain*, and the values of ε in these directions are called the *principal strains* and will be denoted by ε_1 and ε_2 with the convention $\varepsilon_1 \geqslant \varepsilon_2$. If a point is plotted distant $R = k/\varepsilon^{\frac{1}{2}}$ from the origin in the direction θ, this point, whose coordinates are $x = R\cos\theta$, $y = R\sin\theta$, will lie on the conic

$$\varepsilon_x x^2 + \gamma_{xy}xy + \varepsilon_y y^2 = k^2. \qquad . \qquad . \quad (14)$$

This conic is called the *strain conic* and the directions of its axes are given by (13). Referred to principal axes as new x- and y-axes, its equation will be

$$\varepsilon_1 x^2 + \varepsilon_2 y^2 = k^2,$$

where ε_1 and ε_2 are the principal strains. It is an ellipse if ε_1 and ε_2 have the same signs; an hyperbola if they have opposite signs; for a pure shear, $\varepsilon_2 = -\varepsilon_1$, it is a rectangular hyperbola. The strain conic, which gives a measure of the extension of a line in any direction, should be distinguished carefully from the strain ellipse of § 7 which gives the positions in the strained state of the ends of all line elements of unit length drawn from a point; the latter may be obtained by displacing the circumference of the unit circle radially by the amount (11).

Next, the variation of shear strain γ with direction has to be

[1] This discrepancy can be removed by inserting a factor $\frac{1}{2}$ in the definition (3) of γ_{xy}, but this is usually not done because of the very large amount of literature using the present notation. The change is made in developments of the subject which use tensor analysis.

considered. To find this, the change in angle between two directions initially at θ and $\frac{1}{2}\pi+\theta$ is needed: this calculation is precisely the same as that leading to § 7 (13) except that, by (5) and (6), the quantities a, b, c, d are replaced by $1+\varepsilon_x$, $\frac{1}{2}\gamma_{xy}-\omega$, $\frac{1}{2}\gamma_{xy}+\omega$ and $1+\varepsilon_y$, respectively, and in the present instance the quantities ε_x, ε_y, γ_{xy}, ω and $\psi=\gamma$ are so small that their squares and products may be neglected. It follows from § 7 (13) with these modifications that [1]

$$\gamma=(\varepsilon_y-\varepsilon_x)\sin 2\theta+\gamma_{xy}\cos 2\theta. \qquad . \qquad . \quad (15)$$

(11) and (15) may be regarded as formulae for change of axes. If Ox' and Oy' are new axes rotated through θ from Ox and Oy and $\varepsilon_{x'}$, $\varepsilon_{y'}$ and $\gamma_{x'y'}$ are the components of strain relative to them, (11) with θ and $\theta+\frac{1}{2}\pi$ gives

$$\varepsilon_{x'}=\varepsilon_x\cos^2\theta+\gamma_{xy}\sin\theta\cos\theta+\varepsilon_y\sin^2\theta, \qquad . \quad (16)$$

$$\varepsilon_{y'}=\varepsilon_x\sin^2\theta-\gamma_{xy}\sin\theta\cos\theta+\varepsilon_y\cos^2\theta, \qquad . \quad (17)$$

while (15) gives $\gamma_{x'y'}$. Adding (16) and (17) gives

$$\varepsilon_{x'}+\varepsilon_{y'}=\varepsilon_x+\varepsilon_y \qquad . \qquad . \qquad . \qquad . \quad (18)$$

so that this quantity is invariant and equal to $\varepsilon_1+\varepsilon_2$, cf. § 3 (8). This quantity is also the *dilatation* Δ; this follows since the axes of the strain ellipse are $1+\varepsilon_1$ and $1+\varepsilon_2$ so that its area is $\pi(1+\varepsilon_1+\varepsilon_2)$, neglecting the small quantity $\varepsilon_1\varepsilon_2$; the ratio Δ of the change in area to the original area π is therefore

$$\Delta=\varepsilon_1+\varepsilon_2. \qquad . \qquad . \qquad . \qquad . \quad (19)$$

(11) and (15) have precisely the same forms as the expressions § 3 (4) and (5) for the variation of normal and shear stress with direction. Thus the whole of the discussion of § 3 of the variation of σ and τ with direction may be taken over. If the principal axes of strain are chosen as x- and y-axes, the extension ε and shear strain γ for a direction inclined at θ to Ox are by (11) and (15)

$$\varepsilon=\varepsilon_1\cos^2\theta+\varepsilon_2\sin^2\theta=\tfrac{1}{2}(\varepsilon_1+\varepsilon_2)+\tfrac{1}{2}(\varepsilon_1-\varepsilon_2)\cos 2\theta, \quad . \quad (20)$$

$$\gamma=-(\varepsilon_1-\varepsilon_2)\sin 2\theta. \qquad . \qquad . \qquad . \quad (21)$$

These are identical with § 3 (13) and (14) (except for the factor $\frac{1}{2}$ in τ) and it follows as in § 3 that ε and $\frac{1}{2}\gamma$ can be represented by the Mohr diagram of Fig. 17 (a), cf. Fig. 4 (a).

---

[1] (9) may be derived in the same way from the expression § 7 (40) for the quadratic elongation.

The result (20) may be applied to the experimental determination of the principal axes and strains at a point of the surface of a strained solid. This can be done by measuring the extensions in three directions, OP, OQ. OR, inclined at known angles α and β to one another. Such measurements are made by *strain gauges*,[1] and this sort of arrangement is called a rosette. Suppose that OP is inclined at the unknown angle θ to the principal axis

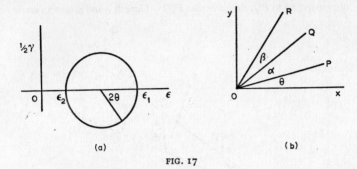

(a)   (b)

FIG. 17

Ox, Fig. 17 (b). Then, if ϵ_P, ϵ_Q, ϵ_R are the measured extensions in the directions OP, OQ, OR, (20) gives

$$\epsilon_P = \tfrac{1}{2}(\epsilon_1 + \epsilon_2) + \tfrac{1}{2}(\epsilon_1 - \epsilon_2)\cos 2\theta,$$
$$\epsilon_Q = \tfrac{1}{2}(\epsilon_1 + \epsilon_2) + \tfrac{1}{2}(\epsilon_1 - \epsilon_2)\cos 2(\theta + \alpha),$$
$$\epsilon_R = \tfrac{1}{2}(\epsilon_1 + \epsilon_2) + \tfrac{1}{2}(\epsilon_1 - \epsilon_2)\cos 2(\theta + \alpha + \beta).$$

These equations can be solved for ϵ_1, ϵ_2 and θ. For example, for the important case $\alpha = \beta = \pi/4$, the solutions are

$$\epsilon_1 + \epsilon_2 = \epsilon_P + \epsilon_R,$$
$$\epsilon_1 - \epsilon_2 = [(\epsilon_P - 2\epsilon_Q + \epsilon_R)^2 + (\epsilon_P - \epsilon_R)^2]^{\frac{1}{2}},$$
$$\tan 2\theta = (\epsilon_P - 2\epsilon_Q + \epsilon_R)/(\epsilon_P - \epsilon_R).$$

The Components of Strain in Plane Polar Coordinates

So far we have only discussed displacement and strain in rectangular Cartesian coordinates, but many important problems can be most simply stated in plane or cylindrical polar coordinates. The development of the theory in polar coordinates follows the same lines as for Cartesians but with minor modifications.

Let P, Q, Fig. 18, be two near points whose polar coordinates are (r, θ) and $(r+r', \theta+\theta')$, respectively, where r' and θ' are small. Suppose that the displacement of P to P' is (u, v) referred to the radial and transverse directions PR and PT at P, and similarly that the displacement of Q to Q'

---

[1] Hetenyi, *Experimental Stress Analysis* (Wiley, 1950); *Strain Gauges* (Philips Technical Library, 1952).

is $(u+u', v+v')$ referred to the corresponding directions for Q. Then, by Taylor's theorem

$$u' = \frac{\partial u}{\partial r}r' + \frac{\partial u}{\partial \theta}\theta', \quad v' = \frac{\partial v}{\partial r}r' + \frac{\partial v}{\partial \theta}\theta'. \quad \cdot \quad \cdot \quad (22)$$

We wish to calculate the extension

$$\epsilon = (P'Q' - PQ)/PQ \quad \cdot \quad \cdot \quad \cdot \quad (23)$$

corresponding to PQ. Suppose that PQ is of length ρ and makes an angle

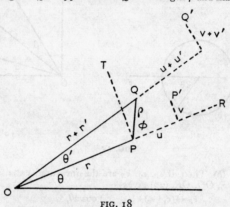

FIG. 18

ϕ with PR. Writing, for shortness, $l = \cos\phi$, $m = \sin\phi$, and neglecting squares of the small quantities r' and θ', we have

$$r' = l\rho, \quad r\theta' = m\rho. \quad \cdot \quad \cdot \quad \cdot \quad (24)$$

Now, again neglecting squares of these small quantities, the coordinates of Q' referred to the rectangular axes PR, PT are

$$\rho l + (u+u') - v\theta', \quad \rho m + u\theta' + (v+v').$$

Therefore, using (22) and (24),

$$P'Q'^2 = [\rho l + u' - v\theta']^2 + [\rho m + u\theta' + v']^2$$

$$= \rho^2\left\{l\left(1 + \frac{\partial u}{\partial r}\right) + \frac{m}{r}\left(\frac{\partial u}{\partial \theta} - v\right)\right\}^2 + \rho^2\left\{l\frac{\partial v}{\partial r} + m\left(1 + \frac{u}{r} + \frac{1}{r}\frac{\partial v}{\partial \theta}\right)\right\}^2.$$

Assuming as before that $\partial u/\partial r$, etc., are small, and in addition that u, v are small,[1] this becomes

$$P'Q'^2 = \rho^2\{1 + 2l^2\epsilon_r + 2lm\gamma_{r\theta} + 2m^2\epsilon_\theta\}, \quad \cdot \quad \cdot \quad (25)$$

---

[1] The reason for this assumption and for the terms such as u/r which appear in (26) is that in this coordinate system the displacements themselves as well as their derivatives contribute to the strain. For example, a radial displacement u of the ends of an arc of a circle of radius r gives a tangential strain u/r of the arc.

where

$$\epsilon_r = \frac{\partial u}{\partial r}, \quad \epsilon_\theta = \frac{1}{r}\left(u + \frac{\partial v}{\partial \theta}\right), \quad \gamma_{r\theta} = \frac{1}{r}\left(\frac{\partial u}{\partial \theta} - v\right) + \frac{\partial v}{\partial r}. \quad . \quad . \quad (26)$$

Taking the square root of (25) gives for the variation with ϕ of the extension given by (23)

$$\epsilon = \epsilon_r \cos^2 \phi + \gamma_{r\theta} \sin \phi \cos \phi + \epsilon_\theta \sin^2 \phi. \quad . \quad . \quad (27)$$

(27) is the analogue of (11) in the present coordinate system, and (26) are the components of strain. ϵ_r and ϵ_θ may be identified with the extensions of lines in the radial and transverse directions, and $\frac{1}{2}\pi - \gamma_{r\theta}$ with the change in angle between these lines. The dilatation Δ is

$$\Delta = \epsilon_r + \epsilon_\theta = \frac{\partial u}{\partial r} + \frac{u}{r} + \frac{\partial v}{r\,\partial \theta}. \quad . \quad . \quad (28)$$

It follows from (26) that the components of strain satisfy the compatibility condition

$$\frac{\partial^2 (r\gamma_{r\theta})}{\partial r\,\partial \theta} = r\frac{\partial^2 (r\epsilon_\theta)}{\partial r^2} - r\frac{\partial \epsilon_r}{\partial r} + \frac{\partial^2 \epsilon_r}{\partial \theta^2}. \quad . \quad . \quad (29)$$

11. INFINITESIMAL STRAIN IN THREE DIMENSIONS

The analysis proceeds exactly as in the two-dimensional case. We take a fixed set of mutually perpendicular axes of reference and suppose that the coordinates of a marked particle P relative to them are (x, y, z) and $(x+u, y+v, z+w)$ in the unstrained and strained states respectively, so that (u, v, w) are the components of displacement at P. Then if Q $(x+x', y+y', z+z')$ is a point near P, its displacement will be $(u+u', v+v', w+w')$, where

$$u' = \frac{\partial u}{\partial x}x' + \frac{\partial u}{\partial y}y' + \frac{\partial u}{\partial z}z', \quad . \quad . \quad (1)$$

$$v' = \frac{\partial v}{\partial x}x' + \frac{\partial v}{\partial y}y' + \frac{\partial v}{\partial z}z', \quad . \quad . \quad (2)$$

$$w' = \frac{\partial w}{\partial x}x' + \frac{\partial w}{\partial y}y' + \frac{\partial w}{\partial z}z', \quad . \quad . \quad (3)$$

by Taylor's theorem, neglecting the terms in x'^2, $x'y'$, etc.

Since in (1) to (3) the displacement of the particle at Q relative to that at P is linear in x', y', z', it follows that *in the immediate neighbourhood of any point* the strain is homogeneous and so the results of § 8 hold locally. In particular, a small sphere with centre at P becomes an ellipsoid, the strain ellipsoid, and there is one ellipsoid with centre at P which becomes a sphere; this is the reciprocal strain ellipsoid and its axes are the principal axes of strain.

The fundamental notation is

$$\varepsilon_x = \frac{\partial u}{\partial x}, \quad \varepsilon_y = \frac{\partial v}{\partial y}, \quad \varepsilon_z = \frac{\partial w}{\partial z}, \quad \cdot \quad \cdot \quad \cdot \quad (4)$$

$$\gamma_{yz} = \gamma_{zy} = \frac{\partial w}{\partial y} + \frac{\partial v}{\partial z}, \quad \gamma_{zx} = \gamma_{xz} = \frac{\partial u}{\partial z} + \frac{\partial w}{\partial x}, \quad \gamma_{xy} = \gamma_{yx} = \frac{\partial v}{\partial x} + \frac{\partial u}{\partial y}, \quad \cdot \quad (5)$$

$$2\omega_x = \frac{\partial w}{\partial y} - \frac{\partial v}{\partial z}, \quad 2\omega_y = \frac{\partial u}{\partial z} - \frac{\partial w}{\partial x}, \quad 2\omega_z = \frac{\partial v}{\partial x} - \frac{\partial u}{\partial y}. \quad \cdot \quad (6)$$

Using this notation, (1) to (3) become

$$u' = x'\varepsilon_x + \tfrac{1}{2}y'\gamma_{xy} + \tfrac{1}{2}z'\gamma_{xz} + z'\omega_y - y'\omega_z, \quad \cdot \quad \cdot \quad (7)$$

$$v' = \tfrac{1}{2}x'\gamma_{yx} + y'\varepsilon_y + \tfrac{1}{2}z'\gamma_{yz} + x'\omega_z - z'\omega_x, \quad \cdot \quad \cdot \quad (8)$$

$$w' = \tfrac{1}{2}x'\gamma_{zx} + \tfrac{1}{2}y'\gamma_{zy} + z'\varepsilon_z + y'\omega_x - x'\omega_y. \quad \cdot \quad (9)$$

The last terms, namely

$$z'\omega_y - y'\omega_z, \quad x'\omega_z - z'\omega_x, \quad y'\omega_x - x'\omega_y, \quad \cdot \quad (10)$$

are just the components of the displacement of the point (x', y', z') due to a small rotation of components $(\omega_x, \omega_y, \omega_z)$. These are called the *components of rotation* and it may be noted that if $\boldsymbol{\omega}$ is the vector of components $(\omega_x, \omega_y, \omega_z)$ specifying the rotation and $\boldsymbol{u}$ is the vector of components (u, v, w) then by (6)

$$2\boldsymbol{\omega} = \operatorname{curl} \boldsymbol{u}. \quad \cdot \quad \cdot \quad \cdot \quad (11)$$

If $\omega_x = \omega_y = \omega_z = 0$, the strain is *irrotational*.

The quantities $\varepsilon_x, \varepsilon_y, \varepsilon_z, \gamma_{yz}, \gamma_{zx}, \gamma_{xy}$ are the *components of strain*. $\varepsilon_x, \varepsilon_y, \varepsilon_z$ are the extensions of lines in the directions of the axes, while $\tfrac{1}{2}\pi - \gamma_{yz}$ is the angle in the strained state between lines initially parallel to the y- and z-axes.

Next, precisely as in § 10, we determine how the length of the line PQ has been altered by straining to $P'Q'$. Using (1) to (3) and making the assumption of infinitesimal strain, namely, that squares and products of the derivatives $\partial u/\partial x$, etc., are negligible, we find

$$P'Q'^2 = (x' + u')^2 + (y' + v')^2 + (z' + w')^2$$

$$= \left\{ x'\left(1 + \frac{\partial u}{\partial x}\right) + y'\frac{\partial u}{\partial y} + z'\frac{\partial u}{\partial z} \right\}^2$$

$$+\left\{x'\frac{\partial v}{\partial x}+y'\left(1+\frac{\partial v}{\partial y}\right)+z'\frac{\partial v}{\partial z}\right\}^2+\left\{x'\frac{\partial w}{\partial x}+y'\frac{\partial w}{\partial y}+z'\left(1+\frac{\partial w}{\partial z}\right)\right\}^2 \quad (12)$$

$$=x'^2+y'^2+z'^2+2x'^2\varepsilon_x+2y'^2\varepsilon_y+2z'^2\varepsilon_z+2y'z'\gamma_{yz}+2z'x'\gamma_{zx}$$
$$+2x'y'\gamma_{xy}. \qquad . \qquad (13)$$

Now suppose that PQ has length r and direction cosines (l, m, n) so that $x'=lr$, $y'=mr$, $z'=nr$, and (13) becomes

$$P'Q'^2=r^2\{1+2l^2\varepsilon_x+2m^2\varepsilon_y+2n^2\varepsilon_z+2mn\gamma_{yz}+2nl\gamma_{zx}+2lm\gamma_{xy}\}, \quad (14)$$

and, finally, taking the square root and neglecting terms in ε_x^2, etc., the extension ε corresponding to the direction (l, m, n) in the unstrained state at P is found to be

$$\varepsilon=\frac{P'Q'-r}{r}$$
$$=l^2\varepsilon_x+m^2\varepsilon_y+n^2\varepsilon_z+mn\gamma_{yz}+nl\gamma_{zx}+lm\gamma_{xy}. \quad . \qquad (15)$$

If a point is plotted in the direction (l, m, n) whose distance from the origin is $k/\varepsilon^{\frac{1}{2}}$, it will lie on the quadric

$$x^2\varepsilon_x+y^2\varepsilon_y+z^2\varepsilon_z+yz\gamma_{yz}+zx\gamma_{zx}+xy\gamma_{xy}=k^2. \qquad . \qquad (16)$$

This is the *strain quadric* whose theory may be developed in the same way as that of the stress quadric in § 4. In particular, its axes will be the principal axes of strain and the extensions ε_1, ε_2, ε_3 in these directions will be the principal strains. As before,

$$\Delta=\varepsilon_x+\varepsilon_y+\varepsilon_z=\varepsilon_1+\varepsilon_2+\varepsilon_3 \quad . \qquad . \qquad (17)$$

is an invariant. It is, in fact, the *dilatation* or the ratio of the change in volume to the initial volume.

Finally, it should be remarked that, as was seen in the two-dimensional case in § 10, the six components of strain are not independent: they are derived by differentiation from the components of displacement, and because of this there are in fact six identical relations between them, namely, § 10 (7) and two similar equations involving y, z and z, x, and also

$$2\frac{\partial^2\epsilon_x}{\partial y\,\partial z}=\frac{\partial}{\partial x}\left(-\frac{\partial\gamma_{yz}}{\partial x}+\frac{\partial\gamma_{zx}}{\partial y}+\frac{\partial\gamma_{xy}}{\partial z}\right), \quad . \qquad . \qquad (18)$$

and two similar equations. These relations are the compatibility conditions satisfied by the components of strain.

The formulae for change of axes are also often needed. Suppose that Ox', Oy', Oz' are new axes whose direction cosines relative to Ox, Oy, Oz

are (l, m, n), (l', m', n'), (l'', m'', n''), respectively, then the components of strain $\epsilon_{x'}$, $\epsilon_{y'}$, $\epsilon_{z'}$, $\gamma_{y'z'}$, $\gamma_{z'x'}$, $\gamma_{x'y'}$ relative to them are

$$\epsilon_{z'}=\epsilon_x l^2+\epsilon_y m^2+\epsilon_z n^2+\gamma_{yz}mn+\gamma_{zx}nl+\gamma_{xy}lm, \qquad . \qquad . \quad (19)$$

$$\gamma_{y'z'}=2\epsilon_x l'l''+2\epsilon_y m'm''+2\epsilon_z n'n''$$
$$+\gamma_{yz}(m'n''+m''n')+\gamma_{zx}(n'l''+n''l')+\gamma_{xy}(l'm''+l''m'), \quad (20)$$

and four similar equations. Of these, (19) has been derived in (15), and (20) follows from the three-dimensional analogue of the calculation leading to § 10 (15).

Finally, the way in which the analytic theory of finite strain is begun may be indicated. Exactly as above, we consider the points P, (x, y, z) and Q, $(x+x', y+y', z+z')$, where x', y', z' are so small that their squares and products are negligible, and find the length $P'Q'$ of the line PQ in the strained state. For this (1) to (3) and (12) still hold, but in the case of finite strain the squares and products of $\partial u/\partial x$, $\partial u/\partial y$, etc., are not negligible so that (13) is replaced by

$$P'Q'^2=x'^2+y'^2+z'^2+2(\epsilon_x^* x'^2+\epsilon_y^* y'^2+\epsilon_z^* z'^2+\gamma_{yz}^* y'z'+\gamma_{zx}^* z'x'+\gamma_{xy}^* x'y'), \quad (21)$$

where

$$\epsilon_x^*=\frac{\partial u}{\partial x}+\tfrac{1}{2}\left\{\left(\frac{\partial u}{\partial x}\right)^2+\left(\frac{\partial v}{\partial x}\right)^2+\left(\frac{\partial w}{\partial x}\right)^2\right\}, \qquad . \qquad . \quad (22)$$

$$\gamma_{yz}^*=\frac{\partial w}{\partial y}+\frac{\partial v}{\partial z}+\frac{\partial u}{\partial y}\frac{\partial u}{\partial z}+\frac{\partial v}{\partial y}\frac{\partial v}{\partial z}+\frac{\partial w}{\partial y}\frac{\partial w}{\partial z}, \qquad . \qquad . \quad (23)$$

with similar formulae for ϵ_y^*, γ_{zx}^*, etc. These quantities ϵ_x^*, ..., γ_{yz}^*, ... are the components of strain in the general case and reduce to (4) and (5) for the case of infinitesimal strain. It follows from (21) with $y'=z'=0$ that the extension in the x-direction is

$$\frac{P'Q'-x'}{x'}=(1+2\epsilon_x^*)^{\frac{1}{2}}-1, \qquad . \qquad . \qquad . \quad (24)$$

with similar formulae for those in the y- and z-directions. It also appears that, just as in § 9, the most satisfactory way of studying (21) is by considering the quadratic elongation $P'Q'^2/PQ^2$ which can be represented by a quadric surface. The way in which the angle between two lines varies may also be calculated. Finally, the dilatation Δ, the ratio of the change in volume to the original volume of an element of volume, is found to be given by

$$(1+\Delta)^2=(1+2\epsilon_x^*)(1+2\epsilon_y^*)(1+2\epsilon_z^*)+2\gamma_{yz}^*\gamma_{zx}^*\gamma_{xy}^*$$
$$-(1+2\epsilon_x^*)\gamma_{yz}^{*2}-(1+2\epsilon_y^*)\gamma_{zx}^{*2}-(1+2\epsilon_z^*)\gamma_{xy}^{*2}. \quad (25)$$

A full discussion along these lines is given in Love, *loc. cit.*, Chap. I (Appendix).

CHAPTER II

BEHAVIOUR OF ACTUAL MATERIALS

12. INTRODUCTORY

THE notions of stress and strain developed quantitatively in Chapter 1 are universal notions, the one being essentially a part of statics and the other a part of geometry. Any substance may be regarded as being in a state of stress and strain, the relationship between them depending on the nature of the substance. The procedure for finding this relationship is the same as that at the outset of any branch of mathematical physics: certain simple experiments are made (for example in a tensile testing machine) in which both the stress and strain are measured and the connexion between them is determined; this is idealized into a simple mathematical formula connecting stress and strain on the basis of which the behaviour of bodies under more complicated conditions can be calculated and in some cases (e.g., hollow cylinders under tension or torsion combined with internal pressure) compared with experiment.

It should be remarked that the idealizations studied are to some extent determined by the simple experiments such as tension, compression, and torsion which are possible, and also by the fact that most of the experimental work has been done on metals because of their technical importance and of the ease of experimenting with them; thus, for example, the perfectly plastic solid which has been much studied is a much more useful approximation to the behaviour of metals than of rock material. It should also be said that the type of behaviour of a substance [1] varies enormously with temperature, confining pressure, and rate of strain, and, again, that new effects appear when stresses are repeatedly reversed, so that the idealizations introduced are only reasonable

For the properties of metals see Barrett, *Structure of Metals* (McGraw-Hill, Ed. 2, 1952); Chalmers, *The Structure and Mechanical Properties of Metals* (Chapman and Hall, 1951). For the behaviour of rock materials see Nadai, *loc. cit.*; Birch, Schairer and Spicer, *Handbook of Physical Constants, Geol. Soc. Am. Special paper* No. 36; Scheidegger, 'Examination of the physics of the theories of orogenesis', *Bull. Geol. Soc. Am.*, **64** (1953), 127.

approximations to the behaviour of actual substances under very limited conditions.

Suppose, first, that a rod of a ductile metal is stressed in tension in a testing machine. The observable quantities are the stress σ_c,

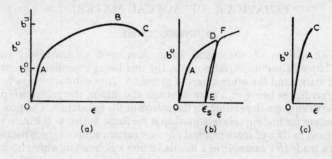

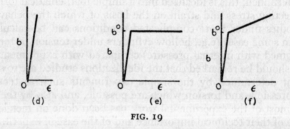

FIG. 19

which is the load applied by the machine divided by the original [1] area of the rod, and the strain

$$\varepsilon = (l - l_0)/l_0 , \qquad . \qquad . \qquad . \qquad . \qquad (1)$$

where l_0 is the original length of the rod and l is its length when the stress is σ_c. If σ_c is plotted against ε a *stress-strain curve* such as Fig. 19 (a) is obtained. For low stresses it is found that if the stress is reduced to zero the rod returns to its original length, that is, there is no permanent deformation. This is the property of elas-

[1] The area of the rod varies during the test, so that strictly σ_c as defined above is not the stress; it is often called the *conventional stress* and the diagram of Fig. 19 (a) is a *conventional stress-strain curve*. The effects of the changes in area are considered in § 26.

ticity, and the range of stresses in which there is no permanent deformation is called the *elastic region*. In this region it is also found to a very good approximation that stress is proportional to strain. The stress σ_0 for which permanent deformation first appears is called the *yield stress*, and it is at the point A, Fig. 19 (*a*), corresponding to it that curvature of the stress-strain curve first becomes apparent.[1] The strain at the point A is usually quite small, of the order of 0·001, so that its square is negligible and the theory of infinitesimal strain is applicable. Elastic behaviour may be idealized in the *perfectly elastic* solid of Fig. 19 (*d*) in which stress is proportional to strain for all stresses and there is no yield stress.

Deformation at stresses above the yield stress is described as plastic deformation, and a material with a yield stress may be idealized by the *perfectly plastic solid* of Fig. 19 (*e*), whose behaviour is elastic for stresses below the yield stress but which can sustain no stress greater than this and flows indefinitely under this stress unless distortion is restricted by some outside agency. The typical stress-strain diagram of Fig. 19 (*a*) shows a rise in the region AB beyond the yield stress. This increase is due to *strain hardening* which may be regarded as an increase in the yield stress of the material caused by deformation. If the material is stressed beyond its yield stress and the load is then removed and reapplied, the strain will diminish to ε_s (the permanent set) and a narrow loop DEF, very nearly parallel to OA, will be described, Fig. 19 (*b*). Thus after stressing beyond its yield stress the solid is found to behave as if its elastic properties were unchanged but its yield stress was increased.

At C in the curve of Fig. 19 (*a*) the specimen breaks; the fall in the region BC is associated with 'necking' of the specimen.

The whole of the above discussion applies to ductile materials, that is, those which exhibit plastic deformation at sufficiently great stresses. There is also a class of materials called *brittle* in which little, if any, plastic deformation takes place. If a brittle material such as cast iron or any rock material is tested, a stress-strain curve such as Fig. 19 (*c*) is obtained, the specimen breaking at the point

---

[1] A distinction is usually made between the *proportional limit* at which stress ceases to be proportional to strain and the yield stress at which permanent deformation is first observed. If this is done, there is a region of non-linear elasticity between the two values. Since neither is very well defined and they are usually close it is simpler to take it that they coincide.

C. Sometimes the curve is initially linear and shows curvature only as C is approached, sometimes it has a small curvature throughout, but it may be roughly idealized by the straight line of Fig. 19 (d), ending abruptly in fracture with no significant amount of plastic deformation.

A fact of the greatest importance for geology is that brittle materials such as rocks tend to become ductile when subjected to compression from all sides. In the classic experiments of von Karman, extended by Griggs,[1] cylinders of marble and limestone were

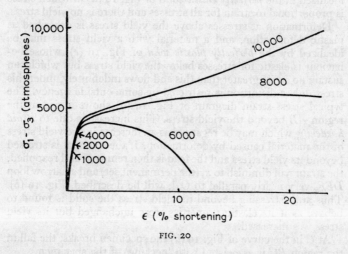

FIG. 20

tested in compression while an additional 'confining' pressure was applied by fluid to their curved surfaces.

In Fig. 20, for limestone, compressive strain is plotted against stress-difference (the excess of the axial compressive stress over the confining pressure) for various values of the confining pressure. The numbers on the curves are the values of the confining pressure in atmospheres. It appears that for confining pressures up to about 4,000 atmospheres limestone behaves as a brittle

[1] *J. Geol.*, **44** (1936), 541. Details of a great deal of work of this type are given in Nadai (*loc. cit.*) and Bridgman, *Studies in Large Plastic Flow and Fracture* (McGraw-Hill, 1952).

material, but for confining pressures of 6,000 atmospheres and over (corresponding to depths of 20 km. and over in the crust) it is capable of considerable plastic deformation. Similar results have been obtained for many rocks and minerals, though quartz shows no plastic deformation at the highest stresses yet attained.

The results described above may be regarded as typical of those which would be obtained by reasonably slow application of the load in a testing machine. If the load is applied more rapidly additional effects appear: in the elastic range these are described as time-dependent elasticity or *anelasticity*.[1] For example, it is found that when a load is applied suddenly the resulting strain does not appear instantaneously, but approaches its final value exponentially as in the curve OD of Fig. 21 (a); similarly, if the load is

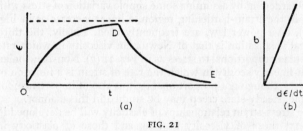

FIG. 21

removed the strain returns exponentially to zero as in curve DE of Fig. 21 (a).

In the plastic range, it is found also that when a load is applied the resulting strain is not taken up instantaneously but is approached asymptotically (transient creep) and also that the portion AB of the stress-strain curve of Fig. 19 (a) is raised as the rate of strain increases.

Finally, when long time intervals are in question, other types of *creep* appear. The most important of these, called steady state creep, consists of a slow steady deformation under load. This occurs at all stresses, even in the elastic range, though its rate increases greatly (approximately exponentially) with the stress and is also greatly accelerated at high temperatures (the creep rate depends on exp $(-A/kT)$, where T is the absolute temperature

[1] Zener, *Elasticity and Anelasticity of Metals* (Chicago, 1948).

and A and k are constants). Creep has been much studied [1] in metals, but it also occurs in rocks, particularly in the presence of solutions, and provides a possible mechanism for slow deformation of rocks, more particularly at the higher temperatures in the deeper parts of the Earth's crust and interior.

The discussion above provides a greatly simplified account of the behaviour of metals and rocks under stress. In developing a mathematical theory, some simple idealization of this behaviour must be taken and its consequences calculated. The simplest is that of the perfectly elastic body of Fig. 19 (d) on which the classical theory of elasticity is based. In an attempt to discuss plasticity, the simplest assumption is that of the perfectly plastic or St-Venant substance of Fig. 19 (e); when this theory has been fully worked out the next step is to introduce the additional complication of strain-hardening by assuming some simple variation of stress with strain in the strain-hardening region, a linear increase as in Fig. 19 (f), or a power law, are frequently used. Finally, the third classical idealization is that of Newtonian viscosity in which rate of strain is proportional to stress as in Fig. 21 (b). Non-Newtonian or non-linear viscosity in which the rate of strain is a function of the stress, though not proportional to it, is also of importance; for example, steady-state creep may be studied in this manner.

The stress-strain relationships of elasticity will be developed in §§ 13–17; those of viscosity in § 19; and those of plasticity in §§ 27–29. These, however, are still not adequate to describe phenomena of anelasticity such as Fig. 21 (a) or the behaviour of many important substances such as paints, clays, doughs, etc. The general study of the flow of such substances is included in the subject of Rheology, where it is found that their behaviour can be expressed in terms of elements containing elastic, viscous, and plastic properties: some examples are given in § 30.

13. THE STRESS-STRAIN RELATIONS FOR A PERFECTLY ELASTIC ISOTROPIC SOLID

The fundamental assumpton of the theory of elasticity, generalizing the notion that strain is proportional to stress in the simple

---

[1] Sully, *Metallic Creep and Creep-resistant Alloys* (Butterworth, 1949): Rotheram, *Creep of Metals* (Inst. of Phys., 1951): Griggs, 'Creep of Rocks', *J. Geol.*, **47** (1939), 225.

extension of a wire, is that each of the six components of stress at every point must be a linear function [1] of the six components of strain at that point so that in all 36 coefficients are involved. These, however, are not all independent, and in this section it will be found that for isotropic substances only two coefficients are involved in the complete expression of the relation between stress and strain. A material is said to be *isotropic* if its characteristics at every point are independent of direction. It will be assumed throughout this book (except in § 16) that the materials discussed are isotropic. If the properties of the material are not the same in all directions it is called *anisotropic* or aeolotropic.

First, we remark that the principal axes of stress and the principal axes of strain, defined quite independently in §§ 4 and 11, respectively, must be identical if the solid is isotropic. This follows since the stresses are purely normal in the directions of the principal axes of stress and thus must produce a system of displacements which are symmetrical with respect to these axes, since no asymmetrical displacement is to be preferred to any other. Now the displacements are symmetrical about the principal axes of strain, and so the two sets must coincide. An analytical proof of this result may be given by the methods of § 16.

If σ_1, σ_2, σ_3 and ε_1, ε_2, ε_3 are the principal stresses and strains, we may then assume as the stress-strain relations referred to principal axes

$$\sigma_1=(\lambda+2G)\varepsilon_1+\lambda\varepsilon_2+\lambda\varepsilon_3, \quad . \quad . \quad . \quad (1)$$

$$\sigma_2=\lambda\varepsilon_1+(\lambda+2G)\varepsilon_2+\lambda\varepsilon_3, \quad . \quad . \quad . \quad (2)$$

$$\sigma_3=\lambda\varepsilon_1+\lambda\varepsilon_2+(\lambda+2G)\varepsilon_3, \quad . \quad . \quad . \quad (3)$$

---

[1] If the equations connecting a number of variables contain all the variables to the first power only (or, if the equations are differential equations, contain successive differential coefficients to the first power only), they are said to be linear. The importance of linearity is twofold, firstly, the equations are relatively easy to solve, and, secondly, the principle of superposition holds in the form that if E_1 is the effect of a cause C_1, and E_2 that of a cause C_2, then E_1+E_2 is the effect of the combined causes C_1+C_2. Because of the difficulty of handling non-linear equations it is usually assumed at the outset of a theory that its equations are linear, the effect of non-linearity being studied later. Thus, while it is found that calculations based on the linear theory of this section give results which agree adequately with experiment for small strains, it is necessary to develop a non-linear theory when large strains are in question.

where λ and G are constants, and the form is chosen so that one parameter, $\lambda+2G$, relates stress and strain in the same direction, and another, λ, relates them in perpendicular directions. The physical significance of λ and G will appear later.

Introducing the dilatation

$$\Delta=\varepsilon_1+\varepsilon_2+\varepsilon_3, \quad . \quad . \quad . \quad . \quad (4)$$

equations (1) to (3) may be written

$$\sigma_1=\lambda\Delta+2G\varepsilon_1, \quad \sigma_2=\lambda\Delta+2G\varepsilon_2, \quad \sigma_3=\lambda\Delta+2G\varepsilon_3. \quad . \quad (5)$$

Now suppose that the axes Ox, Oy, Oz are inclined to the principal axes, their direction cosines being (l, m, n), (l', m', n'), (l'', m'', n''), respectively, so that by § 4 (6) and (7), and § 11 (19) and (20),

$$\sigma_x=l^2\sigma_1+m^2\sigma_2+n^2\sigma_3, \quad \tau_{yz}=\sigma_1l'l''+\sigma_2m'm''+\sigma_3n'n'', \quad . \quad (6)$$

$$\varepsilon_x=l^2\varepsilon_1+m^2\varepsilon_2+n^2\varepsilon_3, \quad \gamma_{yz}=2(\varepsilon_1l'l''+\varepsilon_2m'm''+\varepsilon_3n'n'') \quad . \quad (7)$$

Then, substituting (5) in (6) and then using (7), we get

$$\sigma_x=(l^2+m^2+n^2)\lambda\Delta+2G(l^2\varepsilon_1+m^2\varepsilon_2+n^2\varepsilon_3)$$

$$=\lambda\Delta+2G\varepsilon_x, \quad . \quad . \quad . \quad . \quad . \quad (8)$$

$$\tau_{yz}=(l'l''+m'm''+n'n'')\lambda\Delta+2G(l'l''\varepsilon_1+m'm''\varepsilon_2+n'n''\varepsilon_3)$$

$$=G\gamma_{yz}, \quad . \quad . \quad . \quad . \quad . \quad . \quad (9)$$

the term in Δ in (9) disappearing because (l', m', n') and (l'', m'', n'') are perpendicular. The complete set of equations connecting stress and strain is thus

$$\sigma_x=\lambda\Delta+2G\varepsilon_x, \quad \sigma_y=\lambda\Delta+2G\varepsilon_y, \quad \sigma_z=\lambda\Delta+2G\varepsilon_z, \quad . \quad (10)$$

$$\tau_{yz}=G\gamma_{yz}, \quad \tau_{zx}=G\gamma_{zx}, \quad \tau_{xy}=G\gamma_{xy}. \quad . \quad . \quad (11)$$

Adding (10) and using (4) gives

$$\sigma_x+\sigma_y+\sigma_z=(3\lambda+2G)\Delta. \quad . \quad . \quad . \quad (12)$$

The quantities λ and G are *Lamé's parameters* and are perhaps the most convenient elastic constants to use in theoretical work when it is required to express stress in terms of strain. We now proceed to define the other commonly occurring elastic constants and to express them in terms of λ and G.

The Modulus of Rigidity is defined as the ratio of shear stress to shear strain in simple shear, so by (11) is just the quantity G.

The Bulk Modulus or *Incompressibility* K is defined as the ratio of hydrostatic pressure to the dilatation it produces. In this case $\sigma_1=\sigma_2=\sigma_3=-p$, so, by (12), $(3\lambda+2G)\Delta=-3p$, so that

$$K=-\frac{p}{\Delta}=(\lambda+\tfrac{2}{3}G). \qquad . \qquad . \qquad . \quad (13)$$

The reciprocal of K is called the compressibility.

Young's Modulus E is defined as the ratio of tension to extension in a cylinder which is under axial tension and which is unrestricted laterally. In this case we have $\sigma_2=\sigma_3=0$ in (1) to (3) so that these become

$$\sigma_1=(\lambda+2G)\varepsilon_1+\lambda\varepsilon_2+\lambda\varepsilon_3, \qquad . \qquad . \quad (14)$$
$$0=\lambda\varepsilon_1+(\lambda+2G)\varepsilon_2+\lambda\varepsilon_3, \qquad . \qquad . \quad (15)$$
$$0=\lambda\varepsilon_1+\lambda\varepsilon_2+(\lambda+2G)\varepsilon_3. \qquad . \qquad . \quad (16)$$

It follows from (15) and (16) that

$$\varepsilon_2=\varepsilon_3=-\frac{\lambda}{2(\lambda+G)}\varepsilon_1, \qquad . \qquad . \quad (17)$$

and then from (14) that

$$E=\frac{\sigma_1}{\varepsilon_1}=\frac{G(3\lambda+2G)}{\lambda+G}. \qquad . \qquad . \quad (18)$$

Poisson's Ratio ν is defined as the ratio of lateral contraction to longitudinal extension for the cylinder in the case above, that is, by (17),

$$\nu=\frac{\lambda}{2(\lambda+G)}. \qquad . \qquad . \qquad . \quad (19)$$

There are many relations between the various elastic constants [1] λ, G, K, E, ν, of which the following are frequently useful:

$$\lambda=\frac{E\nu}{(1+\nu)(1-2\nu)}, \qquad G=\frac{E}{2(1+\nu)}, \qquad . \qquad . \quad (20)$$

$$K=\frac{2(1+\nu)G}{3(1-2\nu)}=\frac{E}{3(1-2\nu)}, \qquad . \qquad . \quad (21)$$

$$E=\frac{9KG}{3K+G}, \qquad \nu=\frac{(3K-2G)}{2(3K+G)}, \qquad \frac{\lambda}{G}=\frac{2\nu}{1-2\nu}. \qquad . \quad (22)$$

It follows from the last of (22) that $\nu<\tfrac{1}{2}$, and from the last of (20) that $\nu>-1$.

[1] Many writers use μ in place of G for the rigidity, and σ in place of ν for Poisson's ratio.

5

The equations (10) and (11) give the components of stress in terms of those of strain. Solving them and using (20), gives for strain in terms of stress

$$E\varepsilon_x=\sigma_x-\nu(\sigma_y+\sigma_z), \quad E\varepsilon_y=\sigma_y-\nu(\sigma_x+\sigma_z), \quad E\varepsilon_z=\sigma_z-\nu(\sigma_x+\sigma_y), \quad . \quad (23)$$

$$E\gamma_{yz}=2(1+\nu)\tau_{yz}, \quad E\gamma_{zx}=2(1+\nu)\tau_{zx}, \quad E\gamma_{xy}=2(1+\nu)\tau_{xy} . \quad . \quad (24)$$

In Table I typical values of the elastic constants are shown in order to give an idea of the orders of magnitude involved. It may be remarked that for many solids and rocks λ is very nearly equal to G: the assumption $\lambda=G$, which is often made to simplify calculations, is known as *Poisson's relation* and leads to

$$K=5G/3, \quad E=5G/2, \quad \nu=1/4. \quad . \quad . \quad (25)$$

Another simplifying assumption sometimes made is that the solid is incompressible so that $K=\infty$, this requires

$$\lambda=K=\infty, \quad \nu=1/2, \quad G=E/3.$$

The dimensions of all the elastic moduli λ, G, E, K are those of stress, since strain, being a ratio, is dimensionless. The units commonly used are dyne cm.$^{-2}$, lb.in.$^{-2}$, or kg.cm.$^{-2}$, the latter being approximately equal to 1 atmosphere. Values in the table are given in dyne cm.$^{-2}$: to convert to lb.in.$^{-2}$ multiply by 1.45×10^{-5}, and to convert to kg.cm.$^{-2}$ multiply by 1.02×10^{-6}. There is, of course, a very large variation between the elastic properties of rocks of the same type.

TABLE I

	$E\times10^{-11}$	$G\times10^{-11}$	$K\times10^{-11}$	ν
Steel	20·9	8·1	16·6	0·29
Copper	12·3	4·5	15·4	0·37
Lead	1·6	0·56	3·8	0·43
Quartz fibre	5·2	3·0	1·4	—
Rubber	0·05	—	—	0·46
Granite	4·6	1·9	2·6	0·21
Limestone	5·8	2·3	4·0	0·26
Sandstone	5·7	2·6	2·3	0·10

14. SPECIAL CASES: BIAXIAL STRESS AND STRAIN

In §§ 3, 7, 10 the variation of stress and strain in two dimensions was considered in detail because of its great simplicity relative to that in three dimensions, but since in general stress or strain in one direction is accompanied by effects in perpendicular directions, it is desirable to see precisely what practical systems can be represented adequately in two dimensions. The simple special cases, when referred to principal axes, may be classified as follows:

(i) *Uniaxial stress* $\sigma_1 \neq 0$, $\sigma_2 = \sigma_3 = 0$

This is the case of a bar uniformly stressed in one direction, and free in the perpendicular directions, which has already been discussed in § 13 (14)–(19). There is extension $\varepsilon_1 = \sigma_1/E$ in the direction of the stress and contraction $\varepsilon_2 = \varepsilon_3 = -\nu\varepsilon_1$ in perpendicular directions. The dilatation Δ is $(1-2\nu)\sigma_1/E$, so that since $\nu < \frac{1}{2}$ there is an increase of volume if $\sigma_1 > 0$ and a decrease if $\sigma_1 < 0$.

(ii) *Uniaxial strain* $\varepsilon_1 \neq 0$, $\varepsilon_2 = \varepsilon_3 = 0$

Here by § 13 (1)–(3)

$$\sigma_1 = (\lambda + 2G)\varepsilon_1, \quad \sigma_2 = \sigma_3 = \lambda\varepsilon_1. \quad \cdot \quad \cdot \quad (1)$$

The assumption is that there is no displacement perpendicular to the x-axis, and stresses σ_2, σ_3 given by (1) are called into play to prevent this displacement.

(iii) *Biaxial Stress or Plane Stress* $\sigma_1 \neq 0$, $\sigma_2 \neq 0$, $\sigma_3 = 0$, as in a thin sheet stressed in its own plane. By § 13 (23)

$$E\varepsilon_1 = \sigma_1 - \nu\sigma_2, \quad E\varepsilon_2 = \sigma_2 - \nu\sigma_1, \quad E\varepsilon_3 = -\nu(\sigma_1 + \sigma_2), \quad \cdot \quad (2)$$

so that there is expansion or contraction in the ε_3 direction according as $\sigma_1 + \sigma_2 < 0$ or > 0. For pure shear, $\sigma_1 + \sigma_2 = 0$, there is no strain in the ε_3 direction. The dilatation is

$$\Delta = (\sigma_1 + \sigma_2)(1 - 2\nu)/E. \quad \cdot \quad \cdot \quad (3)$$

This case occurs in the analysis of stress at any free surface, for, if the x- and y-axes are taken in the plane of the surface and the z-axis normal to it, the condition that there be no normal or shear stresses across the surface is

$$\sigma_z = \tau_{yz} = \tau_{xz} = 0.$$

(iv) *Biaxial Strain or Plane Strain* $\varepsilon_1 \neq 0$, $\varepsilon_2 \neq 0$, $\varepsilon_3 = 0$.

This is by far the most important special case in the theory of elasticity; it contains many important practical problems. By § 13 (1)–(3)

$$\sigma_1 = (\lambda + 2G)\varepsilon_1 + \lambda\varepsilon_2, \quad \sigma_2 = (\lambda + 2G)\varepsilon_2 + \lambda\varepsilon_1, \quad . \qquad . \quad (4)$$

$$\sigma_3 = \lambda(\varepsilon_1 + \varepsilon_2) = \nu(\sigma_1 + \sigma_2), \qquad . \qquad . \qquad . \quad (5)$$

adding (4) and using § 13 (19). Solving (4) gives

$$E\varepsilon_1 = (1 - \nu^2)\sigma_1 - \nu(1 + \nu)\sigma_2, \quad E\varepsilon_2 = (1 - \nu^2)\sigma_2 - \nu(1 + \nu)\sigma_1, \qquad (6)$$

$$\Delta = (\sigma_1 + \sigma_2)(1 - \nu - 2\nu^2)/E. \qquad . \qquad . \qquad . \quad (7)$$

In this case a stress given by (5) must be applied perpendicular to the plane of σ_1 and σ_2 to give zero displacement in this direction. If the x- and y-axes in the plane are not principal axes, we get in the same way by (5) and § 13 (23), (24)

$$E\varepsilon_x = (1 - \nu^2)\sigma_x - \nu(1 + \nu)\sigma_y, \quad E\varepsilon_y = (1 - \nu^2)\sigma_y - \nu(1 + \nu)\sigma_x, \quad . \quad (8)$$

$$E\gamma_{xy} = 2(1 + \nu)\tau_{xy}. \qquad . \qquad . \qquad . \qquad . \quad (9)$$

In both this case and (iii) the two dimensional analysis of stress and strain is the same as that of §§ 3, 10, but the situation in three dimensions is slightly different.

(v) *The Case* $\sigma_1 \neq 0$, $\varepsilon_2 = 0$, $\sigma_3 = 0$,

that is, zero stress and zero extension in two perpendicular directions normal to the stress σ_1. By § 13 (23)

$$E\varepsilon_1 = (1 - \nu^2)\sigma_1, \quad \sigma_2 = \nu\sigma_1, \quad \varepsilon_3 = -(\nu/1 - \nu)\varepsilon_1. \qquad . \quad (10)$$

(vi) *Combined Stress Systems.* Since the stress-strain relations of § 13 (1)–(3) are linear in the σ and ε, it follows that if ε_1, ε_2, ε_3 are the strains corresponding to stresses σ_1, σ_2, σ_3, and ε_1', ε_2', ε_3' correspond to σ_1', σ_2', σ_3', then $\varepsilon_1 + \varepsilon_1'$, etc., will be the strains corresponding to the combined stresses $\sigma_1 + \sigma_1'$, etc.

(vii) *Systems with Rotational Symmetry*

If two principal stresses are equal, say $\sigma_2 = \sigma_3$, it follows that $\varepsilon_2 = \varepsilon_3$ and the stress and strain ellipsoids become ellipsoids of revolution. The variation of stress and strain in any plane through the ε_1-axis follows from the two-dimensional theory.

One difference between the case of rotational symmetry and the general case appears in the circular sections of the strain ellipsoid, cf.

§ 8 (7). In the case of rotational symmetry, $\epsilon_2=\epsilon_3$, all sections of the strain ellipsoid perpendicular to the ϵ_1-axis are circles, but by § 8 (6), neglecting squares of ϵ_1, etc., the lines of unchanged length lie on a cone about the ϵ_1-axis whose semi-vertical angle is

$$\tan^{-1} (-\epsilon_1/\epsilon_2)^{\frac{1}{2}}. \qquad . \qquad . \qquad . \qquad . \qquad (11)$$

For example, in uniaxial stress, (i) above, the lines of unchanged length lie on a cone of semi-vertical angle

$$\tan^{-1} (\nu^{-\frac{1}{2}}). \qquad . \qquad . \qquad . \qquad (12)$$

For the general case, $\epsilon_1 > \epsilon_2 > \epsilon_3$, the strain ellipsoid has two circular sections passing through the ϵ_2-axis, and by § 8 (8) these make angles

$$\pm\tan^{-1} [(\epsilon_1-\epsilon_2)/(\epsilon_2-\epsilon_3)]^{\frac{1}{2}} \qquad . \qquad . \qquad . \qquad (13)$$

with the ϵ_1-axis. If $\epsilon_2=0$ the lines of unchanged length lie in these circular sections, and in case (v) above they make angles of

$$\pm\tan^{-1} [(1-\nu)/\nu]^{\frac{1}{2}} \qquad . \qquad . \qquad . \qquad (14)$$

with the ϵ_1-axis. These results are of interest in connection with strain theories of failure, § 25.

When studying problems on regions with rotational symmetry it is

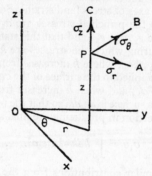

FIG. 22

usually convenient to use cylindrical polar coordinates, the z-axis being the axis of symmetry. In these coordinates the position of a point P is specified by its distance z from a plane perpendicular to the z-axis and the polar coordinates (r, θ) of its projection on this plane, Fig. 22.

The components of stress at P are measured relative to the orthogonal r, θ, z directions PA, PB, PC; they are $\sigma_r, \sigma_\theta, \sigma_z, \tau_{r\theta}, \tau_{\theta z}, \tau_{zr}$. In the same way, if u, v, w are the displacements in the r, θ, z directions, the components of strain are found by an extension of the analysis of § 10 (26) to be

$$\epsilon_r = \frac{\partial u}{\partial r}, \quad \epsilon_\theta = \frac{1}{r}\left(u + \frac{\partial v}{\partial \theta}\right), \quad \epsilon_z = \frac{\partial w}{\partial z}, \qquad . \qquad . \qquad (15)$$

$$\gamma_{\theta z}=\frac{1}{r}\frac{\partial w}{\partial \theta}+\frac{\partial v}{\partial z}, \quad \gamma_{rz}=\frac{\partial u}{\partial z}+\frac{\partial w}{\partial r}, \quad \gamma_{r\theta}=\frac{1}{r}\left(\frac{\partial u}{\partial \theta}-v\right)+\frac{\partial v}{\partial r}, \quad (16)$$

$$\Delta=\frac{\partial u}{\partial r}+\frac{\partial w}{\partial z}+\frac{1}{r}\left(u+\frac{\partial v}{\partial \theta}\right). \quad . \quad . \quad . \quad (17)$$

The stress-strain relations § 13 (10), (11) referred to these axes become

$$\sigma_r=\lambda\Delta+2G\epsilon_r, \quad \sigma_\theta=\lambda\Delta+2G\epsilon_\theta, \quad \sigma_z=\lambda\Delta+2G\epsilon_z, \quad . \quad (18)$$

$$\tau_{\theta z}=G\gamma_{\theta z}, \quad \tau_{zr}=G\gamma_{zr}, \quad \tau_{r\theta}=G\gamma_{r\theta}. \quad . \quad . \quad (19)$$

15. STRAIN-ENERGY

The potential energy per unit volume stored in the body by elastic straining is a quantity of great theoretical importance and also has been made fundamental in several of the criteria for fracture and flow.

Consider a small cube of side length a with its faces perpendicular to the principal axes of stress (and strain). Suppose that in the final state of stress the principal stresses are σ_1, σ_2, σ_3 and the principal strains are ε_1, ε_2, ε_3, and that this state is built-up by a gradual increase during which the stresses are $k\sigma_1$, $k\sigma_2$, $k\sigma_3$ and the strains $k\varepsilon_1$, $k\varepsilon_2$, $k\varepsilon_3$, where k increases from 0 to 1. Then at any stage the force applied to the surface of the cube perpendicular to the σ_1 axis is $ka^2\sigma_1$, and when k increases from k to $k+dk$ the displacement of this surface is $a\varepsilon_1 dk$, so that the total work done by forces in the σ_1-direction in producing the final state of strain is

$$\sigma_1\varepsilon_1 a^3 \int_0^1 k\,dk = \tfrac{1}{2}\sigma_1\varepsilon_1 a^3. \quad . \quad . \quad . \quad (1)$$

There will be similar contributions from the other directions, and adding these and dividing by the volume a^3 gives

$$W=\tfrac{1}{2}(\sigma_1\varepsilon_1+\sigma_2\varepsilon_2+\sigma_3\varepsilon_3) \quad . \quad . \quad (2)$$

for W, the *potential energy per unit volume or strain energy per unit volume* of the body. Clearly, by conservation of energy, the results (1) and (2) must be independent of the way in which the final state of stress is reached, and the linear increase was chosen above as the simplest to calculate.

The result (2) may be put in a variety of forms. Using § 13 (5) it becomes

$$W=\tfrac{1}{2}\lambda\Delta^2+G(\varepsilon_1{}^2+\varepsilon_2{}^2+\varepsilon_3{}^2), \quad . \quad . \quad (3)$$

and using § 13 (23) it becomes

$$W = \frac{1}{2E}\{\sigma_1^2 + \sigma_2^2 + \sigma_3^2 - 2\nu(\sigma_2\sigma_3 + \sigma_3\sigma_1 + \sigma_1\sigma_2)\}. \qquad (4)$$

By § 4 (22) and (23), this becomes

$$W = \frac{1}{2E}\{\sigma_x^2 + \sigma_y^2 + \sigma_z^2 - 2\nu(\sigma_y\sigma_z + \sigma_z\sigma_x + \sigma_x\sigma_y) + 2(1+\nu)(\tau_{yz}^2 + \tau_{zx}^2 + \tau_{xy}^2)\}$$

$$= \tfrac{1}{2}(\sigma_x\varepsilon_x + \sigma_y\varepsilon_y + \sigma_z\varepsilon_z + \tau_{yz}\gamma_{yz} + \tau_{zx}\gamma_{zx} + \tau_{xy}\gamma_{xy}), \qquad \cdot \qquad \cdot \qquad (5)$$

on using § 13 (23) and (24). (5) might have been proved directly by the type of argument leading to (1). It follows from (5) that

$$\frac{\partial W}{\partial \sigma_x} = \varepsilon_x, \quad \frac{\partial W}{\partial \varepsilon_x} = \sigma_x, \quad \frac{\partial W}{\partial \gamma_{yz}} = \tau_{yz}, \text{ etc.} \quad \cdot \qquad (6)$$

Another important expression for W is given in § 27 (26).

16. ANISOTROPIC SUBSTANCES

These may be regarded as being of two types, firstly crystals, and secondly substances such as sedimentary rocks or wood which have different properties in different directions. Only the simplest cases can be treated here to give an indication of the way in which the theory is developed and of the new effects which appear.

It is usual to choose for axes of reference directions related to the symmetry of the substance under consideration so that all six components of stress and strain will appear, and we assume the most general linear relation between them, namely,

$$\sigma_x = c_{11}\varepsilon_x + c_{12}\varepsilon_y + c_{13}\varepsilon_z + c_{14}\gamma_{yz} + c_{15}\gamma_{zx} + c_{16}\gamma_{xy}, \qquad \cdot \qquad \cdot \qquad (1)$$

$$\sigma_y = c_{21}\varepsilon_x + c_{22}\varepsilon_y + c_{23}\varepsilon_z + c_{24}\gamma_{yz} + c_{25}\gamma_{zx} + c_{26}\gamma_{xy}, \qquad \cdot \qquad \cdot \qquad (2)$$

$$\sigma_z = c_{31}\varepsilon_x + c_{32}\varepsilon_y + c_{33}\varepsilon_z + c_{34}\gamma_{yz} + c_{35}\gamma_{zx} + c_{36}\gamma_{xy}, \qquad \cdot \qquad \cdot \qquad (3)$$

$$\tau_{yz} = c_{41}\varepsilon_x + c_{42}\varepsilon_y + c_{43}\varepsilon_z + c_{44}\gamma_{yz} + c_{45}\gamma_{zx} + c_{46}\gamma_{xy}, \qquad \cdot \qquad \cdot \qquad (4)$$

$$\tau_{zx} = c_{51}\varepsilon_x + c_{52}\varepsilon_y + c_{53}\varepsilon_z + c_{54}\gamma_{yz} + c_{55}\gamma_{zx} + c_{56}\gamma_{xy}, \qquad \cdot \qquad \cdot \qquad (5)$$

$$\tau_{xy} = c_{61}\varepsilon_x + c_{62}\varepsilon_y + c_{63}\varepsilon_z + c_{64}\gamma_{yz} + c_{65}\gamma_{zx} + c_{66}\gamma_{xy}. \qquad \cdot \qquad \cdot \qquad (6)$$

The 36 constants c_{rs} are called the elastic coefficients and for various types of crystal symmetry there are relations between them. Firstly, it will be shown that it is always true that

$$c_{rs} = c_{sr}, \qquad \cdot \qquad \cdot \qquad \cdot \qquad \cdot \qquad (7)$$

so that there are at most 21 independent coefficients.

To prove this, it follows from [1] § 15 (6) that

$$\frac{\partial \sigma_x}{\partial \epsilon_y} = \frac{\partial^2 W}{\partial \epsilon_x \partial \epsilon_y} = \frac{\partial \sigma_y}{\partial \epsilon_x}, \qquad \cdot \qquad \cdot \qquad \cdot \qquad (8)$$

and, using the values (1) and (2) of σ_x and σ_y, this gives $c_{12}=c_{21}$, and in the same way the equality of the other pairs of (7) may be derived.

In most cases a further reduction of the number of coefficients follows from the symmetry properties of the material in question, though the most general case, that of a triclinic crystal, contains the full 21 coefficients. The simplest special cases are discussed below.

(i) *Material with Different Properties in Three Orthogonal Directions.* Taking the axes Ox, Oy, Oz in these directions, the material has the

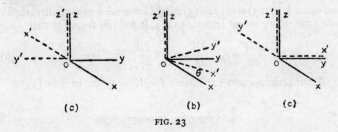

FIG. 23

property that any plane perpendicular to one of these axes is a plane of symmetry. The stress-strain relations relative to these axes are given by (1) to (6), subject, of course, to (7).

It follows from the nature of the material that the stress-strain relations must be precisely the same if, instead of looking at it in the direction Ox, we look at it in the opposite direction. That is, we must get precisely the same set of stress-strain relations for the axes Ox', Oy', Oz' of Fig. 23 (a) which are just the original axes rotated through 180°. That is, referred to these new axes, we must have

$$\sigma_{x'}=c_{11}\epsilon_{x'}+c_{12}\epsilon_{y'}+c_{13}\epsilon_{z'}+c_{14}\gamma_{y'z'}+c_{15}\gamma_{z'x'}+c_{16}\gamma_{x'y'}, \qquad \cdot \qquad (9)$$

and five equations similar to (2)–(6) with $x, y, \ldots$ replaced by $x', y'. \ldots$ Now the quantities $\sigma_{x'}, \ldots, \epsilon_{x'}$, etc., in these are related to the $\sigma_x, \ldots, \epsilon_x$ of (1) to (6) by the formulae § 4 (6), (7) and § 11 (19), (20) for change of axes, the connection being

$$\epsilon_{x'}=\epsilon_x, \quad \epsilon_{y'}=\epsilon_y, \quad \epsilon_{z'}=\epsilon_z, \quad \gamma_{y'z'}=-\gamma_{yz}, \quad \gamma_{z'x'}=-\gamma_{zx}, \quad \gamma_{x'y'}=\gamma_{xy}, \quad (10)$$

$$\sigma_{x'}=\sigma_x, \quad \sigma_{y'}=\sigma_y, \quad \sigma_{z'}=\sigma_z, \quad \tau_{y'z'}=-\tau_{yz}, \quad \tau_{z'x'}=-\tau_{zx}, \quad \tau_{x'y'}=\tau_{xy}. \quad (11)$$

Using these, (9) becomes

$$\sigma_x=c_{11}\epsilon_x+c_{12}\epsilon_y+c_{13}\epsilon_z-c_{14}\gamma_{yz}-c_{15}\gamma_{zx}+c_{16}\gamma_{xy}. \qquad \cdot \qquad \cdot \qquad (12)$$

---

[1] As remarked in § 15, the result § 15 (5) is a general one and independent of the simple arguments used in that section to prove it. The equations (8) are the conditions for dW to be a perfect differential, that is, for W to be a single-valued function of the strains.

Comparing (12) and (1), it follows that

$$c_{14}=0, \quad c_{15}=0,$$

and treating the other five equations corresponding to (9) in the same way gives

$$c_{24}=c_{25}=c_{34}=c_{35}=c_{46}=c_{56}=0. \quad \quad . \quad . \quad . \quad (13)$$

Also, a rotation of 180° about Ox gives in addition

$$c_{16}=c_{26}=c_{36}=c_{45}=0. \quad . \quad \quad . \quad \quad . \quad (14)$$

Thus, finally, the stress-strain relations for *a solid with three mutually perpendicular planes of symmetry* are

$$\sigma_x=c_{11}\epsilon_x+c_{12}\epsilon_y+c_{13}\epsilon , \quad . \quad \quad . \quad \quad . \quad (15)$$

$$\sigma_y=c_{12}\epsilon_x+c_{22}\epsilon_y+c_{23}\epsilon_z , \quad . \quad \quad . \quad \quad . \quad (16)$$

$$\sigma_z=c_{13}\epsilon_x+c_{23}\epsilon_y+c_{33}\epsilon_z , \quad . \quad \quad . \quad \quad . \quad (17)$$

$$\tau_{yz}=c_{44}\gamma_{yz} , \quad \tau_{zx}=c_{55}\gamma_{zx} , \quad \tau_{xy}=c_{66}\gamma_{xy} , \quad \quad . \quad \quad . \quad (18)$$

which involve nine independent coefficients.

(ii) *Material with an Axis of Symmetry.* Suppose the z-axis is an axis of symmetry in the sense that the properties of the material are the same in all directions at right angles to it (as in a sedimentary rock with z-axis perpendicular to the bedding). In this case the same system of equations has to be obtained, not only for a reversal in direction of the z-axis, but also for x- and y-axes rotated through any angle θ about it as in Fig. 23 (*b*). Proceeding as in (i), the equations are found to be

$$\sigma_x=c_{11}\epsilon_x+(c_{11}-2c_{66})\epsilon_y+c_{13}\epsilon_z , \quad . \quad \quad . \quad (19)$$

$$\sigma_y=(c_{11}-2c_{66})\epsilon_x+c_{11}\epsilon_y+c_{13}\epsilon_z , \quad . \quad \quad . \quad (20)$$

$$\sigma_z=c_{13}\epsilon_x+c_{13}\epsilon_y+c_{33}\epsilon_z , \quad \quad . \quad \quad . \quad \quad . \quad (21)$$

$$\tau_{yz}=c_{44}\gamma_{yz} , \quad \tau_{zx}=c_{44}\gamma_{zx} , \quad \tau_{xy}=c_{66}\gamma_{xy} , \quad \quad . \quad \quad . \quad (22)$$

involving five independent coefficients.

(iii) *The Cubic Crystal.* This is the simplest and most important of the crystal classes. In this case the equations must have the same form relative to any right-handed set of mutually perpendicular axes chosen from the axes of symmetry; that is, not merely for the axes, Ox, Oy, Oz and Ox', Oy', Oz' of Fig. 23 (*a*) corresponding to a rotation through 180° but also for the axes Ox', Oy', Oz' of Fig. 23 (*c*) corresponding to rotation through 90°. For such a rotation

$$\epsilon_{x'}=\epsilon_y , \quad \epsilon_{y'}=\epsilon_x , \quad \epsilon_{z'}=\epsilon_z , \quad \gamma_{y'z'}=-\gamma_{zx} , \quad \gamma_{z'x'}=\gamma_{yz} , \quad \gamma_{x'y'}=-\gamma_{xy} ,$$

$$\sigma_{x'}=\sigma_y , \quad \sigma_{y'}=\sigma_x , \quad \sigma_{z'}=\sigma_z , \quad \tau_{y'z'}=-\tau_{zx} , \quad \tau_{z'x'}=\tau_{yz} , \quad \tau_{x'y'}=-\tau_{xy} ,$$

and using these in the same way as (10) and (11) gives finally

$$\sigma_x=c_{11}\epsilon_x+c_{12}\epsilon_y+c_{12}\epsilon_z , \quad . \quad \quad . \quad \quad . \quad (23)$$

$$\sigma_y=c_{12}\epsilon_x+c_{11}\epsilon_y+c_{12}\epsilon_z , \quad . \quad \quad . \quad \quad . \quad (24)$$

$$\sigma_z=c_{12}\epsilon_x+c_{12}\epsilon_y+c_{11}\epsilon_z , \quad . \quad \quad . \quad \quad . \quad (25)$$

$$\tau_{yz}=c_{44}\gamma_{yz} , \quad \tau_{zx}=c_{44}\gamma_{zx} , \quad \tau_{xy}=c_{44}\gamma_{xy} , \quad \quad . \quad \quad . \quad (26)$$

which involve three independent coefficients.

A complete collection of the equations for all the crystal classes is given in Love's *Elasticity* or Wooster's *Crystal Physics* (Cambridge, 1949).

The stress-strain relations above and the expressions for the components of stress and strain referred to any axes give any information required, although the algebra involved usually is very heavy.

Considering, for example, the set (15)–(17), suppose $\sigma_y = \sigma_z = 0$, then, solving

$$\epsilon_x = \sigma_x(c_{22}c_{33} - c_{23}{}^2)/D, \quad \epsilon_y = \sigma_x(c_{23}c_{13} - c_{12}c_{33})/D, \quad \epsilon_z = \sigma (c_{12}c_{23} - c_{22}c_{13})/D, \quad (27)$$

where

$$D = \begin{vmatrix} c_{11} & c_{12} & c_{13} \\ c_{12} & c_{22} & c_{23} \\ c_{13} & c_{23} & c_{33} \end{vmatrix}. \qquad (28)$$

Young's modulus for uniaxial stress in the x-direction is

$$\sigma_x/\epsilon_x = D/(c_{22}c_{33} - c_{23}{}^2), \qquad (29)$$

and for stress in this direction there will be different Poisson's ratios for the y- and z-directions, namely,

$$\frac{\epsilon_y}{\epsilon_x} = \frac{c_{23}c_{13} - c_{12}c_{33}}{c_{22}c_{33} - c_{23}{}^2}, \quad \frac{\epsilon_z}{\epsilon_x} = \frac{c_{12}c_{23} - c_{22}c_{13}}{c_{22}c_{33} - c_{23}{}^2}. \qquad (30)$$

Each direction of stress will have its own Young's Modulus and a variation of Poisson's ratio about it.

In general, the six relations (1)–(6) can be solved for $\epsilon_x, \ldots, \gamma_{xy}$ leading to six equations of which the first is

$$\epsilon_x = s_{11}\sigma_x + s_{12}\sigma_y + s_{13}\sigma_z + s_{14}\tau_{yz} + s_{15}\tau_{zx} + s_{16}\tau_{xy}, \qquad (31)$$

where the 36 quantities s_{rs} (actually at most 21 since $s_{rs} = s_{sr}$) can be written out as determinants involving the c_{rs}. The s_{rs} are called elastic moduli [1] and it may be noticed that they, rather than the c_{rs}, are the quantities accessible to experiment.

17. FINITE HYDROSTATIC STRAIN

In discussing the behaviour of matter under high pressures, both in laboratory experiments and in the interior of the Earth, the assumptions of infinitesimal strain break down and a theory of finite strain must be developed. The general theory is given in Murnaghan (*loc. cit.*); here, to indicate the ideas involved, only the simplest and most important case, that of finite hydrostatic strain in an isotropic material, will be considered.

In this case the extension is independent of direction, so by § 11 (21)

$$\epsilon_x^* = \epsilon_y^* = \epsilon_z^* \qquad (1)$$

$$\gamma_{yz}^* = \gamma_{zx}^* = \gamma_{xy}^* = 0. \qquad (2)$$

Also, by § 11 (24), the extension in any direction is

$$(1 + 2\epsilon_x^*)^{1/2} - 1 \qquad (3)$$

---

[1] There is a considerable variation in the names given to the c_{rs} and s_{rs}. That used above is common in crystallography: on the other hand, Love, *loc. cit.*, calls $1/s_{rs}$ a modulus in conformity with the usage of § 13.

and therefore the volume of a sphere whose radius is r_0 in the unstrained state will be $4\pi r_0{}^3(1+2\epsilon_x^*)^{3/2}/3$ and so the dilatation Δ will be

$$\Delta = (1+2\epsilon_x^*)^{3/2} - 1. \qquad \qquad (4)$$

Writing for shortness $-\epsilon$ for ϵ_x^*, the negative sign being chosen since ϵ_x^* is negative for the case of hydrostatic pressure, the densities ρ and ρ_0 in the strained and unstrained states will by (4) be connected by

$$\rho/\rho_0 = (1-2\epsilon)^{-3/2}. \qquad \qquad (5)$$

It follows from (5) that

$$\frac{d\rho}{d\epsilon} = \frac{3\rho_0}{(1-2\epsilon)^{5/2}}. \qquad \qquad (6)$$

At this stage it is necessary to make some assumption about the relationship between stress and strain, and the simplest general assumption is that the pressure can be expanded as a power series in the strain, that is,

$$p = a_1\epsilon + a_2\epsilon^2 + \ldots, \qquad \qquad (7)$$

where a_1 and a_2 are constants. Murnaghan (*loc. cit.*) gives theoretical reasons for expanding the strain energy in a power series—this is equivalent to (7). In practice, only the first few terms of (7) are needed: even in the extreme case of the deep interior of the Earth the density is of the order of 16, and comparing this with the density of iron at the surface, 7·9, gives by (5) a strain of $\epsilon = 0·19$ so that the series (7) should be rapidly convergent.

Because of the importance of the quantity $(1-2\epsilon)$, an alternative assumption to (7) which is sometimes made is

$$p = (1-2\epsilon)^{-\beta}\{b_1\epsilon + b_2\epsilon^2 + \ldots\}, \qquad \qquad (8)$$

where $\beta, b_1, \ldots$ are constants.

Alternatively, again, assumptions may be made about the incompressibility as a function of pressure. For finite strains, the incompressibility K at any pressure p is defined as the ratio of the increment of pressure δp to the increment of volumetric strain $-\delta v/v$, that is,

$$K = -\lim_{\delta p \to 0} \frac{v\delta p}{\delta v} = -v\frac{dp}{dv} = \rho\frac{dp}{d\rho}. \qquad \qquad (9)$$

The simplest assumption $K = K_0$, independent of pressure, gives by (9)

$$p - p_1 = K_0 \ln(\rho/\rho_1), \qquad \qquad (10)$$

where ρ_1 is the value of ρ when $p = p_1$. This is useful only for small changes of pressure.

The next possibility, K a linear function of p, or

$$K = K_0 + \alpha p, \qquad \qquad (11)$$

where K_0 and α are constants, leads to

$$p = (K_0/\alpha)\{(\rho/\rho_0)^\alpha - 1\}, \qquad \qquad (12)$$

where ρ_0 is the value of ρ when $p = 0$.

If the relations (7) or (8) are assumed, the incompressibility can be expressed as a function of density by (5) and (9): for example, (7) gives

$$K = \tfrac{1}{3}(\rho_0/\rho)^{2/3}\{a_1 + a_2[1-(\rho/\rho_0)^{-2/3}] + \ldots\}, \quad . \quad . \quad (13)$$

and putting $\rho = \rho_0$ gives $a_1 = 3K_0$, where K_0 is the incompressibility when $p=0$. Similarly, (8) gives $b_1 = 3K_0$.

Retaining only the first term of (8) gives

$$p = (3/2)K_0(\rho/\rho_0)^{2(\beta-1)/3}\{(\rho/\rho_0)^{2/3} - 1\}. \quad . \quad . \quad (14)$$

Density and compressibility can be measured as functions of pressure up to pressures of hundreds of thousands of atmospheres,[1] and from the results of such experiments attempts are made to select most suitable values for the constants in the various possible expressions such as (7), (8), (12). For example, Birch has found that (14) with $\beta = 7/2$ is the one-parameter formula which best fits the behaviour of all substances in the pressure range from 0 to 100,000 atmospheres.

18. NATURAL STRAIN

The definition of extension $\epsilon = (l'-l)/l$ of § 6 (1) is not very suitable for large strains since its form for small changes, namely,

$$\delta\epsilon = \delta l'/l, \quad . \quad . \quad . \quad . \quad (1)$$

relates the change in length $\delta l'$ to the original length l. Clearly, it would be more satisfactory to relate $\delta l'$ to the actual length l', that is, to write

$$\delta\bar{\epsilon} = \delta l'/l', \quad . \quad . \quad . \quad . \quad (2)$$

cf. § 17 (9) for a similar definition.

The quantity $\bar{\epsilon}$ defined by (2) is called a *natural* or *logarithmic* strain. Integrating (2) over the whole change in length from l to l' gives

$$\bar{\epsilon} = \int_l^{l'} \frac{dl'}{l'} = \ln\frac{l'}{l} = \ln(1+\epsilon). \quad . \quad . \quad (3)$$

Much of the theory of §§ 7-9 can be rewritten in this new notation; thus the quadratic elongation λ of § 6 (2) is given by

$$\lambda = \exp(2\bar{\epsilon}), \quad . \quad . \quad . \quad (4)$$

and similarly the three principal quadratic elongations of § 9 (4) can be expressed in terms of the three principal natural strains $\bar{\epsilon}_1$, $\bar{\epsilon}_2$, $\bar{\epsilon}_3$. Also, by § 9 (7), the dilatation Δ is given by

$$\Delta = (\lambda_1\lambda_2\lambda_3)^{\frac{1}{2}} - 1 = \exp\{\bar{\epsilon}_1 + \bar{\epsilon}_2 + \bar{\epsilon}_3\} - 1, \quad . \quad . \quad (5)$$

so that the condition for the strain to be equivoluminal is

$$\bar{\epsilon}_1 + \bar{\epsilon}_2 + \bar{\epsilon}_3 = 0. \quad . \quad . \quad . \quad (6)$$

This holds accurately, however large the strain, while the condition $\epsilon_1 + \epsilon_2 + \epsilon_3 = 0$ is only valid for infinitesimal strains.

---

[1] Bridgman, *Physics of High Pressure* (Bell, Ed. 2, 1949); Birch, *J. Geophys. Res.*, **57** (1952), 227.

For a complete theory of natural strain it is also necessary to introduce natural shears. These are usually defined relative to a set of mutually perpendicular axes fixed in space, the increments of the three components of natural shear being the changes in the angles between pairs of lines in the body which instantaneously coincide with two of the axes.

The importance of natural strain arises from the fact that at any stage of deformation the stress-strain relations may be regarded as connecting increments of stress with increments of natural strain.

As an example we consider some problems of finite plane strain in a perfectly elastic material. By § 14 (4) the relations connecting the increments of stress and natural strain referred to principal axes will be

$$\delta\sigma_1=(\lambda+2G)\delta\bar{\epsilon}_1+\lambda\delta\bar{\epsilon}_2, \quad \delta\sigma_2=\lambda\delta\bar{\epsilon}_1+(\lambda+2G)\delta\bar{\epsilon}_2. \qquad (7)$$

For the case of finite *pure shear*, $\sigma_2=-\sigma_1$, these give

$$\delta\bar{\epsilon}_1=-\delta\bar{\epsilon}_2=\delta\sigma_1/2G. \qquad . \qquad . \qquad . \qquad (8)$$

Since the principal axes of stress and strain remain coincident and the same throughout the deformation, (8) may be integrated and gives

$$\bar{\epsilon}_1=-\bar{\epsilon}_2=\sigma_1/2G, \qquad . \qquad . \qquad . \qquad (9)$$

or

$$1+\epsilon_1=1/(1+\epsilon_2)=\exp(\sigma_1/2G). \qquad . \qquad . \qquad (10)$$

The case of *finite simple shear* is also interesting and introduces an important new point. It was shown at the end of § 7 that when the amount of the shear is s, § 7 (4), the axes of the strain ellipse make angles of $\alpha'=\frac{1}{4}\pi-\frac{1}{2}\tan^{-1}s$ and $\frac{1}{2}\pi+\alpha'$ with the x-axis and their lengths are $(s^2+1)^{\frac{1}{2}}\pm s$. It follows that the principal natural strains are

$$\bar{\epsilon}_1=\ln[s+(s^2+1)^{\frac{1}{2}}]=\sinh^{-1}s, \quad \bar{\epsilon}_2=-\bar{\epsilon}_1. \qquad . \qquad (11)$$

The new feature is that the principal axes of strain rotate during straining, and, since the principal axes of stress must coincide with them at all stages, these latter must also rotate and the nature of the stress must change—in particular it cannot be a constant shear stress τ_{xy}. Suppose that a known shear stress τ_{xy} is applied to the material; we calculate the additional shear stress, specified by $\sigma_x=-\sigma_y$, which is necessary to bring the principal axes of stress into the required position. By § 3 (11) these axes make angles α' and $\alpha'+\frac{1}{2}\pi$ with the x-axis given by

$$\tan 2\alpha'=\frac{2\tau_{xy}}{\sigma_x-\sigma_y}=\frac{\tau_{xy}}{\sigma_x}, \qquad . \qquad . \qquad . \qquad (12)$$

and equating this to the value of α' found above from the amount of the shear gives

$$\sigma_x=s\tau_{xy}. \qquad . \qquad . \qquad . \qquad . \qquad (13)$$

This determines σ_x in terms of s and τ_{xy}, and the maximum shear stress τ_0 is, by § 3 (18),

$$\tau_0^2=\sigma_x^2+\tau_{xy}^2=\tau_{xy}^2(s^2+1). \qquad . \qquad . \qquad (14)$$

Since referred to principal axes the shear is now a pure shear $\bar{\epsilon}_2=-\bar{\epsilon}_1$ and the stress system is a pure shear stress $\sigma_1=-\sigma_2=\tau_0$, we can use (11) and (14) in (9) which gives

$$\sinh^{-1}s=(\tau_0/2G)=\tau_{xy}(s^2+1)^{\frac{1}{2}}/2G. \qquad . \qquad . \qquad (15)$$

19. THE EQUATIONS OF VISCOSITY

A fundamental property of a fluid is that it can withstand no shear stress, however small, without permanent deformation. A fluid in laminar motion, however, is found to exert a shear stress on its boundaries which is proportional to the rate of shear. On this basis the equations for viscous flow in three dimensions are set up in exactly the same way that the stress-strain relations of elasticity were generalized from Hooke's law for simple tension.

The displacements of the particles of the fluid do not appear (at least in the usual Eulerian equations) but only their derivatives, the velocities. Writing a dot for differentiation with respect to the time, the components of velocity will be $\dot{u}$, $\dot{v}$, $\dot{w}$, in the notation of § 11, and the components of rate of strain will be by § 11 (4), (5)

$$\dot{\varepsilon}_x = \frac{\partial \dot{u}}{\partial x}, \quad \dot{\varepsilon}_y = \frac{\partial \dot{v}}{\partial y}, \quad \dot{\varepsilon}_z = \frac{\partial \dot{w}}{\partial z}, \qquad \cdot \quad \cdot \quad (1)$$

$$\dot{\gamma}_{yz} = \frac{\partial \dot{w}}{\partial y} + \frac{\partial \dot{v}}{\partial z}, \quad \dot{\gamma}_{zx} = \frac{\partial \dot{u}}{\partial z} + \frac{\partial \dot{w}}{\partial x}, \quad \dot{\gamma}_{xy} = \frac{\partial \dot{v}}{\partial x} + \frac{\partial \dot{u}}{\partial y}, \qquad \cdot \quad \cdot \quad (2)$$

and the components of rate of rotation will be given by

$$2\dot{\omega}_x = \frac{\partial \dot{w}}{\partial y} - \frac{\partial \dot{v}}{\partial z}, \quad 2\dot{\omega}_y = \frac{\partial \dot{u}}{\partial z} - \frac{\partial \dot{w}}{\partial x}, \quad 2\dot{\omega}_z = \frac{\partial \dot{v}}{\partial x} - \frac{\partial \dot{u}}{\partial y}. \quad \cdot \quad (3)$$

The vector (3) is called the vorticity, and if it vanishes the motion is called irrotational.

These velocities and strain rates are to be understood as those at a fixed point referred to fixed axes. The components of stress in the fluid defined in § 4 will be referred to the same axes. The fundamental assumption, then, is that each of the components of stress must be a linear function of the components of rate of strain, and the discussion is precisely the same as that of § 13 with ε_x replaced by $\dot{\varepsilon}_x$, etc., except that, since in a liquid there is usually a hydrostatic pressure p superposed on the viscous stresses which vanish when the velocity is zero, terms $-p$ are added to σ_1, σ_2 and σ_3 to allow for this. Thus in place of § 13 (1) to (3) we get

$$\sigma_1 = -p + (\lambda' + 2\eta)\dot{\varepsilon}_1 + \lambda'\dot{\varepsilon}_2 + \lambda'\dot{\varepsilon}_3, \qquad \cdot \quad \cdot \quad (4)$$

$$\sigma_2 = -p + \lambda'\dot{\varepsilon}_1 + (\lambda' + 2\eta)\dot{\varepsilon}_2 + \lambda'\dot{\varepsilon}_3, \qquad \cdot \quad \cdot \quad (5)$$

$$\sigma_3 = -p + \lambda'\dot{\varepsilon}_1 + \lambda'\dot{\varepsilon}_2 + (\lambda' + 2\eta)\dot{\varepsilon}_3, \qquad \cdot \quad \cdot \quad (6)$$

where λ' and η are the constants of proportionality appropriate to the present case.

Precisely the same analysis as that leading to § 13 (10), (11), (12) gives the fundamental relations

$$\sigma_x=\lambda'\dot{\Delta}+2\eta\dot{\varepsilon}_x-p, \quad \sigma_y=\lambda'\dot{\Delta}+2\eta\dot{\varepsilon}_y-p, \quad \sigma_z=\lambda'\dot{\Delta}+2\eta\dot{\varepsilon}_z-p, \qquad (7)$$

$$\tau_{yz}=\eta\dot{\gamma}_{yz}, \quad \tau_{zx}=\eta\dot{\gamma}_{zx}, \quad \tau_{xy}=\eta\dot{\gamma}_{xy}, \quad . \qquad . \qquad (8)$$

$$\sigma_x+\sigma_y+\sigma_z=-3p+(3\lambda'+2\eta)\dot{\Delta}. \qquad . \qquad . \qquad (9)$$

(9) is a connexion between pressure and rate of change of volume so that $\lambda'+2\eta/3$ is a bulk viscosity analogous to the bulk modulus of § 13 (13). An effect of this type, though it presumably exists, is of no general importance so that we may assume it to vanish and take

$$3\lambda'+2\eta=0. \qquad . \qquad . \qquad . \qquad (10)$$

Using this, (7) and (9) become

$$\sigma_x=2\eta\dot{\varepsilon}_x-\tfrac{2}{3}\eta\dot{\Delta}-p, \quad \sigma_y=2\eta\dot{\varepsilon}_y-\tfrac{2}{3}\eta\dot{\Delta}-p, \quad \sigma_z=2\eta\dot{\varepsilon}_z-\tfrac{2}{3}\eta\dot{\Delta}-p, \quad (11)$$

$$\sigma_x+\sigma_y+\sigma_z=-3p. \qquad . \qquad . \qquad (12)$$

These are the equations of viscosity. For an incompressible fluid Δ and $\dot{\Delta}$ vanish, and (11) becomes

$$\sigma_x=2\eta\dot{\varepsilon}_x-p, \quad \sigma_y=2\eta\dot{\varepsilon}_y-p, \quad \sigma_z=2\eta\dot{\varepsilon}_z-p. \qquad . \qquad (13)$$

The condition

$$\dot{\Delta}=\frac{\partial\dot{u}}{\partial x}+\frac{\partial\dot{v}}{\partial y}+\frac{\partial\dot{w}}{\partial z}=0 \qquad . \qquad . \qquad . \qquad (14)$$

for an incompressible fluid is the *equation of continuity* which expresses the fact that the mass of fluid within any imaginary fixed closed surface remains constant.

In the simplest case of simple shearing motion of planes z=constant in the direction of the x-axis, we have $\dot{u}=U$, the velocity, which is a function of z only, $\dot{v}=\dot{w}=0$, so that the only non-vanishing component of rate of strain is

$$\dot{\gamma}_{zx}=\frac{\partial U}{\partial z},$$

and (8) gives

$$\tau_{zx}=\eta\frac{\partial U}{\partial z}. \qquad . \qquad . \qquad (15)$$

η is called the coefficient of viscosity, its dimensions are those of plastic deformation called 'necking', which usually is terminated by a 'cup and cone' fracture, Fig. 24 (*a*), of which the sides *AB* and *CD* are conical while the central portion *BC* (in which fracture actually begins) is flat. This process of failure in ductile materials by localized plastic deformation is frequently called *rupture*.

(ii) For brittle materials in tension, fracture, known as *brittle*

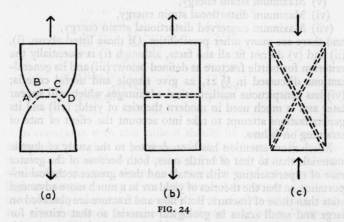

FIG. 24

fracture (sometimes as tensile or cleavage fracture), takes place across a surface perpendicular to the direction of tension, Fig. 24(*b*).

(iii) For brittle materials in compression, fracture, called *shear fracture*, takes place along a pair of planes or a cone approximately in the direction of greatest shear stress but always lying between this direction and the direction of the compressive stress, Fig. 24 (*c*). Shear fracture also occurs in the cone *AB* of the 'cup and cone' in (i).

Other types of fracture,[1] for example, those due to fatigue caused by repeated reversal of stress, and those due to creep at high temperatures, are also recognized and have been studied.

The tensile and compressive strengths of a brittle material are the stresses necessary to cause fracture. For a ductile material the

[1] For a full discussion of fracture in general see Orowan, *Reports on Progress in Physics*, **12** (1949), 185.

'ultimate' stress defined in § 26 is that usually given. Some typical values are given in Table III.

TABLE III

Material	Tension (kg./cm.²)	Compression (kg./cm.²)
Granite	40	1,400
Gabbro		1,800
Marble	60	1,000
Limestone	40	900
Sandstone	20	700
Brick		300
Cast iron	1,500	
Mild steel	4,600	
Copper	1,600	
Glass	600	
Quartz fibre	10,000	

21. THE MAXIMUM SHEAR STRESS THEORY OF
FRACTURE AND ITS GENERALIZATIONS

The maximum shear stress theory, which dates back to Coulomb, states that failure occurs at a point when the maximum shear stress is equal to some definite value which is called the shear strength of the material. Now, if σ_1, σ_2, σ_3 are the principal stresses at a point, it is known from § 4 that the maximum shear stress has magnitude

$$\tfrac{1}{2}(\sigma_1 - \sigma_3)$$

and occurs across a plane whose normal bisects the angle between the greatest and least principal stresses. This implies that, if C_0 is the compressive strength of the material in a pure compression test in which $\sigma_1 = \sigma_2 = 0$, $\sigma_3 = -C_0$, the material may fail across any plane inclined at $45°$ to the direction of compression. The angle is in fact usually less than $45°$ and there are more serious difficulties, notably that the theory implies that the tensile and compressive strengths are equal.

This theory has been modified by Navier into a form which qualitatively fits most of the facts, and which has been used by

Anderson [1] in a discussion of the types of geological faulting. Instead of assuming that fracture takes place across the plane over which the shear stress first becomes equal to a constant S_0 (the shear strength of the medium), it assumes that this shear strength is increased by a constant μ times the normal pressure across the plane. This is analogous to ordinary friction in which the tangential force is μ times the normal reaction, so that μ is frequently called the *coefficient of internal friction*. If σ and τ are the normal and shear stresses across a plane, the criterion states that fracture takes place for the plane at which the magnitude of τ first becomes equal to $S_0-\mu\sigma$ (the negative sign is due to the convention that σ is positive if it is a tension). This criterion

$$|\tau|=S_0-\mu\sigma \quad . \qquad . \qquad . \qquad . \quad (1)$$

may be reached in a number of other ways. Thus, if it is assumed that the general criterion can be expressed by the vanishing of some unknown function of σ and τ, the linear function (1) would be studied first. Another interpretation of (1) will appear in connexion with Mohr's theory, § 22.

We now discuss (1) in detail, taking the case of two dimensions first. If σ_1 and σ_2 are the principal stresses, by § 3 (13) and (14)

$$\sigma=\tfrac{1}{2}(\sigma_1+\sigma_2)+\tfrac{1}{2}(\sigma_1-\sigma_2)\cos 2\theta, \quad . \qquad . \quad (2)$$

$$\tau=-\tfrac{1}{2}(\sigma_1-\sigma_2)\sin 2\theta, \quad . \qquad . \qquad . \quad (3)$$

$$\mu\sigma+|\tau|=\tfrac{1}{2}\mu(\sigma_1+\sigma_2)+\tfrac{1}{2}(\sigma_1-\sigma_2)\{\sin 2\theta+\mu\cos 2\theta\}. \quad . \quad (4)$$

Values of θ between o and $90°$ only need be considered, since only the magnitude of τ occurs in (1): changing the sign of θ only changes the sign of $\sin 2\theta$ and does not affect either σ or $|\tau|$, so that the result is symmetrical about $\theta=0$.

Fracture is assumed to take place when the quantity $\mu\sigma+|\tau|$ first attains the value S_0. Now (4) has its maximum value when

$$\tan 2\theta=1/\mu, \quad . \qquad . \qquad . \quad (5)$$

and the value of this maximum is

$$\tfrac{1}{2}\mu(\sigma_1+\sigma_2)+\tfrac{1}{2}(\sigma_1-\sigma_2)(\mu^2+1)^{\frac{1}{2}}. . \quad . \qquad . \quad (6)$$

Thus by (1) failure takes place across the plane whose normal is specified by (5) when

$$\sigma_1\{\mu+(\mu^2+1)^{\frac{1}{2}}\}+\sigma_2\{\mu-(\mu^2+1)^{\frac{1}{2}}\}=2S_0. . \quad . \quad (7)$$

[1] *The Dynamics of Faulting* (Oliver and Boyd, Ed. 2, 1954).

Considering first the direction of the normal to the plane of failure, if $\mu=0$, $\theta=45°$; if $\mu=1$, $\theta=22\frac{1}{2}°$; if $\mu\rightarrow\infty$, $\theta\rightarrow0$, that is, as μ increases the normal moves towards the direction of maximum stress (reckoned algebraically, tension being positive) and the plane of fracture moves towards the direction of least stress, that is, the direction of maximum compression if one or both of the stresses is compressive. Values of μ of the order of 1 are inferred from the directions of fracture of rocks in testing machines and also from geological faulting. It should be remarked that, because of the symmetry in θ mentioned above, the theory leads to two possible planes of fracture equally inclined to the principal stresses and gives no reason for preferring either.

The formula (7) leads to a criterion for failure under combined stress in terms of the compressive and tensile strengths, C_0 and T_0, of the material.

Failure in pure tension corresponds to $\sigma_1=T_0$, $\sigma_2=0$ in (7) so that

$$T_0\{\mu+(\mu^2+1)^{\frac{1}{2}}\}=2S_0. \quad . \quad . \quad . \quad (8)$$

Failure in compression corresponds to $\sigma_1=0$, $\sigma_2=-C_0$ in (7) so that

$$C_0\{(\mu^2+1)^{\frac{1}{2}}-\mu\}=2S_0. \quad . \quad . \quad . \quad (9)$$

It follows that

$$\frac{C_0}{T_0}=\frac{(\mu^2+1)^{\frac{1}{2}}+\mu}{(\mu^2+1)^{\frac{1}{2}}-\mu}, \quad . \quad . \quad (10)$$

and that (7) may be written

$$\frac{\sigma_1}{T_0}-\frac{\sigma_2}{C_0}=1. \quad . \quad . \quad . \quad (11)$$

This may be represented on the (σ_1, σ_2) plane of Fig. 25 (a). Since $\sigma_1>\sigma_2$ only the region to the right of the line POQ is in question, and (11) is the straight line AB. Then if the point corresponding to principal stresses σ_1, σ_2 lies in the angle ABQ the material will fail, while if it lies in the angle ABP the material can sustain this state of stress. It should be added that this simple representation holds also for axial symmetry in which two of the principal stresses are equal, but has to be modified along the lines of § 28 if the three principal stresses are different.

It follows from (10) that the theory predicts that the compressive strength of a material is always greater than its tensile strength, but the ratio is rather smaller than that found in practice, for example, $\mu=1$ gives $C_0=5\cdot8T_0$ which may be compared with the values in the table of § 20. Another inadequacy of the theory is that it predicts that under any conditions the normal to the plane of fracture makes the same angle, $\frac{1}{2}\tan^{-1}(1/\mu)$, with the direction of greatest principal stress. This is approximately true for compressive stresses but is very far from the truth in the case of pure tension when, as remarked in § 20, the failure is usually by brittle fracture with the plane of fracture normal to the direction of tension. The reason for this is presumably that the above theory

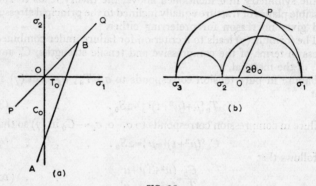

FIG. 25

assumes shear fracture, so that T_0 should not be the actual (brittle) tensile strength but the value at which shear failure in tension would take place if in fact brittle fracture did not occur in practice before this value is reached. This is in line with geological thought which distinguishes sharply between shear faults and tension faults. Despite the above criticisms which refer to systems with a predominant tensile principal stress, the theory gives a reasonably accurate quantitative account of the behaviour of rocks under combined compressive stresses.

In three dimensions the matter is best discussed by using Mohr's representation of Fig. 7 (a) or Fig. 25 (b). (5) may be expressed by the statement that $\mu\sigma+|\tau|$ for planes whose normals lie in the plane of σ_1 and σ_3 is a maximum at the point P of Fig. 25 (b) where OP makes an angle $2\theta_0=\tan^{-1}(1/\mu)$ with the direction of greatest principal stress. It follows by inspection of Fig. 25 (b) that its value at this point is greater than that for any other direction in three dimensions. We thus have the result that the *planes of fracture pass through the axis of the intermediate principal stress and their normals make angles $\pm\frac{1}{2}\tan^{-1}(1/\mu)$ of between* 0 *and* 45° *with the greatest principal stress.* If two of the principal stresses are equal the two-dimensional theory can be taken over immediately, but instead of

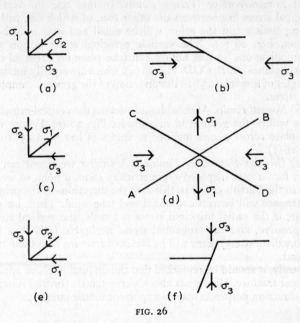

FIG. 26

the two possible planes of fracture there will be a cone of fracture with the direction of the third principal stress as axis.

One important application of these results is the study of faults which are fractures of the rocks of the Earth's crust (they may be on any scale, large or small). Geologists distinguish three major types of fault, and Anderson (*loc. cit.*) has shown that these are determined by the relative magnitudes of the principal stresses. One principal stress should always be nearly vertical, and three cases arise according as this is the greatest, intermediate, or least.

(i) *Thrust Faults.* In this case the vertical principal stress is the least in magnitude and the other two principal stresses are compressive, Fig. 26 (*a*). The planes of fracture pass through the direction of the intermediate principal stress and make angles of less than 45° with the direction of the greatest compressive stress (and also with the horizontal), Fig. 26 (*b*).

(ii) *Transcurrent or Wrench Faults.* In this case the vertical principal stress lies between the other two, of which one will be a compression and the other will be small and may even be a tension, Fig. 26 (c). The verticle principal stress is now the intermediate one so that failure can take place on either of two vertical planes *AOB*, *COD*, Fig. 26 (*d*), which are equally inclined at angles of less than 45° to the direction of the greatest compressive stress.

(iii) *Normal Faults.* At considerable depths the vertical principal stress will be the greatest in magnitude, Fig. 26 (*e*). Failure will take place across planes inclined at angles of less than 45° to it, Fig. 26 (*f*).

(iv) *Circular Systems of Faulting.* A similar treatment can be given for stresses disposed symmetrically about a point of weakness in the Earth's crust. In this case the directions of the principal stresses will be vertical, radial and tangential. Then, for example, if the radial principal stress is tensile, the vertical stress compressive, and the tangential stress negligible (and thus the intermediate stress) there will be cones of fracture with their axes vertical.

Finally, it should be remarked that the discussion above applies to shear fracture. Geologists also observe tensile (brittle) fracture in a direction perpendicular to important tensile stresses.

22. MOHR'S THEORY OF FRACTURE

Mohr's theory assumes that at failure across a plane the normal and shear stresses across the plane, σ and τ, are connected by some functional relation,

$$\tau = f(\sigma), \qquad . \qquad . \qquad . \qquad (1)$$

characteristic of the material. This relation may be plotted on the (σ, τ) plane and, since changing the sign of τ simply changes the direction of failure but not the condition for it, the curve must be symmetrical about the σ-axis. For the present we shall consider the two-dimensional theory only.

Suppose that AB, $A'B'$, Fig. 27 (a), is portion of the curve (1)—the way in which the curve is completed beyond BB' and AA' will be discussed later. Any state of stress can be represented by a Mohr circle on the (σ, τ) plane: if this circle lies wholly within the curve $ABA'B'$ the stresses involved nowhere attain the critical values: is any portion lies outside it the material could not withstand the stresses. The limiting case is that of a circle such as that of centre C, Fig. 27 (a), which just touches the curve AB; in this case failure will take place under conditions corresponding to the points PP', that is, over planes whose normals are inclined at angles of half the

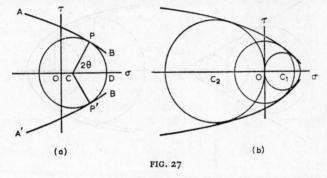

FIG. 27

angle PCD to the direction of the greatest principal stress. The curve AB will be the envelope of all the circles corresponding to all conditions at which fracture takes place, and for this reason is known as the *Mohr envelope*. In principle, three circles which touch it can be found from simple experiments, namely, those of centres C_1, O, and C_2, Fig. 27 (b), corresponding to tension, simple shear, and compression, respectively. In practice, it is difficult to perform shear or tensile tests on rock material, and the *triaxial test* is preferred. In this, the material is subjected to axial compression and to hydrostatic pressure in the perpendicular directions. By varying the hydrostatic pressure any number of circles, all to the left of the τ-axis in Fig. 27 (b), may be found. Since increasing the hydrostatic pressure in general increases the resistance to fracture, it seems probable that the Mohr envelope is open to the left.

The simplest possible Mohr envelope is the pair of straight lines of Fig. 28 (a),

$$\tau = \pm(\tau_1 - \mu\sigma). \qquad . \qquad . \qquad . \qquad (2)$$

In all cases the normal to the plane of fracture makes an angle

$$\tfrac{1}{2}\tan^{-1}(1/\mu)$$

with the direction of the greatest principal stress. Thus the straight line Mohr envelope gives the Coulomb–Navier theory of § 21. It is found that the results of triaxial tests on most rock materials may be represented quite well by a straight line Mohr envelope and it is usual to determine their shear strengths in this way.

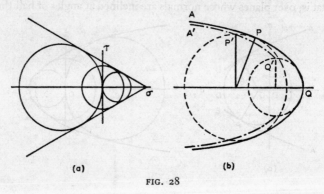

(a)   (b)

FIG. 28

In three dimensions the theory leads to the result that only the Mohr circles for the plane containing the greatest and least principal stresses need be considered, and that fracture always takes place in planes passing through the direction of the intermediate principal stress: this is not altogether consistent with the experimental results.

Mohr's theory, as enunciated above, is an empirical attempt to set up a criterion which gives not only the stresses necessary to cause fracture but also the direction of fracture: it has the merit that these quantities involve both the mean stress $\sigma_m = \tfrac{1}{2}(\sigma_1 + \sigma_2)$ and the maximum shear $\tau_m = \tfrac{1}{2}(\sigma_1 - \sigma_2)$. The more usual point of view is that an experimental relation can be found connecting the principal stresses σ_1 and σ_2 at which fracture occurs; since σ_1 and σ_2 can be expressed in terms of σ_m and τ_m this gives a 'fracture curve' such as $A'P'Q'$ of Fig. 28 (b), the point P' of which corresponds to the point P of the Mohr envelope. If either of the curves APQ or $A'P'Q'$ is known, the other can be found; except that, if the Mohr envelope has a finite radius of curvature at the point Q at which it crosses the σ-axis, any points on the fracture curve $A'P'Q'$ within the circle through Q and Q' will have a Mohr circle lying wholly within the Mohr envelope and so the original assumption breaks down. This case is not of any practical importance since the point Q, corresponding to triaxial or hydrostatic tension, has not yet been attained experimentally.

23. EARTH PRESSURE

It is found experimentally that the behaviour of soil materials above the water table can be fairly adequately represented by the straight-line Mohr envelope of §§ 21, 22, which, for the present purpose, may be written in the form

$$|\tau| = c - \sigma \tan \phi. \qquad . \qquad . \qquad . \qquad (1)$$

Here the constant c, which is the shear stress which the material can sustain at zero normal stress, is called the *cohesion*, and ϕ is called the *angle of friction*. Since soil cannot sustain tension, only the portion of the

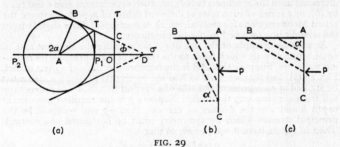

FIG. 29

Mohr envelope (1) to the left of the τ-axis is in question: this is shown by the full lines in Fig. 29 (a). Two special cases are of importance: (i) for very soft clay $\phi = 0$; (ii) for dry [1] sand, which is cohesionless, $c = 0$ so that the straight lines of the Mohr envelope pass through the origin, in this case ϕ has the physical interpretation that it is the maximum possible angle of slope of a sand surface.

Many important results follow from the geometry of the Mohr envelope, Fig. 29 (a). Since we are only concerned with compressive stresses,

---

[1] For wet sand the value of σ is to be increased by a constant representing the pore-water pressure.

we write $\sigma_1 = -p_1$, $\sigma_2 = -p_2$ for the principal stresses so that the lengths OP_1 and OP_2 are p_1 and p_2. Also, it is convenient to introduce as a new parameter the angle α defined by

$$\alpha = 45° + \tfrac{1}{2}\phi . \qquad . \qquad . \qquad . \qquad (2)$$

so that in Fig. 29 (a) the angles BAP_2 and BTP_1 are both 2α. When failure takes place, the plane of sliding will make an angle α with the direction of lesser compression. It follows from (2) that

$$\cot \phi = -\tan 2\alpha = \frac{2 \tan \alpha}{\tan^2 \alpha - 1}. \qquad . \qquad . \qquad (3)$$

Now from the geometry of Fig. 29 (a),

$$P_1T = P_1A \cot \alpha = \tfrac{1}{2}(p_2 - p_1) \cot \alpha, \qquad . \qquad . \qquad (4)$$

and also

$$P_1T = c + p_1 \tan \phi. \qquad . \qquad . \qquad . \qquad (5)$$

From (3), (4) and (5) it follows that

$$p_2 = 2c \tan \alpha + p_1 \tan^2 \alpha. \qquad . \qquad . \qquad (6)$$

This is the fundamental relation which connects the principal stresses at which failure takes place with the properties of the material. These properties are usually measured by the *triaxial test* in which the soil in the form of a finite cylinder is enclosed in a waterproof cover and subjected to external hydrostatic pressure p_1 and an axial load p_2 which is increased until the specimen fails [1]: two such experiments give c and $\tan \alpha$ by (6), or a series of such tests at different values of p_1 will determine the actual Mohr envelope for the soil, which of course will differ slightly from the straight line assumed in the simple theory.

As another example of the use of (6) we consider the simplest case of equilibrium of soils which leads to the theory of earth pressure on retaining walls, etc. Suppose that AB is the horizontal surface of a mass of soil, Fig. 29 (b), and that we wish to find the horizontal pressure which must be applied at each point of the side of a vertical trench AC to prevent the soil from slipping into the trench. Suppose p is the required pressure at depth h and ρ is the density of the soil, then $-p$ and $-\rho h$ will be the principal stresses which by symmetry must be horizontal and vertical. Then in (6) we have $p_1 = p$, $p_2 = \rho h$, so that

$$p \tan^2 \alpha = \rho h - 2c \tan \alpha. \qquad . \qquad . \qquad (7)$$

If a pressure given by (7) is applied at each point of AC, the material will be in a state of incipient slip down the dotted planes in Fig. 29 (b) which are inclined at α to the horizontal. This is known as the *active Rankine state of plastic equilibrium*.

The pressure p was less than ρh in the above. It is also possible to have plastic equilibrium (Rankine's passive state) with $p > \rho h$, corresponding to the pressure being sufficiently great to cause the soil to slip upward.

---

[1] In practice, various types of test are distinguished according to the speed of testing and the arrangements made for the escape or otherwise of pore water from the soil.

In this case $p_1 = \rho h$, $p_2 = p$, and by (6)

$$p = 2c \tan \alpha + \rho h \tan^2 \alpha, \quad . \quad . \quad . \quad (8)$$

and the material is in a state of incipient slip upwards along the dotted planes of Fig. 29 (c) inclined at α to the vertical.

24. THE GRIFFITH THEORY OF BRITTLE STRENGTH

The mathematical theory involved is too difficult to give here, but the results are indicated as an example of an important method of attack and of another criterion of failure.

It is well known that attempts to calculate the tensile strengths of simple crystals give results which are very much higher than those observed experimentally. Griffith explained this by the presence of a large number of minute cracks, *Griffith cracks*, in the material, and demonstrated their existence and the general validity of the formulae below by experiments on glass.

The effect of a crack is to produce a very high concentration of stress at its edge. The amount of this can be calculated from the result that the maximum tensile stress in a flat plate containing an elliptical hole of major axis $2l$ and subjected to an average tensile stress σ in a direction perpendicular to the major axis is given by

$$2\sigma(l/\rho)^{\frac{1}{2}}, \quad . \quad . \quad . \quad . \quad (1)$$

where ρ is the radius of curvature at the ends of the major axis. The maximum stress (1) occurs at the ends of the major axis, and as $\rho \rightarrow 0$, that is, the ellipse tends to a flat crack, the stress tends to infinity. For the type of crack under consideration ρ may be estimated to be of the order of the intermolecular spacing a.

The crack will spread if the stress given by (1) is equal to σ_m, the maximum tensile stress which can be sustained by the material without cracking. To estimate this, the process of cracking must be considered: this produces two new surfaces within the material whose distance apart is of the order of the intermolecular spacing a and which each possess surface energy α per unit area which may be regarded as an intrinsic and measurable property of the material. This surface energy must be provided by the strain energy stored in the solid before cracking, and the quantity available will be of the order of that stored in the volume of the crack, this is $a\sigma_m^2/2E$ per unit area of the crack (assuming § 15 (4) to hold up till the moment of fracture). Equating these two expressions for the energy gives

$$\sigma_m = 2(E\alpha/a)^{\frac{1}{2}}. \quad . \quad . \quad . \quad (2)$$

Equating (2) to (1) with $\rho = a$ gives for the tensile strength T_0 in uniaxial tension in a direction perpendicular to the crack

$$T_0 = (E\alpha/l)^{\frac{1}{2}}. \quad . \quad . \quad . \quad (3)$$

Values of T_0 calculated from (3) prove to be of the right order of magnitude.

This theory can be extended to biaxial stress, the assumption being that the material contains a large number of incipient cracks, randomly orientated, and that failure takes place when the highest local stress at the longest crack of the most dangerous orientation is equal to σ_m given by (2). This leads to the criterion of failure

$$\sigma_1 = T_0, \quad \text{if } 3\sigma_1 + \sigma_2 > 0, \quad \cdot \quad \cdot \quad \cdot \quad (4)$$

$$(\sigma_1 - \sigma_2)^2 + 8T_0(\sigma_1 + \sigma_2) = 0, \quad \text{if } 3\sigma_1 + \sigma_2 < 0, \quad \cdot \quad \cdot \quad (5)$$

where T_0 is the tensile strength (3) in uniaxial tension and σ_1 and σ_2 are the principal stresses with $\sigma_1 > \sigma_2$. That is, failure takes place when the point (σ_1, σ_2) crosses the curve ABC of Fig. 30, composed of straight lines and portion of a parabola.

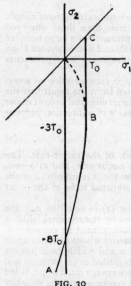

FIG. 30

25. STRAIN THEORIES OF FAILURE

In geological, as distinct from engineering work, strain or displacement is the only observed quantity so that it is natural to attempt to set up criteria for flow or fracture in terms of strain rather than stress. It is to be understood that finite strain is in question here, and this must for simplicity be assumed to be finite homogeneous strain; since this is completely described by the strain ellipsoid, it is natural to set up criteria for failure in terms of the strain ellipsoid.

The most obvious assumption is that fracture will occur across planes for which the shear strain is a maximum, though experience with stress criteria shows that it might well prove that this simple assumption would have to be modified subsequently. The history of the matter is rather curious. Becker, in 1893, (cf. § 7), made this assumption, but incorrectly concluded that, in the case in which there is no change in area, the directions of maximum shear coincide with the directions of unchanged length; in three dimensions this led to the statement that the planes of maximum shear coincide with the circular sections of the strain ellipsoid. For this reason the criterion that the planes of fracture are the planes of the circular sections of the strain ellipsoid was for many years used extensively in geological literature. It may be seen to be inconsistent with the fairly generally observed fact that the planes of fracture make angles of less than 45° with the direction of maximum compressive stress. Thus, for example, in the system of § 14 (v) it was shown in § 14 (14) that the circular sections make angles $\pm\tan^{-1}[(1-\nu)/\nu]^{\frac{1}{2}}$ with the direction of compression. This angle is determined only by Poisson's ratio ν, and since $\nu < \frac{1}{2}$, it is always greater than 45°. It may be remarked also that in uniaxial compression the lines of unchanged length also make angles greater than 45° with the direction of compression (cf. § 14 (12)).

Apart from this mistake, Becker's analysis is interesting because it offers a possible line of attack on the common and puzzling phenomenon that of the two directions of fracture which on the stress theories should be equally probable (and usually appear so in laboratory experiments), one system is usually preferred in geological fractures. Becker's theory in two dimensions may be stated as follows: suppose that the criterion of failure (whatever it may be) indicates two planes which in the unstrained state make angles $\pm\eta$ with a principal axis of strain, and in the strained state make angles $\pm\eta'$ with the axis into which this is strained. These two axes,

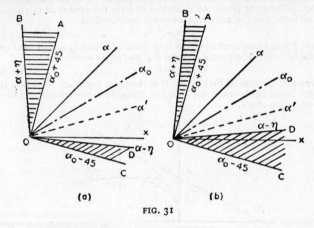

(a)   **(b)**

FIG. 31

as in § 7, make angles α and α' with Ox, and the planes in question make angles $\alpha\pm\eta$ with Ox before straining. Now suppose the strain is increased steadily from an infinitesimal amount to its final value. When the strain is infinitesimal the principal axis will, by § 7 (39), make an angle $\alpha_0=\frac{1}{2}(\alpha+\alpha')$ with Ox, also in many cases η tends to 45°: we shall assume this to be the case, if it is not a similar argument can be used. For infinitesimal strain the initial positions of the lines in question, OA and OC, make angles of $\alpha_0\pm45°$ with Ox, while for the finite strain they are OB and OD which make angles of $\alpha\pm\eta$ with Ox. Thus, as the strain is increased to its final value these lines sweep through the two wedges AOB and COD of Fig. 31 (a) and (b), which are drawn for $\eta>45°$ and $\eta<45°$, respectively. The angles of these wedges differ by the amount of rotation $\alpha-\alpha'$, and inspection of Fig. 31 (a) shows that if $\eta>45°$ the wedge in the direction of rotation is the smaller, while if $\eta<45°$, Fig. 31 (b), that in the direction of rotation is the larger, and if $\eta=45°$ the two wedges are equal. The fact that these wedges are unequal implies an asymmetry which may lead to a preferred direction of failure. Becker suggested that in the larger wedge through which the line must sweep more rapidly during straining, fracture would be more likely, and, in the smaller wedge, flow would be expected.

If maximum shear strain is taken as the criterion of failure it follows from § 7 (13) that $\eta = 45°$, so that for this particular criterion the two wedges are equal and neither would be preferred. But, as remarked above, almost any other criterion would lead to unequal wedges and a preferred direction of fracture, provided, of course, that the strain is rotational.

26. THE TENSILE TEST ON DUCTILE MATERIALS

This has been described in § 12; further discussion of the plastic region ABC will now be given. As remarked in § 12, the strains in this region are so large that the conventional stress σ_c defined by

$$\sigma_c = P/a_0, \qquad . \qquad . \qquad . \qquad (1)$$

where P is the load applied by the testing machine and a_0 is the initial area of the bar, differs appreciably from the true stress σ which is

$$\sigma = P/a, \qquad . \qquad . \qquad . \qquad . \qquad (2)$$

where a is the area at that stress. It is therefore necessary to reduce the conventional stress-strain curve of Fig. 19 (a) to a *true stress-strain curve* connecting σ and ϵ.

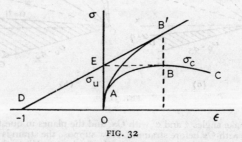

FIG. 32

Suppose that $OABC$, Fig. 32, is the conventional stress-strain curve connecting σ_c and the strain ϵ given by

$$\epsilon = (l - l_0)/l_0, \qquad . \qquad . \qquad . \qquad (3)$$

where l is the length and l_0 the original length of the bar. As remarked in § 12, it shows a yield point at A, a maximum at B, and at C the specimen breaks. The value σ_u of σ_c corresponding to the maximum at B is called the *ultimate stress*.

In the region AB it is found that the bar remains uniform in cross-section, and since it is found that in processes of plastic deformation the change in volume is very small, its area will be given by

$$a = l_0 a_0/l = a_0/(1 + \epsilon), \qquad . \qquad . \qquad (4)$$

and thus the true stress σ is given by

$$\sigma = P/a = (1 + \epsilon)P/a_0 = (1 + \epsilon)\sigma_c \qquad . \qquad . \qquad (5)$$

Using (5), the true stress-strain curve OAB' of Fig. 32 can be obtained from the conventional stress-strain curve OAB. Since at the point B of the latter, $\sigma_e = \sigma_u$, $d\sigma_e/d\epsilon = 0$, it follows from (5) that at the corresponding point B'

$$\frac{d\sigma}{d\epsilon} = \sigma_u . \qquad . \qquad . \qquad . \qquad . \qquad (6)$$

That is, the (σ, ϵ) curve has slope σ_u at the point B', and the tangent to it at this point has intercepts $OD = -1$ on the ϵ-axis and $OE = \sigma_u$ on the σ-axis.

At B in the stress-strain curve some sort of instability [1] sets in, the cross-section of the bar ceases to be uniform and a 'neck' develops at some point at which fracture ultimately takes place. To discuss the portion BC of the curve the shape of this neck and the stresses in it must be considered, cf. Bridgman, *loc. cit.*

If the natural strain $\bar{\epsilon}$ defined in § 18 is introduced, a natural stress-strain curve of σ against $\bar{\epsilon}$ is obtained. It follows by the arguments leading to § 18 (9) that for a perfectly elastic material this curve would be $\sigma = E\bar{\epsilon}$, and attempts have been made to represent the early portion of the curve OB' by a power relation of the form $\sigma = k\bar{\epsilon}^n$ with $n < 1$.

27. YIELD CRITERIA

In this section the mathematical formulation of yield criteria for the perfectly plastic solid will be discussed and some of the more commonly used criteria studied.

So far as is known at present, hydrostatic pressure alone does not cause appreciable plastic deformation in metals and crystalline rocks. Thus, in developing criteria for yielding, it is usual to subtract a hydrostatic part from the actual stresses, calling the remainder a stress deviation, and assuming that this quantity alone produces yield and that conditions for yield may be expressed in terms of it alone. The necessary preliminary theory, (1)–(13) and (17)–(22) below, is quite general and might have been given in § 4.

---

[1] If a small additional strain $\delta\epsilon$ is imposed when the stress is σ, strain-hardening requires the load to be increased by $a_0(d\sigma/d\epsilon)\delta\epsilon/(1+\epsilon)$, while the reduction of area corresponds to a reduction of the load by

$$-\sigma\delta a = \sigma a_0 \delta\epsilon/(1+\epsilon)^2.$$

For $\sigma_e < \sigma_u$ the latter quantity is the less, so that an increase of strain corresponds to an increase of load, but when $\sigma_e = \sigma_u$ the two quantities balance exactly by (6) so that the strain may be increased without increasing the load.

7

If σ_x, σ_y, σ_z are the normal stresses referred to any system of axes, the *mean normal stress* [1] is defined as

$$s=(\sigma_x+\sigma_y+\sigma_z)/3=(\sigma_1+\sigma_2+\sigma_3)/3, \quad . \quad . \quad (1)$$

this quantity being invariant by § 4 (21). The *stress deviation* is defined as having components s_x, s_y, s_z, s_{yz}, s_{zx}, s_{xy} given by

$$s_x=\sigma_x-s, \quad s_y=\sigma_y-s, \quad s_z=\sigma_z-s, \quad . \quad . \quad (2)$$

$$s_{yz}=\tau_{yz}, \quad s_{zx}=\tau_{zx}, \quad s_{xy}=\tau_{xy}. \quad . \quad . \quad (3)$$

This quantity may be reduced to principal axes as in § 4: the principal axes for the stress deviation are the same as the principal axes of stress, and the principal stress deviations s_1, s_2, s_3 are

$$\left.\begin{aligned} s_1=\sigma_1-s=(2\sigma_1-\sigma_2-\sigma_3)/3, \quad s_2=\sigma_2-s=(2\sigma_2-\sigma_1-\sigma_3)/3, \\ s_3=\sigma_3-s=(2\sigma_3-\sigma_1-\sigma_2)/3. \end{aligned}\right\} \quad . \quad (4)$$

It follows from (1) that

$$s_x+s_y+s_z=s_1+s_2+s_3=0. \quad . \quad . \quad (5)$$

In the same way the components of strain can be decomposed into the *mean normal strain e* defined by

$$e=(\varepsilon_x+\varepsilon_y+\varepsilon_z)/3=(\varepsilon_1+\varepsilon_2+\varepsilon_3)/3=\Delta/3, \quad . \quad . \quad (6)$$

which by § 11 (17) is one-third of the dilatation Δ and is invariant, and the *strain deviation* whose components e_x, ..., e_{yz}, ... are defined as

$$e_x=\varepsilon_x-e, \quad e_y=\varepsilon_y-e, \quad e_z=\varepsilon_z-e, \quad . \quad . \quad (7)$$

$$e_{yz}=\gamma_{yz}, \quad e_{zx}=\gamma_{zx}, \quad e_{xy}=\gamma_{xy}. \quad . \quad . \quad (8)$$

As in the case of stress, the principal axes of the strain deviation coincide with the principal axes of strain, and the *principal strain deviations* e_1, e_2, e_3 are

$$e_1=\varepsilon_1-e, \quad e_2=\varepsilon_2-e, \quad e_3=\varepsilon_3-e, \quad . \quad . \quad (9)$$

so that by (6)

$$e_1+e_2+e_3=e_x+e_y+e_z=0. \quad . \quad . \quad (10)$$

The stress-strain relations for an elastic material, § 13 (10)–(12), take a simpler form when expressed in terms of stress and strain deviations. Firstly, using (1) and (6) in § 13 (12), (13) gives

$$s=3Ke, \quad . \quad . \quad . \quad (11)$$

---

[1] Sometimes, particularly in geological literature, the term 'confining pressure' is used in this sense. But it is also used in a different sense in experimental studies of deformation, cf. § 12.

and using this result in § 13 (10), (11) gives by § 13 (13)

$$s_x = 2Ge_x , \quad s_y = 2Ge_y , \quad s_z = 2Ge_z , \qquad . \qquad . \quad (12)$$

$$s_{yz} = Ge_{yz} , \quad s_{zx} = Ge_{zx} , \quad s_{xy} = Ge_{xy} . \qquad . \qquad (13)$$

Only two of (12) are independent since, if they are added, both sides vanish by (5) and (10).

In the same way, the equations of viscosity for an incompressible fluid, § 19 (8), (12), (13) take the simpler form

$$\left. \begin{array}{lll} s_x = 2\eta\dot{e}_x , & s_y = 2\eta\dot{e}_y , & s_z = 2\eta\dot{e}_z , \\ s_{yz} = \eta\dot{e}_{yz} , & s_{zx} = \eta\dot{e}_{zx} , & s_{xy} = \eta\dot{e}_{xy} , \end{array} \right\} \qquad . \qquad (14)$$

$$\dot{e} = 0. \qquad . \qquad . \qquad . \quad (15)$$

The mathematical requirements for a yield criterion may be illustrated by the case of the *maximum shearing stress*, or *Tresca's*, criterion which states that yield occurs at a point when the magnitude of the maximum shearing stress there has a value [1] $\frac{1}{2}\sigma_0$ which is a constant of the material. The maximum shearing stress has been found in § 4 (38) to be $(\sigma_1 - \sigma_3)/2$, so that Tresca's criterion may be written

$$\sigma_1 - \sigma_3 = s_1 - s_3 = \sigma_0 . \qquad . \qquad . \quad (16)$$

It may be remarked that it gives equal yield stresses of σ_0 in uniaxial tension and compression: this is approximately true for the case of yield, though as remarked in § 21 it is far from true for fracture, and so (16) is ruled out as a criterion for fracture. Further consequences of (16) will be discussed later.

In order to use (16), it is necessary to know the principal stresses and to pick out the greatest and least of them: while this can frequently be done in simple problems, it makes (16) unsuitable as a general mathematical formulation (though it may be made so by suitable modification). The most important requirement for a yield criterion is that, since the actual yielding cannot be affected by the choice of axes, the criterion should be invariant with respect to rotation of the axes. Also, as remarked earlier, it is assumed that the mean normal stress does not affect the process so that the criterion must involve stress deviations only.

---

[1] It is a little more convenient in subsequent calculations to have yield criteria stated in terms of the yield stress σ_0 in tension rather than in terms of that in pure shear, though the latter is the more logical in the present connection.

This suggests that the invariants of the stress deviation should be examined. The invariants I_1, I_2, I_3 of the stress have been found in § 4 (18)–(20), and the invariants J_1, J_2, J_3 of the stress deviation are found in precisely the same way. The first two of these are

$$J_1 = s_x + s_y + s_z , \qquad \qquad (17)$$

$$J_2 = -(s_y s_z + s_z s_x + s_x s_y) + s_{yz}^2 + s_{zx}^2 + s_{xy}^2 . \qquad (18)$$

Of these, J_1 vanishes identically by (5). Using this result in (18) gives

$$J_2 = \tfrac{1}{2}(s_x^2 + s_y^2 + s_z^2) + s_{yz}^2 + s_{zx}^2 + s_{xy}^2 \qquad (19)$$

$$= \tfrac{1}{6}\{(\sigma_y - \sigma_z)^2 + (\sigma_z - \sigma_x)^2 + (\sigma_x - \sigma_y)^2\} + \tau_{yz}^2 + \tau_{zx}^2 + \tau_{xy}^2 \qquad (20)$$

$$= \tfrac{1}{6}\{(\sigma_2 - \sigma_3)^2 + (\sigma_3 - \sigma_1)^2 + (\sigma_1 - \sigma_2)^2\} \qquad (21)$$

$$= \tfrac{1}{2}(s_1^2 + s_2^2 + s_3^2), \qquad \qquad (22)$$

where (20) follows from (19) by (2) and (3), and (21) and (22) are (20) and (19) referred to principal axes.

Since, as above, any yield criterion must be expressible in terms of the invariants J_2, J_3, that is, in the form

$$f(J_2, J_3, \sigma_0) = 0, \qquad \qquad (23)$$

where σ_0 is a constant of the material, it is reasonable to examine simple relations of this type. The simplest of all is obtained by assuming J_2 to be constant, that is, by (21) and (22),

$$2J_2 = s_1^2 + s_2^2 + s_3^2 = 2\sigma_0^2/3, \qquad \qquad (24)$$

or

$$(\sigma_2 - \sigma_3)^2 + (\sigma_3 - \sigma_1)^2 + (\sigma_1 - \sigma_2)^2 = 2\sigma_0^2, \qquad (25)$$

where σ_0 is a constant of the material, which, using the values $\sigma_2 = \sigma_3 = 0$, $s = \sigma_1/3$, $s_1 = 2\sigma_1/3$, $s_2 = s_3 = -\sigma_1/3$ appropriate to uniaxial tension, is seen to be the yield stress in uniaxial tension or compression. For pure shear $\sigma_3 = -\sigma_1$, $\sigma_2 = 0$, it gives a yield stress of $\sigma_0/\sqrt{3}$.

(24) is the *von Mises* criterion which is probably the simplest to use and the one whose consequences have been most studied. It was introduced above by purely mathematical arguments, but it can be given a physical interpretation (or if preferred introduced as an empirical criterion) by two other types of argument, based on strain energy and the concept of octahedral stress and strain, respectively.

The strain energy per unit volume in the elastic state was found in § 15 (2) to be given by

$$2W = \sigma_1\varepsilon_1 + \sigma_2\varepsilon_2 + \sigma_3\varepsilon_3 .$$

Using (4) and (9) this becomes

$$2W = (s_1+s)(e_1+e) + (s_2+s)(e_2+e) + (s_3+s)(e_3+e)$$

$$= \frac{1}{2G}(s_1{}^2 + s_2{}^2 + s_3{}^2) + \frac{s^2}{K}, \quad . \quad . \quad . \quad . \quad (26)$$

using (5), (10), (11), (12). It follows that the elastic strain energy per unit volume can be split into a part $s^2/2K$ associated with change of volume and a part

$$(s_1{}^2 + s_2{}^2 + s_3{}^2)/4G \quad . \quad . \quad . \quad (27)$$

associated with distortion. Thus (24) arises if it is assumed that *yield takes place when the elastic strain energy of distortion* [1] *reaches a value characteristic of the material:* in this form the theory is associated with the names of Huber and Hencky.

Another interpretation of (24) has been given by Nadai in terms of the shear stress across the plane whose normal has direction cosines $l=m=n=1/\sqrt{3}$ and so is equally inclined to the principal axes: this plane, he calls the *octahedral plane*. By § 4 (26) the normal stress across it is $(\sigma_1+\sigma_2+\sigma_3)/3$, and so by (1) is just equal to the mean normal stress and may be regarded as playing no part in yield phenomena. By § 4 (29) the shear stress τ_{oc} across it, called the *octahedral shearing stress*, is given by

$$\tau_{oc} = \tfrac{1}{3}\{(\sigma_2-\sigma_3)^2 + (\sigma_3-\sigma_1)^2 + (\sigma_1-\sigma_2)^2\}^{\frac{1}{2}} = (2J_2/3)^{\frac{1}{2}}, \quad . \quad (28)$$

using (21). Thus the yield criterion (25) may be stated in the form that yield takes place when the octahedral shearing stress is equal to $\sqrt{(2/3)}$ times the yield stress in pure shear or $(\sqrt{2})/3$ times the yield stress in uniaxial tension.

The various yield criteria must be judged and compared by the way in which their predictions fit the experimental results. Considering the simple criteria discussed above, Tresca's and von Mises's, it has been remarked that they both predict equal yield stresses in tension and compression, which is in reasonable agreement with experiment.

---

[1] Beltrami and Haigh attempted to use the *total* strain energy as a criterion, but this did not prove satisfactory. For example, it predicts yielding under hydrostatic pressure which is not observed.

The simplest and most satisfactory tests of the theories are made under combined stresses on circular cylinders whose walls are so thin that they may be regarded as being in a state of plane stress. Taking x, y, and z-axes at a point of the cylinder in the axial, tangential, and radial directions, respectively, torsion of the cylinder gives a system of stresses in which the only non-zero component is τ_{xy}. If an axial tension σ_x is superposed on this system, the stresses in the xy-plane are σ_x, $\sigma_y=0$, τ_{xy}. By § 3 (19) the principal stresses σ_1, σ_2, σ_3 are

$$\tfrac{1}{2}\sigma_x + \tfrac{1}{2}(\sigma_x{}^2 + 4\tau_{xy}{}^2)^{\frac{1}{2}}, \quad 0, \quad \tfrac{1}{2}\sigma_x - \tfrac{1}{2}(\sigma_x{}^2 + 4\tau_{xy}{}^2)^{\frac{1}{2}}.$$

Using these values, Tresca's criterion (16) gives

$$\sigma_x{}^2 + 4\tau_{xy}{}^2 = \sigma_0{}^2, \qquad \cdot \qquad \cdot \qquad \cdot \quad (29)$$

while the von Mises criterion (25) gives

$$\sigma_x{}^2 + 3\tau_{xy}{}^2 = \sigma_0{}^2. \qquad \cdot \qquad \cdot \qquad \cdot \quad (30)$$

According to Tresca's criterion the values of σ_x and τ_{xy} for which yield occurs under various conditions lie on the ellipse (29),

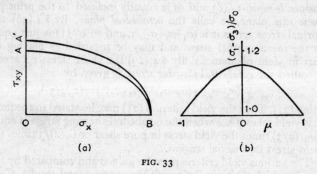

FIG. 33

AB, Fig. 33 (a), while for the von Mises criterion they lie on the ellipse $A'B$ given by (30). In the classical experiments of Taylor and Quinney [1] on metals it was found that the experimental points showed considerable scatter but were better fitted by (30).

Another method of discriminating between the criteria is by studying the influence of the intermediate principal stress σ_2. The

[1] *Phil. Trans. Roy. Soc.*, A, **230** (1931), 323.

value of this relative to σ_1 and σ_3 may be expressed by the parameter

$$\mu = \frac{2\sigma_2 - \sigma_1 - \sigma_3}{\sigma_1 - \sigma_3} \qquad . \qquad . \qquad . \qquad (31)$$

which takes values between -1 and 1 as σ_2 varies from σ_3 to σ_1. In terms of this parameter, Tresca's criterion becomes

$$(\sigma_1 - \sigma_3)/\sigma_0 = 1, \qquad . \qquad . \qquad . \qquad (32)$$

and von Mises's is

$$(\sigma_1 - \sigma_3)/\sigma_0 = 2(3 + \mu^2)^{-\frac{1}{2}}. \qquad . \qquad . \qquad (33)$$

The two curves are shown in Fig. 33 (b), the latter having a maximum of $2/\sqrt{3} = 1 \cdot 155 \ldots$ when $\mu = 0$. Lode studied this curve experimentally by using thin-walled tubes with combined axial tension and internal hydrostatic pressure. In this case there are tensile principal stresses in the axial and tangential directions, and the third principal stress in the radial direction is zero. By varying the amounts of the axial tension and hydrostatic pressure, all values of μ can be obtained. The experimental results again slightly favour the von Mises criterion.

Finally, it should be remarked that many other yield criteria have been proposed and may be studied in the same way. In particular the Mohr theory may be regarded as an example of a criterion in which the mean normal stress is regarded as having an influence. The theory of earth pressure given in § 23 may be regarded as that for yield of a material with this property.

28. THE YIELD SURFACE

Since criteria for yield will be expressible in terms of the principal stresses, it is obviously convenient to represent a state of stress by a point whose coordinates are σ_1, σ_2, σ_3. In doing this, it is convenient to abandon the convention $\sigma_1 \geqslant \sigma_2 \geqslant \sigma_3$ which has always been understood hitherto, so that, for the purposes of this section *only*, σ_1 will be the stress in a given principal direction irrespective of its magnitude relative to the other principal stresses. The σ_1, σ_2, σ_3 space in this sense is called the *stress space*.

The criterion for yield will be expressed by a relation

$$F(\sigma_1, \sigma_2, \sigma_3, \sigma_0) = 0, \qquad . \qquad . \qquad . \qquad (1)$$

where σ_0 is a constant of the material. This may be represented by a surface called the *yield surface*.

First we consider the intersections of this with the plane $\sigma_3=0$ for the yield criteria previously considered.

Tresca's criterion requires the difference between the greatest and least principal stresses to be a constant, σ_0, which is the yield stress in tension. If $\sigma_1>\sigma_2>0$, this requires $\sigma_1=\sigma_0$, giving the line AB, Fig. 34 (*a*); if $\sigma_2>\sigma_1>0$, it requires $\sigma_2=\sigma_0$, giving BC; if

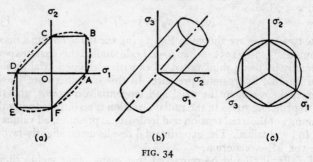

(a)   (b)   (c)

FIG. 34

$\sigma_2>0>\sigma_1$, it requires $\sigma_2-\sigma_1=\sigma_0$, giving CD; and so on, the final locus being the hexagon $ABCDEFA$.

The von Mises criterion, § 27 (25), is

$$\sigma_1^2-\sigma_1\sigma_2+\sigma_2^2=\sigma_0^2, \qquad . \qquad . \qquad . \qquad (2)$$

giving the dotted ellipse in Fig. 34 (*a*) which passes through the vertices of the hexagon. Comparison of the two curves indicates clearly the difference between the criteria. The greatest discrepancy is for pure shear $\sigma_2=-\sigma_1$ for which the values are $\sigma_0/2$ and $\sigma_0/\sqrt{3}$.

In three dimensions, it follows from § 27 (4) that all points on the line

$$\sigma_1=\sigma_2=\sigma_3 \qquad . \qquad . \qquad . \qquad . \qquad (3)$$

have zero stress deviation, and that all points on a line parallel to it have the same stress deviation. Since on the assumptions made here the yield criterion involves only the principal stress deviations, the yield surface must be a cylinder in the stress space with its axis along the line (3) which is equally inclined to the principal directions, Fig. 34 (*b*). For the cases of Tresca's and von Mises's criteria discussed above, Fig. 34 (*a*) gives the intersection of the cylinder with the plane $\sigma_3=0$. The cross-section of the cylinder is a regular hexagon for Tresca's criterion and a circle for von Mises's. Its intersection with the plane $\sigma_1+\sigma_2+\sigma_3=0$ perpendicular to the axis of the cylinder is sometimes known as the yield locus and is shown in Fig. 34 (*c*) for the two cases above. In general it possesses a high degree of symmetry since the yield criterion must be unchanged by interchanging two principal stresses.

The cylindrical form of the yield surface in Fig. 34 (*b*) is caused by the assumption that the mean normal stress has no effect on the process of yield. In the more general case in which this assumption is abandoned, the surface (i) is not a cylinder.

29. THE EQUATIONS OF PLASTICITY

In this section we shall set up stress-strain relations for a perfectly plastic substance under the simplest possible conditions. It is assumed that the substance satisfies some yield condition such as § 27 (16) or (24) and that at every point of a region which is behaving plastically this relation holds. For example, if the maximum shear stress condition is assumed, the maximum shear stress at every point in a region behaving plastically must have the same value $\frac{1}{2}\sigma_0$. In most problems in which a body is subjected to prescribed stresses it will be divided into elastic regions in which the magnitude of the maximum shear stress is less than $\frac{1}{2}\sigma_0$ and plastic regions in which it is equal to $\frac{1}{2}\sigma_0$. Problems are further divided into two classes: (i) those in which the elastic and plastic displacements are of the same order of magnitude, for example in many engineering problems such as highly stressed pressure vessels, (ii) those in which there is unrestricted plastic deformation, as in extrusion; in such cases the elastic displacement can often be neglected in comparison with the plastic deformation and a considerable simplification results.

Each yield criterion will lead to its own set of equations. Here we shall consider only the von Mises criterion, § 27 (24),

$$2J_2=s_1{}^2+s_2{}^2+s_3{}^2=2\sigma_0{}^2/3. \qquad \cdot \qquad \cdot \qquad (1)$$

This is assumed to hold at all times and points in the plastic region so that, in addition,

$$\dot{J}_2=0, \qquad \cdot \qquad \cdot \qquad \cdot \qquad (2)$$

where, as in § 19, a dot denotes differentiation with respect to the time.

To obtain the simplest possible set of equations we shall consider only the case of an incompressible substance for which $\Delta = e = 0$, so that $e_1 = \varepsilon_1$, etc., and also assume that the elastic strains are negligible in comparison with the plastic strains.

The stress-strain relations, due to St-Venant, are then obtained by assuming that the principal axes of rate of strain and of stress deviation are the same, and that the principal stress deviations are proportional to the principal rates of strain, just as in § 13 (1)–(3) or § 19 (4)–(6), except that, because of the assumption of incompressibility $\Delta = 0$, these equations take the simpler form

$$s_1 = 2\phi\dot{\varepsilon}_1, \quad s_2 = 2\phi\dot{\varepsilon}_2, \quad s_3 = 2\phi\dot{\varepsilon}_3, \qquad \cdot \quad \cdot \quad (3)$$

where ϕ is a quantity yet to be determined.

Precisely similar analysis to that leading to § 13 (10), (11) gives for the equations referred to any axes

$$\left.\begin{array}{ll} s_x = 2\phi\dot{\varepsilon}_x, & s_y = 2\phi\dot{\varepsilon}_y, \quad s_z = 2\phi\dot{\varepsilon}_z, \\ s_{yz} = \phi\dot{\gamma}_{yz}, & s_{zx} = \phi\dot{\gamma}_{zx}, \quad s_{xy} = \phi\dot{\gamma}_{xy}. \end{array}\right\} \quad \cdot \quad \cdot \quad (4)$$

These equations are similar in form to the equations of viscosity § 19 (13), (8), but there is a very fundamental difference since, while the viscosity η was an absolute constant, the quantity ϕ is a function of position to be determined from the condition that the stresses must satisfy the yield condition (1). Substituting (3) in (1) gives

$$\phi^2(\dot{\varepsilon}_1{}^2 + \dot{\varepsilon}_2{}^2 + \dot{\varepsilon}_3{}^2) = \sigma_0{}^2/6, \qquad \cdot \quad \cdot \quad (5)$$

and in this $\dot{\varepsilon}_1{}^2 + \dot{\varepsilon}_2{}^2 + \dot{\varepsilon}_3{}^2$ is an invariant of the rate of strain. Putting (5) in (3) gives

$$s_1 = \frac{\sigma_0\dot{\varepsilon}_1\sqrt{2}}{[3(\dot{\varepsilon}_1{}^2 + \dot{\varepsilon}_2{}^2 + \dot{\varepsilon}_3{}^2)]^{\frac{1}{2}}}, \text{ etc.} \quad \cdot \quad \cdot \quad (6)$$

It appears that the stresses are unaffected if all the rates of strain are multiplied by a constant factor. This illustrates the fundamental difference of these effects from those of viscosity in which stress varies linearly with the rate of strain.

The equations (3) may be regarded as connecting small changes of plastic strain $\delta\varepsilon_1$, $\delta\varepsilon_2$, $\delta\varepsilon_3$ with the stress deviations; that is, $s_1 : s_2 : s_3 = \delta\varepsilon_1 : \delta\varepsilon_2 : \delta\varepsilon_3$, or, using § 27 (4),

$$\frac{2\sigma_1 - \sigma_2 - \sigma_3}{2\sigma_2 - \sigma_1 - \sigma_3} = \frac{\delta\varepsilon_1}{\delta\varepsilon_2}, \quad \frac{2\sigma_1 - \sigma_2 - \sigma_3}{2\sigma_3 - \sigma_1 - \sigma_2} = \frac{\delta\varepsilon_1}{\delta\varepsilon_3}. \quad \cdot \quad \cdot \quad (7)$$

Using the result $\delta\varepsilon_1+\delta\varepsilon_2+\delta\varepsilon_3=0$ corresponding to incompressibility, these give

$$\frac{2\sigma_2-\sigma_1-\sigma_3}{\sigma_1-\sigma_3}=\frac{2\delta\varepsilon_2-\delta\varepsilon_1-\delta\varepsilon_3}{\delta\varepsilon_1-\delta\varepsilon_3}. \quad \cdot \quad \cdot \quad (8)$$

This is a relation connecting increments of plastic principal strains with the principal stresses. It can be studied experimentally in the simple situations described in § 27 and shows reasonable agreement with experiment.

30. SUBSTANCES WITH COMPOSITE PROPERTIES

In § 12 the three important first approximations to the behaviour of actual materials were noticed and their properties have been discussed in the preceding sections. It was pointed out that most substances show effects dependent on the time: while these may be neglected in most engineering problems, a proper description of them is of the greatest importance in some geological connexions and in Rheology,[1] which is the study of flow in general.

These time effects may be described phenomenologically by combinations of the simple elements already discussed, which will be described again from the present point of view in (i) to (iii) below. To see the effects involved, it is convenient to study them in one variable which will be taken to be extension (though it might equally well be shear) and to represent them by simple mechanical models. When this has been done, the general mathematical formulation will be discussed.

(i) The Perfectly Elastic or 'Hookean' Substance [2]

In this case the extension ε is instantaneous and is related to the stress σ by

$$\sigma=k\varepsilon, \quad \cdot \quad \cdot \quad \cdot \quad \cdot \quad (1)$$

where k is a constant of the material. Such a substance can be represented by a spring as in Fig. 35 (a).

---

[1] Cf. Reiner, *Deformation and Flow* (Lewis, 1947); Reiner, *Twelve Lectures on Theoretical Rheology* (Amsterdam, 1949); Scott Blair, *Survey of General and Applied Rheology* (Pitman, Ed. 2, 1947).

[2] The practice of attaching names of this sort to the various models avoids the use of terms such as solid and fluid, which are inadequate to describe many of these substances.

(ii) *The Perfectly Viscous Fluid or 'Newtonian' Substance*

In this case the rate of strain $\dot{\varepsilon}$ is connected with the stress σ by

$$\sigma = \eta\dot{\varepsilon}, \qquad . \qquad . \qquad . \qquad . \qquad (2)$$

where η is a constant, and so, if $\varepsilon = 0$ when $t = 0$,

$$\varepsilon = \sigma t/\eta. \qquad . \qquad . \qquad . \qquad . \qquad (3)$$

The substance can be represented by the dashpot of Fig. 35 (*b*).

(iii) *A Yield Stress σ_0*

This may be represented by a frictional contact, Fig. 35 (*c*), which can supply a frictional force σ_0 due to static friction. If the

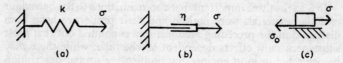

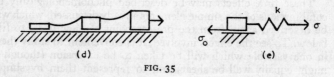

FIG. 35

applied stress $\sigma < \sigma_0$ there is no strain, but if $\sigma > \sigma_0$ the contact yields. Strain hardening, an increase of yield stress with strain, may be represented by a number of such contacts connected by loose strings, Fig. 35 (*d*).

(iv) *The Perfectly Plastic Solid or 'St-Venant' Substance*

In this case the strain is elastic and given by (1) until the yield stress σ_0 is reached. The appropriate model is Fig. 35 (*e*).

(v) *The 'Kelvin', 'Voigt', or 'Firmo-viscous' Substance*

This is represented by a spring and a dashpot in parallel as in Fig. 36 (*a*). Physically, it is the sort of model which might be expected to apply to a cellular elastic material with the holes filled with viscous liquid.

If ε is the strain, the stresses in the spring and dashpot, respectively, will be $k\varepsilon$ and $\eta\dot\varepsilon$, by (1) and (2), so that σ, which is the sum of these, will be given by

$$\eta\dot\varepsilon + k\varepsilon = \sigma. \qquad \cdot \qquad \cdot \qquad \cdot \qquad (4)$$

If at $t=0$, when the strain $\varepsilon=0$, a constant stress S is applied, the solution of the differential equation (4) is

$$\varepsilon = (S/k)\{1 - e^{-kt/\eta}\}, \qquad \cdot \qquad \cdot \qquad (5)$$

and thus the strain S/k, which would occur instantaneously in

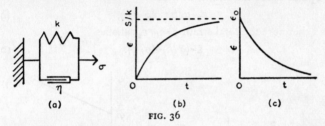

FIG. 36

the absence of the dashpot, is approached exponentially as in Fig. 36 (b).

Similarly, if the system is extended till the strain is ε_0 and then is released, the strain at time t is

$$\varepsilon = \varepsilon_0 e^{-kt/}, \qquad \cdot \qquad \cdot \qquad \cdot \qquad (6)$$

and the strain decreases exponentially to zero, Fig. 36 (c). This is described as relaxation of strain under zero stress, and the time η/k in which the strain falls to $1/e$ of its initial value is called the *relaxation time*.

If a mass m per unit area is attached to such a substance its equation of motion will be

$$m\ddot\varepsilon + \eta\dot\varepsilon + k\varepsilon = 0. \qquad \cdot \qquad \cdot \qquad (7)$$

This is the differential equation of the damped harmonic oscillator and its solution is

$$\varepsilon = Ae^{-\eta t/2m} \cos \{(\eta^2 - 4km)^{\frac{1}{2}}t/2m + B\}, \qquad \cdot \qquad (8)$$

where A and B are constants determined by the initial conditions. Thus this model can represent the damping of vibrations by internal friction and η can be estimated from the decrement.

This model is the simplest which corresponds to a solid in which vibrations are damped by internal friction and in consequence has been much used in connexion with the damping of earthquake waves. While it represents the behaviour of some substances such as cork and rubber reasonably well, the model (vii) discussed below is in general much more satisfactory.

(vi) The 'Maxwell' or 'Elastico-viscous' Substance

In this case the spring and dashpot are in series, Fig. 37 (a). The same stress σ acts across both the spring and the dashpot, so that if ε_1 and ε_2 are the strains in them

$$\varepsilon_1 = \sigma/k, \quad \varepsilon_2 = \sigma/\eta, \qquad \qquad (9)$$

and therefore the total strain $\varepsilon = \varepsilon_1 + \varepsilon_2$ satisfies

$$\dot{\varepsilon} = (\dot{\sigma}/k) + (\sigma/\eta). \qquad \qquad (10)$$

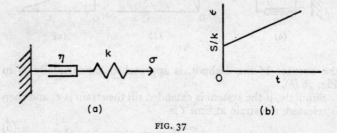

(a)   (b)

FIG. 37

If the system is suddenly given a strain ε_0 at time $t=0$, the stress at time t is given by

$$\sigma = k\varepsilon_0 e^{-kt/\eta}. \qquad \qquad (11)$$

In this case the stress relaxes at constant strain, falling to $1/e$ of its value in time η/k. This time is Maxwell's relaxation time.

If the substance is unstrained at time $t=0$ and constant stress S is then applied, the strain ε is found from (9) to be given by

$$\varepsilon = (S/k) + St/\eta \qquad \qquad (12)$$

and so there is an instantaneous elastic strain, S/k, followed by a linearly increasing strain, Fig. 37 (b). The two are equal at the relaxation time η/k.

This model was introduced by Maxwell to describe substances such as pitch which show instantaneous elasticity but flow in a viscous manner under small stresses. It has been applied to the study of the material in the Earth's mantle which must behave elastically for short times since it transmits shear waves, but at the same time may flow very slowly under continuously applied stresses.

(vii) The General Linear Substance

This may be regarded as consisting of a spring in parallel with a Maxwell element, Fig. 38 (a). If σ_1 is the stress on the Maxwell

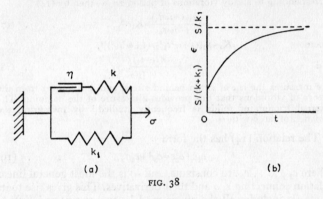

FIG. 38

element and σ_2 that on the spring, and ε is the strain, (1) and (10) give

$$k_1\varepsilon=\sigma_2, \quad \dot{\varepsilon}=(\dot{\sigma}_1/k)+(\sigma_1/\eta), \qquad . \quad (13)$$

therefore, if $\sigma=\sigma_1+\sigma_2$ is the total stress,

$$\sigma+t_0\dot{\sigma}=k_1(\varepsilon+t_1\dot{\varepsilon}), \qquad . \quad . \quad (14)$$

where

$$t_0=\eta/k, \quad t_1=\eta(k+k_1)/kk_1 . \qquad . \quad . \quad (15)$$

If constant stress S is applied at $t=0$ when the substance is unstrained, there is an instantaneous strain of $S/(k+k_1)$ given by (13), and solving (14) with this initial value of ε gives

$$\varepsilon=\frac{S}{k_1}\left\{1-\frac{k}{k+k_1}e^{-t/t_1}\right\} \qquad . \quad . \quad (16)$$

which tends exponentially to a final value of S/k_1, Fig. 38 (b). This is a much better approximation to the behaviour of most substances than the Kelvin model.

It follows from (14) that the general linear substance has two relaxation times, t_0 for relaxation of stress at constant strain, and t_1 for relaxation of strain at constant stress.

Like the Kelvin model, the present one gives a representation of the damping of vibrations by internal friction. This is usually measured by studying steady periodic oscillations. Suppose that

$$\epsilon=\xi e^{i\omega t}, \qquad \sigma=s e^{i\omega t}$$

corresponding to steady vibrations of period $2\pi/\omega$, then by (14)

$$\frac{s}{\xi}=\frac{k_1(1+i\omega t_1)}{1+i\omega t_0}=K_1 e^{i\delta}, \qquad \cdot \qquad \cdot \qquad \cdot \qquad (17)$$

where

$$K_1=k_1[(1+\omega^2 t_1^2)/(1+\omega^2 t_0^2)]^{\frac{1}{2}},$$

and

$$\tan \delta=\frac{\omega(t_1-t_0)}{1+\omega^2 t_1 t_0}. \qquad \cdot \qquad \cdot \qquad \cdot \qquad (18)$$

δ measures the lag of strain behind stress, and it is known from the theory of vibrations that this provides a measure of the damping. The internal friction of solids is frequently studied [1] by measuring the variation of $\tan \delta$ with ω.

The relation (14) has the form

$$c_1\dot{\epsilon}+c_2\epsilon=c_3\dot{\sigma}+c_4\sigma, \qquad \cdot \qquad \cdot \qquad (19)$$

where $c_1, \ldots, c_4$ are constants, and so is the most general linear relation connecting ϵ, σ and their derivatives. This gives rise to its name. It includes all the above models, except (iii) and (iv), as special cases.

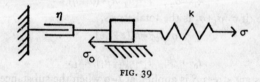

FIG. 39

(viii) *The Bingham Substance*

The perfectly plastic substance of (iv) has no restriction on its movement once the yield point is passed. This disadvantage is removed in the Bingham body, Fig. 39, which is the simplest model which gives a reasonable representation of the flow of a substance possessing a yield point. It behaves as an elastic body for stresses

[1] For complete details see Zener, *loc. cit.*

less than the yield point, and for greater stresses gives a steadily increasing strain. That is, for constant stress σ applied at $t=0$,

$$\varepsilon=\sigma/k, \quad \text{if } \sigma<\sigma_0, \qquad \cdot \qquad \cdot \qquad \cdot \quad (20)$$

$$\varepsilon=(\sigma-\sigma_0)t/\eta+\sigma/k, \quad \text{if } \sigma>\sigma_0. \qquad \cdot \qquad \cdot \quad (21)$$

(ix) *Other Substances*

The models described above, that is, essentially, the general linear substance and the Bingham substance, are adequate to describe most engineering and geological phenomena, but more complicated systems are needed to describe the behaviour of materials such as flour dough.

The models above are intended for descriptive purposes only, though the formulae given apply in simple shear or extension. We now have to consider how they may be applied to three-dimensional situations. For an incompressible substance, the equations of elasticity § 27 (12), (13) state that each component of the stress deviation is proportional to the corresponding component of the strain deviation; similarly, in the equations of viscosity, § 27 (14), they are proportional to the corresponding components of rate of strain deviation. The generalization of these corresponding to the general linear body (19) is to assume a linear connexion between the components of stress and strain deviations and their time-derivatives, that is,

$$c_1\dot{e}_x+c_2e_x=c_3\dot{s}_x+c_4s_x , \qquad \cdot \qquad \cdot \qquad \cdot \quad (22)$$

with five similar equations for the other components. This set of equations, being linear, is not difficult to handle mathematically. Equations of motion for a Bingham substance in three dimensions have also been set up and studied but their theory is relatively difficult.

Finally, the question of failure of these bodies should be mentioned. Reiner and Weissenberg (cf. Reiner, *loc. cit.*) have proposed the criterion that failure takes place when the conserved strain energy reaches some definite value. This may be illustrated by considering the Maxwell substance (vi). In the process of straining, some energy is dissipated in friction in the dashpot, while an amount

$$\tfrac{1}{2}k\varepsilon_1{}^2=\sigma^2/2k$$

is stored as potential energy in the spring. The hypothesis is that

8

failure takes place when this quantity reaches a value E characteristic of the material, that is, when the stress is

$$\sigma = \sqrt{(2kE)}. \qquad . \qquad . \qquad . \qquad (23$$

Now by (10) the rate of strain when the material fails is

$$\dot{\varepsilon} = (\dot{\sigma}/k) + (2kE)^{\frac{1}{2}}/\eta, \qquad . \qquad . \qquad . \qquad (24)$$

so that the rate of strain at which the material fails increases with the rate at which the load is applied.

CHAPTER III

EQUATIONS OF MOTION AND EQUILIBRIUM

31. INTRODUCTORY

IN the previous chapters the general theories of stress and strain and their relationship in actual materials have been studied in some detail. The final stage in the development of the mathematical theory is the setting up of the equations of motion for the various types of substance considered: the equations of equilibrium follow from these as the special case in which there is no motion. These equations will be derived in §§ 33, 39, 41.

While mathematical methods for the solution of problems in elasticity and viscosity have been standard for many years, those for problems in plasticity and on the flow of more complicated materials such as the Bingham substance are both less well developed and more difficult. At the same time it is important to appreciate the differences in behaviour between the various substances, and to illustrate this a number of simple problems will be solved from first principles in § 32. In the later sections more general methods will be employed.

In treatises on the mathematical theories of elasticity and viscosity the fundamental equations are derived at a very early stage and the vast bulk of the theory is concerned with methods for their solution. But for practical applications it is the equations themselves and the detailed analysis of the stress and strain patterns represented by their solutions which are of importance, rather than the actual mathematical processes involved in finding the solutions. Accordingly, only a few typical problems will be solved here, partly to show how the whole of the theory fits together, and partly to illustrate points of practical importance.

32. SIMPLE PROBLEMS ILLUSTRATING
THE BEHAVIOUR OF ELASTIC, VISCOUS, PLASTIC
AND BINGHAM SUBSTANCES

In this section a number of problems on flow in a cylindrical tube, flow between rotating cylinders, and torsion of a circular cylinder will be solved. It has been remarked above that the discussion of the general equations of motion of perfectly plastic and Bingham substances involves relatively difficult mathematics so that the best way of comparing the behaviour of the different types of substance is by studying simple situations of practical importance for which the equations can be written down from first principles.[1]

(i) *Elastic Displacement of a Circular Cylinder of Radius a and Length l due to Uniform Pressure P at One End and Zero Pressure at the Other, there being no Displacement over the Curved Surface*

We shall assume that the displacements are in the direction of the axis of the cylinder, so that, choosing the z-axis in this direction and writing r for the distance from it, Fig. 40 (a), the only

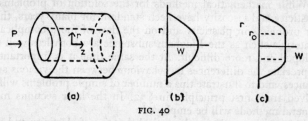

FIG. 40

non-vanishing component of displacement is w in the direction of the z-axis, and the only non-zero components of shear stress and strain are τ_{rz} and $\gamma_{rz} = dw/dr$, so the stress-strain relations, § 14 (19), become

$$\tau_{rz} = G\frac{dw}{dr}. \qquad . \qquad . \qquad . \qquad (1)$$

If, in addition, we assume that the solid is incompressible, w must be independent of z, and therefore, by (1), τ_{rz} must also. Now, considering the equilibrium of a cylinder of radius r and length l in the material, the forces on the ends of this are $\pi r^2 P$ and zero, and the force over the curved surface is $2\pi r l \tau_{rz}$, so the condition for equilibrium of the cylinder is

$$\tau_{rz} = -rP/2l. \qquad . \qquad . \qquad . \qquad (2)$$

[1] For the discussion of many other problems on these lines the standard works on Rheology may be consulted, e.g. Reiner, *loc. cit.*

This is the fundamental relation which will be used again in (ii) to (v) below. Using (1) gives

$$\frac{dw}{dr} = -\frac{Pr}{2Gl}, \qquad . \qquad . \qquad . \quad (3)$$

and integrating and using the condition $w=0$ when $r=a$ gives

$$w = P(a^2 - r^2)/4Gl. \qquad . \qquad . \qquad . \quad (4)$$

Thus the effect of uniform pressure P across the cross-section is to distort it into a parabolic form.

(ii) *Flow of an Incompressible Viscous (Newtonian) Fluid through a Circular Cylinder of Radius a and Length l caused by Pressure P at one End*

We assume laminar flow, that is, that the only non-zero component of velocity is W in the direction of the z-axis. Then, as in § 19 (8), the stress-strain relation is

$$\tau_{rz} = \eta \frac{dW}{dr}. \qquad . \qquad . \qquad . \quad (5)$$

Also the argument leading to (2) still holds, so using (5) in (2) gives

$$\frac{dW}{dr} = -\frac{Pr}{2\eta l}. \qquad . \qquad . \qquad . \quad (6)$$

If it is assumed that $W=0$ when $r=a$, that is, that there is no slip between the fluid and the cylinder, integrating (6) gives

$$W = P(a^2 - r^2)/4\eta l. \qquad . \qquad . \qquad . \quad (7)$$

The parabolic distribution of velocity over the cross-section, shown in Fig. 40 (*b*), is characteristic of laminar flow. The observed quantity is the discharge Q, the quantity of fluid flowing from the tube per second, this is

$$Q = \int_0^a 2\pi r W dr = \pi P a^4 / 8\eta l. \qquad . \qquad . \quad (8)$$

(8) is Poiseuille's relation which is much used for the measurement of viscosity.

(iii) *Non-Newtonian Viscosity*

In this case the rate of shear is not proportional to τ_{rz} and thus the problem is non-linear and exact solution becomes difficult. One of the simplest and most important cases is the power law

$$\frac{dW}{dr} = k\tau_{rz}|\tau_{rz}|^{n-1} . \qquad . \qquad . \qquad . \qquad (9)$$

The form of (9) is chosen so as to make dW/dr change sign with τ_{rz} and be proportional to the nth power of its magnitude. The case $n=1$ reduces to (5).

Using (2) in (9) gives

$$\frac{dW}{dr} = -\frac{kr^n P^n}{2^n l^n} ,$$

so that, assuming as before that $W=0$ when $r=a$,

$$W = \frac{kP^n(a^{n+1} - r^{n+1})}{(n+1)2^n l^n} . \qquad . \qquad . \qquad . \qquad (10)$$

(iv) *The Perfectly Plastic Substance under the Conditions of* (ii)

In this case the maximum shear stress which the material can sustain is S_0, and the substance behaves elastically until this stress is attained. Now by (2) the maximum shear occurs at the boundary $r=a$ so that when the pressure P reaches the value

$$2lS_0/a \qquad . \qquad . \qquad . \qquad . \qquad (11)$$

slip occurs at the boundary. The material will then move through the tube as a solid plug at a rate determined from outside.

(v) *The Bingham Substance under the Conditions of* (ii)

This behaves elastically until the maximum shear stress attains the value S_0. By (iv) this occurs at the boundary $r=a$ when the applied pressure attains the value (11). When this value has been passed in any region there will be flow in that region, and the magnitudes of the shear stress and rate of shear will, as in § 30 (viii), be connected by

$$|\tau_{rz}| = S_0 + \eta \left| \frac{dW}{dr} \right| . \qquad . \qquad . \qquad . \qquad (12)$$

Just as in problems on friction in elementary dynamics, the direction of the frictional force does not determine itself automatically but has to be chosen to conform with the direction of motion. In the present problem both τ_{rz} and dW/dr are negative, therefore (12) becomes

$$-\tau_{rz} = S_0 - \eta \frac{dW}{dr} . \qquad . \qquad . \qquad . \qquad (13)$$

τ_{rz} is given by (2), so that if $r<r_0$, where

$$r_0 = 2lS_0/P, \qquad . \qquad . \qquad . \qquad . \qquad (14)$$

$\tau_{rz}<S_0$ and there is no yield. In the region $r_0<r<a$, by (2) and (13),

$$\eta\frac{dW}{dr}-S_0 = -\frac{rP}{2l}. \qquad . \qquad . \qquad . \qquad (15)$$

Integrating, and using the condition $W=0$ when $r=a$ for no slip at the boundary, gives for the velocity

$$W = -S_0(a-r)/\eta + P(a^2-r^2)/4l\eta. \qquad . \qquad . \qquad (16)$$

When $r=r_0$, given by (14), W has the value

$$P(a-r_0)^2/4\eta l. \qquad . \qquad . \qquad . \qquad (17)$$

Thus in the region $r_0<r<a$ there is a velocity distribution given by (16), while a plug $0<r<r_0$ moves as if solid with velocity given by (17), Fig. 40 (c). This illustrates the characteristic difference between the Bingham substance and viscous fluid: in the latter case there is some motion at all points; in the former it frequently happens that flow is confined to certain regions, the remainder moving as if solid.

(vi) *Viscous Motion in the Region between Two Coaxial Rotating Cylinders*

Suppose that the region is $a<r<b$, that the inner cylinder is of radius a and at rest, and the outer cylinder is of radius b and is rotated with angular velocity ω_0 about its axis. There is supposed to be no motion in the axial or radial directions so that all quantities are functions of r only.

If $\tau_{r\theta}$ is the shear stress at radius r, the couple per unit length on a cylinder of fluid of radius r must be $2\pi r^2\tau_{r\theta}$ and this must be constant and equal to the couple per unit length M on the inner cylinder, that is,

$$\tau_{r\theta} = M/2\pi r^2. \qquad . \qquad . \qquad . \qquad (18)$$

The equations of viscosity § 19 (8) give, cf. § 14 (19),

$$\tau_{r\theta} = \eta\dot{\gamma}_{r\theta}. \qquad . \qquad . \qquad . \qquad (19)$$

If V is the tangential velocity at radius r it follows from § 14 (16) that

$$\dot{\gamma}_{r\theta} = \frac{dV}{dr}-\frac{V}{r}, \qquad . \qquad . \qquad . \qquad (20)$$

and therefore, by (18) and (19),

$$\frac{dV}{dr} - \frac{V}{r} = \frac{M}{2\pi\eta r^2} . \qquad . \qquad . \qquad . \quad (21)$$

The differential equation (21) for V has to be solved with $V=0$ when $r=a$, and $V=\omega_0 b$ when $r=b$; this, of course, assumes that there is no slip between the fluid and its boundaries. The general solution of (21) is

$$V = Ar - M/4\pi\eta r,$$

where A is a constant to be determined, together with the un-

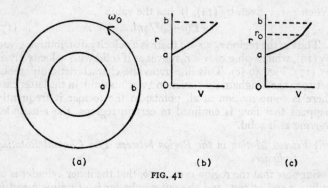

(a)   (b)   (c)

FIG. 41

known M, from the two boundary conditions stated above. These give

$$M = 4\pi\eta\omega_0 a^2 b^2/(b^2-a^2), \quad A = \omega_0 b^2/(b^2-a^2), \qquad . \quad (22)$$

so that the velocity distribution is given by

$$V = \omega_0 b^2 (r^2-a^2)/r(b^2-a^2), \qquad . \qquad . \quad (23)$$

as shown in Fig. 41 (b). This method has been much used for determination of the viscosity from the value of M given by (22).

(vii) *A Bingham Substance between Rotating Cylinders*

By (18) the shear stress is greatest when $r=a$, if the value here is less than S_0 there will be no motion. If it is greater than S_0, flow will take place in the region $a<r<r_0$ where r_0 is given by

$$r_0 = (M/2\pi S_0)^{\frac{1}{2}}. \qquad . \qquad . \qquad . \quad (24)$$

In this region we have

$$\tau_{r\theta}=S_0+\eta\dot{\gamma}_{r\theta},$$

or, using (18) and (20),

$$\frac{dV}{dr}-\frac{V}{r}=-\frac{S_0}{\eta}+\frac{M}{2\pi\eta r^2}. \qquad . \qquad . \qquad . \qquad (25)$$

The solution of (25) with $V=0$ when $r=a$ is

$$\frac{V}{r}=\frac{M}{4\pi\eta}\left(\frac{1}{a^2}-\frac{1}{r^2}\right)-\frac{S_0}{\eta}\ln\frac{r}{a}. \qquad . \qquad . \qquad . \qquad (26)$$

The region $r_0<r<b$ in which the shear stress is less than S_0 rotates as if solid with the angular velocity ω_0 of the outer cylinder, so the tangential velocity when $r=r_0$ must be $\omega_0 r_0$. Using this in (26) gives

$$M=\frac{4\pi\eta a^2 r_0^2}{(r_0^2-a^2)}\left(\omega_0+\frac{S_0}{\eta}\ln\frac{r_0}{a}\right). \qquad . \qquad . \qquad (27)$$

(24) and (27) determine r_0 and M, and the velocity distribution is then given by (26), cf. Fig. 41 (c). If

$$2\pi a^2 S_0 < M < 2\pi b^2 S_0,$$

portion of the material rotates as a solid mass. If $M>2\pi b^2 S_0$, there is flow throughout the material.

(viii) *Elastic Torsion of a Circular Cylinder*

Suppose that a circular cylinder of radius a and length l is twisted by a couple M applied at its ends and that the relative angular displacement of the ends is Θ.

The stress-strain relation § 14 (19) gives

$$\tau_{\theta z}=G\gamma_{\theta z}=G\frac{dv}{dz}, \qquad . \qquad . \qquad (28)$$

where v is the tangential displacement at radius r. The relative tangential displacement between the ends is just $r\Theta$, so that $dv/dz=r\Theta/l$ and (28) becomes

$$\tau_{\theta z}=Gr\Theta/l. \qquad . \qquad . \qquad . \qquad (29)$$

The total couple M is

$$M=\int_0^a 2\pi r^2\tau_{\theta z}dr=\pi G\Theta a^4/2l. \qquad . \qquad . \qquad (30)$$

This relation provides one of the simplest methods of determining G.

(ix) *Elastic and Plastic Torsion of a Circular Cylinder*

In the problem (viii) the shear stress (29) reaches the value S_0 first at the outer surface $r=a$ when the applied couple is

$$\tfrac{1}{2}\pi a^3 S_0 .$$

If the applied couple exceeds this value the cross-section will be divided into two parts, the elastic region $0 < r < r_0$ in which $\tau_{\theta z} < S_0$, and the plastic region $r_0 < r < a$ in which $\tau_{\theta z} = S_0$, the maximum shear which the material can sustain. By (29), the radius r_0 is given by

$$r_0 = \frac{lS_0}{G\Theta}. \qquad . \qquad . \qquad . \quad (31)$$

The couple M is given by

$$
\begin{aligned}
M &= \int_0^{r_0} 2\pi r^2 (Gr\Theta/l)dr + \int_{r_0}^{a} 2\pi r^2 S_0 dr \\
&= \tfrac{2}{3}\pi(a^3 - r_0^3)S_0 + \frac{\pi Gr_0^4\Theta}{2l} \\
&= \tfrac{2}{3}\pi a^3 S_0 - \frac{\pi l^3 S_0^4}{6G^3\Theta^3}. \qquad . \qquad . \quad (32)
\end{aligned}
$$

Thus, if the angle of twist is increased steadily, the couple increases linearly until the yield stress is reached at the outside of

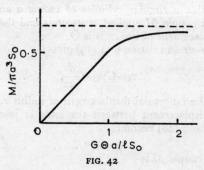

FIG. 42

the cylinder and subsequently tends asymptotically to the value $2\pi a^3 S_0/3$, Fig. 42.

It should be remarked that this simple treatment is not exact since it has used (29) which, from its derivation, is only valid if Θ is small. It is given to indicate the main features of the problem, namely, the division into elastic and plastic regions. In engineering practice this frequently occurs also in highly stressed beams and pressure vessels.

33. THE ELASTIC EQUATIONS OF MOTION

To calculate the actual stresses and strains in a body subjected to given applied forces the equations of motion have to be set up. The forces on the body will be of two kinds; *surface forces* (which may be pre-scribed or may have to be calculated) applied over the surface of the body, and *body forces*, such as gravity or magnetic forces which act on all portions of the body.

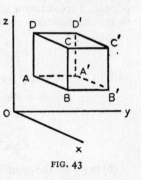

FIG. 43

Choosing axes Ox, Oy, Oz, let (X, Y, Z) be the components of body force per unit mass at the point (x, y, z). We write down the equations of motion of the small rectangular parallelepiped $ABCDA'B'C'D'$, Fig. 43, whose centre is at (x, y, z) and whose sides have lengths $\delta x, \delta y, \delta z$ and are parallel to the axes.

Suppose that σ_x, σ_y, σ_z, τ_{yz}, τ_{zx}, τ_{xy} are the components of stress at the point P, (x, y, z), then the forces on the parallelepiped in the x-direction across the forces $AA'D'D$, and $BB'C'C$ at $x-\frac{1}{2}\delta x$ and $x+\frac{1}{2}\delta x$ are, respectively,

$$\left\{-\sigma_x+\tfrac{1}{2}\frac{\partial\sigma_x}{\partial x}\delta x\right\}\delta y\,\delta z \quad \text{and} \quad \left\{\sigma_x+\tfrac{1}{2}\frac{\partial\sigma_x}{\partial x}\delta x\right\}\delta y\,\delta z. \quad (1)$$

Across the faces $ABCD$ and $A'B'C'D'$ they are

$$\left\{-\tau_{yx}+\tfrac{1}{2}\frac{\partial\tau_{yx}}{\partial y}\delta y\right\}\delta x\,\delta z \quad \text{and} \quad \left\{\tau_{yx}+\tfrac{1}{2}\frac{\partial\tau_{yx}}{\partial y}\delta y\right\}\delta x\,\delta z, \quad (2)$$

and across the faces $ABB'A'$ and $DCC'D'$ they are

$$\left\{-\tau_{zx}+\tfrac{1}{2}\frac{\partial\tau_{zx}}{\partial z}\delta z\right\}\delta x\,\delta y \quad \text{and} \quad \left\{\tau_{zx}+\tfrac{1}{2}\frac{\partial\tau_{zx}}{\partial z}\delta z\right\}\delta x\,\delta y. \quad (3)$$

Also, if ρ is the density of the solid, the component of body force in the x-direction is

$$\rho X \, \delta x \, \delta y \, \delta z. \qquad . \qquad . \qquad . \qquad (4)$$

Adding (1) to (4) it appears that the total force on the parallelepiped in the x-direction is

$$\left\{\frac{\partial \sigma_x}{\partial x} + \frac{\partial \tau_{yx}}{\partial y} + \frac{\partial \tau_{zx}}{\partial z} + \rho X\right\}\delta x \, \delta y \, \delta z. \qquad . \qquad . \qquad (5)$$

Now the mass of the parallelepiped is $\rho \, \delta x \, \delta y \, \delta z$ and, if (u, v, w) are the components of the displacement of the point P, its component of acceleration in the x-direction is very nearly [1] $\partial^2 u/\partial t^2$ so that by Newton's second law

$$\rho \frac{\partial^2 u}{\partial t^2} = \frac{\partial \sigma_x}{\partial x} + \frac{\partial \tau_{yx}}{\partial y} + \frac{\partial \tau_{zx}}{\partial z} + \rho X, \qquad . \qquad . \qquad (6)$$

and, in the same way for the y- and z-directions

$$\rho \frac{\partial^2 v}{\partial t^2} = \frac{\partial \tau_{xy}}{\partial x} + \frac{\partial \sigma_y}{\partial y} + \frac{\partial \tau_{zy}}{\partial z} + \rho Y, \qquad . \qquad . \qquad (7)$$

$$\rho \frac{\partial^2 w}{\partial t^2} = \frac{\partial \tau_{xz}}{\partial x} + \frac{\partial \tau_{yz}}{\partial y} + \frac{\partial \sigma_z}{\partial z} + \rho Z. \qquad . \qquad . \qquad (8)$$

(6) to (8) are the *equations of motion in terms of stresses*. For many purposes it is more convenient to have equations of motion in terms of the displacements. To find these equations, we express the stresses in (6) to (8) in terms of the strains by § 13 (10), (11) and then express the strains in terms of displacements by § 11 (4), (5). In this way, assuming that λ and G are constants, we get from (6)

$$\rho \frac{\partial^2 u}{\partial t^2} = \frac{\partial}{\partial x}(\lambda \Delta + 2G\varepsilon_x) + \frac{\partial}{\partial y}(G\gamma_{yx}) + \frac{\partial}{\partial z}(G\gamma_{zx}) + \rho X$$

$$= \lambda \frac{\partial \Delta}{\partial x} + G\left\{2\frac{\partial}{\partial x}\left(\frac{\partial u}{\partial x}\right) + \frac{\partial}{\partial y}\left(\frac{\partial v}{\partial x} + \frac{\partial u}{\partial y}\right) + \frac{\partial}{\partial z}\left(\frac{\partial w}{\partial x} + \frac{\partial u}{\partial z}\right)\right\} + \rho X$$

$$= (\lambda + G)\frac{\partial \Delta}{\partial x} + G\nabla^2 u + \rho X, \qquad . \qquad . \qquad . \qquad (9)$$

[1] Actually it is the quantity $D^2 u/Dt^2$ discussed in § 39, but for small velocities this reduces to $\partial^2 u/\partial t^2$.

using the result § 11 (17)

$$\Delta=\frac{\partial u}{\partial x}+\frac{\partial v}{\partial y}+\frac{\partial w}{\partial z}, \qquad . \qquad . \qquad . \quad (10)$$

and writing ∇^2 for the operator

$$\nabla^2=\frac{\partial^2}{\partial x^2}+\frac{\partial^2}{\partial y^2}+\frac{\partial^2}{\partial z^2}. \qquad . \qquad . \quad (11)$$

In the same way (7) and (8) give the equations

$$\rho\frac{\partial^2 v}{\partial t^2}=(\lambda+G)\frac{\partial\Delta}{\partial y}+G\nabla^2 v+\rho Y, \qquad . \qquad . \quad (12)$$

$$\rho\frac{\partial^2 w}{\partial t^2}=(\lambda+G)\frac{\partial\Delta}{\partial z}+G\nabla^2 w+\rho Z. \qquad . \qquad . \quad (13)$$

(9), (12) and (13) are the *equations of motion in terms of displacements*.

Differentiating (9), (12) and (13) partially with respect to x, y, and z, respectively, and adding gives, using (10) and assuming ρ to be constant,

$$\rho\frac{\partial^2\Delta}{\partial t^2}=(\lambda+2G)\nabla^2\Delta+\rho\left(\frac{\partial X}{\partial x}+\frac{\partial Y}{\partial y}+\frac{\partial Z}{\partial z}\right), \qquad . \quad (14)$$

and, if the body forces are constant or zero,

$$\frac{\partial^2\Delta}{\partial t^2}=\left(\frac{\lambda+2G}{\rho}\right)\nabla^2\Delta. \qquad . \qquad . \quad (15)$$

(15) is the so-called wave equation. It will be shown in § 37 that it has the property that its solutions are propagated with speed

$$\left(\frac{\lambda+2G}{\rho}\right)^{\frac{1}{2}}=\left(\frac{3K+4G}{3\rho}\right)^{\frac{1}{2}} \qquad . \qquad . \quad (16)$$

so that, since Δ is the dilatation, it follows from (15) that waves of dilatation are propagated in the solid with speed (16). These correspond, in fact, to the primary seismic waves, cf. § 38.

Again it follows from (12) and (13) for the case of no body forces and ρ constant, that

$$\rho\frac{\partial^2}{\partial t^2}\left(\frac{\partial w}{\partial y}-\frac{\partial v}{\partial z}\right)=G\nabla^2\left(\frac{\partial w}{\partial y}-\frac{\partial v}{\partial z}\right)$$

and so, using the definition § 11 (6) of the components of rotation,

$$\frac{\partial^2 \omega_x}{\partial t^2} = \frac{G}{\rho} \nabla^2 \omega_x . \qquad . \qquad . \qquad . \quad (17)$$

In the same way ω_y and ω_z satisfy the wave equation, and they will be propagated with speed

$$(G/\rho)^{\frac{1}{2}} \qquad . \qquad . \qquad . \qquad . \quad (18)$$

which will be found in § 38 to correspond with secondary seismic waves. For a fluid, $G=0$ and these waves will not be present.

In certain cases, the displacements u, v, w themselves satisfy the wave equation; thus in the equivoluminal case, $\Delta=0$, it follows from (9), (12), (13) that in the absence of body forces

$$\rho\frac{\partial^2 u}{\partial t^2} = G\nabla^2 u, \quad \rho\frac{\partial^2 v}{\partial t^2} = G\nabla^2 v, \quad \rho\frac{\partial^2 w}{\partial t^2} = G\nabla^2 w. \quad . \quad (19)$$

Also in the irrotational case, $\omega_x = \omega_y = \omega_z = 0$,

$$\frac{\partial\Delta}{\partial x} = \frac{\partial^2 u}{\partial x^2} + \frac{\partial}{\partial y}\left(\frac{\partial v}{\partial x}\right) + \frac{\partial}{\partial z}\left(\frac{\partial w}{\partial x}\right) = \nabla^2 u,$$

so that (9) becomes (for the case of no body forces)

$$\rho\frac{\partial^2 u}{\partial t^2} = (\lambda + 2G)\nabla^2 u, \qquad . \qquad . \qquad . \quad (20)$$

and, similarly, v and w satisfy this equation.

34. THE ELASTIC EQUATIONS OF EQUILIBRIUM

These are the special case of the equations of motion in which all particles are at rest. Putting $\partial^2 u/\partial t^2$, etc., equal to zero, § 33 (6) to (8) give the *equations of equilibrium in terms of stresses*

$$\frac{\partial\sigma_x}{\partial x} + \frac{\partial\tau_{yx}}{\partial y} + \frac{\partial\tau_{zx}}{\partial z} + \rho X = 0, \qquad . \qquad . \qquad (1)$$

$$\frac{\partial\tau_{xy}}{\partial x} + \frac{\partial\sigma_y}{\partial y} + \frac{\partial\tau_{zy}}{\partial z} + \rho Y = 0, \qquad . \qquad . \qquad (2)$$

$$\frac{\partial\tau_{xz}}{\partial x} + \frac{\partial\tau_{yz}}{\partial y} + \frac{\partial\sigma_z}{\partial z} + \rho Z = 0. \qquad . \qquad . \qquad (3)$$

Similarly, § 33 (9) to (13) give the *equations of equilibrium in terms of displacements*

$$(\lambda+G)\frac{\partial\Delta}{\partial x}+G\nabla^2 u+\rho X=0, \qquad . \quad . \quad (4)$$

$$(\lambda+G)\frac{\partial\Delta}{\partial y}+G\nabla^2 v+\rho Y=0, \qquad . \quad . \quad (5)$$

$$(\lambda+G)\frac{\partial\Delta}{\partial z}+G\nabla^2 w+\rho Z=0. \qquad . \quad . \quad (6)$$

Also, by § 33 (15), (17) it follows that if the body forces vanish

$$\nabla^2\Delta=0, \qquad . \qquad . \qquad . \qquad . \quad (7)$$

$$\nabla^2\omega_x=\nabla^2\omega_y=\nabla^2\omega_z=0 \quad . \qquad . \qquad . \quad (8)$$

that is, Δ, ω_x, ω_y, ω_z all satisfy Laplace's equation.

These differential equations have to be satisfied within the body of the solid subject to certain conditions at its surface which are called boundary conditions. These usually take the form of prescribed stress or displacement over portions of the surface.

It should be remarked that these equations do not apply to initial stresses (the 'locked-up' stresses produced in engineering or geological material in the process of forming) or to thermal stresses (the stresses produced by inequalities of temperature). Thus, for example, in the latter case, it can be shown that if T is the temperature at the point (x, y, z), (4) is replaced by

$$(\lambda+G)\frac{\partial\Delta}{\partial x}+G\nabla^2 u-\frac{\alpha E}{1-2\nu}\frac{\partial T}{\partial x}=0, \qquad . \quad . \quad (9)$$

where α is the coefficient of (linear) thermal expansion of the body.

The complete formulation of problems in elasticity can now be seen. The stresses have to satisfy (1) to (3), while the boundary conditions may involve either stress or displacement. This, in effect, covers the statics of the problem. The strains are related to the stresses by the stress-strain relations § 13 (8), (9), (23), (24), and finally, since the strains are not independent but have to satisfy the compatibility conditions § 11 (18), § 10 (7), these require additional connections between the stresses so that a self-consistent set of stresses and strains may be obtained. This is discussed in more detail in § 35. Finally, when the strains are known, their definitions § 11 (4), (5) may be regarded as a set of equations from which the displacements may be found.

As in most branches of applied mathematics, there is a unique-ness theorem which states that, under fairly general conditions (for example, if either the surface displacements or the surface stresses are given), if a solution can be found by any means this is the unique solution of the problem. This is of great importance because (as in the problem discussed below) at least part of the solution of many problems is by inspection or artifice and it is important to know that the solution so obtained is, in fact, the only one possible.

As a simple but important example to illustrate the way in which the various sets of equations are involved in a final solution we con-sider the semi-infinite region under gravity. Taking x- and y-axes in the surface and the z-axis vertically upwards, the region con-sidered is $z < 0$ and the body force is $X = Y = 0$, $Z = -g$.

The stress equations (1) to (3) are satisfied if

$$\sigma_z = \rho g z, \qquad . \qquad . \qquad . \qquad (10)$$
$$\tau_{yz} = \tau_{zx} = \tau_{xy} = 0,$$

and σ_x and σ_y are functions of z only. (10) also makes σ_z vanish at the surface $z = 0$.

In addition we know that, from the conditions of the problem, there can be no displacement in the x- and y-directions so that w is the only non-vanishing displacement, and, since it must be in-dependent of x and y, ε_z is, by § 11 (4), (5), the only non-vanishing strain. Then, by § 13 (4), (10)

$$\Delta = \varepsilon_z, \qquad . \qquad . \qquad . \qquad . \qquad (11)$$
$$\sigma_x = \sigma_y = \lambda \varepsilon_z, \qquad \sigma_z = (\lambda + 2G) \varepsilon_z. \qquad . \qquad . \qquad (12)$$

From (10), (12) and § 13 (22),

$$\sigma_x = \sigma_y = \frac{\lambda}{\lambda + 2G} \sigma_z = \frac{\nu}{1-\nu} \sigma_z = \frac{\nu}{1-\nu} \rho g z. \qquad . \qquad . \qquad (13)$$

It may be verified that the strains satisfy the compatability con-ditions.

From the definition of the strain ε_z, we have

$$\frac{\partial w}{\partial z} = \varepsilon_z = \frac{\rho g z}{\lambda + 2G} = \frac{(1+\nu)(1-2\nu)\rho g z}{E(1-\nu)},$$

and therefore

$$w = \frac{(1+\nu)(1-2\nu)\rho g z^2}{2E(1-\nu)} + \text{Const.}$$

(13) gives the stresses at shallow depths below the Earth's surface. σ_x, σ_y, σ_z are, of course, principal stresses: the vertical principal stress σ_z is just the load or the weight of a column of rock of unit area above the point considered; since ν is approximately $1/4$, the horizontal principal stresses are roughly $1/3$ of the vertical principal stress so the stresses are far from hydrostatic. There is some evidence that, even at the depths involved in mining, creep in the rocks causes the stresses to approach nearer to the hydrostatic values. It may also be remarked that since the relative densities of rock and water are roughly in the ratio 3:1, the (hydrostatic) pressure in a fissure containing water will be of the same order as the horizontal principal stress for solid rock.

35. SPECIAL CASES OF THE EQUATIONS OF ELASTICITY

Because of the complexity of the general equations of § 34, most of the special problems which have been solved are either two-dimensional problems of plane stress or strain, or problems which can be simply expressed by reference to one of the other important coordinate systems such as cylindrical coordinates, spherical polar coordinates, etc. The equations for the most important case of all, plane strain, will be given below in both rectangular and polar coordinates.

Plane Strain in Rectangular Coordinates

This has been discussed in § 14 (iv), where it was found that, to keep the displacement in the z-direction zero, stress

$$\sigma_z = \nu(\sigma_x + \sigma_y) \qquad . \qquad . \qquad . \qquad (1)$$

had to be supplied. The stress-strain relations § 14 (8), (9) are

$$E\varepsilon_x = (1-\nu^2)\sigma_x - \nu(1+\nu)\sigma_y, \quad E\varepsilon_y = -\nu(1+\nu)\sigma_x + (1-\nu^2)\sigma_y, \qquad . \qquad (2)$$

$$E\gamma_{xy} = 2(1+\nu)\tau_{xy}. \qquad . \qquad (3)$$

The compatibility relation for strains, § 10 (7), is

$$\frac{\partial^2 \varepsilon_x}{\partial y^2} + \frac{\partial^2 \varepsilon_y}{\partial x^2} = \frac{\partial^2 \gamma_{xy}}{\partial x \, \partial y}, \qquad . \qquad . \qquad . \qquad (4)$$

and expressing the strains in (4) in terms of stresses by (2) and (3) gives the compatibility relation for stresses

$$(1-\nu)\frac{\partial^2 \sigma_x}{\partial y^2} - \nu \frac{\partial^2 \sigma_x}{\partial x^2} + (1-\nu)\frac{\partial^2 \sigma_y}{\partial x^2} - \nu \frac{\partial^2 \sigma_y}{\partial y^2} = 2\frac{\partial^2 \tau_{xy}}{\partial x \, \partial y}. \qquad . \qquad (5)$$

9

If body forces are absent, the equations of equilibrium, § 34 (1)–(3), become in this case

$$\frac{\partial \sigma_x}{\partial x} + \frac{\partial \tau_{yx}}{\partial y} = 0, \qquad \qquad (6)$$

$$\frac{\partial \tau_{xy}}{\partial x} + \frac{\partial \sigma_y}{\partial y} = 0, \qquad \qquad (7)$$

and, using these, (5) may be written

$$\left(\frac{\partial^2}{\partial x^2} + \frac{\partial^2}{\partial y^2}\right)(\sigma_x + \sigma_y) = 0. \qquad \qquad (8)$$

Now suppose that there is a function ϕ such that

$$\sigma_x = \frac{\partial^2 \phi}{\partial y^2}, \quad \sigma_y = \frac{\partial^2 \phi}{\partial x^2}, \quad \tau_{xy} = -\frac{\partial^2 \phi}{\partial x\, \partial y}, \qquad (9)$$

then, using (9) in (6) and (7), it appears that these equations are satisfied identically. Also, using (9) in (8) it appears that ϕ must satisfy

$$\left(\frac{\partial^2}{\partial x^2} + \frac{\partial^2}{\partial y^2}\right)\left(\frac{\partial^2 \phi}{\partial x^2} + \frac{\partial^2 \phi}{\partial y^2}\right) = 0, \qquad (10)$$

that is

$$\frac{\partial^4 \phi}{\partial x^4} + 2\frac{\partial^4 \phi}{\partial x^2\, \partial y^2} + \frac{\partial^4 \phi}{\partial y^4} = 0. \qquad \qquad (11)$$

Such a function ϕ is called a *stress function*, and the above analysis shows that any solution of (11) is such that its derivatives (9) give a system of stresses which automatically satisfy the equations of equilibrium and the compatibility conditions. Thus most of the mathematics will be concerned with the solution of (11); this is called the *biharmonic equation*, which is sometimes written for shortness, using the notation § 33 (11),

$$\nabla^2(\nabla^2 \phi) = 0 \quad \text{or} \quad \nabla^4 \phi = 0. \qquad \qquad (12)$$

The use of stress functions is perhaps the most powerful method used in the solution of problems in elasticity. The method is not confined to plane problems, and stress functions are also available for the solution of problems in three dimensions.

Plane Strain in Polar Coordinates

Polar coordinates and the components of strain with reference to them have been discussed in § 10. The components of stress are the *radial stress* σ_r in the direction PR, Fig. 18, the *tangential stress* σ_θ in the direction PT, and the shear stress $\tau_{r\theta} = \tau_{\theta r}$ associated with these directions.

To find the equations of equilibrium, we consider the region $ABCD$ of Fig. 44 bounded by circles BC and AD of radii $r \pm \frac{1}{2}\delta r$ and by the rays DC and AB at angles $\theta \pm \frac{1}{2}\delta\theta$, where δr and $\delta\theta$ are so small that their squares and product are negligible.

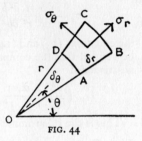

FIG. 44

Then if σ_r, σ_θ, $\tau_{r\theta}$ are the components of stress at the point (r, θ), the forces (per unit length perpendicular to the plane) in the radial and tangential directions on the faces DC and AB are, respectively,

$$\pm\left(\tau_{r\theta} \pm \frac{1}{2}\frac{\partial \tau_{r\theta}}{\partial \theta}\delta\theta\right)\delta r \quad \text{and} \quad \pm\left(\sigma_\theta \pm \frac{1}{2}\frac{\partial \sigma_\theta}{\partial \theta}\delta\theta\right)\delta r,$$

while the radial and tangential forces on the faces BC and AD are, respectively,

$$\pm\left(\sigma_r \pm \frac{1}{2}\frac{\partial \sigma_r}{\partial r}\delta r\right)(r \pm \frac{1}{2}\delta r)\delta\theta \quad \text{and} \quad \pm\left(\tau_{r\theta} \pm \frac{1}{2}\frac{\partial \tau_{r\theta}}{\partial r}\delta r\right)(r \pm \frac{1}{2}\delta r)\delta\theta.$$

Resolving in the radial direction gives, for the case of no body forces,

$$\left(\tau_{r\theta} + \frac{1}{2}\frac{\partial \tau_{r\theta}}{\partial \theta}\delta\theta\right)(\delta r)\cos\frac{1}{2}\delta\theta - \left(\sigma_\theta + \frac{1}{2}\frac{\partial \sigma_\theta}{\partial \theta}\delta\theta\right)(\delta r)\sin\frac{1}{2}\delta\theta$$

$$- \left(\tau_{r\theta} - \frac{1}{2}\frac{\partial \tau_{r\theta}}{\partial \theta}\delta\theta\right)(\delta r)\cos\frac{1}{2}\delta\theta - \left(\sigma_\theta - \frac{1}{2}\frac{\partial \sigma_\theta}{\partial \theta}\delta\theta\right)(\delta r)\sin\frac{1}{2}\delta\theta$$

$$+ \left(\sigma_r + \frac{1}{2}\frac{\partial \sigma_r}{\partial r}\delta r\right)(r + \frac{1}{2}\delta r)\delta\theta - \left(\sigma_r - \frac{1}{2}\frac{\partial \sigma_r}{\partial r}\delta r\right)(r - \frac{1}{2}\delta r)\delta\theta = 0.$$

Neglecting all terms of higher order than $\delta r\, \delta\theta$ gives

$$\frac{\partial \sigma_r}{\partial r} + \frac{1}{r}\frac{\partial \tau_{r\theta}}{\partial \theta} + \frac{\sigma_r - \sigma_\theta}{r} = 0. \quad \cdot \quad \cdot \quad \cdot \quad (13)$$

Similarly, resolving in the tangential direction gives

$$\frac{1}{r}\frac{\partial \sigma_\theta}{\partial \theta} + \frac{\partial \tau_{r\theta}}{\partial r} + \frac{2\tau_{r\theta}}{r} = 0. \quad \cdot \quad \cdot \quad \cdot \quad (14)$$

(13) and (14) are the equations of equilibrium in terms of stresses.

Next, a stress function ϕ can be introduced as in (9) to (11). If there is a function ϕ such that

$$\sigma_r = \frac{1}{r}\frac{\partial \phi}{\partial r} + \frac{1}{r^2}\frac{\partial^2 \phi}{\partial \theta^2}, \quad \sigma_\theta = \frac{\partial^2 \phi}{\partial r^2}, \quad \tau_{r\theta} = -\frac{\partial}{\partial r}\left(\frac{1}{r}\frac{\partial \phi}{\partial \theta}\right), \quad \cdot \quad (15)$$

the equations (13) and (14) are satisfied automatically, and it may be verified that the compatibility condition for strains, § 10 (29), is satisfied if

$$\left(\frac{\partial^2}{\partial r^2} + \frac{1}{r}\frac{\partial}{\partial r} + \frac{1}{r^2}\frac{\partial^2}{\partial \theta^2}\right)\left(\frac{\partial^2 \phi}{\partial r^2} + \frac{1}{r}\frac{\partial \phi}{\partial r} + \frac{1}{r^2}\frac{\partial^2 \phi}{\partial \theta^2}\right) = 0. \quad \cdot \quad (16)$$

This is the biharmonic equation (10) in polar coordinates.

Plane Stress

In this case $\sigma_3 = 0$, and by § 14 (2) the stress-strain equations are

$$E\varepsilon_x = \sigma_x - \nu\sigma_y, \quad E\varepsilon_y = -\nu\sigma_x + \sigma_y, \quad E\gamma_{xy} = 2(1+\nu)\tau_{xy}. \quad (17)$$

The equations of equilibrium in terms of stresses are the same; and it is found that (8) still holds so that the theory of the stress function (9), (11) is still valid. The position is that the determination of stresses is the same as for the case of plane strain; in the calculation of strains and displacements a difference arises because the constants in (17) and (2) are different.

36. SPECIAL PROBLEMS IN ELASTICITY

In this section a number of special problems will be discussed to indicate the way in which the various branches of the theory previously studied are involved in the process of solution.

The simplest and most instructive method of attack, already used in § 34 and used again in (i) below, is to write down all the equations involved and to solve them step by step with appropriate simplifying assumptions, thus finally building up a solution of the required type. A related approach, frequently used in the early stages of the development of a subject, is to take a fundamental solution of a simple type, see what problem it solves, and build up solutions of more complicated problems by superposition of these simple solutions, cf. (ii) below.

For more complicated problems, more sophisticated methods involving additional mathematical theory are needed and a great many such methods have been developed for torsion, flexure, behaviour of thin plates, and so on. Here, only the use of the stress function for problems in plane stress and strain will be discussed. In effect this states that every solution of the biharmonic equation, § 35 (11), provides the solution of some problem in elasticity. By studying solutions of this equation in various coordinate systems, a large number of results for regions bounded by simple surfaces may be obtained, cf. (iii) and (iv), and by using the theory of the complex variable in its solution [1] others may be obtained for regions of less regular shapes.

(i) *The Cylindrical Pressure Vessel.* The problem is that of the calculation of the stresses in the hollow cylinder $a<r<b$ with applied pressures p_1 at $r=a$ and p_2 at $r=b$. It is assumed that the situation is one of plane strain.

Since all quantities are independent of θ, the equation of equilibrium § 35 (13) becomes

$$\frac{d\sigma_r}{dr}+\frac{\sigma_r-\sigma_\theta}{r}=0, \quad . \quad . \quad . \quad . \quad (1)$$

also § 35 (14) and all subsequent equations involving $\tau_{r\theta}$ are satisfied by $\tau_{r\theta}=0$. Since the displacements are purely radial, $v=0$ in § 10 (26) and the components of strain are given by

$$\varepsilon_r=\frac{du}{dr}, \quad \varepsilon_\theta=\frac{u}{r}. \quad . \quad . \quad . \quad (2)$$

The stress-strain relations § 14 (4) for the case of plane strain $\varepsilon_z=0$ are

$$\sigma_r=(\lambda+2G)\varepsilon_r+\lambda\varepsilon_\theta, \quad \sigma_\theta=\lambda\varepsilon_r+(\lambda+2G)\varepsilon_\theta. \quad . \quad (3)$$

Using (3) and (2) in (1), the radial displacement u has to satisfy

$$\frac{d}{dr}\left(\frac{du}{dr}+\frac{u}{r}\right)=0,$$

the general solution of which is

$$u=Ar+B/r, \quad . \quad . \quad . \quad . \quad (4)$$

where A and B are constants which have to be found from the

---

[1] Cf. Muskhelishvili, *Some Basic Problems of the Mathematical Theory of Elasticity* (Noordhoff, 1953).

known values of σ_r at $r=a$ and $r=b$. Strains calculated from (4) satisfy the compatibility conditions § (29). By (2) and (3)

$$\sigma_r = 2A(\lambda+G)-2GB/r^2, \quad \sigma_\theta = 2A(\lambda+G)+2GB/r^2. \quad (5)$$

The conditions $\sigma_r = -p_1$ when $r=a$, $\sigma_r = -p_2$ when $r=b$ give

$$2A(\lambda+G)-2GB/a^2 = -p_1, \quad 2A(\lambda+G)-(2GB/b^2) = -p_2.$$

Solving and substituting in (5) gives finally

$$\sigma_r = \frac{a^2p_1-b^2p_2}{b^2-a^2} - \frac{a^2b^2(p_1-p_2)}{r^2(b^2-a^2)}, \quad \cdot \quad \cdot \quad (6)$$

$$\sigma_\theta = \frac{a^2p_1-b^2p_2}{b^2-a^2} + \frac{a^2b^2(p_1-p_2)}{r^2(b^2-a^2)}. \quad \cdot \quad \cdot \quad (7)$$

The tangential stress σ_θ has its maximum value of

$$\frac{(a^2+b^2)p_1-2b^2p_2}{b^2-a^2} \quad \cdot \quad \cdot \quad \cdot \quad (8)$$

when $r=a$. If p_2 is negligible, this is always greater than p_1, and it tends to p_1 for a very thick cylinder $b\to\infty$.

For the case $p_1=0$, $b\to\infty$, (6) and (7) give

$$\sigma_r = -p_2\left(1-\frac{a^2}{r^2}\right), \quad \sigma_\theta = -p_2\left(1+\frac{a^2}{r^2}\right). \quad \cdot \quad (9)$$

(9) gives the stresses around a cylindrical opening in a solid subjected to a pressure which is effectively hydrostatic at large distances and has magnitude p_2 there. The greatest stress is the tangential compressive stress $2p_2$ at the surface of the hole, and this value is independent of the radius of the hole. This is the simplest example of stress concentration near openings.

(ii) *The Semi-infinite Region with a Line Load*

Results for this case will be derived by studying the properties of the simple stress system.

$$\sigma_r = \frac{A\cos\theta}{r}, \quad \sigma_\theta = 0, \quad \tau_{r\theta} = 0, \quad \cdot \quad (10)$$

which satisfies the equations of equilibrium § 35 (13), (14). Also the components of strain derived from it satisfy the compatibility condition § 10 (29).

The system (10) gives zero stress in the plane $\theta = \pm\frac{1}{2}\pi$ except near the origin $r \to 0$. Thus it may be regarded as a solution for the region $x > 0$ with no surface forces except at the origin. To find the force at the origin, consider a small circle of radius a about the origin, Fig. 45 (a). The stresses over this give a resultant force in the x-direction of

$$2 \int_0^{\pi/2} a\sigma_r \cos\theta \, d\theta = 2A \int_0^{\pi/2} \cos^2\theta \, d\theta = \pi A/2,$$

and so, if $A = -2P/\pi$ in (10), this solution is appropriate to a concentrated line force at the origin of P per unit length in the z-direction.

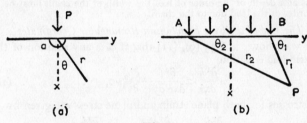

FIG. 45

Using § 3 (4) and (5), the components of stress in the x, y coordinate system are found to be

$$\sigma_x = -\frac{2P}{\pi} \frac{\cos^3\theta}{r} = -\frac{2Px^3}{\pi r^4}, \qquad . \qquad . \qquad (11)$$

$$\sigma_y = -\frac{2Pxy^2}{\pi r^4}, \qquad \tau_{xy} = -\frac{2Px^2y}{\pi r^4}. \qquad . \qquad . \qquad (12)$$

The stresses for any loading distributed over the face $x = 0$ can be obtained by integration. For a uniformly distributed load p per unit length over the region $-a < y < a$ it follows from (11) that

$$\sigma_x = -\frac{2px^3}{\pi} \int_{-a}^{a} \frac{d\eta}{[x^2 + (y-\eta)^2]^2}$$

$$= (p/\pi)\{\theta_1 - \theta_2 + x(y-a)/r_1^2 - x(y+a)/r_2^2\}, \qquad . \qquad (13)$$

where θ_1 and θ_2 are the angles PBy, PAy, and r_1, r_2 are the distances PB and PA in Fig. 45 (b). Similarly

$$\sigma_y = (p/\pi)\{\theta_1 - \theta_2 - x(y-a)/r_1^2 + x(y+a)/r_2^2\}, \qquad . \qquad (14)$$

$$\tau_{xy} = -px^2(r_2^2 - r_1^2)/\pi r_1^2 r_2^2. \qquad . \qquad . \qquad (15)$$

By § 3 (19) the principal stresses at (x, y) are

$$p(\theta_1 - \theta_2)/\pi \pm 2pax/\pi r_1 r_2 \quad . \quad . \quad . \quad (16)$$

Thus the maximum shear stress at (x, y) is $2pax/\pi r_1 r_2$. It follows from elementary trigonometry that this has the value

$$p/\pi \quad . \quad . \quad . \quad . \quad (17)$$

at all points of the circle $x^2 + y^2 = a^2$, and it is easy to show that this is the greatest value it attains.

This analysis gives the stresses when a smooth, two-dimensional stamp is pressed onto the surface of a semi-infinite solid. Assuming Tresca's criterion of yielding, § 27 (16), yield will take place over the surface $x^2 + y^2 = a^2$ when $p = \pi \sigma_0/2$. This result has been used to estimate the strength which the Earth's crust must possess in order to be able to support inequalities of load such as mountain chains. By (17) its yield stress at a depth of the order of half the width of the chain must be of the order of the load due to the chain.

(iii) *The Use of a Stress Function in Rectangular Coordinates*

It was shown in § 35 (9), (11) that if ϕ is any solution of the biharmonic equation

$$\frac{\partial^4 \phi}{\partial x^4} + 2 \frac{\partial^4 \phi}{\partial x^2 \, \partial y^2} + \frac{\partial^4 \phi}{\partial y^4} = 0, \quad . \quad . \quad (18)$$

the stresses for both plane strain and plane stress are given by

$$\sigma_x = \frac{\partial^2 \phi}{\partial y^2}, \quad \sigma_y = \frac{\partial^2 \phi}{\partial x^2}, \quad \tau_{xy} = -\frac{\partial^2 \phi}{\partial x \, \partial y}. \quad . \quad (19)$$

We proceed to see what problems can be solved by simple solutions of (18). The simplest solutions of all are polynomials in x and y; if the degree of the polynomial is less than the fourth, (18) is

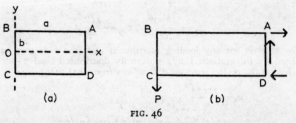

FIG. 46

satisfied automatically; for polynomials of the fourth or higher degree there must be relations between the coefficients. The solutions will be interpreted with reference to the rectangle $ABCD$, $0 < x < a$, $-b < y < b$ of Fig. 46 (a).

$$\text{(i)} \quad \phi=Ax^2, \quad \sigma_y=2A, \quad \sigma_x=\tau_{xy}=0, \qquad . \qquad (20)$$

a uniform tension in the direction of the y-axis.

$$\text{(ii)} \quad \phi=Bxy, \quad \sigma_x=\sigma_y=0, \quad \tau_{xy}=-B, \qquad . \qquad (21)$$

a pure shear.

$$\text{(iii)} \quad \phi=Cy^3, \quad \sigma_x=6Cy, \quad \sigma_y=\tau_{xy}=0. \qquad . \qquad (22)$$

In this case there is no stress over the surfaces AB, CD, and there are normal stresses over AD and BC varying linearly from $6Cb$ at A and B to $-6Cb$ at C and D. The resultant force on these surfaces is zero, but the forces have a moment

$$M=\int_{-b}^{b} 6Cy^2dy=4Cb^3. \qquad . \qquad . \qquad (23)$$

The problem solved is thus that of a beam bent by couples M applied at its ends.

As an example of the calculation of displacements, consider the case of plane stress (that is, assume that the beam is thin in the direction perpendicular to the plane $ABCD$). Then, using (22) in § 35 (17) gives for the strains and displacements

$$E\epsilon_x=E\frac{\partial u}{\partial x}=6Cy, \quad E\epsilon_y=E\frac{\partial v}{\partial y}=-6vCy, \qquad . \qquad (24)$$

$$E\gamma_{xy}=E\left(\frac{\partial u}{\partial y}+\frac{\partial v}{\partial x}\right)=0. \qquad . \qquad . \qquad (25)$$

Integrating (24) gives

$$Eu=6Cxy+f(y), \quad Ev=-3vCy^2+g(x), \qquad . \qquad (26)$$

where $f(y)$ and $g(x)$ are unknown functions. Substituting (26) in (25) gives

$$6Cx+f'(y)+g'(x)=0,$$

that is,

$$g'(x)=-6Cx+A, \quad f'(y)=-A, \qquad . \qquad . \qquad (27)$$

where A is a constant. Integrating (27) and substituting in (26), gives finally

$$Eu=6Cxy-Ay+B, \qquad . \qquad . \qquad . \qquad (28)$$

$$Ev=-3vCy^2-3Cx^2+Ax+D, \qquad . \qquad . \qquad (29)$$

where B and D are constants.

In (28) and (29), B and D correspond to uniform translations in the x- and y-directions, and the terms $-Ay/E$ and Ax/E to a rotation as a rigid body through the small angle A/E. These displacements do not affect the system of stresses and strains; the calculation of displacements always involves this uncertainty. Putting $A=B=D=0$ in (28) and (29), the displacement of the centre line $y=0$ is found to be $-3Cx^2/E$. Its radius of curvature is

$$E/6C=2Eb^3/3M \qquad . \qquad . \qquad . \qquad (30)$$

which agrees with that given by the elementary Euler-Bernouilli theory of the deflection of beams.

This solution, and others such as (iv) below, is exact only if the forces over BC and AD are applied accurately according to (22) and, strictly, is not valid for any other system of forces of the same moment M. There is, however, a general principle in elasticity, *St-Venant's principle*, which states that if statically equivalent systems of forces are applied over a restricted area of a body their effects will be the same at distances large compared with the diameter of the area although they will be very different at points near to the area.

(iv) $\phi=Dxy^3+Fxy$, $\sigma_x=6Dxy$, $\sigma_y=0$, $\tau_{xy}=-3Dy^2-F$.   (31)

On AB and CD, $\sigma_y=0$ and $\tau_{xy}=-3Db^2-F$, so if we choose $F=-3Db^2$ there will be no stress over these surfaces. With this value of F we have $\sigma_x=0$, $\tau_{xy}=3D(b^2-y^2)$ on BC, and so the stress over this surface is wholly tangential and its total amount P is

$$P=\int_{-b}^{b} 3D(b^2-y^2)dy=4Db^3. \qquad . \qquad . \qquad . \qquad (32)$$

This stress function thus solves the problem of a cantilever bent by a concentrated load P at one end BC and held in position by stresses over the face AD. Using the above values of D and F in (31) gives the stresses

$$\sigma_x=3Pxy/2b^3, \quad \sigma_y=0, \quad \tau_{xy}=3P(b^2-y^2)/4b^3. \qquad . \qquad (33)$$

The displacements may be calculated as in (iii). Proceeding in this way, and using polynomials of higher orders, a great variety of problems on beams with various types of loading can be solved (cf. Timoshenko, *loc. cit.*).

Polynomials are not the only simple solutions of (18). As another example it is easily verified that both

$$e^{\omega y} \cos \omega x \quad \text{and} \quad ye^{\omega y} \cos \omega x \qquad . \qquad . \qquad . \qquad (34)$$

satisfy it, and, because of the exponential factors, they are appropriate to the semi-infinite region $y<0$. For example, if $\phi=A(1-\omega y)e^{\omega y} \cos \omega x$,

$$\sigma_x=-\omega^2A(1+\omega y)e^{\omega y} \cos \omega x, \quad \sigma_y=-\omega^2A(1-\omega y)e^{\omega y} \cos \omega x,$$
$$\tau_{xy}=-A\omega^3ye^{\omega y} \sin \omega x.$$

This gives

$$\sigma_y=-\omega^2A \cos \omega x, \quad \tau_{xy}=0 \qquad . \qquad . \qquad . \qquad (35)$$

in the plane $y=0$, and is thus the solution for harmonic loading on the surface of the semi-infinite region $y<0$. It appears that the stresses in the material become negligible at depths of a few wave lengths.

(iv) *Stress Functions in Polar Coordinates*

In polar coordinates the biharmonic equation takes the form § 35 (16). It may be verified that

$$\phi=(A+Br^2) \ln r+(C+Dr^2) \qquad . \qquad . \qquad . \qquad (36)$$

satisfies it and leads to the results of (i) above. Also that

$$\phi=-(P/\pi)r\theta \sin \theta \qquad . \qquad . \qquad . \qquad . \qquad (37)$$

satisfies it and leads to the results in (ii) above.

Many important results follow from seeking solutions of the form $f(r) \cos n\theta$. (36) above is the case $n=0$, while that for $n=2$ is

$$(A+Br^2+Cr^4+D/r^2) \cos 2\theta. \quad . \quad . \quad . \quad (38)$$

As an important example of the latter and (36),

$$\phi=\tfrac{1}{4}T(2a^2-r^2-a^4/r^2) \cos 2\theta+\tfrac{1}{4}Tr^2-\tfrac{1}{2}a^2T \ln r \quad . \quad . \quad (39)$$

gives the solution for a circular hole of radius a in an infinite region subjected to stresses which at great distances from the hole are a uniform tension T in the direction of the x-axis.

37. WAVE PROPAGATION

It was found in § 33 that Δ, ω_x, ω_y, ω_z all satisfy the wave equation which may be written

$$\nabla^2\psi-\frac{1}{c^2}\frac{\partial^2\psi}{\partial t^2}=0, \quad . \quad . \quad . \quad (1)$$

where c is a constant. The theory of this equation is well known. The most important results can be seen by considering propagation in one dimension, in which case (1) becomes

$$\frac{\partial^2\psi}{\partial x^2}-\frac{1}{c^2}\frac{\partial^2\psi}{\partial t^2}=0. \quad . \quad . \quad . \quad (2)$$

The simplest method of attack is to seek solutions of (2) which contain the time factor $\exp i\kappa(x-ct)$, real or imaginary parts being taken subsequently. Such solutions correspond to harmonic vibrations of wave-length $2\pi/\kappa$ which are propagated with speed c. By superposing waves of this type more general cases can be studied.

It is easy to show from first principles that any disturbance is propagated with speed c. If $f(x)$ and $F(x)$ are any differentiable functions of x, it follows by differentiation that both $f(x-ct)$ and $F(x+ct)$ satisfy (2). Now $f(x-ct)$ corresponds to a disturbance which moves to the right with speed c, keeping its form (which is $f(x)$ at $t=0$) unchanged. Similarly, $F(x+ct)$ corresponds to a disturbance, whose form at $t=0$ is $F(x)$, which moves to the left with speed c. A typical problem is to solve (2) in the region $-\infty<x<\infty$ with a given initial value of ψ, say $\psi=f(x)$, when $t=0$. From the above it appears that

$$\psi=\tfrac{1}{2}f(x-ct)+\tfrac{1}{2}f(x+ct) \quad . \quad . \quad . \quad (3)$$

satisfies (2) and has the required value when $t=0$. This corresponds to one wave of form $\frac{1}{2}f(x)$ being propagated to the right and another to the left with speed c, the situation being as in Fig. 47.

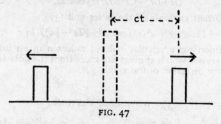

FIG. 47

Thus (2), and in fact (1) also, correspond to propagation of waves with speed c, so that if a disturbance takes place at the origin at time $t=0$, no effect is perceived at distance x until a wave front arrives at time $t=x/c$.

38. ELASTIC WAVES

In § 33 the equations of motion of an elastic solid were derived and it was found that both the dilatation Δ and the rotation ω satisfy the wave equation, waves of dilatation being propagated with speed V_P and waves of rotation with speed V_S, where

$$V_P=[(\lambda+2G)/\rho]^{\frac{1}{2}}=[G(2-2\nu)/\rho(1-2\nu)]^{\frac{1}{2}}, \quad . \quad . \quad (1)$$
$$V_S=(G/\rho)^{\frac{1}{2}}=[(1-2\nu)/(2-2\nu)]^{\frac{1}{2}}V_P. \quad . \quad . \quad (2)$$

We now proceed to examine the situation more closely, starting with the study of plane waves. Without loss of generality the waves may be assumed to be propagated along the x-axis so that all quantities will contain the factor $\exp i\kappa(x-ct)$ where c is the (as yet unknown) speed of propagation. Thus we assume that the displacements are of the form

$$u=u_1e^{i\kappa(x-ct)}, \quad v=v_1e^{i\kappa(x-ct)}, \quad w=w_1e^{i\kappa(x-ct)}, \quad . \quad (3)$$

where u_1, v_1, w_1 are constants.

By § 33 (9), (12), (13) the displacements have to satisfy

$$\rho\frac{\partial^2u}{\partial t^2}=(\lambda+G)\frac{\partial\Delta}{\partial x}+G\nabla^2u, \quad . \quad . \quad . \quad (4)$$

where

$$\Delta=\frac{\partial u}{\partial x}+\frac{\partial v}{\partial y}+\frac{\partial w}{\partial z}, \quad . \quad . \quad . \quad (5)$$

and two equations similar to (4) for v and w. Substituting (3) in these and cancelling the exponential factors gives

$$\rho\kappa^2 c^2 u_1 = (\lambda+G)\kappa^2 u_1 + G\kappa^2 u_1, \quad \rho\kappa^2 c^2 v_1 = G\kappa^2 v_1, \quad \rho\kappa^2 c^2 w_1 = G\kappa^2 w_1. \quad (6)$$

The set of equations (6) may be satisfied in two simple ways:

(i) *Primary or P waves* in which

$$v_1 = w_1 = 0, \quad c = [(\lambda+2G)/\rho]^{\frac{1}{2}} = V_P, \quad . \quad . \quad (7)$$

corresponding to a longitudinal wave in which the directions of motion of the particles are in the direction of propagation. This motion is irrotational and the wave is one of dilatation propagated with speed V_p given by (1).

(ii) *Secondary or shear or S waves* in which

$$u_1 = 0, \quad c = (G/\rho)^{\frac{1}{2}} = V_S, \quad . \quad . \quad . \quad (8)$$

and v_1 and w_1 may have any values, corresponding to a transverse wave in which the direction of motion of the particles is perpendicular to the direction of propagation. In this case $\Delta = 0$, the motion is rotational, and the wave is propagated with speed V_S given by (2). Since $V_P > V_S$ the first waves to arrive from any disturbance will be P waves.

Precisely as in the theory of light, the reflection and refraction of plane waves at the boundary between two media may be studied.[1] The situation is a little more complicated since, in general, when a wave of one type is incident on a surface of separation it gives rise to reflected and refracted waves of both types. Just as in optics, also, the behaviour of waves may be adequately represented by a ray theory in which propagation along the ray (normal to the wave front) takes place with the speed of wave propagation and the path of the ray between two points is determined by the principle of least time, namely, that the path of a ray between two points is such that the time for the actual path is less than that for any possible neighbouring path.

In a uniform, infinite medium the simple types (7) and (8) are the only ones which appear, and more general wave motions can be built up by superposition of them. But if the medium is bounded or non-uniform other simple types appear, the most important of which are the surface waves which it is found can be

[1] Cf. Bullen, *An Introduction to the Theory of Seismology* (Cambridge, 1947), *Seismology* (Methuen, 1954).

propagated near the surface of a solid without much penetration into its interior: these will now be discussed.

Rayleigh Waves. Suppose the region $z > 0$ is filled with solid with a free surface in the plane $z=0$: we investigate the possibility of waves whose amplitude diminishes exponentially in the z-direction being propagated along the x-axis. That is, we seek solutions of the equations of motion (4), etc., for u, v, w of the form

$$u=u_1 e^{-\alpha z + i\kappa(x-ct)}, \quad v=v_1 e^{-\alpha z + i\kappa(x-ct)}, \quad w=w_1 e^{-\alpha z + i\kappa(x-ct)}, \quad (9)$$

where α is a real and positive constant and u_1, v_1, w_1 are constants. Substituting in the equations of motion, (4), etc., gives

$$-\rho\kappa^2 c^2 u_1 = i\kappa(\lambda+G)(i\kappa u_1 - \alpha w_1) + G(\alpha^2-\kappa^2)u_1, \quad (10)$$

$$-\rho\kappa^2 c^2 v_1 = Gv_1(\alpha^2-\kappa^2), \quad (11)$$

$$-\rho\kappa^2 c^2 w_1 = -\alpha(\lambda+G)(i\kappa u_1 - \alpha w_1) + G(\alpha^2-\kappa^2)w_1. \quad (12)$$

(10) and (12) give

$$\frac{u_1}{w_1} = \frac{i\kappa\alpha(\lambda+G)}{\rho\kappa^2 c^2 + G\alpha^2 - \kappa^2(\lambda+2G)} = \frac{\rho\kappa^2 c^2 + \alpha^2(\lambda+2G) - G\kappa^2}{i\kappa\alpha(\lambda+G)}. \quad (13)$$

The second equation of (13) gives

$$\{\rho\kappa^2 c^2 + G(\alpha^2-\kappa^2)\}\{\rho\kappa^2 c^2 + (\lambda+2G)(\alpha^2-\kappa^2)\}=0. \quad (14)$$

This gives two values of α, namely,

$$\alpha^2 = \kappa^2(1 - c^2/V_S^2), \quad (15)$$

$$\alpha^2 = \kappa^2(1 - c^2/V_P^2). \quad (16)$$

Since α must be real, c must be less than V_S. Writing α_s for the value of α in (15), and substituting this in the first of (13), gives one type of wave with

$$\alpha=\alpha_s=\kappa(1-c^2/V_S^2)^{\frac{1}{2}}, \quad \text{and} \quad u_1/w_1=-i\alpha_s/\kappa. \quad (17)$$

Writing α_P for the value of α in (16), and substituting this in the second of (13), gives another type of wave with

$$\alpha=\alpha_P=\kappa(1-c^2/V_P^2)^{\frac{1}{2}}, \quad \text{and} \quad u_1/w_1=-i\kappa/\alpha_P. \quad (18)$$

Since v_1 enters only in (11) we may take it to be zero (if this is not done the boundary condition $\tau_{yz}=0$ requires it to vanish), so the simplest general solution is

$$u=-iA\alpha_s \exp\{-\alpha_s z + i\kappa(x-ct)\} - i\kappa B \exp\{-\alpha_P z + i\kappa(x-ct)\}, \quad (19)$$

$$v=0,$$

$$w=\kappa A \exp\{-\alpha_s z + i\kappa(x-ct)\} + B\alpha_P \exp\{-\alpha_P z + i\kappa(x-ct)\}, \quad (20)$$

where A and B are constants and c is as yet undetermined. The displacements (19) and (20) have to satisfy the boundary conditions in the plane $z=0$, namely,

$$\tau_{zx} = G\left(\frac{\partial u}{\partial z} + \frac{\partial w}{\partial x}\right) = 0, \quad (21)$$

$$\sigma_z = \lambda\Delta + 2G\frac{\partial w}{\partial z} = \lambda\frac{\partial u}{\partial x} + (\lambda+2G)\frac{\partial w}{\partial z} = 0. \quad (22)$$

Substituting (19) and (20) in these gives

$$A(\kappa^2+\alpha_s^2)+2\kappa B\alpha_P=0, \qquad . \qquad . \quad (23)$$

$$A\{\lambda\kappa\alpha_s-(\lambda+2G)\kappa\alpha_s\}+B\{\lambda\kappa^2-(\lambda+2G)\alpha_P^2\}=0. \qquad . \quad (24)$$

Eliminating A and B gives

$$\left(2-\frac{c^2}{V_s^2}\right)^2=4\left(1-\frac{c^2}{V_s^2}\right)^{\frac{1}{2}}\left(1-\frac{c^2}{V_P^2}\right)^{\frac{1}{2}},$$

which is the equation for the velocity of the waves. On squaring and multiplying out it becomes

$$\frac{c^6}{V_s^6}-8\frac{c^4}{V_s^4}+\frac{c^2}{V_s^2}\left(24-16\frac{V_s^2}{V_P^2}\right)-16\left(1-\frac{V_s^2}{V_P^2}\right)=0. \qquad . \quad (25)$$

This has a real root between o and V_s which makes α_s and α_P in (17) and (18) real, as they should be, and so all conditions are satisfied.

In the important case $\nu=1/4$, so that, by (2), $V_P=V_s\sqrt{3}$, the roots of (25) are $c^2=4V_s^2$ and $c^2=2V_s^2(1\pm1/\sqrt{3})$. The value of c less than V_s gives

$$c=0\cdot919V_s, \quad \alpha_P=0\cdot848\kappa, \quad \alpha_s=0\cdot393\kappa. \qquad . \quad (26)$$

Then from (23) $B=-0\cdot68A$, and (19) and (20) become

$$u=[-iA\kappa\times0\cdot393e^{-0\cdot393\kappa z}+i\kappa\times0\cdot68Ae^{-0\cdot848\kappa z}]e^{i\kappa(x-ct)},$$

$$w=[\kappa Ae^{-0\cdot393\kappa z}-0\cdot68\times0\cdot848\kappa Ae^{-0\cdot848\kappa z}]e^{i\kappa(x-ct)}.$$

Taking the real parts and writing C for $-0\cdot68\kappa A$ gives the complete displacement

$$u=C(e^{-0\cdot848\kappa z}-0\cdot578e^{-0\cdot393\kappa z})\sin\kappa(x-0\cdot919V_st), \quad . \quad (27)$$

$$w=C(0\cdot848e^{-0\cdot848\kappa z}-1\cdot468e^{-0\cdot393\kappa z})\cos\kappa(x-0\cdot919V_st). \quad . \quad (28)$$

Rayleigh waves are not the only simple type of surface wave which can be predicted and identified. If the solid is stratified so that the regions $0<z<a$ and $z>a$ are of different materials, another type, called *Love waves*, appears. The study of waves in a stratified region is of considerable importance because there appears to be a fairly sharp change in properties in the Earth at a depth of about 33 km. (the base of the crust). It should be remarked that while in the cases of P, S, and Rayleigh waves the speed of propagation is independent of the wave-length $2\pi/\kappa$, this is not always the case and is not so for Love waves. This is the phenomenon of dispersion well known in connexion with water waves and electromagnetic waves.

Seismology is the study of earthquake waves and the deduction of the properties of the Earth's material at depth from their records. From what has been said above it appears that P waves will arrive first, followed by S waves, the Rayleigh and Love waves, and a great many multiply reflected waves. From the times of arrival of these the position of any shock may be determined; and from the totality of information on all shocks, the speed of propagation of P and S waves at any depth below the Earth's surface can be calculated (cf. Bullen, *loc. cit.*). Since by (1) and (2)

$$\frac{V_P{}^2}{V_s{}^2}=\frac{2(1-\nu)}{1-2\nu}, \quad V_P{}^2-4V_s{}^2/3=K/\rho, \qquad . \qquad . \quad (29)$$

it follows that ν is known at any depth, and, since the density can be calculated independently, all the elastic constants can be determined.

The object of *seismic prospecting* is the determination of the position of sub-surface changes in geological structure by the study of waves reflected from (or refracted into) them. The source of the waves is an explosion at the shot point S, and in the simplest situation the times of arrival of the waves at a string of detectors

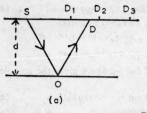 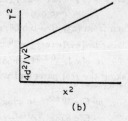

(a)   (b)

FIG. 48

D_1, D_2, ..., Fig. 48 (a), are recorded. From an analysis of the records, the time of arrival T of the P wave may be determined as a function of distance x from the shot point.

Suppose, for example, that the reflecting layer is horizontal and at distance d below the surface, Fig. 48 (a), the speed of the waves in the region above it being V. The wave which reaches D after reflection from the lower layer will have traversed the path SOD of length $(4d^2+x^2)^{\frac{1}{2}}$ and its time of arrival T will be

$$T=(4d^2+x^2)^{\frac{1}{2}}/V. \qquad . \qquad . \qquad . \quad (30)$$

Plotting T^2 against x^2 as in Fig. 48 (b) gives a straight line of slope $1/V^2$ and intercept $4d^2/V^2$ on the T^2 axis and so, in principle, both d and V can be determined. The case in which the bed is not horizontal may be treated similarly, the geometry being slightly more complicated. This *reflection method* is the most commonly used: it has the disadvantage that a direct wave from S to D

always arrives before the reflected wave so that the latter may be difficult to identify.

The older *refraction method* avoids this difficulty, but it is applicable only to the (very common) case in which the lower bed has a higher speed of propagation.

Suppose that a bed of thickness d in which the speed of propagation is V_1 lies on material in which the speed is $V_2 > V_1$, the surface of separation being horizontal, Fig. 49 (a). In this case a

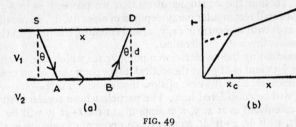

FIG. 49

wave may travel from S to D by a path $SABD$ as well as by the path SD, and if x is sufficiently large the former may arrive first. The time T taken to traverse the path $SABD$ may be calculated as follows: if SA and DB are inclined at angles θ to the vertical

$$T = (2d \sec \theta)/V_1 + (x - 2d \tan \theta)/V_2 . \quad . \quad . \quad (31)$$

Here θ is known from the laws of refraction or, alternatively, it may be found from the principle of least time which states that θ must be such as to make the time in this path a minimum, that is,

$$\frac{dT}{d\theta} = \frac{2d \sin \theta}{V_1 \cos^2 \theta} - \frac{2d \sec^2 \theta}{V_2} = 0.$$

This gives $\sin \theta = V_1/V_2$, and using this in (31) gives

$$T = 2d(V_2{}^2 - V_1{}^2)^{\frac{1}{2}}/V_1 V_2 + x/V_2 . \quad . \quad . \quad (32)$$

The wave by the direct path SD arrives at time x/V_1. This is equal to (32) if x has the critical value x_c given by

$$x_c = 2d[(V_2 + V_1)/(V_2 - V_1)]^{\frac{1}{2}}, \quad . \quad . \quad (33)$$

so that if $x < x_c$ the direct wave arrives first and

$$T = x/V_1 . \quad . \quad . \quad . \quad (34)$$

Thus if T is plotted against x as in Fig. 49 (b), a straight line of

10

slope $1/V_1$ is obtained for $x<x_c$, and a straight line of slope $1/V_2$ and intercept $2d(V_2{}^2-V_1{}^2)^{\frac{1}{2}}/V_1V_2$ on the T axis for $x>x_c$. It follows that, in principle, V_1, V_2 and d can be determined.

39. THE EQUATIONS OF MOTION OF A VISCOUS FLUID

Let (U, V, W) be the components of the velocity of the fluid at the point (x, y, z) at time t. Each of these is a function of x, y, z and t. To find the equations of motion we proceed as in § 33, taking a small rectangular parallelepiped of sides δx, δy, δz parallel to the axes with its centre at (x, y, z) and equating the force on this to its mass times its acceleration.

In calculating the acceleration a point arises which was slurred over in § 33 and is of great theoretical importance, but of no practical importance for the case of slow motion which is the only one which will be considered here. The particle whose acceleration is being calculated is at x, y, z at time t; at time $t+\delta t$ it will be at $x+U\,\delta t, y+V\,\delta t, z+W\,\delta t$, so that its component of velocity in the x-direction at this time will be $U+\delta U$ given by

$$U(x+U\,\delta t,\quad y+V\,\delta t,\quad z+W\,\delta t,\quad t+\delta t)$$

$$=U+\left(U\frac{\partial U}{\partial x}+V\frac{\partial U}{\partial y}+W\frac{\partial U}{\partial z}+\frac{\partial U}{\partial t}\right)\delta t,$$

neglecting terms in $(\delta t)^2$, and its component of acceleration in the x-direction will be

$$\lim_{\delta t \to 0}\frac{\delta U}{\delta t}=\frac{\partial U}{\partial t}+U\frac{\partial U}{\partial x}+V\frac{\partial U}{\partial y}+W\frac{\partial U}{\partial z}.\quad\quad\text{(1)}$$

This quantity is written DU/Dt, and this process of calculation is referred to as *differentiation following the motion of the fluid*. Clearly, the above discussion was quite general, and, if f is any property associated with the particle of the fluid which was at x, y, z at time t,

$$\frac{Df}{Dt}=\frac{\partial f}{\partial t}+U\frac{\partial f}{\partial x}+V\frac{\partial f}{\partial y}+W\frac{\partial f}{\partial z}.\quad\quad\text{(2)}$$

If U, V, W are small, this reduces to $\partial f/\partial t$. This is the justification for taking $\partial^2 u/\partial t^2$ for the x-component of acceleration in deducing the elastic equations § 33 (6)–(8).

The remainder of the derivation of the equations of motion is precisely the same as that of § 33 for the elastic equations. Suppose (X, Y, Z) are the components of body force per unit mass at (x, y, z) and that σ_x, σ_y, σ_z, τ_{yz}, τ_{zx}, τ_{xy} are the components of stress in the fluid, then the x-component of force on the parallele-piped is given by § 33 (5), and equating this to the mass times the component of acceleration in the x-direction gives

$$\rho \frac{DU}{Dt} = \frac{\partial \sigma_x}{\partial x} + \frac{\partial \tau_{yx}}{\partial y} + \frac{\partial \tau_{zx}}{\partial z} + \rho X, \quad . \quad . \quad . \quad (3)$$

and, similarly,

$$\rho \frac{DV}{Dt} = \frac{\partial \tau_{xy}}{\partial x} + \frac{\partial \sigma_y}{\partial y} + \frac{\partial \tau_{zy}}{\partial z} + \rho Y, \quad . \quad . \quad . \quad (4)$$

$$\rho \frac{DW}{Dt} = \frac{\partial \tau_{xz}}{\partial x} + \frac{\partial \tau_{yz}}{\partial y} + \frac{\partial \sigma_z}{\partial z} + \rho Z. \quad . \quad . \quad . \quad (5)$$

(3) to (5) are the equations of motion in terms of the stresses. They may be expressed in terms of the velocities by using § 19 (8), (11) (replacing $\dot{u}$, $\dot{v}$, $\dot{w}$ in these equations by U, V, W) which give

$$\rho \frac{DU}{Dt} = \rho X - \frac{\partial p}{\partial x} + \frac{1}{3} \eta \frac{\partial \dot{\Delta}}{\partial x} + \eta \nabla^2 U, \quad . \quad . \quad (6)$$

$$\rho \frac{DV}{Dt} = \rho Y - \frac{\partial p}{\partial y} + \frac{1}{3} \eta \frac{\partial \Delta}{\partial y} + \eta \nabla^2 V, \quad . \quad . \quad (7)$$

$$\rho \frac{DW}{Dt} = \rho Z - \frac{\partial p}{\partial z} + \frac{1}{3} \eta \frac{\partial \dot{\Delta}}{\partial y} + \eta \nabla^2 W, \quad . \quad . \quad (8)$$

where

$$\dot{\Delta} = \frac{\partial U}{\partial x} + \frac{\partial V}{\partial y} + \frac{\partial W}{\partial z}, \quad . \quad . \quad . \quad (9)$$

and if the fluid is incompressible $\Delta = 0$.

For relatively slow motion DU/Dt, etc., may be replaced by $\partial U/\partial t$ as in the equations of elasticity. This is allowable in many important problems: if it cannot be done the equations are non-linear (since by (1) squares and products of the components of velocity are involved) and they become extremely difficult to handle. In many problems the motion is so slow that inertia effects, that is, the accelerations DU/Dt, can be neglected altogether.

40. SPECIAL PROBLEMS IN VISCOSITY

The simple standard problems of motion of viscous fluid through a tube and between rotating cylinders have been solved in § 32. In this section some problems on slow viscous motion of incompressible fluid in two dimensions will be studied: the methods and results may be compared with those of §§ 36, 41. Only cases in which there are no body forces will be considered.

Suppose that the plane of motion is the xy-plane so that all quantities are independent of z. The equation of continuity § 19 (14) is

$$\dot{\Delta} = \frac{\partial U}{\partial x} + \frac{\partial V}{\partial y} = 0. \qquad . \qquad . \qquad . \qquad (1)$$

Using this result and assuming that the motion is so slow that the accelerations DU/Dt, etc., are negligible, and putting $X = Y = 0$, the equations of motion § 39 (6), (7) become

$$-\frac{1}{\eta}\frac{\partial p}{\partial x} + \frac{\partial^2 U}{\partial x^2} + \frac{\partial^2 U}{\partial y^2} = 0, \qquad . \qquad . \qquad . \qquad (2)$$

$$-\frac{1}{\eta}\frac{\partial p}{\partial y} + \frac{\partial^2 V}{\partial x^2} + \frac{\partial^2 V}{\partial y^2} = 0. \qquad . \qquad . \qquad . \qquad (3)$$

It follows from (1)–(3) that

$$\frac{\partial^2 p}{\partial x^2} + \frac{\partial^2 p}{\partial y^2} = 0. \qquad . \qquad . \qquad . \qquad (4)$$

Now suppose that there exists a function ψ such that

$$U = -\frac{\partial \psi}{\partial y}, \quad V = \frac{\partial \psi}{\partial x}, \qquad . \qquad . \qquad . \qquad (5)$$

so that (1) is satisfied automatically. Differentiating (2) and (3) partially with respect to y and x, respectively, subtracting and using (5) gives

$$\frac{\partial^4 \psi}{\partial x^4} + 2\frac{\partial^4 \psi}{\partial x^2 \partial y^2} + \frac{\partial^4 \psi}{\partial y^4} = 0. \qquad . \qquad . \qquad . \qquad (6)$$

The method is analogous to that of § 35; ψ is called a *stream function*, and if a solution of the biharmonic equation (6) can be found with suitable boundary conditions the complete solution follows.

(i) The Case of Two Planes approaching One Another

Suppose that there is incompressible fluid of viscosity η between two parallel strips $-l < x < l$, $y = \pm h$, and that these are pressed together by equal and oppositely directed forces parallel to the y-axis, Fig. 50. It is assumed that there is no slip of the fluid across the boundaries $y = \pm h$.

The equations (1) to (4) have to be satisfied with boundary conditions

$$U = 0, \quad -l < x < l, \quad \text{when } y = \pm h, \qquad . \qquad . \qquad (7)$$

$$V = \mp V_0, \quad -l < x < l, \quad \text{when } y = \pm h. \qquad . \qquad (8)$$

where V_0 is the speed with which the strips move. In addition to these U must, by symmetry, be an odd function of x, that is, $U(-x)=-U(x)$.

The method of solution which will be used consists of building up a simple polynomial solution of the equations. Firstly we notice that the second degree polynomial

$$p=\tfrac{1}{2}ky^2-\tfrac{1}{2}kx^2+C, \quad . \quad . \quad . \quad . \quad (9)$$

where k and C are constants, satisfies (4). No first-degree terms have been included since the pressure must be the same if the signs of x or y are

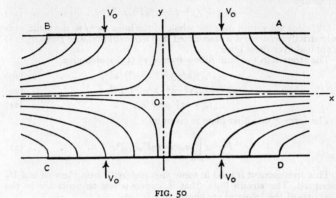

FIG. 50

changed. Also, since U is to be an odd function of x, it cannot contain a term in x^2 so we seek a solution of (2) with $\partial^2 U/\partial x^2=0$. Using this and (9), (2) becomes

$$\frac{\partial^2 U}{\partial y^2}=-\frac{kx}{\eta}. \quad . \quad . \quad . \quad . \quad (10)$$

The solution of (10) is

$$U=-\tfrac{1}{2}kxy^2/\eta+yf(x)+g(x), \quad . \quad . \quad (11)$$

where $f(x)$ and $g(x)$ are unknown functions of x. The conditions (7) require $f(x)=0$, $g(x)=kxh^2/2\eta$, and so (11) becomes finally

$$U=kx(h^2-y^2)/2\eta. \quad . \quad . \quad . \quad (12)$$

Using (12) in (1) gives

$$\frac{\partial V}{\partial y}=-k(h^2-y^2)/2\eta, \quad . \quad . \quad . \quad (13)$$

and integrating this,

$$V=-ky(3h^2-y^2)/6\eta+F(x), \quad . \quad . \quad (14)$$

where $F(x)$ is an unknown function of x. The conditions (8) give $F(x)=0$ and

$$k=3\eta V_0/h^3, \quad . \quad . \quad . \quad (15)$$

and therefore

$$U = 3V_0x(h^2-y^2)/2h^3, \quad V = V_0y(y^2-3h^2)/2h^3, \qquad (16)$$

$$p = 3\eta V_0(y^2-x^2)/2h^3 + C. \qquad (17)$$

(16) and (17) satisfy all the equations and boundary conditions but do not involve the length of the plates. For the practical case of fluid being squeezed from between parallel plates, we may assume $p=0$ when $x=\pm l$, $y=\pm h$, that is at the points $ABCD$, Fig. 50. This gives C in (17), and we get finally

$$p = 3\eta V_0(y^2-h^2-x^2+l^2)/2h^3. \qquad (18)$$

(18) does not vanish over the whole of the lines $x=\pm l$ so the solution is only strictly accurate if it is assumed that a (small) pressure given by (18) is applied over these lines.

The stresses in the fluid follow from § 19 (13) which give

$$\sigma_x = 3\eta V_0[3(h^2-y^2)+x^2-l^2]/2h^3, \qquad (19)$$

$$\sigma_y = 3\eta V_0[y^2-h^2+x^2-l^2]/2h^3, \qquad (20)$$

$$\tau_{xy} = -3V_0\eta xy/h^3. \qquad (21)$$

The force P on either plate is given by

$$P = -2\int_0^l \sigma_y dx = 2\eta V_0 l^3/h^3. \qquad (22)$$

This arrangement is used in some viscometers, P being known and V_0 measured. The stream lines (that is, curves whose tangents are in the direction of the velocity) are shown in Fig. 50.

(ii) *Motion in the Semi-infinite Region $y<0$ due to a Surface-Disturbance*

As in § 36 (34)

$$\psi = Ae^{\omega y}\sin \omega x \qquad (23)$$

satisfies (6) and so is a stream function which vanishes exponentially for large negative y and thus is appropriate for the study of surface motions in the region $y<0$. By (5) the velocities are given by

$$U = -A\omega e^{\omega y}\sin \omega x, \quad V = A\omega e^{\omega y}\cos \omega x, \qquad (24)$$

and by § 19 (13) the stresses are (taking $p=0$)

$$\sigma_x = -2\eta\omega^2 Ae^{\omega y}\cos \omega x, \qquad (25)$$

$$\sigma_y = 2\eta\omega^2 Ae^{\omega y}\cos \omega x, \qquad (26)$$

$$\tau_{xy} = -2\eta\omega^2 Ae^{\omega y}\sin \omega x. \qquad (27)$$

Suppose, now, that the surface $y=0$ is distorted into the harmonic shape

$$y = h\cos \omega x, \qquad (28)$$

so that, if the material is of density ρ, the stress over the plane $y=0$ is

$$\sigma_y = -\rho gh\cos \omega x, \qquad (29)$$

that is, the constant A in (24) is $-\rho gh/2\eta\omega^2$. Also the value of V when

$x=y=0$ will be dh/dt, the rate of subsidence of the surface, and therefore

$$\frac{dh}{dt}=A\omega=-\frac{\rho g h}{2\eta\omega}.$$

It follows that if h_0 is the height of the disturbance when $t=0$, its value at t will be

$$h=h_0 \exp\left(-\rho g t/2\eta\omega\right). \qquad . \qquad . \qquad (30)$$

This solution is only approximate since the value of τ_{xy} in the surface has not been discussed, but it is correct in order of magnitude. Calculations of this type have been used to estimate a viscosity for the Earth's interior from the observed rate of rise of the surface after the melting of a large ice-cap.

41. PLASTIC FLOW IN TWO DIMENSIONS

In this section two-dimensional plastic flow will be discussed on the assumption of § 29 that the elastic strains may be neglected. It will be assumed that there is no motion in the z-direction, so that $\dot{\varepsilon}_z=0$ and so by § 29 (4) $s_z=0$, and thus by § 27 (4) the principal stress in the z-direction will be $\frac{1}{2}(\sigma_1+\sigma_2)$, where σ_1 and σ_2 are the principal stresses in the xy-plane. In this case both Tresca's and von Mises's criteria of yield take the same form, namely,

$$\sigma_1-\sigma_2=2k, \qquad . \qquad . \qquad . \qquad (1)$$

where, by § 27 (16), (25), k has the value $\frac{1}{2}\sigma_0$ in the former case and $\sigma_0/\sqrt{3}$ in the latter.

If σ_x, σ_y, τ_{xy} are the components of stress referred to the xy-axes, (1) becomes by § 3 (18)

$$\tfrac{1}{4}(\sigma_x-\sigma_y)^2+\tau_{xy}{}^2=k^2. \qquad . \qquad . \qquad (2)$$

The stresses in the material are determined by (2) in conjunction with the equations of equilibrium, § 35, (6), (7), namely

$$\frac{\partial \sigma_x}{\partial x}+\frac{\partial \tau_{xy}}{\partial y}=0, \qquad . \qquad . \qquad . \qquad (3)$$

$$\frac{\partial \tau_{xy}}{\partial x}+\frac{\partial \sigma_y}{\partial y}=0. \qquad . \qquad . \qquad . \qquad (4)$$

(3) and (4) give

$$\frac{\partial^2 \tau_{xy}}{\partial x^2}-\frac{\partial^2 \tau_{xy}}{\partial y^2}=\frac{\partial^2(\sigma_x-\sigma_y)}{\partial x\,\partial y},$$

and using this in (2) gives

$$\frac{\partial^2 \tau_{xy}}{\partial x^2}-\frac{\partial^2 \tau_{xy}}{\partial y^2}=\pm 2\frac{\partial^2}{\partial x\,\partial y}(k^2-\tau_{xy}{}^2)^{\frac{1}{2}}. \qquad . \qquad . \qquad (5)$$

Alternatively, if the stress function Φ defined in § 35 is used, substituting § 35 (9) in (2) gives

$$\left(\frac{\partial^2\Phi}{\partial y^2}-\frac{\partial^2\Phi}{\partial x^2}\right)^2+4\left(\frac{\partial^2\Phi}{\partial x\,\partial y}\right)^2=4k^2. \qquad . \qquad . \qquad (6)$$

(5) is a partial differential equation for τ_{xy}: if the boundary conditions of the problem involve stresses only, the solution is particularly simple since (5) and the boundary conditions determine the stresses immediately: on the other hand, if the boundary conditions involve displacements the situation is more complicated as the stress-strain relations also have to be used. The same remarks apply to (6).

Assuming that the stresses have been found, the stress-strain relations § 29 (4)

$$s_x=2\phi\dot{\varepsilon}_x, \quad s_y=2\phi\dot{\varepsilon}_y, \quad s_{xy}=\phi\dot{\gamma}_{xy}, \qquad . \qquad . \qquad (7)$$

give the rates of strain, and from these the velocity $\dot{u}$, $\dot{v}$ may be determined.

In most problems, however, the greatest interest centres on the determination of the slip lines. By the assumptions of § 29, which led to the stress-strain relations (7), the principal axes of stress and rate of strain coincide. Now it was shown in § 3 (14) that the directions of maximum shear stress bisect the angles between the principal axes of stress, and in § 10 (15) that for infinitesimal strain the directions of maximum shear strain bisect the angles between the principal axes of strain (and also that for an incompressible material the extension vanishes in these directions). In these *shear directions* the relative movement between neighbouring parallel planes is a maximum, so they may be regarded as the directions of slip at the point. A curve whose tangent at every point is one of the shear directions at that point is called a *slip line* or *shear line*. Clearly in general there are two orthogonal slip lines through every point.

For example, in the case of radially symmetrical stress in two dimensions, the principal stresses at every point are radial and tangential, so that the slip lines are inclined at $45°$ to these directions. Therefore, by the geometry of Fig. 51 (a),

$$\frac{dr}{rd\theta}=\pm 1, \qquad . \qquad . \qquad . \qquad . \qquad (8)$$

and these are the differential equations of the two systems of slip lines. Solving (8) gives the two families of equiangular spirals.

$$r = ae^{\pm\theta}, \qquad . \qquad . \qquad . \qquad (9)$$

where a is an arbitrary constant; these are shown in Fig. 51 (b).

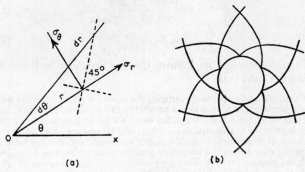

FIG. 51

In the general case, suppose that the principal axes are inclined at angles α and $\alpha + \frac{1}{2}\pi$ to the x-axis, then the shear directions will be inclined to it at β and $\beta + \frac{1}{2}\pi$, where $\beta = \alpha + \pi/4$, Fig. 52.

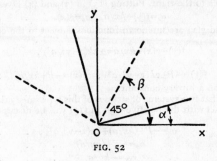

FIG. 52

Writing σ for $\frac{1}{2}(\sigma_1 + \sigma_2)$ and $2k$ for $(\sigma_1 - \sigma_2)$ by (1), it follows from § 3 (5), (6), (7) that

$$\sigma_x = \sigma + k \cos 2\alpha, \quad \sigma_y = \sigma - k \cos 2\alpha, \quad \tau_{xy} = k \sin 2\alpha.$$

Replacing α by $\beta - \pi/4$, these become

$$\sigma_x = \sigma + k \sin 2\beta, \quad \sigma_y = \sigma - k \sin 2\beta, \quad \tau_{xy} = -k \cos 2\beta \quad . \quad (10)$$

The differential equations of the two systems of slip lines are thus

$$\frac{dy}{dx} = \tan \beta = \frac{1 - \cos 2\beta}{\sin 2\beta} = \frac{2(k + \tau_{xy})}{\sigma_x - \sigma_y}, \quad . \quad . \quad (11)$$

$$\frac{dy}{dx} = -\cot \beta = -\frac{\sigma_x - \sigma_y}{2(k + \tau_{xy})}. \quad . \quad . \quad (12)$$

When the stresses are known, the slip lines can be found by solving (11) and (12).

As a simple and important example, the case of a plastic material compressed between the planes $y = \pm a$ parallel to the x-axis will be considered in detail. First, the equation (5) has to be solved and, as usual, we take a simple solution of this equation and (3) and (4) and see what conditions it satisfies. If it is assumed that the planes are rough, and that the material is slipping over them, the boundary conditions at $y = \pm a$ will be $|\tau_{xy}| = k$, which is independent of x. This suggests that we seek a solution of (5) in which τ_{xy} is a function of y only. In this case (5) becomes

$$\frac{\partial^2 \tau_{xy}}{\partial y^2} = 0,$$

which is satisfied by the linear function

$$\tau_{xy} = -ky/a, \quad . \quad . \quad . \quad (13)$$

and this gives $\tau_{xy} = \mp k$ when $y = \pm a$, corresponding to the material moving over the planes to the right. Putting (13) in (3) and (4) gives

$$\sigma_x = f(y) + kx/a, \quad \sigma_y = g(x), \quad . \quad . \quad (14)$$

where $f(y)$ and $g(x)$ are unknown functions subject to the condition (2). This requires

$$f(y) - g(x) + kx/a = \pm 2k(1 - y^2/a^2)^{\frac{1}{2}},$$

and it follows that

$$f(y) = -P \pm 2k(1 - y^2/a^2)^{\frac{1}{2}}, \quad g(x) = -P + kx/a, \quad . \quad . \quad (15)$$

where $-P$ is an arbitrary constant.

It appears that two systems of stresses of this type satisfy the equations, of these, the set with the positive sign in (15) will be discussed in detail; this gives

$$\sigma_x = -P + (kx/a) + 2k(1 - y^2/a^2)^{\frac{1}{2}}, \quad . \quad . \quad (16)$$

$$\sigma_y = -P + (kx/a), \quad . \quad . \quad . \quad (17)$$

$$\tau_{xy} = -ky/a. \quad . \quad . \quad . \quad (18)$$

Putting (16) to (18) in (11) gives for the differential equation of one system of slip lines

$$\frac{dy}{dx} = \frac{a - y}{(a^2 - y^2)^{\frac{1}{2}}}. \quad . \quad . \quad . \quad (19)$$

The integral of (19) is

$$x = \int \frac{(a^2 - y^2)^{\frac{1}{2}} dy}{a - y},$$

or, putting

$$y = a \cos \theta, \quad . \quad . \quad . \quad . \quad (20)$$

$$x = -a \int (1 + \cos \theta) d\theta = -a(\theta + \sin \theta) + C. \quad . \quad . \quad (21)$$

(20) and (21) are the equations of a family of cycloids, in which, since by (19) dy/dx is always positive, only the portions in which y increases with x must be taken. Similarly, the second system of slip lines given by (12) is the cycloids

$$y = a \cos \theta, \quad x = a(\theta - \sin \theta) + D, \quad . \quad . \quad (22)$$

of which only the portions with y decreasing must be taken. The two systems of slip lines are shown in Fig. 53.

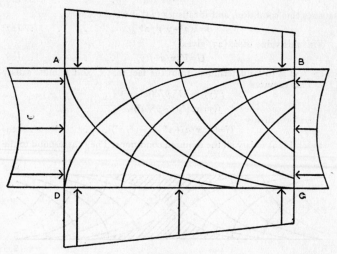

FIG. 53

To see the physical significance of this solution, suppose the plastic mass is in the region $ABCD$, Fig. 53, bounded by the lines $y = \pm a$, $x = 0$, and $x = l$.

On AB and CD, $\sigma_y = -P + (kx/a)$; on AD, $\sigma_x = -P + 2k(1 - y^2/a^2)^{\frac{1}{2}}$; on BC, $\sigma_x = -P + (kl/a) + 2k(1 - y^2/a^2)^{\frac{1}{2}}$; these normal pressures are indicated by the lengths of the arrows pointing inwards towards the surfaces in Fig. 53.

Like most simple exact solutions it is valid only if this precise system of stresses is applied: its physical interpretation will be discussed later.

To find the velocity distribution corresponding to the stresses (16) to (18), it follows from (16) and (17) that

$$s_x = -s_y = k(1-y^2/a^2)^{\frac{1}{2}},$$

and, using this and (18) in (7) gives, writing U and V for $\dot{u}$, and $\dot{v}$,

$$s_x = k(1-y^2/a^2)^{\frac{1}{2}} = 2\phi\dot{\epsilon}_x = 2\phi\frac{\partial U}{\partial x}, \qquad . \qquad . \qquad . \qquad (23)$$

$$s_y = -k(1-y^2/a^2)^{\frac{1}{2}} = 2\phi\dot{\epsilon}_y = 2\phi\frac{\partial V}{\partial y}, \qquad . \qquad . \qquad . \qquad (24)$$

$$\tau_{xy} = -ky/a = \phi\dot{\gamma}_{xy} = \phi\left(\frac{\partial U}{\partial y} + \frac{\partial V}{\partial x}\right), \qquad . \qquad . \qquad . \qquad (25)$$

where ϕ is an unknown function involving the strain rate. We seek a solution of these corresponding to the plates approaching with speed V_0. Clearly

$$V = -yV_0/a \qquad . \qquad . \qquad . \qquad . \qquad (26)$$

satisfies this condition, and it satisfies (24) if we choose

$$\phi = k(a^2-y^2)^{\frac{1}{2}}/2V_0 . \qquad . \qquad . \qquad . \qquad (27)$$

With this value of ϕ, (23) gives

$$U = V_0x/a + f(y), \qquad . \qquad . \qquad . \qquad (28)$$

where $f(y)$ is to be determined from the fact that U and V must satisfy (25). This requires

$$f'(y) = -2V_0y/a(a^2-y^2)^{\frac{1}{2}},$$

$$f(y) = 2V_0(1-y^2/a^2)^{\frac{1}{2}}.$$

Therefore, finally

$$U = (V_0x/a) + 2V_0(1-y^2/a^2)^{\frac{1}{2}}. \qquad . \qquad . \qquad (29)$$

(26) and (29) satisfy all the required conditions. They correspond to the

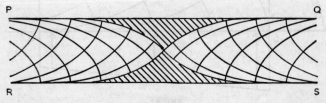

P   Q

R   S

FIG. 54

plastic material being squeezed to the right as the planes approach, its speed past the planes being V_0x/a.

(26) and (29) illustrate the important result mentioned in § 29, namely, that U and V are proportional to the externally prescribed speed V_0, while the stresses are unaffected if this is changed. This is in striking

contrast to the results for the corresponding problem for viscous flow discussed in § 40.

The other solution, corresponding to choosing the negative sign in (15), represents a situation in which material is forced in over BC, causing AB and CD to move outwards.

In the practical case of a plastic material compressed between rough parallel plates PQ and RS, a more refined analysis shows that there are regions towards the centre, shown shaded in Fig. 54, in which the yield stress is not exceeded so that they remain undistorted: in the region beyond these the material is extruded in a manner well represented by the preceding discussion.

CHAPTER IV

APPLICATIONS

42. INTRODUCTORY

IN this chapter some applications and extensions of the preceding theory will be made which will refer mainly to geological matters such as faulting and stresses in the Earth's crust, and to engineering problems on rock mechanics.[1] Such problems are essentially those of fracture and of the behaviour of fractured material, and the relevant criteria will be studied in some detail. The more mathematical problems are those of the stresses around boreholes, tunnels and cracks.

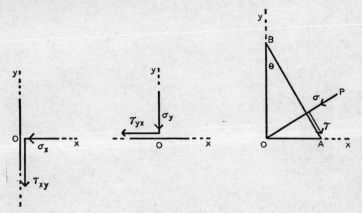

FIG. 55

The conditions are such that the stresses are so frequently compressive that it is an advantage to use a convention in which compressive stresses are reckoned positive. This will be done throughout this chapter. This implies that the convention of Fig. 2 is replaced by that of Fig. 55.

[1] The most complete discussion of this subject is given by J. Talobre, *La Mécanique des Roches* (Dunod, 1957).

With this change, the whole of the results of §§ 2–5 remain unchanged in form. $\sigma_1, \sigma_2, \sigma_3$ with $\sigma_1 > \sigma_2 > \sigma_3$ will be the principal stresses, σ_1 being the greatest compressive stress. Similar modifications apply to strains.

43. EXPERIMENTAL RESULTS ON THE MECHANICAL PROPERTIES OF ROCKS

In the past few years many series of experiments on the mechanical properties of rocks have been made. Some of these have been for engineering purposes to determine the elastic moduli and compressive strengths of rocks for design purposes. Others, from the geophysical point of view, have been intended to study the brittle–ductile transition and the plastic behaviour of rocks at as high temperatures and pressures as possible.

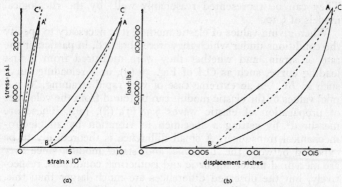

FIG. 56. (a) Stress-strain curve for an altered granite: $OABC$ longitudinal strain, $OA'OC'$ lateral strain. (b) Load-displacement curve for a 12″ circular disk pressed into unsound rock

(i) *Elastic Moduli and their Variation with Stress*

In practice, curves of stress σ as a function of strain ε depart from simple proportionality, and the elastic modulus corresponding to stress σ can be defined either as the *tangent modulus* $d\sigma/d\varepsilon$ or the *secant modulus* σ/ε.

Several different effects contribute to this non-linearity. In some cases, such as basalt, the typical behaviour of Fig. 19 (*c*) occurs.

In many others, however, the stress-strain curves are concave upwards for low stresses. This effect, which is probably caused by the presence of pores or minute cracks in the rock, is shown in the curve OA, Fig. 56 (a), which represents longitudinal strain for the first loading of a specimen of an altered granite in unconfined compression. In this case the tangent modulus is approximately linear in the stress, so that the early part of the stress-strain curve can be represented approximately by the formula

$$\sigma = A[\exp{(k\varepsilon)} - 1]. \qquad . \qquad . \qquad . \qquad (1)$$

If in Fig. 56 (a) the stress is reduced from its value at A, the unloading curve AB is traced out, leading to strain OB at zero stress. Reloading gives BC, and further cycles of unloading and reloading to the same maximum stress give loops similar to ABC but moving slightly to the right. These effects may be associated with anelasticity (involving no permanent set) or transient creep. They can be represented reasonably well[1] by the rheological models of § 30.

When giving values of elastic moduli, it is necessary to specify the conditions under which they were obtained, in particular the rate of strain, and whether they were measured from a first loading curve, such as OA of Fig. 56 (a), or a reloading curve such as BC. As an extreme case of very rapid straining, 'dynamic' values of the elastic moduli can be found from the velocities of propagation of elastic waves § 38 (7), (8), (29). These are measured[2] by setting a specimen in vibration by an electromechanical transducer. A small difference is theoretically to be expected between the 'dynamic' and 'static' moduli, since they are measured under adiabatic and isothermal conditions, respectively, but the observed differences are much larger than this, the dynamic moduli usually being higher. This effect may be associated with the existence of pores and minute cracks.

The variation of the elastic 'constants' with stress is large enough to be of importance in engineering and mining contexts and measurements have been made on rocks of practical interest.[3]

[1] M. Nishihara, *Doshida Engng Rev.*, **8** (1958), 32, 85.

[2] F. Birch, *J. Geophys. Res.*, **66** (1961), 2199.

[3] N. J. Price, *Mechanical Properties of Brittle Materials* (ed. Walton, Butterworths, London, 1958), p. 106; D. W. Phillips, *Colliery Engineering*, **25** (1948), 199; U.S. Bureau of Reclamation, Concrete Laboratory Report SP-39 (1953).

Phillips found that for sandstones and siltstones in unconfined compression the values of v and E increased considerably with stress over the range 0–10,000 p.s.i. (by a factor of two or more). Price made triaxial tests on a number of sedimentary rocks. In such tests the specimen is cylindrical and subjected to axial stress σ_1 as well as radial stress $\sigma_2 = \sigma_3$ provided by oil pressure. The specimen is enclosed in a rubber or copper jacket to exclude the oil. He studied the influence of σ_3 on v and E. v was found always to increase with the stress-difference $\sigma_1 - \sigma_3$; at the higher confining pressures (>4,000 p.s.i.) it depended only on $\sigma_1 - \sigma_3$. E increased with $\sigma_1 - \sigma_3$, and, for a given value of $\sigma_1 - \sigma_3$, increased slowly with σ_3.

(ii) *Unsound Rock and Measurements* in situ

Laboratory measurements are usually made on selected specimens of sound rock. In practice, values for the overall elastic properties of a mass of rock are often needed, and this mass may contain joints and broken and unsound rock. Many attempts have been made to measure elastic properties of rock *in situ*. One such method consists of applying a force P normal to a circular pad of radius a cemented to a rock face, and measuring the displacement u of this pad: the situation is the three-dimensional analogue of that of Fig. 45 (b) and the elastic theory is well known, the average displacement being given by[1]

$$u = 0.54P(1 - v^2)/aE. \qquad . \qquad . \qquad (2)$$

Fig. 56 (b) shows a load-displacement curve for poor rock taken under such conditions. The general behaviour is similar to, but more extreme than that of Fig. 56 (a) and figures deduced from it probably provide a reasonable approximation to the actual behaviour of the rock. Thus, knowing $a = 6''$, and assuming $v = 0.2$, the portion BC of the curve gives a secant modulus of

$$E = 1.2 \times 10^6 \text{ p.s.i.}$$

[1] Timoshenko, *loc. cit.*, p. 339. He also gives the result for a rigid circular disk pressed into the surface of a semi-infinite elastic solid; in this case the displacement is again given by (2) except that the numerical factor 0.54 is replaced by 0.5. The theory of uniform loading along a strip on the surface of a semi-infinite solid is considered by Prager and Hodge, *loc. cit.*, for the case of a perfectly plastic solid, and by K. von Terzaghi, *Theoretical Soil Mechanics* (Wiley, 1943), for the case of a solid obeying the laws of soil mechanics: these solutions give the forces corresponding to flow or slip but no information about the displacement.

(iii) *Fracture and Ductility*

The general nature of the phenomena and the pioneer work of von Karman and Griggs were referred to in § 12. Recently, several series of experiments[1] have been made to determine the behaviour of various types of rock under a wide range of values of confining pressure, temperature, rate of strain, and pressure of pore fluid.[2] Most of these have been triaxial tests in which a stress-strain curve is obtained which connects differential stress with longitudinal strain.

In uniaxial compression at room temperature, many rocks fail suddenly by slabbing outwards. This is probably a subsidiary effect due to tensile stresses caused by a wedging action. It disappears at quite small confining pressures.

At moderate confining pressures and room temperature, failure is almost invariably by shearing across a single plane and the results can be reasonably well expressed in terms of the Coulomb–Navier theory, or, better, by a slightly curved Mohr envelope. Some typical values of S_0 and the angle of internal friction ϕ for various rock types taken from the Bureau of Reclamation Report (*loc. cit.*) are shown in Table IV. It should be emphasized that the variation between different rocks of the same general type can be very large.

As the confining pressure is increased, there is a great increase in strength and, at higher pressures, in ductility. In most cases, shear failure at low confining pressures occurs across a well-defined plane; as the confining pressure is increased this broadens into a shear zone; at still higher confining pressures deformation takes place throughout most of the volume of the specimen and considerable plastic strain can be introduced with little increase of load. In this condition the rock is said to be ductile. This brittle–ductile transition for limestone has been illustrated in Fig. 20 and has been studied in great detail by Heard.[3] The effect of raising the temperature is, in general, to lower the strength

---

[1] J. Handin and R. V. Hager, *Bull. Amer. Ass. Petroleum Geol.*, **41** (1957), 1, and **42** (1958), 2892, also R. O. Bredthauer, *Trans. Amer. Soc. Mech. Engrs*, **79** (1957), 695, have studied a wide range of sedimentary rocks at moderate temperatures and pressures up to 5,000 bars.

[2] In this case fluid is supplied at a known pressure to the ends of the (slightly porous) specimen. It is, of course, separated from the oil which provides the confining pressure by the jacket around the specimen.

[3] H. C. Heard, *Geol. Soc. Amer. Memoir* 79 (1960), 193.

and increase the ductility. Some typical results for sediments, taken from Handin and Hager, *loc. cit.*, are given in Table V.

Since the temperature below the Earth's surface increases with depth, temperature and pressure there are related. Measurements such as those of Table V allow the differential stress which can be withstood by rocks at various depths below the surface to be computed: for example, with the normal geothermal gradient this is 4,400, 3,500, and 9,200 bars, respectively, at 25,000 feet

TABLE IV

Shear strength S_0 (bars) and angles of internal friction for some typical rocks. Under each heading two values are given corresponding to specimens with extreme values of S_0.

	S_0	ϕ
Basalt	420	48°
	300	50°
Granite	220	58°
	140	56°
Greywacke	110	45°
	60	50°
Limestone	350	35°
	140	58°
Sandstone	160	48°
	110	48°
Schist	140	27°
	20	54°

for the three rocks listed in Table V. The behaviour of halite is anomalous and is important in connexion with the formation of salt domes: at depths of about 20,000 feet it may be expected to behave like a perfectly plastic solid with a yield stress of only 100 bars (cf. Handin and Hager, *loc. cit.*).

It should be understood that the figures above do not include the effect of pressure of pore-water; also they are for rapid straining, and in general slow straining raises the strength.

At relatively high temperatures,[1] many rocks become extremely ductile and very considerable distortions of the individual crystals

[1] Cf. D. T. Griggs, F. J. Turner and H. C. Heard, 'Deformation of rocks at 500° C to 800° C', *Geol. Soc. Amer. Memoir* 79 (1960), 39.

TABLE V

Triaxial tests on some typical rocks: L, limestone; Ss, a rather soft sandstone; $Sq.$, sandstone with a silicious cement. 'Max. stress' and 'Max. strain' indicate the maxima attained in the experiment (at which the specimen may or may not have failed). In the last column N.B. indicates that the specimen has not been broken; Sh. indicates explosive shattering; when failure took place across a single shear plane the angle of this to the σ_3-direction is given.

Rock	Confining Pressure σ_3 (bars)	Temperature	Max. Stress Difference $\sigma_1 - \sigma_3$ (bars)	Max. Strain (per cent)	Angle
L	0	24	830	1·0	Sh.
	1,000	24	4,190	26·5	steep
	1,000	300	3,860	27·2	N.B.
	2,000	24	6,200	30	N.B.
	2,000	300	4,700	27·3	N.B.
Ss	0	24	400	0·6	cone
	1,000	24	2,650	21·8	70°
	1,000	300	2,400	28·4	54°
	2,000	24	4,750	24·2	N.B.
	2,000	300	3,980	19·6	N.B.
$Sq.$	0	24	1,000	0·5	cone
	1,000	24	6,000	2·5	
	1,000	300	7,050	1·4	74°
	2,000	24	10,300	3·8	61°
	2,000	300	9,300	2·4	58°

take place. This mechanism of plastic deformation at high temperatures may well be different from that at low temperatures. When rocks such as marble are plastically deformed at room temperature, it was pointed out by von Karman and Orowan[1] that they are in effect broken up into a granular mass which then deforms as such, cf. § 44.

(iv) Criteria for Failure

When observations on fracture are represented by Mohr envelopes, these may vary from nearly linear, Fig. 57 (a), to those

[1] E. Orowan, *Geol. Soc. Amer. Memoir* 79 (1960), 323.

for more ductile rocks such as Fig. 57 (b) which show considerable curvature. There is, in general, reasonably good agreement between observed directions of fracture and those deduced from the Mohr envelope. Of the two available theories with a simple physical interpretation, the Coulomb–Navier theory predicts a

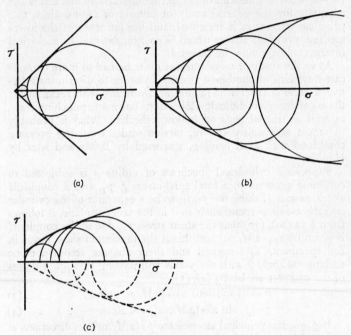

FIG. 57. Some typical Mohr envelopes. (a) Silicious sandstone. (b) Dolomite. (c) Yule marble: upper curve torsion, lower curve compression

linear Mohr envelope and the Griffith theory a parabolic one, cf. § 46. Triaxial tests may be carried out either in compression or extension (in which case the longitudinal stress is less than the confining pressure) and the results should lie on the same Mohr envelope: this is not the case, though there is no very serious discrepancy. On the Griffith theory, the same values of the

Griffith constant T_0, § 24 (5), should be given by all experiments on the same rock, whether in compression or extension, but observed values differ by up to 30 per cent, cf. Heard, *loc. cit.*

The behaviour of rocks in the triaxial test may be regarded as reasonably well known and reasonably well represented by the two-dimensional theories of failure. Unfortunately this test is not adequate for the general study of criteria of failure since two principal stresses in it are equal, and the influence of the intermediate principal stress, which is so fundamental in geological interpretation, cannot be assessed.

As in the study of metals, resort must be had to more complicated systems of combined stresses in order to discriminate between various criteria of failure, and working with rocks under these conditions is difficult. Robertson[1] has made punching tests, as well as triaxial tests on hollow cylinders. What is probably the most satisfactory system, torsion under confining pressure combined with axial loading, was used by Boker and later by Handin.[2]

Suppose a cylindrical specimen of radius a is subjected to confining pressure p, a total axial stress $p+p_1$, and a couple M about its axis. Taking the y-axis to be a generator of the cylinder and the x-axis perpendicular to it in the tangent plane, it follows from § 32 (29), (30) that the shear stress τ_{xy} due to the couple M is given by $\tau_{xy}=2M/\pi a^3$ and this is the maximum shear stress in the specimen. The normal and shear stresses across a plane making an angle θ with the y-axis and passing through a radius of the cylinder are by § 3 (4), (5),

$$\sigma=p+\tfrac{1}{2}p_1(1-\cos 2\theta)+(2M/\pi a^3)\sin 2\theta, \quad . \quad . \quad (3)$$

$$\tau=\tfrac{1}{2}p_1 \sin 2\theta+(2M/\pi a^3)\cos 2\theta \quad . \quad . \quad . \quad (4)$$

If $p_1=0$, the principal stresses are $p\pm(2M/\pi a^3)$ in directions at $45°$ to the axes. If M is large enough, one principal stress will be tensile, and tensile fracture may be expected (and is observed) along a helix inclined at $45°$ to the axis. If p_1 is not zero, the situation is more complicated, but it follows from (4) that the directions of maximum shearing stress are given by

$$\tan 2\theta=\pi a^3 p_1/4M. \quad . \quad . \quad . \quad (5)$$

[1] E. C. Robertson, *Bull. Geol. Soc. Amer.*, **66** (1955), 1275.

[2] J. Handin, D. V. Higgs and J. K. O'Brien, *Geol. Soc. Amer. Memoir* **79** (1960), 245.

The principal stresses at failure can be calculated from (3) and (4) and a Mohr envelope drawn. In general this differs from the Mohr envelope derived from triaxial tests and shows a higher value for the shear strength (cf. Fig. 57 (c) for Yule marble in which the full curve refers to the compression-torsion and the dotted curve to the triaxial test). Also the directions of shear failure appear to agree better with the directions of maximum shear stress calculated from (5) than with the Coulomb–Navier directions. However, the Yule marble on which most experiments have been made is highly anisotropic so that no definite conclusions can yet be drawn.

44. SYSTEMS HAVING ONE OR MORE PLANES OF WEAKNESS

(i) *The General Formulae in Two Dimensions for Slip on a Plane of Weakness*

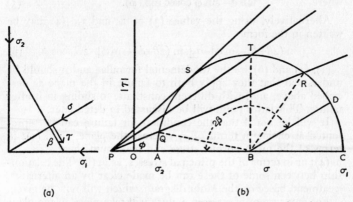

FIG. 58. The Mohr representation for failure in a plane of weakness

In many cases, relatively homogeneous rock is intersected by a plane of weakness which on a small scale might be a joint plane or on a larger scale might be an old fault plane. It is important to find conditions under which failure will take place in such a plane. If σ and τ are the normal and shear stresses across the plane, the assumption of Coulomb–Navier type is that failure will take place when

$$| \tau | = S_0 + \sigma \tan \phi, \qquad \qquad (1)$$

where S_0 is the shear strength of the material in the plane (e.g., joint-filling material) and $\mu = \tan \phi$ is a coefficient of internal friction for it.

Considering first the two-dimensional case, suppose that the plane is inclined at β to the direction of the greatest principal stress, Fig. 58 (a), then putting $\beta = \frac{1}{2}\pi - \theta$ in § 3 (13), (14) gives

$$\sigma = \sigma_m - \tau_m \cos 2\beta, \quad \tau = -\tau_m \sin 2\beta, \qquad (2)$$

where

$$\sigma_m = \tfrac{1}{2}(\sigma_1 + \sigma_2) \quad \text{and} \quad \tau_m = \tfrac{1}{2}(\sigma_1 - \sigma_2) \qquad (3)$$

are, respectively, the mean normal stress and the maximum shear stress.

Substituting (2) in (1) gives for the criterion of failure

$$\tau_m = (\sigma_m + S_0 \cot \phi) \tan \delta, \qquad \qquad (4)$$

where

$$\tan \delta = \sin \phi \operatorname{cosec} (2\beta + \phi). \qquad \qquad (5)$$

Alternatively, using the values (3) of σ_m and τ_m, (4) may be written in the form

$$\sigma_1 [\sin (2\beta + \phi) - \sin \phi] - \sigma_2 [\sin (2\beta + \phi) + \sin \phi] = 2S_0 \cos \phi. \qquad (6)$$

(1), (4) and (6) are the fundamental formulae and it should be understood that they apply both to failure in the plane as described above, and, with different constants, to sliding in it after failure. This latter point will be discussed in detail later.

It will be noted that the condition for failure can be represented at choice in terms of σ, τ across the plane, as in (1); in terms of the mean normal stress and maximum shear stress, as in (4); or in terms of the principal stresses, as in (6). The relationship between some of these can be made clear by an alternative treatment, based on the Mohr diagram, which will now be given.

For any system of stresses, failure will take place in the plane when $| \tau |$ and σ are related by (1) which is the line PQR in Fig. 58 (b) inclined at ϕ to OC and making an intercept $OP = -S_0 \cot \phi$ on the σ-axis. Now suppose the principal stresses are σ_1 and σ_2, corresponding to the Mohr circle on AC as diameter. For any inclination β of the plane, the values of σ and $| \tau |$ across it will be the coordinates of the point D on the Mohr circle. If D lies in either of the arcs AQ or RC, these stresses will not cause failure in the plane, but if D lies in the arc QSR they will. From either of the triangles PQB or PRB it follows that at the limiting condition for failure

$$(\sigma_m + S_0 \cot \phi) \operatorname{cosec} (\phi + 2\beta) = \tau_m \operatorname{cosec} \phi$$

which is the condition (4). This relationship between σ_m and τ_m is represented by the line PT in Fig. 58 (b), where BT is perpendicular to OB.

Finally, the envelope of all Mohr circles corresponding to failure in a plane at β is PS whose slope is $\sin^{-1} (\tan \delta)$, but this envelope has little physical significance since failure takes place at points such as Q, R within it.

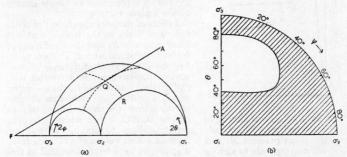

FIG. 59. (a) An assumed system of stresses and criterion for failure in a plane. (b) Directions (shaded) of the normal to the plane for which failure will not occur. ψ is the angle between the planes EOx and zOx in Fig. 7

(ii) Extension to Three Dimensions

This theory may be extended to three dimensions with the aid of the Mohr representation of Fig. 8. The problem now is: given a set of principal stresses σ_1, σ_2, σ_3, it is required to find the direction cosines of the normals to planes in which slip cannot take place. Suppose that the Mohr circles for the stresses are as shown in Fig. 59 (a), and that PA is the line (1), then each point in this line gives values of the angles θ and ϕ defined in § 5 which lie on a curve separating regions in which slip in the plane can or cannot occur. For example, the point Q is $\theta = 60°$, $\phi = 55°$, and failure cannot occur on QR for which $\theta = 60°$, $90° > \phi > 55°$. For any system of stresses and assumed properties of the plane of weakness, regions in which slip cannot occur can be plotted on a stereographic projection. The shaded area in Fig. 59 (b) shows this region for the system of Fig. 59 (a).

If there are several planes of weakness, corresponding, for example, to different joint systems, one such curve can be drawn for each set.

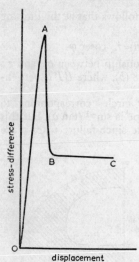

FIG. 60. Failure and sliding in a triaxial test. Shear failure takes place at A, and BC corresponds to sliding along the sheared surface

(iii) *Sliding Friction*

If two surfaces are sliding over each other, Amonton's law of solid friction should hold, so that $|\tau| = \mu\sigma$, where τ and σ are the shear stress and normal stress across the surface and μ is now a coefficient of ordinary sliding friction. If sliding takes place between two rough rock surfaces such as joint or shear surfaces, it is reasonable to generalize this to the form (1) where the constant S_0 allows for the roughness of the sliding surfaces. Thus the whole of the preceding theory applies also to simple sliding across a plane surface.

Effects of this sort appear in the shear failure of rocks in the triaxial test and allow values of S_0 and the coefficient of friction to be measured. For example, Fig. 60 shows stress-difference plotted against displacement in a triaxial test. OA corresponds to loading the specimen which failed at A with considerable energy release, the stress-difference falling to B. BC is the stress-difference corresponding to sliding across this fracture plane. Values of μ ranging from 0·47 to 0·86 have been measured in this way.[1]

(iv) *Solid Material with a Plane of Weakness: Fracture Cutting across the Plane*

Suppose that solid rock with shear strength S_0' and angle of internal friction ϕ' is intersected by a single plane of weakness with shear strength S_0 and angle of internal friction (or ordinary sliding friction) ϕ. It may be expected that S_0' will be much larger than S_0, and ϕ' probably slightly larger than ϕ, so that if DE, Fig. 61, is the curve (1) for the solid material and PS is that for the plane of weakness, the relationship of the curves will be as shown in Fig. 61. Now suppose that σ_3 is held constant and σ_1 increased. For lower values of σ_1, corresponding to the dotted circle AW, slip in the plane of weakness will be possible for some orientations of this plane but failure in the solid material is not possible. When σ_1 is so large that the Mohr circle for σ_1 and σ_3 touches DE at F, failure may take place in the plane of weakness as in Fig. 58 if 2β lies in the arc QFR: if 2β lies in the arcs AQ or RC, failure in the plane of weakness is not possible, but failure will take place through the solid material at the Coulomb–Navier angle of $(\pi/4) - \tfrac{1}{2}\phi'$ and this plane will intersect the plane of weakness.

---

[1] J. C. Jaeger, *Geofis. pura e appl.*, **43** (1959), 148.

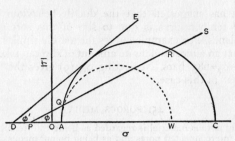

FIG. 61. Failure through solid material across a plane of weakness

(v) *The Case of Rock with Random Fracturing in All Directions*

If the rock has fractures in all directions so that the weakest direction can be selected, this weakest direction will correspond to the case $Q=R$ in Fig. 58 (*b*) so that $\beta=(\pi/4)-\frac{1}{2}\phi$. In this case (4) becomes

$$\tau_m=S_0\cos\phi+\sigma_m\sin\phi, \qquad . \qquad . \qquad . \qquad (7)$$

or, in a general coordinate system, by § 3 (19)

$$\{(\sigma_x-\sigma_y)^2+4\tau^2_{xy}\}^{\frac{1}{2}}=2S_0\cos\phi+(\sigma_x+\sigma_y)\sin\phi. \qquad . \qquad (8)$$

Also (6) becomes

$$\sigma_1=2S_0\tan\alpha+\sigma_2\tan^2\alpha, \qquad . \qquad . \qquad . \qquad (9)$$

where

$$\alpha=(\pi/4)+\frac{1}{2}\phi. \qquad . \qquad . \qquad . \qquad (10)$$

Here we have regained, by a different method, the Coulomb–Navier theory of § 21 and also (with $p_1=\sigma_2$ and $p_2=\sigma_1$) the soil mechanics theory of § 23 (6). The formulae (7), (8), (9) are useful alternatives to § 21 (7).

The position then is this: a 'solid' rock according to the theory of § 21 will select its own plane of fracture; a mass of rock with a single plane of weakness will fail along this plane of weakness if the principal stresses satisfy (6); a rock with many planes of weakness such as a shattered or brecciated rock will also select its plane of failure and behave according to the laws of soil mechanics. This provides the justification for treating many engineering problems on rock mechanics which involve grossly jointed or shattered rock on the basis of the methods of soil mechanics.

Orowan has suggested that the ductile behaviour of marble at normal temperatures is due to slip of this sort over many fracture planes. For example curves for marble similar to Fig. 20 suggest that an almost indefinite amount of slip can take place for $\sigma_1 = 3{,}565$, $\sigma_3 = 685$ bars. Neglecting S_0, (9) gives the reasonable value $\phi = 42°$ in this case.

45. POROUS MEDIA

An ideally porous material is regarded as being traversed by a system of minute, interconnected pores and as being homogeneous in the sense that the *surface porosity* e, defined as the ratio of the area of voids to total area for an arbitrary element of surface of the region, is independent of the position of the surface. It follows that the volume porosity, the ratio of pore space to total volume for any element of volume, is also equal to e. It varies from 0·01 or 0·02 for 'solid' rocks to as much as 0·5 for sand. The general theory has to cover all cases from sand, which is an aggregate of particles touching at a few points, to materials such as concrete and rocks, which may be regarded as solid material traversed by a network of fine capillaries or cracks. Since it is assumed that the pores are interconnected, it follows that the pressure p of pore-fluid in them varies continuously with position. For simplicity, it will be assumed that the pore-fluid is incompressible and completely fills the pores.

(i) *The Equations of Equilibrium and Consolidation*

The components of stress are defined precisely as in § 3 for the system as a whole. The element of area δA in Fig. 1 is assumed to be large enough to be intersected by a large number of pores and the force δF across it is in fact compounded of the force across the solid part and a normal force $ep\,\delta A$ across the pores. Similarly the components of strain are defined for the whole medium as in § 11 by considering the distortion of surfaces in it. To complete the specification of the system, the pore-pressure p at every point is needed, and also a quantity θ to specify the change in pore volume. θ will be defined as the increment of pore volume per unit volume, by analogy with the dilatation Δ which is the fractional change in total volume, cf. § 11 (17).

Just as in § 13, linear stress-strain relations can be assumed connecting p and the six components of stress with θ and the six components of strain. These may be written

$$\sigma_x = 2G'\epsilon_x + \lambda'\Delta + \lambda''\theta, \quad \tau_{yz} = G'\gamma_{yz}, \text{ etc.} \qquad (1)$$

$$p = k\Delta + k'\theta, \qquad \qquad \qquad (2)$$

where G', λ', λ'', k, k' are constants. In addition, it follows[1] from a relation of type § 16 (8) that $\lambda'' = k$. The physical significance of the constants in (1) and (2) has to be determined as in § 13 by consideration of simple stress-systems. For example, $(\lambda' - k\lambda''/k')$ and G' are Lamé's

---

[1] For the argument see R. V. Southwell, *loc. cit.*, p. 10.

parameters for the material at zero pore-pressure. A full discussion is given by Biot.[1]

The equations of equilibrium in terms of stresses, § 34 (1)–(3), hold as before.

Finally, a relation specifying the movement of fluid through the pores is needed. This is provided by Darcy's law

$$V_x = -b\,\partial p/\partial x, \quad V_y = -b\,\partial p/\partial y, \quad V_z = -b\,\partial p/\partial z, \qquad (3)$$

where b is a constant and V_x, V_y, V_z are the components of the velocity of the fluid. For incompressible fluid, the equation of continuity, obtained by equating the rate of flow of fluid into a small rectangular parallelepiped to the rate of increase of pore volume in that region, is

$$\frac{\partial \theta}{\partial t} = -\frac{\partial V_x}{\partial x} - \frac{\partial V_y}{\partial y} - \frac{\partial V_z}{\partial z} = b\nabla^2 p. \qquad (4)$$

These are the equations of the problem, and their solution has been discussed by Biot, *loc. cit.* They are of the greatest importance, particularly in connexion with the consolidation of soils. As a simple illustration the problem of one-dimensional consolidation along the z-axis will be considered. In this case, all quantities are independent of x and y so that (1) and (2) give

$$\sigma_z = (\lambda' + 2G')\Delta + k\theta, \qquad (5)$$

$$p = k\Delta + k'\theta, \qquad (6)$$

using $k = \lambda''$ and $\Delta = \epsilon_z = \partial w/\partial z$. The stress-equations of equilibrium reduce to $\partial \sigma_z/\partial z = 0$ so that $\sigma_z = C$, constant, and, from (5) and (6),

$$[k'(\lambda' + 2G') - k^2]\theta = (\lambda' + 2G')p - kC. \qquad (7)$$

Finally, using (7) in (4) gives

$$\frac{\partial^2 p}{\partial z^2} = \frac{1}{c}\frac{\partial p}{\partial t}, \qquad (8)$$

where

$$c = b[k'(\lambda' + 2G') - k^2]/(\lambda' + 2G'), \qquad (9)$$

so that p, and hence also Δ and θ, satisfy the equation of diffusion.

Considering, as a specific case, the consolidation of the region $0 < z < h$ under applied stress p_0 in the z-direction applied for times $t > 0$, with no flow of pore-fluid at $z = h$ and free flow at $z = 0$, the boundary conditions derived from (3) are

$$p = 0, \quad z = 0, \quad t > 0, \qquad (10)$$

$$\partial p/\partial z = 0, \quad z = h, \quad t > 0. \qquad (11)$$

The initial condition is that the material is undisturbed, so that $\theta = 0$, $0 < z < h$, for $t < 0$. When $t = 0$, σ_z is suddenly raised to p_0 and maintained constant so that

$$\sigma_z = p_0, \quad t \geqslant 0. \qquad (12)$$

Putting $\theta = 0$ and $\sigma_z = p_0$ in (5) and (6) gives for the initial value of p

$$p = kp_0/(\lambda' + 2G'), \quad 0 < z < h, \quad t = 0. \qquad (13)$$

---

[1] M. A. Biot, *J. Appl. Phys.*, **12** (1941), 155; *J. Appl. Mech.*, **23** (1956) 91. See also K. von Terzaghi, *loc. cit.*

The solution of (8) subject to the initial condition (13) and boundary conditions (10) and (11) is well known: it is[1]

$$p = \frac{4kp_0}{\pi(\lambda'+2G')} \sum_{n=0}^{\infty} \frac{1}{(2n+1)} e^{-(2n+1)^2\pi^2ct/4h^2} \sin\frac{(2n+1)\pi z}{2h}. \quad (14)$$

From this all other quantities, such as the settling of the surface $z=0$ under the load, are readily calculated.

(ii) *Criteria for Failure for Materials with Pore-pressure*

This is a matter of considerable geological importance. At depth z below the Earth's surface in material of density ρ the vertical stress is ρgz and the pressure p of a column of liquid of density ρ' and height z would be $\rho'gz$. Many instances have been encountered in which the fluid pressure is greater than this, and in some cases it has been observed to be as large as the over-burden pressure ρgz, cf. Hubbert and Rubey, *loc. cit.* Another case in which pore-pressure is of geological importance is that in which the pores are filled with volatiles from igneous intrusions.

The criterion for failure of material containing pore-water under pressure may be considered in the following way.[2] For a porous medium consisting of small spherical grains under no stress except hydrostatic pressure p, the stress in those grains would be just the hydrostatic pressure p. This suggests that, in a general porous medium, the pore-pressure p produces an approximately hydrostatic pressure p in the surrounding solid material, and that this base state of pressure will have no effect on its mechanical properties. This in turn suggests that failure will be determined by the *effective stress* σ_1-p, σ_2-p, σ_3-p, and, in particular, that the Coulomb–Navier criterion § 21 (1) is to be replaced by

$$|\tau| = S_0 + \mu(\sigma-p). \quad . \quad . \quad . \quad (15)$$

This may be regarded, like the Coulomb–Navier criterion itself, as an hypothesis to be tested experimentally, and, in general, the results of triaxial tests in which pore-water is supplied to the specimen under pressure are in agreement with it.

Fig. 62 shows some results by Handin on sandstone reported by Hubbert (*loc. cit.*). They represent triaxial tests at pore-pressures of between zero and 2,000 bars, and when plotted as suggested by (15) in terms of σ_1-p and σ_2-p they are seen all to fit the same Mohr envelope extremely well, irrespective of the value of p. Other experiments on concrete also agree well with (15).

The way in which pore-pressure contributes to failure is shown in Fig. 62. Curve I, for $p=500$ bars, corresponds to failure at $\sigma_1=5,400$, $\sigma_2=2,000$ bars. For zero pore-pressure, the Mohr circle for these stresses would be the dotted circle II which lies well within the Mohr envelope so that failure could not occur. As the pore-pressure is increased, this

---

[1] H. S. Carslaw and J. C. Jaeger, *Conduction of Heat in Solids* (Oxford, Ed. 2, 1959), § 3.4.

[2] A full discussion is given by M. King Hubbert and W. W. Rubey, *Bull. Geol. Soc. Amer.*, **70** (1959), 115, 167; *ibid.*, **71** (1960), 611.

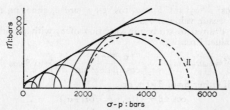

FIG. 62. Mohr envelope for failure of sandstone under triaxial conditions
including pore-pressure p

circle is moved to the left until it touches the Mohr envelope and failure
takes place.

For tensile failure, the assumption corresponding to (15) is that, if
T_0 is the tensile strength for zero pore-pressure, the criterion for failure is

$$\sigma_3 - p + T_0 = 0. \qquad . \qquad . \qquad . \qquad . \qquad . \qquad (16)$$

It will be shown in § 46 that this result follows from the Griffith theory.

46. FURTHER DISCUSSION OF CRITERIA FOR FAILURE

(1) *The Griffith Criterion*

A brief discussion of the Griffith criterion has already been given in
§ 24. In view of its increasing importance and the fact that the basic
theory is given in § 51, some further discussion is given here. There are
two aspects of the theory: (i) the energetics of the situation and the condition that the crack will propagate, and (ii) the detailed study of stresses
around the crack leading to the criterion § 24 (4), (5). It is the latter question which will be studied here.

Using the elliptic coordinates and notation of § 51 (23), suppose the
crack to be the ellipse $\xi = \xi_0$, where ξ_0 is small, and that the principal
stresses at infinity are σ_1 and σ_2, inclined, respectively, at $\frac{1}{2}\pi + \beta$ and β
to the major axis. The tangential stress σ_η in the surface of the ellipse is by
§ 51 (28)

$$\sigma_\eta = \frac{(\sigma_1 + \sigma_2) \sinh 2\xi_0 + (\sigma_1 - \sigma_2)[e^{2\xi_0} \cos 2(\beta - \eta) - \cos 2\beta]}{\cosh 2\xi_0 - \cos 2\eta}. \quad . \quad (1)$$

To find the positions of the extreme values of σ_η in the surface we
differentiate with respect to η. Since ξ_0 is small, it is found that maxima
or minima of σ_η occur at η and $\pi + \eta$, where η is small and to the first
order in ξ_0 is given by

$$\eta = -\xi_0[\sigma_1 \cos^2 \beta + \sigma_2 \sin^2 \beta \pm (\sigma_1^2 \cos^2 \beta + \sigma_2^2 \sin^2 \beta)^{\frac{1}{2}}]$$
$$[(\sigma_1 - \sigma_2) \sin \beta \cos \beta]^{-1}, \quad . \quad . \quad (2)$$

provided $\sigma_1 \neq \sigma_2$. The extreme values σ_e of σ_η at these points are found
to be

$$\xi_0 \sigma_e = \sigma_1 \cos^2 \beta + \sigma_2 \sin^2 \beta \pm (\sigma_1^2 \cos^2 \beta + \sigma_2^2 \sin^2 \beta)^{\frac{1}{2}}. \quad . \quad (3)$$

Since $(\sigma_1^2 \cos^2 \beta + \sigma_2^2 \sin^2 \beta)^{\frac{1}{2}} > \sigma_1 \cos^2 \beta + \sigma_2 \sin^2 \beta$, choosing the negative sign gives a tensile value of σ_e.

It is now desired to study the variation of σ_e with β and to find its maximum value. From (3)

$$\xi_0 \frac{d\sigma_e}{d\beta} = \left\{ 2\sigma_2 - 2\sigma_1 + \frac{\sigma_1^2 - \sigma_2^2}{(\sigma_1^2 \cos^2 \beta + \sigma_2^2 \sin^2 \beta)^{\frac{1}{2}}} \right\} \sin \beta \cos \beta, \qquad . \quad (4)$$

and is zero if either $\beta = 0$, $\beta = \frac{1}{2}\pi$, or

$$\cos 2\beta = -\tfrac{1}{2}(\sigma_1 - \sigma_2)/(\sigma_1 + \sigma_2). \qquad . \qquad . \qquad . \quad (5)$$

The inclined position (5) only exists if $|\cos 2\beta| < 1$, or

$$\sigma_1 + 3\sigma_2 > 0, \qquad . \qquad . \qquad . \qquad . \qquad . \quad (6)$$

and the corresponding value of σ_e is

$$\sigma_e = -\frac{(\sigma_1 - \sigma_2)^2}{4(\sigma_1 + \sigma_2)\xi_0}. \qquad . \qquad . \qquad . \qquad (7)$$

For the inclined positions, it follows from (5) that as $\sigma_2 \to \sigma_1$, $\beta \to 45°$. If $\sigma_2 = 0$, $\beta = 60°$, and the plane of the most dangerous crack is inclined at $30°$ to the direction of the compression σ_1. As $\sigma_2 \to -\sigma_1/3$, $\beta \to 90°$, and the plane of the most dangerous crack becomes perpendicular to the tensile direction.

If $\sigma_2 < -\sigma_1/3$, the inequality (6) is not satisfied and there is no inclined solution of (4). The maximum value of σ_e occurs when $\beta = 90°$. In this case the maximum tangential stress occurs when $\eta = 0$ and by (1) it is

$$\sigma_e = \frac{(\sigma_1 + \sigma_2) \sinh 2\xi_0 - (\sigma_1 - \sigma_2)(e^{2\xi_0} - 1)}{\cosh 2\xi_0 - 1} = \frac{2\sigma_2}{\xi_0}, \qquad . \qquad (8)$$

since ξ_0 is small. If T_0 is the tensile strength, so that $\sigma_2 = -T_0$ in (8), the maximum stress in the crack at failure is in this case

$$\sigma_e = -2T_0/\xi_0. \qquad . \qquad . \qquad . \qquad . \qquad (9)$$

If it is assumed that under all conditions failure occurs when the maximum tangential tension in the most dangerous crack reaches this value, $\sigma_e \xi_0$ may be eliminated between (7) and (9), and the criterion for failure is

$$(\sigma_1 - \sigma_2)^2 - 8T_0(\sigma_1 + \sigma_2) = 0, \quad \text{if } \sigma_1 + 3\sigma_2 > 0, \qquad . \quad (10)$$

$$\sigma_2 + T_0 = 0, \quad \text{if } \sigma_1 + 3\sigma_2 < 0. \qquad . \qquad (11)$$

This is the result quoted in § 24 and represented in Fig. 30, with the change that in that section stresses were taken positive when tensile.

Introducing $\sigma_m = \frac{1}{2}(\sigma_1 + \sigma_2)$, $\tau_m = \frac{1}{2}(\sigma_1 - \sigma_2)$, the σ_m, τ_m curve for failure is

$$\left. \begin{array}{l} \tau_m^2 = 4T_0 \sigma_m, \quad \text{if } 2\sigma_m > \tau_m, \\ \tau_m = \sigma_m + T_0, \quad \text{if } 2\sigma_m < \tau_m. \end{array} \right\} \qquad . \qquad . \quad (12)$$

This consists of the line AB of slope $45°$ for $-T_0 < \sigma_m < T_0$, and portion BC of a parabola for $\sigma_m > T_0$, Fig. 63. The Mohr circles for all points of the line AB touch at the point A. The Mohr envelope for points on the parabola is the envelope of the circles

$$f(\sigma_m) \equiv \tau^2 + (\sigma - \sigma_m)^2 - 4\sigma_m T_0 = 0, \qquad . \qquad . \qquad (13)$$

and so is obtained by eliminating σ_m between (13) and $\partial f / \partial \sigma_m = 0$, or

$$\sigma - \sigma_m + 2T_0 = 0.$$

Thus the equation of the Mohr envelope is

$$\tau^2 = 4T_0(\sigma + T_0), \qquad . \qquad . \qquad . \qquad . \qquad (14)$$

which is a parabola AD passing through the point A, Fig. 63.

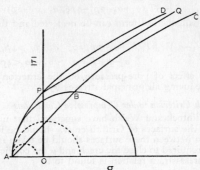

FIG. 63. The Griffith criterion. ABC is the σ_m, τ_m curve for failure and APD its Mohr envelope. APQ is the modified Mohr envelope for compressional conditions

It is easy to show that the direction of fracture derived from this Mohr envelope is also the direction of the major axis of the crack in which fracture occurs. This cannot be taken as an argument for propagation of the crack in this direction since the maximum tensile stress in the crack is not in general at the ends of the crack.

A parabolic form of the Mohr envelope has been advocated by Leon (cf. Nadai, *loc. cit.*). It has the advantage of allowing continuous variation of the directions of fracture between the 'tensile' and shear directions which is consistent with some field observations.[1] The parabolic form is also in many cases a nearer representation of the actual Mohr envelope for high σ_m, cf. Fig. 57 (*b*). Finally, it is shown in § 48 that the parabolic form has some theoretical status as being derived from the simple yield condition § 48 (9).

(ii) *The Case of Fluid Pressure in a Griffith Crack*

Suppose that, in addition to the external stresses σ_1, σ_2 there is an internal fluid pressure p in the crack. The solution § 50 (13) for this case has to be added to (1) which is replaced by

$$\sigma_\eta = p + \frac{(\sigma_1 + \sigma_2 - 2p) \sinh 2\xi_0 + (\sigma_1 - \sigma_2)[e^{2\xi_0} \cos 2(\beta - \eta) - \cos 2\beta]}{\cosh 2\xi_0 - \cos 2\eta}. \qquad (15)$$

---

[1] W. R. Muehlberger, *J. Geol.*, **69** (1961), 211

The essential change is that σ_1 and σ_2 are replaced by σ_1-p and σ_2-p, and most of the previous work can be taken over immediately. In particular, (6) and (7) are replaced by

$$\sigma_e = p - \frac{(\sigma_1-\sigma_2)^2}{4(\sigma_1+\sigma_2-2p)\xi_0}, \quad \text{if } \sigma_1+3\sigma_2>4p. \qquad . \qquad . \quad (16)$$

Combining this with (9) gives

$$(\sigma_1-\sigma_2)^2-8T_0(\sigma_1+\sigma_2-2p)-4p\xi_0(\sigma_1+\sigma_2-2p)=0.$$

Since ξ_0 is small, the last term can be neglected and the criterion for failure becomes

$$(\sigma_1-\sigma_2)^2-8T_0(\sigma_1+\sigma_2-2p)=0, \quad \sigma_1+3\sigma_2>4p, \quad . \qquad (17)$$

$$\sigma_2-p+T_0=0, \quad \sigma_1+3\sigma_2<4p. \qquad . \quad (18)$$

That is, the effect of pore-pressure on the criterion for failure is equivalent to reducing all principal stresses by p.

(iii) *The Griffith Criterion under Compressive Conditions*

Brace,[1] McClintock and Walsh have suggested that under compressive conditions the surfaces of Griffith cracks should be forced together and that friction between these surfaces should be taken into account. If σ_c is the stress required to close the crack and μ the coefficient of friction across it, the stress-strain relation is found to be

$$\sigma_1[(1+\mu^2)^{\frac{1}{2}}-\mu]-\sigma_2[(1+\mu^2)^{\frac{1}{2}}+\mu]=4T_0(1+\sigma_c/T_0)^{\frac{1}{2}}-2\mu\sigma_c, \quad . \quad (19)$$

which is a linear relationship of form § 44 (7). For the case $\sigma_c=0$ it reduces to § 44 (7) with $S_0=2T_0$, and its Mohr envelope for $\sigma>0$ will be the straight line PQ of slope μ, Fig. 63, which joins the Griffith parabola at P.

(iv) *Anisotropic Materials*

Since many rocks are highly anisotropic it is desirable to have some simple criterion for failure which takes this into account. A simple generalization of the Coulomb–Navier theory can be made if it is assumed that the shear strength of the rock in a plane, instead of being constant, contains a term in $\cos 2\theta$ where θ specifies the direction of the plane. Thus, with axes as in Fig. 58 (*a*), suppose the shear strength of the rock in a plane inclined at β to the greatest principal stress is

$$S_1-S_2 \cos 2\,(\omega-\beta), \qquad . \qquad . \qquad . \quad (20)$$

so that it has a minimum value of S_1-S_2 in a plane inclined at ω to the greatest principal stress and a maximum S_1+S_2 in the perpendicular direction. Replacing S_0 by (20) in § 44 (1) and using § 44 (2), the condition for failure in a plane inclined at β becomes

$$\tau_m \sin (2\beta+\phi)+S_2 \cos 2(\omega-\beta) \cos \phi=S_1 \cos \phi+\sigma_m \sin \phi. \quad . \quad (21)$$

For fixed τ_m, the left-hand side of (21) has a maximum when

$$\tan 2\beta=\frac{\tau_m+S_2 \sin 2\omega}{\tau_m \tan \phi+S_2 \cos 2\omega}. \qquad . \qquad . \quad (22)$$

---

[1] W. F. Brace, *J. Geophys. Res.*, **65** (1960), 3477.

The value of this maximum is

$$[(\tau_m + S_2 \sin 2\omega)^2 + (\tau_m \tan \phi + S_2 \cos 2\omega)^2]^{\frac{1}{2}} \cos \phi, . \qquad (23)$$

and at failure this must be equal to $S_1 \cos \phi + \sigma_m \sin \phi$. This leads to the criterion

$$(\sigma_m + S_1 \cot \phi)^2 - (\tau_m + b)^2 \operatorname{cosec}^2 \phi = S_2{}^2 \cot^2 \phi \cos^2 (2\omega + \phi), \qquad (24)$$

where

$$b = S_2 \sin (2\omega + \phi) \cos \phi. \qquad (25)$$

The curve (24) is an hyperbola in the (σ_m, τ_m) plane with centre at $(-S_1 \cot \phi, -b)$ and asymptotes inclined to the σ_m-axis at $\tan^{-1} (\sin \phi)$.

To determine the directions of failure for any system of stresses it is necessary to substitute τ_m from (24) into (22). When this is done, it is found that, instead of the two possible directions of failure on the Coulomb–Navier theory, there is *only one*, which lies between the plane of minimum shear strength and the nearest to it of the two Coulomb–Navier directions.

The criterion (24) has been found to be in reasonable agreement with laboratory experiments.[1]

47. STRESSES AND FAULTING IN THE CRUST

(i) *The Assumption of No Horizontal Displacement*

It was shown in § 34 that, on the assumption that there is no horizontal displacement, the principal stresses at depth z below the surface are

$$\sigma_z = \rho g z, \quad \sigma_x = \sigma_y = (\nu/1 - \nu)\sigma_z, \qquad (1)$$

and these values, which have a simple mathematical status, are sometimes regarded as the normal state of stress. An additional horizontal tectonic stress c_x along the x-axis may be taken into account[2] approximately by superposing on (1) the stress-state § 14 (10), $\sigma_x = c_x$, $\varepsilon_y = 0$, $\sigma_z = 0$, for which $\sigma_y = \nu c_x$ so that the combined stresses are

$$\sigma_x = [\nu/(1-\nu)]\rho g z + c_x, \quad \sigma_y = [\nu/(1-\nu)]\rho g z + \nu c_x, \quad \sigma_z = \rho g z. \qquad (2)$$

Certain deductions can be drawn from this. For example, for transcurrent faulting, it is necessary that $\sigma_x > \sigma_z > \sigma_y$ and this leads to limits for c_x, namely

$$\nu(1-2\nu)\sigma_z < \nu(1-\nu)c_x < (1-2\nu)\sigma_z, \qquad (3)$$

[1] F. A. Donath, *Bull. Geol. Soc. Amer.*, **72** (1961), 985; J. C. Jaeger, *Geol. Mag.*, **97** (1960), 65.
[2] N. J. Price, *Geol. Mag.*, **96** (1959), 149.

and using this condition it follows that

$$\sigma_x/\sigma_y < (1-\nu)/\nu. \qquad . \qquad . \qquad . \qquad (4)$$

Price (*loc. cit.*) has carried this hypothesis further by assuming that if a rock mass is uplifted by an amount u, $v=0$ during this uplift, so that by § 14 (15) there is a tangential strain $\varepsilon_\theta = u/R$, where R is the Earth's radius. This gives rise to a horizontal tension $-Eu/R$ which may be added to σ_x and σ_y in (2). The effect of this is to make the horizontal stresses tensile at some levels, and provides a possible explanation of some types of jointing.

(ii) *The Hydrostatic Hypothesis and the Experimental Results*

The validity of the assumption that all horizontal displacements are zero which was made in (i) is open to question. An alternative assumption, known as Heim's rule (cf. Talobre, *loc. cit.*), is that the stresses at any depth will tend to become hydrostatic due to the action of creep over long periods of time so that at depth z

$$\sigma_x = \sigma_y = \sigma_z = \rho g z. \qquad . \qquad . \qquad . \qquad (5)$$

While this hypothesis has no particular justification it is the simplest possible and has the advantage that calculations of stresses in underground excavations based on it are especially simple. Anderson, *loc. cit.*, regards it as a standard reference state and speaks of increase or relief of pressure relative to it.

A few experimental measurements of underground stresses have been made from engineering works at relatively shallow depths. Some of these results are shown by Talobre (*loc. cit.*), p. 56. In general, such measurements yield values of the horizontal stresses which are of the same size as, and occasionally greater than the vertical stresses and so they may be regarded as giving some support for the rule (5). However, it must be emphasized that such measurements are usually made in irregular terrain, which is often tectonically active.

The assumption that one principal stress is vertical also needs examination. Near a horizontal free surface this must be the case, but any horizontal forces would cause inclination of the principal stresses such as those shown in Fig. 66. When stresses are measured in engineering structures underground, the principal stresses usually show considerable inclination, but such measurements are not typical, usually being in irregular terrain.

(iii) *Deductions from the Coulomb–Navier–Mohr Theory*

According to this theory in three dimensions the criterion of failure § 44 (9) is

$$\sigma_1 = 2S_0 \tan\alpha + \sigma_3 \tan^2\alpha, \qquad . \qquad . \qquad . \qquad (6)$$

where $\alpha = (\pi/4) + \frac{1}{2}\phi$, and failure takes place in a plane through the σ_2-axis at an angle α to the σ_3-direction.

Laboratory experiments on rocks, referred to in § 43, give values of S_0 ranging, usually, between 100 and 300 bars, and values of ϕ between 30° and 55°, corresponding to α between 60° and 72°.

Alternatively, the theory of shear faulting[1] given in § 21 may be regarded as providing a value of α and hence ϕ for rock on a large scale. For example 1,650 normal faults in the Netherlands coal measures are reported by Hubbert[2] as having an average dip of 63°, that is $\alpha = 63°$, $\phi = 36°$, while 450 thrust faults have an average dip of 22°, corresponding to $\alpha = 68°$ or $\phi = 46°$. For trans-current faults $\phi = 30°$ is commonly measured, and taken as a reasonable average value.[3] These values, which are typical, are well within the range quoted above for laboratory experiments.

(iv) *The Use of the Mohr Diagrams in Discussing Faulting*

A very instructive treatment of shear faulting on the basis of the Mohr representation has been given by Hubbert, *loc. cit.*

As a numerical illustration, suppose $S_0 = 150$ bars and $\phi = 40°$, the Mohr envelope for failure being PQ in Fig. 64. In this case the criterion (6) for failure in terms of principal stresses becomes

$$\sigma_1 = 640 + 4{\cdot}6\sigma_3. . \qquad . \qquad . \qquad . \qquad (7)$$

For normal faulting to occur at depth z, $\sigma_1 = \rho g z$ is fixed and σ_3 has to be reduced until the Mohr circle on σ_1 and σ_3 touches PQ, Fig. 64 (*a*). In the present case σ_3 would have to fall to $(\sigma_1 - 640)/4{\cdot}6$. If $\sigma_1 = \rho g z$ is less than the strength of the rock in unconfined compression (for which the Mohr circle passes through the origin) σ_3 must be tensile. Because of the uncertainty

---

[1] The nomenclature of faults is very varied. Transcurrent faults are frequently called wrench faults or strike-slip faults. The descriptive terms strike-slip, dip-slip and oblique-slip define themselves. The terms 'normal' and 'reverse' are also used to denote downward and upward relative motion of the hanging wall, respectively.

[2] M. King Hubbert, *Bull. Geol. Soc. Amer.*, **62** (1951), 355.

[3] J. D. Moody and M. J. Hill, *Bull. Geol. Soc. Amer.*, **67** (1956), 1207; A. Williams, *Trans. Roy. Soc. Edin.*, **63** (1959), 629.

of the numerical values and their variation with depth, much stress cannot be placed on quantitative determinations, but the results strongly suggest that horizontal stresses will be small in regions in which normal faulting occurs.

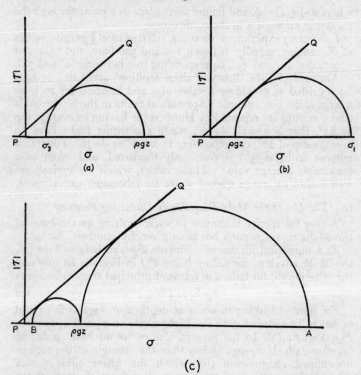

FIG. 64. Positions of the Mohr circles for faulting at depth z. (a) Normal faulting. (b) Thrust faulting. (c) Transcurrent faulting

For thrust faulting, Fig. 64 (b), $\sigma_3 = \rho g z$ is fixed and failure takes place when the horizontal stress σ_1 has built up to a value such that the circle for σ_3 and σ_1 touches PQ.

For transcurrent faulting, $\rho g z$ is to be the intermediate principal stress σ_2, and the other principal stresses must lie between the extreme values A and B in Fig. 64 (c). These correspond to the cases: (i), $\sigma_2=\sigma_3$, $\sigma_1=640+4\cdot6\sigma_2$, for A, and (ii) $\sigma_1=\sigma_2$, $\sigma_3=(\sigma_2-640)/4\cdot6$, for B. In all cases $\sigma_1>\sigma_3\tan^2\alpha$ and if both this criterion and (4) are to be satisfied only restricted ranges of ν and α are possible. This may account for the comparative rarity of transcurrent faults, or it may imply that the assumptions leading to (4) are untenable.

Hubbert, *loc. cit.* has shown that the phenomena of normal and thrust faulting can be elegantly illustrated by experiments on sand for which the theoretical predictions are verified with an angle of friction of about 30°, cf. Fig. 66.

(v) *Oblique Slip and Tectonic Regimes*

In § 4 and elsewhere, only the magnitude τ of the shear stress across a general plane has been discussed. In connexion with oblique slip faulting

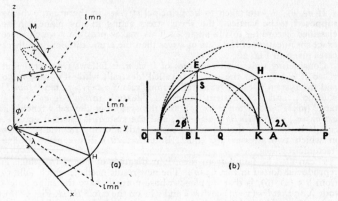

FIG. 65. Determination of the direction of the shear stress in a plane l, m, n. (a) Coordinate system. (b) Mohr representation

and some problems in rock mechanics it is necessary also to know the direction of the shear stress. This may be found by a simple extension[1] of the graphical or analytical methods of §§ 4, 5.

Let the normal to the plane have direction cosines (l, m, n) specified in terms of θ and ϕ as in Fig. 7 (b) and Fig. 65 (a) relative to principal

---

[1] C. A. Zizicas, *J. Appl. Mech.*, **22** (1955), 273; M. H. A. Bott, *Geol. Mag.*, **96** (1959), 109. Note that in the present discussion ϕ is the angle defined in Fig. 7 (b) and not the angle of friction.

stresses σ_x, σ_y, σ_z. Suppose a right-handed system of axes is defined by (l, m, n), (l', m', n'), (l'', m'', n'') where $(l', m'\ n')$ is in the plane EOH Fig. 65 (a). Then, if λ is the longitude of OH,

$$\left.\begin{array}{lll} l=\sin\phi\cos\lambda, & m=\sin\phi\sin\lambda, & n=\cos\phi, \\ l'=\cos\phi\cos\lambda, & m'=\cos\phi\sin\lambda, & n'=-\sin\phi, \\ l''=-\sin\lambda, & m''=\cos\lambda, & n''=0. \end{array}\right\} \quad . \quad . \quad (8)$$

Using these values in § 4 (7) the components τ' and τ'' of the shear stress in the directions l', m', n' and l'', m'', n'' are found to be

$$\tau'=\sin\phi\cos\phi[(\sigma_x\cos^2\lambda+\sigma_y\sin^2\lambda)-\sigma_z] \quad . \quad . \quad (9)$$

$$=n\{m^2(\sigma_y-\sigma_x)-(1-n^2)(\sigma_z-\sigma_x)\}(1-n^2)^{-\frac{1}{2}}, \quad . \quad (10)$$

$$\tau''=\sin\phi\sin\lambda\cos\lambda(\sigma_y-\sigma_x)=ml(\sigma_y-\sigma_x)(1-n^2)^{-\frac{1}{2}}. \quad . \quad (11)$$

With the present convention of sign, τ' and τ'' will be positive in the directions EM and EN, respectively, Fig. 65 (a). The angle ω which the resultant shear stress τ makes with EN is given by

$$\tan\omega=\frac{n}{lm}\left\{m^2-(1-n^2)\frac{\sigma_x-\sigma_z}{\sigma_x-\sigma_y}\right\}. \quad . \quad . \quad (12)$$

If σ_x, σ_y, σ_z, are taken to be principal stresses in the crust, σ_z being supposed to be vertical, the shear stress acting in any plane can be classified according to the angle ω. This makes possible a much more exact specification of the state of stress than the crude division into three cases given in Fig. 26.

Considering only positive values of l, m, n, it follows from (11) that $\tau''>0$ if $\sigma_y>\sigma_x$ and the system is called 'dextral', while if $\sigma_y<\sigma_x$, $\tau''<0$ and the system is called 'sinistral'. From (12): if $\sigma_y>\sigma_x>\sigma_z$, $\tan^{-1}(nm/l)$ $<\omega<90°$, and the system is called 'dextral thrust'; if $\sigma_y>\sigma_z>\sigma_x$, $\tan^{-1}(nm/l)>\omega>-\tan^{-1}(ln/m)$, and the system is 'dextral wrench'; if $\sigma_z>\sigma_y>\sigma_x$, $-\tan^{-1}(ln/m)>\omega>-90°$, and the system is 'dextral gravity'. Similarly there are three sinistral cases, and, allowing for the six cases in which two stresses are equal, Bott (loc. cit.) distinguishes twelve 'tectonic regimes'.

τ' can also be found from the Mohr diagram of Fig. 7 (a) which is reproduced dotted in Fig. 65 (b). The new result needed, which follows from § 5 (4), (6), is that for planes whose normals have the same longitude λ, so that $l^2=(1-n^2)\cos^2\lambda$, σ and τ lie on the circle REH, Fig. 65 (b), where the angle HAP is 2λ. Any two of θ, ϕ, λ determine the third, and OL and LE are the normal and shear stresses across the plane so specified. Also OK is the normal stress across the plane whose normal is OH, Fig. 65 (a). Thus the circle on RK as diameter is the Mohr circle for the plane OEH and the shear stress τ' in this plane corresponding to the normal stress OL will be SL.

(vi) Stress and Fracture Patterns in the Crust

Hitherto only the simplest systems of stress, and directions of fracture at a point, have been considered. It is obviously necessary next to consider typical two-dimensional situations likely to arise in the crust. A number of these have been studied in detail by Hafner[1] and Sandford.[2]

As an example, consider the two-dimensional system of stresses

$$\sigma_x = \rho g x, \quad \sigma_y = p - ky + \rho g x, \quad \tau_{xy} = kx, \qquad \qquad (13)$$

acting on the block $OABC$ of Fig. 66. Here the x-axis is vertically downwards and the y-axis is in the Earth's surface. The stresses (13) satisfy the equations of equilibrium § 34 (1), (2), with the modification that compressive stresses are now reckoned positive. They may be regarded as the stresses in a crustal block $OABC$ of depth d acted on by horizontal pressure p from an active area to

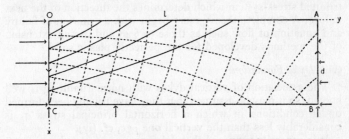

FIG. 66. Stress-trajectories (dotted) in a rectangle subjected to the stresses shown. The full lines intersect the stress-trajectories at 30°

the left. This is resisted by the shear stress kd over the surface BC. The forces on the block are shown in Fig. 66, and, of course, keep it in static equilibrium. The length l of the block is chosen to be p/k so that the excess horizontal pressure has disappeared at the face AB. By § 3 (11), the directions of the principal axes at x, y are given by

$$\tan 2\theta = \frac{2kx}{ky - p} = \frac{2x}{y - l}. \qquad \qquad (14)$$

When $x = 0$, $\theta = 0$, and the principal axes are horizontal and vertical. At depth, they are rotated by a variable amount in a clockwise direction. The stress-trajectories (curves whose directions at any point are the directions of the principal axes there, cf. § 49) are shown dotted in Fig. 66.

If the stresses at any point are sufficient to cause failure, this

[1] *Bull. Geol. Soc. Amer.*, **62** (1951), 373.   [2] *Ibid.*, **70** (1959), 19.

will occur in a direction at $(\pi/4)-\frac{1}{2}\phi$ to the greatest principal stress and shear failure might be expected to take place along a family of curves which cut the stress-trajectories at this angle. Such a family, drawn for $\phi=30°$, is shown by the full lines in Fig. 66. As remarked by Hubbert, *loc. cit.*, such curves show a striking resemblance both to the pattern of failure of sand in compression in sand-box experiments and also to the phenomena of thrust faulting on a geological scale. However, this simple argument must not be pushed too far, since in practice when failure takes place at a point there will be a redistribution of the stress-system before further fracture occurs and it is this redistributed stress-system which determines the direction of the next failure. A complete theory must begin with a criterion of failure and equation of flow such as those of § 48 and use an extension of the methods developed for the perfectly plastic solid.[1]

(vii) *Dyke Formation*

The association of vertical dykes with normal faulting is well known, so it may be assumed that they have usually been formed under conditions in which a horizontal principal stress σ_h is considerably less than the vertical one ρgz, cf. (iv).

It is generally supposed that dykes are opened by the pressure p of the magma, so the theory of the elliptical crack with internal pressure[2] can be applied immediately. The criterion for failure § 46 (18) becomes

$$\sigma_h - p + T_0 = 0, \qquad . \qquad . \qquad . \qquad (15)$$

provided $3\sigma_h + \rho gz < 4p$, which should be satisfied since p may be expected to be of the same order as ρgz, and σ_h is relatively small. As shown in § 46 (ii) the crack will open in the direction perpendicular to the least principal stress, that is, in a vertical plane.

For sill formation, it is necessary to have a horizontal crack propagating. On the present theory this implies that the horizontal stress $\sigma_h > \rho gz$ and the condition for failure becomes

$$\rho gz - p + T_0 = 0, \quad \text{provided } 3\rho gh + \sigma_h < 4p. \qquad . \qquad (16)$$

The mechanics of the feeding of a sill by a dyke presumably is a complicated process connected with the raising of the horizontal stress by the intrusion.

[1] Cf. H. Odé, *Geol. Soc. Amer. Memoir* 79 (1960), 293.
[2] E. M. Anderson, *Proc. Roy. Soc. Edin.*, 58 (1938), 242.

The effect of pressure of pore-water, as well as volatiles from the intrusion, in the country rock may be important and can be allowed for as in § 45.

Other cases of the formation of dykes are attributed to tensile failures caused by magma pressure. Dykes are sometimes observed running radially from a vertical neck. In this case the theory is that of the opening of cracks radially from a circular cylinder with internal pressure which is studied in § 50 in connexion with hydraulic fracturing. The theory of dykes running from a vertical neck in the presence of a parallel impervious barrier is discussed by Odé.[1] Pressure of magma (or uplift due to a low magma density) in a magma chamber of approximately paraboloidal shape with its roof some miles below the surface will give rise to a system of principal stresses of which the least lie in approximately conical surfaces intersecting the paraboloid. Tensile failure across these is believed to give rise to cone sheets.[2]

(viii) *Overthrust Faulting*

If a block of material $OABC$ is to be moved across a horizontal fault surface BC by stress applied over a vertical face OC, this stress at any depth is limited by the strength of the rock, and hence the length l of the block which can be so moved is limited by the strength of its material. Hubbert and Rubey[3] have shown that the great

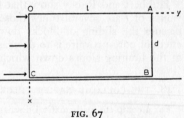

FIG. 67

lengths which appear to have been moved can be accounted for if due allowance is made for the effects of fluid pressure in the pores.

Consider the sliding of the block $OABC$, of length l and thickness d, Fig. 67, over the horizontal surface BC, there being no stress across AB. It is assumed that the vertical stress at depth x is $\sigma_x = \rho g x$ and that the pore-pressure $p = \lambda \rho g x$ where λ is a

[1] H. Odé, *Bull. Geol. Soc. Amer.*, **68** (1957), 567.

[2] E. M. Anderson, *Proc. Roy. Soc. Edin.*, **56** (1936), 128.

[3] M. King Hubbert and W. W. Rubey, *Bull. Geol. Soc. Amer.*, **70** (1959), 115, 167.

constant. The maximum stress σ_y which can be applied at depth x in the surface OC is, using the criterion § 44 (9) and allowing for pore-pressure as in § 45,

$$\sigma_y - \lambda \rho g x = (1-\lambda)\rho g x \tan^2 \alpha + 2S_0 \tan \alpha. \quad . \quad . \quad (17)$$

If the block is to slide along its base CB, the shear stress across this must be, by § 44 (1), again allowing for pore-pressure,

$$\tau = \tau_0 + \rho g d(1-\lambda) \tan \phi', \quad . \quad . \quad . \quad (18)$$

where τ_0 is the shear strength (if any) in the plane BC, and $\tan \phi'$ is the coefficient of sliding friction over it. For the block just to slide it is necessary that

$$\int_0^a \sigma_y \, dx = \int_0^l \tau \, dy, . \quad . \quad . \quad . \quad (19)$$

and substituting (17) and (18) in (19) gives for the length of the block

$$l = \frac{\rho g d^2[\lambda + (1-\lambda) \tan^2 \alpha] + 4dS_0 \tan \alpha}{2\tau_0 + 2\rho g d(1-\lambda) \tan \phi'}. \quad . \quad . \quad (20)$$

Hubbert and Rubey show that for reasonable values of λ the values of l are several times those for the case $\lambda=0$. They also discuss the sliding of blocks down slopes, and show that the effect of pore-pressure is to decrease substantially the inclination of the limiting slopes down which sliding is just possible.

48. THE COULOMB–NAVIER THEORY IN TERMS OF INVARIANTS

For a complete mathematical discussion of flow in a material obeying the Coulomb–Navier criterion, a development of the subject similar to that for the perfectly plastic solid is needed. Here only the beginnings of this theory will be given and it will be shown that, for the case of plane flow, the Coulomb–Navier theory can be expressed in terms of the invariants of § 27.

It was shown in § 27 that any yield criterion should be expressible in terms of the invariants I of the stress or J of the stress-deviation, so that it may be written

$$f(I_1, I_2, \ldots, J_1, J_2, \ldots) = 0. \quad . \quad . \quad . \quad (1)$$

Von Mises and later Drucker and Prager[1] have proposed a formulation of the relations connecting rate of strain with stress in which the yield function (1) is regarded as a 'plastic potential' and rates of strain are

---

[1] D. C. Drucker and W. Prager, *Quart. Appl. Math.*, **10** (1952), 157.

obtained by differentiating it with respect to the appropriate stress, that is,

$$\dot{\epsilon}_x = \lambda \frac{\partial f}{\partial \sigma_x}, \quad \dot{\epsilon}_y = \lambda \frac{\partial f}{\partial \sigma_y}, \quad \dot{\gamma}_{xy} = \lambda \frac{\partial f}{\partial \tau_{xy}}, \quad \text{etc.} \qquad . \qquad . \qquad (2)$$

where λ may be a function of position. This generalizes the assumption § 29 (3), and reduces to it in the case $f = J_2 - k$ previously considered. In other cases it has slightly different properties, and provides a more satisfactory formulation mathematically.

The yield function

$$f(I_1, J_2) \equiv a I_1 - J_2^{\frac{1}{2}} + k = 0. \qquad . \qquad . \qquad . \qquad (3)$$

will now be considered, and will be shown to be equivalent to the Coulomb–Navier criterion for the case of plane flows. If the system is referred to principal axes, the yield surface (3) is a circular cone whose axis is equally inclined to the σ_1, σ_2, σ_3 axes. In the case $a = 0$, this becomes the cylinder of Fig. 34 (b).

Using the values § 4 (18) and § 27 (21) for I_1 and J_2 in (3), (2) gives

$$\dot{\epsilon}_1 = \lambda \left\{ a - \frac{1}{2} J_2^{-\frac{1}{2}} \frac{\partial J_2}{\partial \sigma_1} \right\} = \lambda \left\{ a - \frac{1}{6} J_2^{-\frac{1}{2}} (2\sigma_1 - \sigma_2 - \sigma_3) \right\}, \qquad . \qquad (4)$$

with similar equations for $\dot{\epsilon}_2$ and $\dot{\epsilon}_3$.

In the case of plane flow in the σ_1, σ_2 plane, $\dot{\epsilon}_3 = 0$, so, by the equation for $\dot{\epsilon}_3$ of type (4),

$$6 a J_2^{\frac{1}{2}} = 2\sigma_3 - \sigma_1 - \sigma_2. \qquad . \qquad . \qquad . \qquad (5)$$

Squaring (5) and subtracting the value § 27 (21) of $12 J_2$ gives

$$J_2 = \frac{1}{4} (\sigma_1 - \sigma_2)^2 (1 - 3a^2)^{-1}. \qquad . \qquad . \qquad (6)$$

Using (5) and (6) in (3), the yield condition becomes

$$\frac{1}{2} (\sigma_1 - \sigma_2) = \frac{3a(\sigma_1 + \sigma_2)}{2(1 - 3a^2)^{\frac{1}{2}}} + \frac{k}{(1 - 3a^2)^{\frac{1}{2}}}, \qquad . \qquad . \qquad (7)$$

which is identical with the form § 44 (7) of the Coulomb–Navier criterion if

$$\sin \phi = \frac{3a}{(1 - 3a^2)^{\frac{1}{2}}}, \quad \cos \phi = \left(\frac{1 - 12a^2}{1 - 3a^2} \right)^{\frac{1}{2}}, \quad S_0 = \frac{k}{(1 - 12a^2)^{\frac{1}{2}}}. \qquad . \qquad (8)$$

In the same way it may be shown that the yield criterion

$$f(I_1, J_2) \equiv J_2 - A I_1 - B = 0 \qquad . \qquad . \qquad . \qquad (9)$$

leads to the parabolic relation of Griffith type

$$\tau_m^2 = 3 A \sigma_m + B + 3 A^2 / 4. \qquad . \qquad . \qquad . \qquad (10)$$

It follows from (2), and the form (7) of the yield condition, that the ratio of the principal strain rates is

$$-\frac{\dot{\epsilon}_2}{\dot{\epsilon}_1} = \frac{1 + \sin \phi}{1 - \sin \phi} = \tan^2 \left(\frac{\pi}{4} + \frac{\phi}{2} \right). \qquad . \qquad . \qquad (11)$$

Also, adding the three equations of type (4),

$$\dot{\epsilon}_1 + \dot{\epsilon}_2 + \dot{\epsilon}_3 = 3 \lambda a, \qquad . \qquad . \qquad . \qquad (12)$$

so that there is a change of volume on straining. This is a well-known property of granular materials.

This change of volume implies that, if faulting is restricted to a thin shear zone with a discontinuity of velocity δu along it, there must also be a discontinuity of velocity δv normal to it. To see this, suppose that the shear zone is of small thickness t; then the strain rate normal to it will be $\dot{\epsilon} = -\delta v/t$ and the rate of shear across it will be $\dot{\gamma} = \delta u/t$. If σ and τ are the normal and shear stresses, the yield criterion can be written in the form § 44 (1) as $f \equiv \tau - \sigma \tan \phi - S_0 = 0$, and using (2) gives

$$-\frac{\delta v}{\delta u} = \frac{\dot{\epsilon}}{\dot{\gamma}} = \frac{\partial f/\partial \sigma}{\partial f/\partial \tau} = -\tan \phi,$$

so that
$$\delta v = \delta u \tan \phi. \qquad . \qquad . \qquad . \qquad (13)$$

It follows, for example, that rigid body sliding around a circular arc is not possible: the circle has to be replaced by an equiangular spiral with the direction of sliding at $\frac{1}{2}\pi + \phi$ to the radius vector.

49. THE REPRESENTATION OF TWO-DIMENSIONAL STRESS FIELDS

A complete specification of the field requires a knowledge of σ_1, σ_2 and the principal directions at all points and, clearly, would be very complicated. However, certain simple combinations of these quantities appear, either mathematically or experimentally through photoelasticity, which give useful representations of some aspects of the situation. These are:

(i) *Isochromatics* which are curves along which the principal stress-difference is constant. They are the most directly obtained, and the most commonly reproduced, photoelastic results.

(ii) *Isoclinics* are curves on which the principal axes make a constant angle with a reference direction. They, also, are obtained immediately by photoelastic observations.

(iii) *Stress-trajectories* or *isostatics* are an orthogonal system of curves whose directions at any point are the directions of the principal axes. They intersect a free boundary at right angles. They can be calculated from photoelastic results but are not obtained directly.

(iv) *Isopachs* are curves of constant mean stress $\sigma_1 + \sigma_2$. The quantity $\sigma_1 + \sigma_2$ satisfies Laplace's equation [cf. § 35 (8)] and may be found by a subsidiary photoelastic measurement (of the thickness of the plate). It may be noted that $\sigma_1 + \sigma_2$ is readily determined at a free boundary since one principal stress vanishes at such a boundary and $\sigma_1 - \sigma_2$ can be found photoelastically.

(v) *Slip lines*, or lines of maximum shear stress, are an ortho-

gonal family of curves which at all points bisect the angles
between the directions of the principal stresses.

(vi) *Isobars* are lines of constant principal stress: there will be
one set for σ_1 and another for σ_2.

Systems with complicated boundaries, such as underground
excavations with irregular shapes, are commonly studied photoelastically; photographs of the isochromatics, together with calculated stress-trajectories, give a very good indication of the
stress-situation, and, in particular, show stress concentrations
very clearly. Many calculated isochromatics and stress-trajectories
for rectangular openings under various conditions are shown by
Savin (*loc. cit.*).

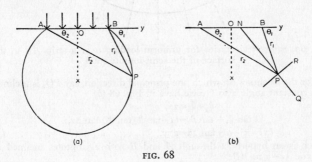

FIG. 68

Special Cases

In a few simple cases the curves mentioned above have simple mathematical forms so that the relationship between them can be clearly seen.
As an example, the problem of stress p over a strip of width $2a$ in the
surface of the semi-infinite solid will be discussed.

The principal stresses σ_1, σ_2 have been found in § 36 (16), and it follows
that

$$\sigma_1+\sigma_2=2p(\theta_1-\theta_2)/\pi, \quad \sigma_1-\sigma_2=(2p/\pi) \sin (\theta_1-\theta_2), \qquad (1)$$

so that *both* the isopachs $\sigma_1+\sigma_2=\text{Const.}$, and the isochromatics
$\sigma_1-\sigma_2=\text{Const.}$, are circles through AB, cf. Fig. 68 (*a*). For example on
the semi-circle $\theta_1-\theta_2=\frac{1}{2}\pi$, $\sigma_1+\sigma_2=p$, $\sigma_1-\sigma_2=2p/\pi$. To find the angle θ
which the principal axes at P make with Ox, the values § 36 (14), (15) of
σ_x, σ_y, τ_{xy} are used in § 3 (11) which gives

$$\tan 2\theta =\frac{x(r_2{}^2-r_1{}^2)}{(y+a)r_1{}^2-(y-a)r_2{}^2}=-\tan (\theta_1+\theta_2). \qquad (2)$$

It follows that one principal axis PQ makes an angle $\frac{1}{2}[\pi-\theta_1-\theta_2]$ with
Ox and thus bisects the angle APB Fig. 68 (*b*). Now it is a property of

the ellipse of foci A and B that the normal PN at P bisects the angle between the lines PA and PB joining P to the foci. It follows that the directions of the principal axes at any point are the tangent and normal to an ellipse of foci A and B, and thus that the stress-trajectories are a system of confocal ellipses and the orthogonal system of confocal hyperbolae. This system is shown in Fig. 69.

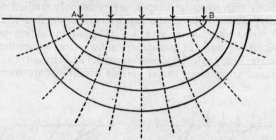

FIG. 69. Stress-trajectories for uniform loading over a strip AB in the surface of the semi-infinite solid

For the isoclinics, in which one principal direction, say PQ, is inclined at a constant angle α to Oy we have in Fig. 68 (b)

$$\theta_1 + \theta_2 = 2\alpha,$$

or
$$\tan \theta_1 + \tan \theta_2 = (1 - \tan \theta_1 \tan \theta_2) \tan 2\alpha,$$

or
$$(y^2 - x^2 - a^2) \tan 2\alpha = 2xy, \qquad . \qquad . \qquad . \qquad (3)$$

which is an hyperbola through A and B with asymptotes inclined at $-\alpha$ and $\tfrac{1}{2}\pi - \alpha$ to AB.

Photoelastic Observations[1]

The way in which the isochromatics and isoclinics appear as photo-elastic patterns may be seen by considering the simple case of plane polarization. Suppose a beam of plane-polarized light is incident normally on a sheet of material cut to the shape of the body to be studied and suitably stressed. Under the influence of stress the material becomes doubly refracting, and at each point there are two principal directions of vibration, coinciding with the directions of the principal stresses σ_1, σ_2, in which the indices of refraction are n_1 and n_2, where it is known experimentally that

$$n_1 - n_2 = C(\sigma_1 - \sigma_2), \qquad . \qquad . \qquad . \qquad . \qquad (4)$$

where C is a constant of the material.

---

[1] For fuller accounts see E. G. Coker and L. N. G. Filon, *Photoelasticity* (Cambridge, Ed. 2, 1957); M. Hetényi, *Handbook of Experimental Stress Analysis* (Wiley, 1950); A. J. Durelli, E. A. Phillips and C. H. Tsao, *Introduction to the Theoretical and Experimental Analysis of Stress and Strain* (McGraw-Hill, 1958).

Now suppose that Ox and Oy are the directions of the principal axes at a point O of the sheet, and that a ray of monochromatic plane-polarized light is incident normally on the sheet and that its vibration is $OF = a \sin \omega t$ in the plane OP inclined at α to Ox, Fig. 70. This vibration will be resolved into components $OG = a \sin \omega t \cos \alpha$ and $OH = a \sin \omega t \sin \alpha$ along the principal directions Ox and Oy, and these will be propagated with refractive indices n_1 and n_2. If the emergent beam is observed

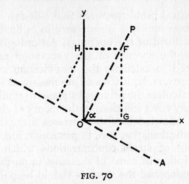

FIG. 70

through an analyser which only accepts vibrations in the plane OA perpendicular to OP ('crossed Nicols') the vibration seen through this will be

$$a \cos \alpha \sin \omega(t - n_1 l/c) \sin \alpha - a \sin \alpha \sin \omega(t - n_2 l/c) \cos \alpha$$
$$= a \sin 2\alpha \sin [\omega l(n_1 - n_2)/2c] \sin [\omega(t - (n_1 + n_2)l/2c) - \tfrac{1}{2}\pi], \quad (5)$$

where l is the thickness of the plate and c is the speed of light in vacuo.

If the material is unstressed, (5) is zero. For the stressed material, the amplitude of the vibration (5) is zero if either

$$\sin 2\alpha = 0, \qquad \qquad (6)$$

or $\qquad \omega l(n_1 - n_2)/c = 2m\pi, \quad m = 1, 2, \ldots . \qquad (7)$

The condition (6) implies that no light is transmitted when $\alpha = 0$ or $\alpha = \tfrac{1}{2}\pi$, that is, at all points at which the directions of the principal axes coincide with the directions OP and OA of the polarizer and analyser. Such points thus lie on a curve which is an isoclinic, and by rotating the polarizer (with the analyser remaining perpendicular to it) all isoclinics may be obtained.

Using (4), the second condition (7) may be written in the form

$$\sigma_1 - \sigma_2 = m\lambda/lC, \quad m = 1, 2, \ldots, \qquad (8)$$

where λ is the wavelength of the light. Thus curves on which the stress difference is constant and an integral multiple of λ/lC will appear dark. By knowing this constant and counting the number of curves, the stress difference can be determined absolutely. If white light is used instead of monochromatic, different wavelengths will be extinguished in different

13

positions and the curves will exhibit a regular gradation of colours: hence the name isochromatics.

With this simple arrangement both the isoclinics and the isochromatics appear at the same time. A simple modification, using circular polarization, allows the isochromatics to be observed alone.

50. STRESSES AROUND OPENINGS

In many practical problems, such as the design of support for underground excavations, it is necessary to estimate the stresses in the neighbourhood of the openings. Assuming that the principal stresses in the absence of any excavation are known, cf. § 47, it is desired to calculate the modification caused by the excavation, or conversely, if stresses are measured in the walls of an opening, to calculate the principal stresses in undisturbed rock.

There are many exact solutions in the theory of elasticity which give a detailed knowledge of the stresses around openings of simple mathematical shapes, and, in particular, indicate the position and amount of stress concentrations which might cause failure. A description of some of the most important of these is given in this section and the next. It should be pointed out that such solutions are of importance, not merely for sound rock, but to some extent also for unsound material, since, as remarked in § 43, such material also shows a rough proportionality between stress and strain (with different constants). For extensively fractured rock the Coulomb–Navier criterion for slip may be used in the form § 44 (9), and a few simple solutions for this law are also available.

In this section some exact solutions for the stresses around cylindrical openings of various shapes will be given. The z-axis and one principal stress will be assumed to be along the axis of the cylinder. Two-dimensional theory in the xy-plane will be used which includes plane stress and strain, discussed in § 14, as well as the case in which the displacements u, v are functions of x, y only while w is independent of x and y. In this case § 13 (10) can be written in the form

$$E\varepsilon_x = (1-\nu^2)\sigma_x - \nu(1+\nu)\sigma_y - E\nu\varepsilon_z,$$
$$E\varepsilon_y = (1-\nu^2)\sigma_y - \nu(1+\nu)\sigma_x - E\nu\varepsilon_z, \qquad . \qquad . \quad (1)$$
$$\sigma_z = \nu(\sigma_x + \sigma_y) + E\varepsilon_z. \qquad . \qquad . \qquad . \qquad . \quad (2)$$

These replace § 14 (8), (5) and provide a reasonable approximation to conditions in underground tunnels.

(i) *The Circular Hole of Radius a in an Infinite Elastic Region*

If the principal stresses at a great distance from the hole are p_1 in the direction of the x-axis and zero in the perpendicular direction, the stress-components in polar coordinates follow from § 35 (15) and the stress function § 36 (39). They are

$$\sigma_r = \tfrac{1}{2}p_1\left(1-\frac{a^2}{r^2}\right)+\tfrac{1}{2}p_1\left(1-\frac{4a^2}{r^2}+\frac{3a^4}{r^4}\right)\cos 2\theta, \qquad (3)$$

$$\sigma_\theta = \tfrac{1}{2}p_1\left(1+\frac{a^2}{r^2}\right)-\tfrac{1}{2}p_1\left(1+\frac{3a^4}{r^4}\right)\cos 2\theta, \qquad (4)$$

$$\tau_{r\theta} = -\tfrac{1}{2}p_1\left(1+\frac{2a^2}{r^2}-\frac{3a^4}{r^4}\right)\sin 2\theta. \qquad (5)$$

When $r=a$, (3) and (5) give $\sigma_r = 0 = \tau_{r\theta}$ as they should, and as $r\to\infty$

$$\sigma_r \to \tfrac{1}{2}p_1(1+\cos 2\theta), \quad \sigma_\theta \to \tfrac{1}{2}p_1(1-\cos 2\theta), \quad \tau_{r\theta} \to -\tfrac{1}{2}p_1 \sin 2\theta,$$

so that, by § 3 (13), (14), the principal stresses at infinity are p_1 in the direction $\theta=0$ and zero in the direction $\theta=\tfrac{1}{2}\pi$ as required. The stress function § 36 (39) is in fact found by assuming the form § 36 (36), (38) and determining the constants to satisfy the conditions at $r=a$ and $r\to\infty$. An alternative derivation of (3) to (5) will be given in § 51.

It follows from (3) to (5) that the disturbance of the stress field caused by the hole dies away like $(a/r)^2$. The stress trajectories are shown in Fig. 71.

The tangential stress at the surface $r=a$ is by (4)

$$\sigma_\theta = p_1(1-2\cos 2\theta), \qquad (6)$$

and so varies from a tension $-p_1$ at $\theta=0$ to a compression $3p_1$ at $\theta=\tfrac{1}{2}\pi$.

It follows from (3) and (4) that

$$\sigma_r+\sigma_\theta = p_1[1-2(a^2/r^2)\cos 2\theta],$$

and thus that the mean stress is tensile within the region bounded by the curve $r^2=2a^2\cos 2\theta$.

If the principal stresses at a great distance from the hole are p_1 and p_2, results are obtained by superposing two solutions of types (3)–(5). If $p_2=p_1=p$, we regain the result § 36 (9) for a uniform all-round stress at infinity. Subtracting this from p, gives for the stresses due to an internal pressure p with no stress at infinity

$$\sigma_r = pa^2/r^2, \quad \sigma_\theta = -pa^2/r^2. \qquad (7)$$

If the principal stresses at great distances are p_1, p_2, and there is an internal pressure p in the hole, combining (4) and (7) gives

$$\sigma_\theta = \tfrac{1}{2}(p_1+p_2) + \frac{a^2}{2r^2}(p_1+p_2-2p) - \tfrac{1}{2}(p_1-p_2)\left(1+\frac{3a^4}{r^4}\right)\cos 2\theta. \qquad (8)$$

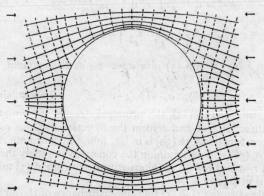

FIG. 71. Stress-trajectories near a circular hole in an infinite solid subjected to uniaxial stress

At the surface $r=a$ this becomes

$$\sigma_\theta = p_1 + p_2 - p - 2(p_1-p_2)\cos 2\theta, \qquad (9)$$

which varies from $3p_2-p_1-p$ at $\theta=0$ to $3p_1-p_2-p$ at $\theta=\tfrac{1}{2}\pi$. If $p_1 > p_2$ and the internal pressure p in the hole is increased, σ_θ becomes negative when $p=3p_2-p_1$ and a tension fracture in the plane $\theta=0$ becomes possible. This mechanism has been assumed by Hubbert and Willis[1] in a study of hydraulic fracturing of boreholes by internal pressure.

[1] M. King Hubbert and D. G. Willis, *Trans Amer. Inst. Min. Met. and Petroleum Engrs*, **210** (1957), 153. In porous rocks the effect of the pressure of pore-water also has to be considered. cf. § 45.

(ii) *Stress Concentrations around Openings of Various Shapes on Elastic Theory*

For the circular opening in a region with principal stresses p_1 and o at infinity, the tangential stress has been shown in (6) to vary from $3p_1$ to $-p_1$ around the periphery. Similar and more extreme variations occur in openings of variable curvature.

For the elliptical hole

$$x = a \cos \eta, \quad y = b \sin \eta \quad . \quad . \quad . \quad (10)$$

in a medium in which the stress at great distances is p_1 in a direction making an angle β with the major axis, the tangential stress σ_t in the surface is shown in § 51 (29) to be

$$\sigma_t = \frac{p_1[2ab + (a^2 - b^2)\cos 2\beta - (a+b)^2 \cos 2(\beta - \eta)]}{a^2 + b^2 - (a^2 - b^2)\cos 2\eta}. \quad . \quad (11)$$

If $\beta = 90°$, so that the stress p_1 is perpendicular to the major axis, σ_t varies from $-p_1$ at the ends of the minor axis to $p_1(1 + 2a/b)$ at the ends of the major axis, so that if b/a is small the stresses there theoretically become very large. If $\beta = 0$, the stresses at the

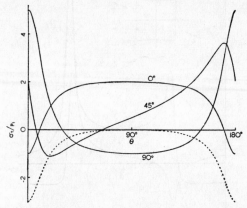

FIG. 72. Tangential stress σ_t as a function of polar angle θ around an elliptical hole $a = 2b$ in an infinite solid with uniaxial stress p_1 in a direction inclined at β to the major axis. The numbers on the curves are the values of β. The dotted curve shows σ_t for the case of internal pressure p_1 in the hole with no stress at infinity

ends of the major and minor axes are $-p_1$ and $p_1(1+2b/a)$, respectively. The variation of σ_t with the polar angle θ defined by $\tan\theta = y/x = (b/a)\tan\eta$ is shown in Fig. 72 for the case $a=2b$ and various values of β.

For the case of an all-round pressure p_1 at infinity, the tangential stress is obtained by adding the value of (11) with $\beta=0$ to that with $\beta=90°$. This gives

$$\sigma_t = 4p_1 ab[a^2+b^2-(a^2-b^2)\cos 2\eta]^{-1}. \qquad . \qquad . \quad (12)$$

The solution for an elliptic hole with internal pressure p_1 and no stress at infinity is obtained by subtracting a hydrostatic stress p_1 at all points from (12) and changing the sign of p_1 which gives

$$\sigma_t = p_1 - 4p_1 ab[a^2+b^2-(a^2-b^2)\cos 2\eta]^{-1}. \qquad . \qquad . \quad (13)$$

Holes of more complicated shapes can be treated by the methods of conformal representation sketched in § 51. In par-

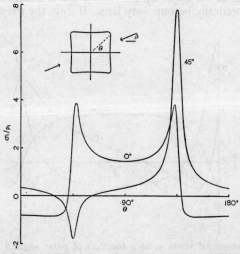

FIG. 73. Tangential stress σ_t as a function of polar angle θ in a nearly square hole (section shown inset) in an infinite solid with uniaxial stress p_1 at infinity in a direction inclined at β to a 'side'. The numbers on the curves are the values of β

ticular, Savin[1] develops transformations for regions whose shapes are approximately those of squares, rectangles and triangles with slightly rounded corners and gives formulae from which the stresses can be found. Fig. 73 shows the tangential stresses calculated from § 51 (39) for a hole of shape § 51 (37) with pressure p_1 at infinity in a direction inclined at β to Ox.

These calculations are of importance as indicating the variations of stress which may occur around openings: they are in good agreement with photoelastic measurements. For still more complicated shapes photoelastic measurements have to be used. It may be mentioned that when stresses are measured in underground openings it is the tangential stresses σ_t which are measured, and a knowledge of the stress concentration around the opening is necessary before the stresses in undisturbed rock can be inferred.

(iii) *The Stresses around a Circular Opening in Fractured Material*[2]

The material around an opening may often be regarded as being in a fractured state in which the stresses at each point are related by the Coulomb–Navier relation, cf. § 44. σ_θ, σ_r will be the principal stresses with $\sigma_\theta > \sigma_r$, so by § 44 (9) this condition becomes

$$\sigma_\theta = 2S_0 t + \sigma_r t^2, \qquad \qquad (14)$$

where
$$t = \tan \alpha, \quad \alpha = (\pi/4) + \tfrac{1}{2}\phi, \qquad \qquad (15)$$

and ϕ is the angle of friction and S_0 the shear strength of the material in the joints. Suppose a is the radius of the opening, p_i the internal pressure applied there to support it, and p the all-round pressure at infinity. The situation is supposed to be symmetrical, corresponding to a vertical shaft or borehole (in which case the radial pressure p is usually taken to be the load pressure) or a horizontal tunnel in which the effects of gravity are ignored. It is assumed that the material in the annulus $a < r < R$, where

---

[1] G. N. Savin, *Stress Concentration around Holes* (Pergamon Press 1961). The case of aeolotropic media is discussed by Savin and also by A. E. Green, *Proc. Roy. Soc.*, A**184** (1945), 181, 231, 289, 301. These authors also discuss a number of problems relating to two circular openings. Bipolar coordinates are used for this latter problem by G. B. Jeffery, *Phil. Trans. Roy. Soc.*, A**221** (1921), 265. The effects of gravity are discussed by R. D. Mindlin, *Proc. Amer. Soc. Civil Engrs*, **65** (1939), 619, and Yi-Yuan Yu, *J. Appl. Mech.*, **19** (1952), 537. Hyperbolic boundaries are discussed by H. Neuber, *Zeits. fur. appl. Math. Mech.*, **13** (1933), 439.

[2] The results given here are essentially solutions of well-known problems in soil mechanics, cf. K. von Terzaghi, *loc. cit.*; R. G. K. Morrison and D. F. Coates, *Canad. Min. Met. Bull.*, **48** (1955), 701; Talobre, *loc. cit.*, Chap. 10.

R is as yet unknown, is of the type described by (14) and that for $r>R$ the material is elastic.

For $a<r<R$, the stress-equation § 35 (13), namely

$$\frac{d\sigma_r}{dr}+\frac{\sigma_r-\sigma_\theta}{r}=0, \qquad . \qquad . \qquad . \qquad . \qquad (16)$$

still holds, and substituting (14) it becomes

$$\frac{d\sigma_r}{(t^2-1)\sigma_r+2S_0t}=\frac{dr}{r}, \qquad . \qquad . \qquad . \qquad (17)$$

the solution of which is

$$\sigma_r=\frac{2S_0t}{1-t^2}+Cr^{(t^2-1)}. \qquad . \qquad . \qquad . \qquad (18)$$

The condition $\sigma_r=p_i$, when $r=a$, gives C, so that

$$\sigma_r=\frac{2S_0t}{1-t^2}+\left(p_i-\frac{2S_0t}{1-t^2}\right)\left(\frac{r}{a}\right)^{t^2-1} \qquad . \qquad . \qquad (19)$$

and by (16)

$$\sigma_\theta=\frac{2S_0t}{1-t^2}+\left(p_i-\frac{2S_0t}{1-t^2}\right)t^2\left(\frac{r}{a}\right)^{(t^2-1)} . \qquad . \qquad . \qquad (20)$$

For $r>R$, by § 36 (5), the solution has the form

$$\sigma_r=p-A/r^2, \qquad \sigma_\theta=p+A/r^2. \qquad . \qquad . \qquad (21)$$

Equating the values (19), (20), (21) of σ_r and σ_θ at $r=R$ gives

$$\frac{R}{a}=\left\{\frac{2[p(t^2-1)+2S_0t]}{[p_i(t^2-1)+2tS_0](1+t^2)}\right\}^{1/(t^2-1)}, \qquad . \qquad (22)$$

$$A=R^2[p(t^2-1)+2tS_0]/(t^2+1), \qquad . \qquad . \qquad (23)$$

so that R is determined if p and p_i are known.

As a simple illustration, suppose $\phi=30°$ so that $\alpha=60°$ and $t=\sqrt{3}$, then

$$\left.\begin{array}{l}R/a=[\tfrac{1}{2}(p+S_0\sqrt{3})/(p_i+S_0\sqrt{3})]^{\frac{1}{4}}\\ \sigma_r=(p_i+S_0\sqrt{3})(r/a)^2-S_0\sqrt{3}, \quad a<r<R,\\ \sigma_r=p-\tfrac{1}{2}(p+S_0\sqrt{3})(R/r)^2, \quad r>R.\end{array}\right\} \qquad . \qquad (24)$$

In the region $a<r<R$ the directions of slip are inclined at α to the direction of least compression which is radial. Thus the equations of the slip lines are

$$\frac{dr}{r d\theta}=\pm\cot\alpha, \qquad . \qquad . \qquad . \qquad . \qquad (25)$$

so that they are the equiangular spirals

$$r=a\exp(\pm\theta\cot\alpha). \qquad . \qquad . \qquad . \qquad (26)$$

Perfectly Plastic Material

This is the case $\phi=0$, $\alpha=\pi/4$, $\tan\alpha=1$, and (14) becomes Tresca's criterion § 41 (1) for yielding in the perfectly plastic solid. (19) is replaced by

$$\sigma_r = 2S_0 \ln (r/a) + p_i, \qquad . \qquad . \qquad . \qquad . \qquad (27)$$

and (22) by

$$R = a \exp \{(p - p_i - S_0)/2S_0\}. \qquad . \qquad . \qquad (28)$$

(iv) *The Effect of Gravity for a Horizontal Tunnel*

A very crude approximation for the effect of the weight of the fractured material above the roof of a tunnel may be obtained by adding a radial body force ρg in the left-hand side of (16), cf. § 34 (1). The solution corresponding to (18) is then

$$\sigma_r = Ar^{t^2-1} - \frac{2S_0 t}{t^2-1} + \frac{\rho g r}{t^2-2}. \qquad . \qquad . \qquad . \qquad (29)$$

If the radius of the sound rock around the tunnel is b, and if it is assumed that the sound and unsound rock tend to separate at this level so that $\sigma_r = 0$ there, the value of A is determined by (29) and so

$$\sigma_r = \left(\frac{2S_0 t}{t^2-1} - \frac{\rho g b}{t^2-2}\right)\left(\frac{r}{b}\right)^{t^2-1} - \frac{2S_0 t}{t^2-1} + \frac{\rho g r}{t^2-2} \qquad . \qquad . \qquad (30)$$

This gives, approximately, the radial stress σ_r necessary to support an opening of radius r under these conditions.

(v) *The Alteration of Stresses Caused by Excavation. Rock Bolting*

Considering only the two-dimensional case, the stresses at depth h may be assumed to be known and a Mohr circle may be drawn for them. The circle AB, Fig. 74 (a), is drawn for vertical and horizontal stresses of $\rho g h$ and $\rho g h/3$, respectively. It may be assumed to lie well within the Mohr envelope for failure.

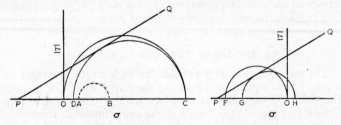

FIG. 74. The normal stress needed to prevent failure in an opening. (a) if the tangential stress in the wall is compressive, (b) if it is tensile

Now suppose that a tunnel is excavated at this depth. The principal stresses in its walls will be zero normal to the surface and $k\rho g h$ tangentially, where k is a numerical factor which can be estimated from the calculations of this section or determined photoelastically. It varies around the cross-section and may be negative. For a circular tunnel with the external stresses mentioned above, its greatest value, by (6), is $8/3$. The corresponding Mohr circle is shown as OC in Fig. 74 (a). This may well cut the Mohr envelope PQ, so that failure would occur. This Mohr envelope is not necessarily that for sound rock, but more probably a lower one corresponding to the disturbed rock in the immediate neighbourhood of the excavation. If a normal stress σ_2 could be applied to the surface of the excavation so that the Mohr circle becomes DC, this failure would be inhibited. Assuming, for simplicity, that σ_2 does not affect the tangential stress, its value is found by § 44 (9) to be given by

$$k\rho gh = \sigma_2 \tan^2 \alpha + 2S_0 \tan \alpha. \qquad . \qquad . \qquad (31)$$

A normal stress of this average magnitude can be applied by a regular pattern of long bolts, running normal to the surface of the excavation, securely anchored in the sound rock beyond the disturbed zone, and tightened. In the same way, the normal stress required in (19) and (30) can be supplied.

A second case arises if k is negative, say $k = -k'$, so that the Mohr circle after excavation is OF, Fig. 74 (b). A pattern of bolts arranged at an angle β to the surface will increase the tangential stress by $p \cos \beta$ and the normal stress by $p \sin \beta$, where p is a constant. The principal stresses will then be $-k'\rho gh + p \cos \beta$ and $p \sin \beta$, and § 44 (9) gives for equilibrium

$$p \sin \beta = (p \cos \beta - k'\rho gh) \tan^2 \alpha + 2S_0 \tan \alpha, \qquad . \qquad . \qquad (32)$$

which determines p, and from this the number and spacing of the bolts can be found. The new Mohr circle is GH.

Finally, similar methods may be applied in other cases. For example, if an average stress P is applied by rock bolts normal to the plane of weakness in § 44 (i), the only change is to add a term $P \tan \phi$ in the right-hand side of § 44 (1) so that the whole of the theory of that section may be taken over with S_0 replaced by $S_0 + P \tan \phi$.

51. THE USE OF THE COMPLEX VARIABLE

The use of the complex variable has very great advantages in the solution of plane problems on elasticity.[1] Firstly, it greatly simplifies the formulae for transformation of stress and strain; secondly, it extends the theory of the stress function; thirdly, it allows regions with complicated boundaries to be studied by the use of conformal representation.

[1] N. I. Muskhelishvili, *Some Basic Problems of the Mathematical Theory of Elasticity* (translated, J. M. Radok, Noordhoff, 1953); a good introductory account is given by I. S. Sokolnikoff, *Mathematical Theory of Elasticity* (McGraw-Hill, 1956), Chap. 5.

(i) *Changes of Axes*

It follows from § 3 (5), (6), (7) that the formulae for change of axes can be put in the form

$$\sigma_{x'} + \sigma_{y'} = \sigma_x + \sigma_y , \qquad . \qquad . \qquad . \quad (1)$$

$$\sigma_{y'} - \sigma_{x'} + 2i\tau_{x'y'} = (\sigma_y - \sigma_x + 2i\tau_{xy})e^{2i\theta}. \qquad . \qquad . \quad (2)$$

Subtracting (1) and (2) gives

$$2(\sigma_{x'} - i\tau_{x'y'}) = \sigma_x + \sigma_y - (\sigma_y - \sigma_x + 2i\tau_{xy})e^{2i\theta}. \qquad . \qquad . \quad (3)$$

This may be used immediately to give the boundary conditions at an element of surface whose normal is inclined at θ to the x-axis; if N and T are the normal and shear stresses across this surface, the boundary condition is

$$2(N - iT) = \sigma_x + \sigma_y - (\sigma_y - \sigma_x + 2i\tau_{xy})e^{2i\theta}. \qquad . \qquad . \quad (4)$$

(ii) *General Solutions for the Stresses*

It will now be shown that the general solutions of the equations of equilibrium can be expressed in terms of analytic[1] functions of the complex variable $z = x + iy$.

Firstly, since by § 35 (8), $\nabla^2(\sigma_x + \sigma_y) = 0$, it follows that $\sigma_x + \sigma_y$ is the real part of some function of the complex variable z which will be written[2] $4\phi'(z)$, the 'dash' denoting differentiation with respect to z, so that

$$\sigma_x + \sigma_y = 2[\phi'(z) + \overline{\phi}'(\bar{z})] = 4\mathbf{R}[\phi'(z)], \qquad . \qquad . \qquad . \quad (5)$$

where the 'bar' denotes the conjugate complex[3] and $\mathbf{R}$ stands for 'the real part of'.

Next, it follows from § 35 (6) and (7) that

$$\frac{\partial \sigma_x}{\partial x} - i\frac{\partial \sigma_y}{\partial y} + \frac{\partial \tau_{xy}}{\partial y} - i\frac{\partial \tau_{xy}}{\partial x} = 0. \qquad . \qquad . \qquad . \quad (6)$$

---

[1] Analytic functions have the following properties: (i) they are finite and single valued in any closed, simply connected region in the z-plane, (ii) they have differential coefficients of all orders, (iii) if u and v are the real and imaginary parts of an analytic function of z, they satisfy the Cauchy–Riemann equations $\partial u/\partial x = \partial v/\partial y$, $\partial u/\partial y = -\partial v/\partial x$, from which it follows that $\nabla^2 u = \nabla^2 v = 0$, (iv) they can be represented by series of powers of z. The theory of functions of a complex variable will not be needed here, but it is of great value in the higher developments of the subject.

[2] This form is chosen since the integral of $\phi'(z)$ appears in some formulae such as (8) and (9). The factor 4 is introduced to conform with Savin (*loc. cit.*).

[3] Note that if $\phi(z) = u(z) + iv(z)$ where u and v are real, $\overline{\phi}(z) = u(z) - iv(z)$, $\phi(\bar{z}) = u(\bar{z}) + iv(\bar{z})$ and the conjugate of $\phi(z)$ is $\overline{\phi}(\bar{z}) = u(\bar{z}) - iv(\bar{z})$.

Using $z=x+iy$ and $\bar{z}=x-iy$ as independent variables in place of x and y, this becomes

$$\frac{\partial}{\partial\bar{z}}\{\sigma_y-\sigma_x+2i\tau_{xy}\}=\frac{\partial}{\partial z}(\sigma_x+\sigma_y)=2\phi''(z),$$

where (5) has been used. Integrating gives

$$\sigma_y-\sigma_x+2i\tau_{xy}=2\{\bar{z}\phi''(z)+\chi''(z)\},\quad\quad\bullet\quad\quad\bullet\quad\quad(7)$$

where $\chi''(z)$ is an unknown function of z.

(5) and (7) are the fundamental expressions for the stresses in terms of two analytic functions $\phi(z)$ and $\chi(z)$. It may be verified that they correspond by § 35 (9) to the stress function

$$\tfrac{1}{2}\{\bar{z}\phi(z)+z\bar{\phi}(\bar{z})+\chi(z)+\bar{\chi}(\bar{z})\},\quad\quad\bullet\quad\quad\bullet\quad\quad(8)$$

which is the general solution of the biharmonic equation § 35 (11).

Displacements will not be studied here, but it may be noted that they, also, can be represented conveniently in complex form and the result obtained by integrating the stress-strain relations for plane strain is

$$2G(u+iv)=(3-4\nu)\phi(z)-z\bar{\phi}'(\bar{z})-\bar{\chi}'(\bar{z}).\quad\quad\bullet\quad\quad(9)$$

(iii) *The Infinite Region Bounded Internally by a Circle of Radius a*

The preceding theory applies immediately to the case of a circular hole in infinite material (or, with obvious modifications, to the region within a circle). Since the stresses must be finite at infinity, we assume for the functions $\phi'(z)$ and $\chi''(z)$ which appear in (5) and (7) power series of the forms

$$\phi'(z)=\sum_{n=0}^{\infty}c_n z^{-n},\quad\chi''(z)=\sum_{n=0}^{\infty}d_n z^{-n},\quad\bullet\quad\quad\bullet\quad\quad(10)$$

where c_n and d_n are complex constants.

As $z\to\infty$, $\phi'(z)\to c_0$ and $\chi''(z)\to d_0$ so that these can be determined from the prescribed principal stresses at infinity. Suppose that these are p_1 and p_2, the direction of p_1 being inclined at β to the x-axis, then (1), (2), (5), (7) and (10) give

$$\left.\begin{aligned}p_1+p_2&=\sigma_x+\sigma_y=2(c_0+\bar{c}_0)\\p_2-p_1&=(\sigma_y-\sigma_x+2i\tau_{xy})e^{2i\beta}=2d_0 e^{2i\beta}\end{aligned}\right\}.\quad\quad\bullet\quad\quad(11)$$

Considering next the boundary condition at the internal boundary $r=a$, the normal and tangential stresses N and T can be represented in the most general case by the complex Fourier series

$$N-iT=\sum_{n=-\infty}^{\infty}A_n e^{in\theta},\quad\quad\bullet\quad\quad\bullet\quad\quad(12)$$

so that, using (12), (5) and (7) in (4), with the values (10) of $\psi'(z)$ and $\chi''(z)$, gives on the circle $z=ae^{i\theta}$

$$\sum_{n=-\infty}^{\infty} A_n e^{in\theta} = \sum_{n=0}^{\infty}(n+1)c_n a^{-n}e^{-in\theta} + \sum_{n=0}^{\infty}\bar{c}_n a^{-n}e^{in\theta} - \sum_{n=0}^{\infty}d_n a^{-n}e^{(2-n)i\theta}. \quad (13)$$

Equating coefficients of $e^{in\theta}$ for all n gives

$$A_n = \bar{c}_n a^{-n}, \quad n \geqslant 3$$

$$A_2 = \bar{c}_2 a^{-2} - d_0; \quad A_1 = \bar{c}_1 a^{-1} - d_1 a^{-1}; \quad A_0 = c_0 + \bar{c}_0 - d_2 a^{-2}, \quad . \quad (14)$$

$$A_{-n} = (n+1)c_n a^{-n} - d_{n+2}a^{-n-2}, \quad n \geqslant 1$$

As an example consider the case $p_2=0$, $\beta=0$ with no applied stress at the interior of the hole so that all the A_n are zero. In this case (11) and (14) give

$$(c_0+\bar{c}_0)=\tfrac{1}{2}p_1, \; \bar{c}_2=-\tfrac{1}{2}a^2 p_1, \; d_0=-\tfrac{1}{2}p_1, \; d_2=\tfrac{1}{2}a^2 p_1, \; d_4=-\tfrac{3}{2}a^4 p_1, \; . \quad (15)$$

and the other c_n and d_n are zero with the exception of $d_1=\bar{c}_1$ and $d_3=2a^2 c_1$ which also are zero.[1]

Also, since c_0 only occurs in the stresses in the form $c_0+\bar{c}_0$, it may be taken to be real. With these values, we get finally

$$\phi'(z)=\tfrac{1}{4}p_1\left(1-\frac{2a^2}{z^2}\right), \quad \chi''(z)=-\tfrac{1}{2}p_1\left(1-\frac{a^2}{z^2}+\frac{3a^4}{z^4}\right). \quad . \quad (16)$$

To find the stress components in polar coordinates we use (1) and (3) which give

$$\sigma_r+\sigma_\theta=\sigma_x+\sigma_y=2\{\phi'(z)+\bar{\phi}'(\bar{z})\}, \quad . \qquad . \qquad . \quad (17)$$

$$\sigma_\theta-\sigma_r+2i\tau_{r\theta}=(\sigma_y-\sigma_x+2i\tau_{xy})e^{2i\theta}=2[\bar{z}\phi''(z)+\chi''(z)]e^{2i\theta}. \quad . \quad (18)$$

Substituting the values (16) of $\phi'(z)$ and $\chi''(z)$ in these gives σ_r, σ_θ and $\tau_{r\theta}$ in the form § 50 (3)–(5). It appears that the present method is more direct and much more general.

(iv) Conformal Representation: Curvilinear Coordinates

Suppose the transformation $z=\omega(\zeta)$ relates a point $z=x+iy$ on the z-plane to a point $\zeta=\xi+i\eta$ on the ζ-plane. The values of z for which $\xi=\xi_0$, Constant, and $\eta=\eta_0$, Constant, will be orthogonal curves in the z-plane specified by the *curvilinear coordinates* ξ_0, η_0. At every point P in the z-plane, Fig. 75, there will be two directions at right angles, $P\xi$, that of constant η, and $P\eta$, that for constant ξ. These may be taken as new axes at P, and the inclination δ of $P\xi$ to Ox is given by arg $[\omega'(\zeta)]$

---

[1] By (9), the terms $c_1 z^{-1}$ and $d_1 z^{-1}$ in $\phi'(z)$ and $\chi''(z)$ contribute a term $(3-4\nu)c_1 \ln z - d_1 \ln \bar{z} = \{(3-4\nu)c_1-d_1\} \ln r + i\{(3-4\nu)c_1+d_1\}\theta$ to $2G(u+iv)$. Now the displacements must remain unchanged when θ is increased by 2π so $(3-4\nu)c_1+d_1$ must be zero. This illustrates a point of some importance: it is possible to derive a great deal of information by fairly elementary considerations involving stresses only, but to obtain an unambiguous solution it is often necessary to refer to the displacements.

since $dx+idy=\omega'(\zeta)d\xi$ for $d\eta=0$. This may be written more conveniently in the form

$$e^{2i\delta}=\omega'(\zeta)/\bar{\omega}'(\bar{\zeta}).\qquad\qquad(19)$$

With this value of δ, the stress-components $\sigma_\xi,\ \sigma_\eta,\ \tau_{\xi\eta}$ relative to the curvilinear coordinates may be obtained from those in the $x,\ y$ system by the transformation formulae (1), (2) which give

$$\sigma_\xi+\sigma_\eta=\sigma_x+\sigma_y=2\{\phi'(z)+\bar{\phi}'(\bar{z})\},\qquad\qquad(20)$$

$$\sigma_\eta-\sigma_\xi+2i\tau_{\xi\eta}=(\sigma_y-\sigma_x+2i\tau_{xy})e^{2i\delta}=2[\bar{z}\phi''(z)+\chi''(z)]\omega'(\zeta)/\bar{\omega}'(\bar{\zeta}),\qquad(21)$$

where $\phi(z)$ and $\chi(z)$ may be expressed as functions of ζ but it must be understood that the differentiations are with respect to z so that

$$\phi'(z)=\frac{d\phi}{d\zeta}\frac{d\zeta}{dz}.\qquad\qquad(22)$$

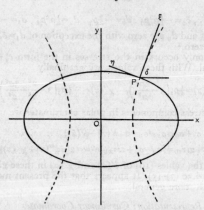

FIG. 75. Curvilinear coordinates

As an example, some results in elliptic coordinates will be sketched. The transformation is

$$z=x+iy=c\cosh\zeta=c\cosh(\xi+i\eta).\qquad\qquad(23)$$

so that

$$x=c\cosh\xi\cos\eta.\quad y=c\sinh\xi\sin\eta.\qquad\qquad(24)$$

If ξ has the constant value ξ_0, the point (24) traces out the ellipse

$$\frac{x^2}{c^2\cosh^2\xi_0}+\frac{y^2}{c^2\sinh^2\xi_0}=1\qquad\qquad(25)$$

as η varies from 0 to 2π. If $\xi_0=0$, the ellipse degenerates into a crack of length $2c$. The lines $\eta=$ Constant are confocal hyperbolae. The situation is as shown in Fig. 75.

The problem of the infinite region bounded internally by the elliptic hole $\xi=\xi_0$ of major axis $a=c\cosh\xi_0$ and minor axis $b=c\sinh\xi_0$ and with stress p_1 at infinity in a direction inclined at β to Ox is solved by[1]

$$\phi(z)=\tfrac{1}{4}p_1ce^{2\xi_0}\cos 2\beta\cosh\zeta+\tfrac{1}{4}p_1c(1-e^{2\xi_0}+2i\beta)\sinh\zeta, \qquad (26)$$

$$\chi(z)=-\tfrac{1}{4}p_1c^2(\cosh 2\xi_0-\cos 2\beta)\zeta-\tfrac{1}{8}p_1c^2e^{2\xi_0}\cosh 2(\zeta-\xi_0-i\beta). \qquad (27)$$

Substituting these expressions in (20) and (21) rather complicated formulae for the stresses may be obtained, and it is found that the boundary conditions at infinity and at $\xi=\xi_0$ are satisfied. Actually expressions involving $\sinh\zeta$, $\cosh\zeta$ which have period 2π in η are assumed, and their coefficients chosen in order to satisfy these boundary conditions. One simple and important result, the tangential stress σ_t at the boundary $\xi=\xi_0$, can be found immediately from (20) since $\sigma_\xi=0$ on the boundary. By (26), (20) and (22)

$$\phi'(z)=\tfrac{1}{4}p_1e^{2\xi_0}\cos 2\beta+\tfrac{1}{4}p_1(1-e^{2\xi_0}+2i\beta)\coth\zeta,$$

so when $\qquad\qquad \zeta=\xi_0+i\eta,$

$$\sigma_t=2[\phi'(z)+\overline{\phi'(\bar z)}]$$

$$=p_1e^{2\xi_0}\cos 2\beta+\tfrac{1}{2}p_1(1-e^{2\xi_0}+2i\beta)\coth(\xi_0+i\eta)$$

$$\qquad\qquad +\tfrac{1}{2}p_1(1-e^{2\xi_0}-2i\beta)\coth(\xi_0-i\eta)$$

$$=p_1\frac{\sinh 2\xi_0+\cos 2\beta-\exp(2\xi_0)\cos 2(\beta-\eta)}{\cosh 2\xi_0-\cos 2\eta} \qquad (28)$$

$$=p_1\frac{2ab+(a^2-b^2)\cos 2\beta-(a+b)^2\cos 2(\beta-\eta)}{a^2+b^2-(a^2-b^2)\cos 2\eta}. \qquad (29)$$

This result and some consequences have been discussed in § 50.

Finally, results for the crack $\xi_0=0$ are of considerable interest[2] both in connexion with the theory of Griffith cracks and energy release in earthquakes. For the crack in pure shear with principal stresses p_1 at $\beta=\pi/4$ and $-p_1$ at $-\pi/4$ the results take a relatively simple form, namely

$$\sigma_\xi=p_1(\cosh 2\xi-1)(\alpha-\alpha^2)\sin 2\eta, \qquad\qquad (30)$$

$$\sigma_\eta=p_1\sin 2\eta[\alpha^2(\cosh 2\xi-1)-\alpha(\cosh 2\xi+1)], \qquad (31)$$

$$\tau_{\xi\eta}=p_1\sinh 2\xi[\alpha\cos 2\eta-\alpha^2(1-\cos 2\eta)], \qquad (32)$$

where $\qquad \alpha=[\cosh 2\xi-\cos 2\eta]^{-1}. \qquad\qquad (33)$

---

[1] These results are given by A. C. Stevenson, *Proc. Roy. Soc.*, A**184** (1945), 129, who derives many others for the circle and ellipse by this method. Another method is used by C. E. Inglis, *Trans. Inst. Naval Arch.*, **55** (1913), 219. Alternatively, again, transformation on to the unit circle may be used, cf. Savin (*loc. cit.*).

[2] A full treatment of the crack in pure shear including a discussion of displacements and strain energy is given by A. T. Starr, *Proc. Camb. Phil. Soc.*, **24** (1928), 489. 'Penny-shaped' cracks are discussed by I. N. Sneddon, *Proc. Roy. Soc.*, A**187** (1946), 229, and R. A. Sack, *Proc. Phys. Soc.*, **58** (1946), 729, in connexion with the Griffith criterion. The case of a crack $|x|<c$, $-\infty<z<\infty$, $y=0$, subjected to shear τ_{yz} is considered by L. Knopoff, *Geophys. J.*, **1** (1958), 44, in connexion with strike-slip faulting.

The shear stress in the plane of the crack $\eta=0$ is

$$p_1 \coth \xi = \frac{p_1 x}{(x^2 - c^2)^{\frac{1}{2}}} \quad . \quad . \quad . \quad . \quad (34)$$

and tends to infinity as $x \to c$.

The mean stress $2\sigma_m = \sigma_1 + \sigma_2 = \sigma_\xi + \sigma_\eta$ is

$$\sigma_m = -p_1 \sin 2\eta [\cosh 2\xi - \cos 2\eta]^{-1}. \quad . \quad . \quad (35)$$

It is negative, tensile, in the first and third quadrants, and positive, compressive, in the second and fourth. These results give an indication of the way in which stress is redistributed after shear failure over a crack. Starr, *loc. cit.*, shows details of the distortion of the stress trajectories.

For the general case of uniaxial stress p_1 at infinity in a direction inclined at β to the major axis of the crack, the results are

$$\sigma_\xi + \sigma_\eta = p_1 \cos 2\beta + \alpha p_1 [(1 - \cos 2\beta) \sinh 2\xi - \sin 2\beta \sin 2\eta], \quad . \quad . \quad (36)$$

$$\sigma_\xi - \sigma_\eta = \alpha p_1 \cosh 2\xi \cos 2(\eta - \beta)$$
$$+ \alpha^2 p_1 \begin{Bmatrix} (1 - \cos 2\beta)(\cos 2\eta - 1) \sinh 2\xi - \cosh 2\xi \cos 2\beta \\ + \cos 2(\eta - \beta) - \cosh 2\xi \sin 2\beta \sin 2\eta \end{Bmatrix}, \quad . \quad (37)$$

$$\tau_{\xi\eta} = \tfrac{1}{2} p_1 \alpha \sinh 2\xi \sin 2(\beta - \eta)$$
$$+ \tfrac{1}{2} p_1 \alpha^2 [\sinh 2\xi \sin 2\beta (\cos 2\eta - 1) + (1 - \cos 2\beta)(\cosh 2\xi - 1) \sin 2\eta], \quad (38)$$

where α is defined in (33).

The case in which the stress p_1 is perpendicular to the crack is of special interest. On the x-axis $\eta=0$, so that, by (24), $\cosh \xi = x/c = X$, where X is a dimensionless ratio, and (36)–(38) give

$$\sigma_x/p_1 = \sigma_\xi/p_1 = X(X^2 - 1)^{-\frac{1}{2}} - 1, \quad \sigma_y/p_1 = \sigma_\eta/p_1 = X(X^2 - 1)^{-\frac{1}{2}} \quad . \quad . \quad (39)$$

so that both σ_x and σ_y tend to infinity as $X \to 1$.

On the y-axis, $\eta = \tfrac{1}{2}\pi$ and $\sinh \xi = y/c = Y$, and (36)–(38) give

$$\sigma_x/p_1 = \sigma_\eta/p_1 = Y(2 + Y^2)(1 + Y^2)^{-3/2} - 1, \quad \sigma_y/p_1 = \sigma_\xi/p_1 = Y^3(1 + Y^2)^{-3/2}. \quad (40)$$

The variation of σ_x and σ_y with $Y=y/c$ for this case is shown in Fig. 76(a). It appears that σ_x is tensile if $Y<0.8$.

These results are often used[1] to discuss the stresses about long thin plane ('tabular') excavations. Suppose that such an excavation of width $2c$ is made horizontally at a depth of kc in material of density ρ. As in §§ 34, 47 the vertical stress at depth z may be expected to be of the order of ρgz so that at depth kc it will be ρgkc. The effect of mining is to reduce the normal stress at the surface of the slit to zero, that is, by (40) to superimpose a 'mining-induced stress' $\{-\rho gkc[1 - Y^3(1 + Y^2)^{-3/2}]\}$ on the stress $\rho gz = \rho gc(k - Y)$ which existed before mining. Adding these gives for the vertical stress

$$\sigma_y = \rho gkc[Y^3(1 + Y^2)^{-3/2} - (Y/k)]. \quad . \quad . \quad (41)$$

This vertical stress is tensile if $Y<Y_0$ where Y_0 is given by

$$Y_0^2(1 + Y_0^2)^{-3/2} = (1/k) \quad . \quad . \quad (42)$$

Values of Y_0 as a function of k calculated from (42) are shown in Fig.

---

[1] J. C. Jaeger and N. G. W. Cook, *Fundamentals of Rock Mechanics* (Methuen, 1969).

76 (b). This gives a useful indication of the region in which tensile stresses exist, but it is approximate only, since the calculation does not accurately take the effects of gravity into account.

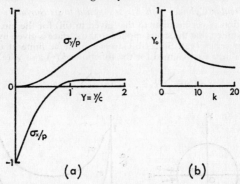

FIG. 76. (a) Stresses σ_x and σ_y on the y-axis of a flat crack with stress p at infinity in the y-direction

(b) The distance cY_o above a flat horizontal crack of width $2c$ at depth ck below the surface for which vertical stresses are tensile.

(v) *Conformal Representation: Transformation on to the Unit Circle*

The most powerful method which the use of the complex variable makes possible is the transformation of the region outside some curve on to the interior (or the exterior) of the unit circle. As an example consider the transformation

$$z=x+iy=\omega(\zeta)=a(\zeta^{-1}-\tfrac{1}{6}\zeta^3), \qquad . \qquad . \qquad . \quad (43)$$

which transforms the circle $\zeta=\exp i\psi$ into the curve

$$x=a(\cos\psi-\tfrac{1}{6}\cos 3\psi), \quad y=-a(\sin\psi+\tfrac{1}{6}\sin 3\psi) . \qquad . \quad (44)$$

and maps the region outside this curve on the interior of the unit circle. The curve (44) is shown in Fig. 73 and resembles a square with rounded corners. Problems on this region may be solved by a slight extension of the previous theory: for example it is found that for the region bounded internally by the cylindrical opening (44) with stress p_1 at infinity in a direction inclined at β to the x-axis, the function $\phi(z)$ is given by

$$\phi(z)=p_1a\left[\frac{1}{4\zeta}+(\tfrac{3}{7}\cos 2\beta+i\tfrac{3}{8}\sin 2\beta)\zeta+\tfrac{1}{24}\zeta^3\right] \qquad . \qquad . \quad (45)$$

so that the tangential stress in the boundary at the point corresponding to $\zeta=\exp i\psi$ is

$$\sigma_t=4p_1a\mathbf{R}[\phi'(\zeta)/\omega'(\zeta)]$$

$$=p_1\{105-360\cos 2\beta\cos 2\psi+168\sin 2\beta\sin 2\psi\}/35(5+4\cos 4\psi). \quad (46)$$

Values of σ_t for $\beta=0$ and $\beta=\pi/4$ have been given in Fig. 73. They are plotted against the polar angle $\theta=-\tan^{-1}(y/x)$ where x and y are given by (44).

14

The result (45) is taken from Savin's book (*loc. cit.*) where many similar results, including better approximations for square and rectangular openings, are given.

(vi) *The Circular Cylinder with Stress Applied to its Surface*

The solution is very similar to that given in (iii) for the circular hole. It will be assumed that the stress applied to the surface is given by the complex Fourier series (12). Since the stresses must be finite at the origin, power series in z are assumed for the functions $\phi'(z)$ and $\chi''(z)$, namely,

$$\phi'(z) = \sum_{n=0}^{\infty} c_n z^n, \quad \chi''(z) = \sum_{n=0}^{\infty} \mathrm{d}_n z^n, \qquad . \qquad . \qquad (47)$$

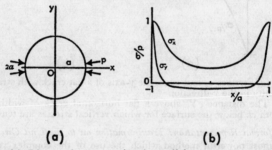

(a)   **(b)**

FIG. 77. (*a*) Diametral compression by radial stress p over arcs of 2α
(*b*) Stresses σ_x and σ_y on the diameter $y=0$

and the solution then proceeds precisely as in (iii). As a specific example of great importance, we consider the case of pressure p applied to a cylinder of radius a over the arcs $-\alpha < \theta < \alpha$, $\pi - \alpha < \theta < \pi + \alpha$, Fig. 77 (*a*). In this case the coefficients A_n of (12) are given by

$$A_0 = 2\alpha p/\pi, \quad A_{2m} = A_{-2m} = (p/m\pi)\sin 2m\alpha, \quad m = 1, 2, \ldots, \quad (48)$$

and $A_{2m+1} = A_{-2m-1} = 0$. The quantities $\phi'(z)$ and $\chi''(z)$ are found to be

$$\phi'(z) = \frac{\alpha p}{\pi} + \frac{p}{\pi}\sum_{m=1}^{\infty}\frac{\sin 2m\alpha}{m}\left(\frac{z}{a}\right)^{2m}, \quad \chi''(z) = -\frac{2p}{\pi}\sum_{m=0}^{\infty}\left(\frac{z}{a}\right)^{2m}\sin 2(m+1)\alpha. \tag{49}$$

Then from (17) and (18) the stress-components in polar coordinates are found to be

$$\sigma_r = \frac{2\alpha p}{\pi} + \frac{2p}{\pi}\sum_{m=1}^{\infty}\left(\frac{r}{a}\right)^{2m-2}\left\{1 - \left(1 - \frac{1}{m}\right)\left(\frac{r}{a}\right)^2\right\}\sin 2m\alpha \cos 2m\theta, \tag{50}$$

$$\sigma_\theta = \frac{2\alpha p}{\pi} - \frac{2p}{\pi}\sum_{m=1}^{\infty}\left(\frac{r}{a}\right)^{2m-2}\left\{1 - \left(1 + \frac{1}{m}\right)\left(\frac{r}{a}\right)^2\right\}\sin 2m\alpha \cos 2m\theta, \tag{51}$$

$$\tau_{r\theta} = \frac{2p}{\pi} \sum_{m=1}^{\infty} \left\{ \left(\frac{r}{a}\right)^{2m} - \left(\frac{r}{a}\right)^{2m-2} \right\} \sin 2m\alpha \sin 2m\theta . \qquad . \qquad (52)$$

On the loaded diameter $\theta=0$, $\tau_{r\theta}=0$, and the series (50) and (51) can be summed[1] to give

$$\sigma_x = (\sigma_r)_{\theta=0} = \frac{2p}{\pi} \left\{ \frac{(1-\rho^2)\sin 2\alpha}{(1-2\rho^2 \cos 2\alpha + \rho^4)} + \tan^{-1}\left[\frac{(1+\rho^2)}{(1-\rho^2)} \tan \alpha\right] \right\}, \quad (53)$$

$$\sigma_y = (\sigma_\theta)_{\theta=0} = -\frac{2p}{\pi} \left\{ \frac{(1-\rho^2)\sin 2\alpha}{(1-2\rho^2 \cos 2\alpha + \rho^4)} - \tan^{-1}\left[\frac{(1+\rho^2)}{(1-\rho^2)} \tan \alpha\right] \right\}, \quad (54)$$

where $\rho=r/a$. The variation of σ_x and σ_y with ρ for the case $2\alpha=15°$ is shown in Fig. 77 (b). If α is small, (53) and (54) tend to

$$\sigma_x = \frac{W(3+\rho^2)}{\pi a(1-\rho^2)}, \quad \sigma_y = -\frac{W}{\pi a}, \qquad . \qquad . \qquad (55)$$

where $W=2pa\alpha$ is the load applied per unit length of the cylinder. (55) implies that there is a constant tensile stress $-W/\pi a$ across the loaded diameter, and Fig. 77 (b) shows that this is nearly true if the load is applied over a small finite angle. This is the theory of the 'diametral compression' or 'Brazilian' test which is discussed from the practical point of view in § 54.

(vii) *A Cylindrical Inclusion in an Infinite Medium with Different Properties*

This problem[2] may be studied by combining solutions of types given in (iii) and (vi). As in (iii), only terms involving $\cos 2\theta$ and $\sin 2\theta$ appear. The simplest result, which illustrates the effects which appear, is that for the case of uniaxial stress σ_1 at infinity, in which the stress σ_1' in the inclusion is found to be homogeneous and to have the value

$$\sigma_1' = \frac{3G_0}{2G_0+G}\sigma_1 \qquad . \qquad . \qquad . \qquad (56)$$

for the case of plane strain and $\nu=\nu_0=\frac{1}{4}$, where G and G_0 are the moduli of rigidity of the outside material and the inclusion, and ν and ν_0 are their Poisson's ratios. The ratio σ_1'/σ_1 varies from zero for a very 'soft' inclusion for which $G_0/G\to0$, to $\frac{3}{2}$ for a very 'hard' inclusion for which $G_0/G\to\infty$.

---

[1] G. Hondros, *Aust. J. Appl. Sci.*, **10** (1959), 243–64, gives a full discussion of these formulae and their applications. See also J. C. Jaeger and N. G. W. Cook, *loc. cit.* Stresses in rings loaded in the same way are discussed by L. N. G. Filon, *Sel. Engng Pap. Inst. Civ. Engrs*, No. 12, 1924, and J. C. Jaeger and E. R. Hoskins, *Brit. J. Appl. Phys.*, **17** (1966), 685–92.

[2] Muskhelishvili, *loc. cit.*, and Wilson, *Proc. Fourth Symp. Rock Mechs. Penn. State*, 1961, 185–95. Goodier, *Trans. Amer. Soc. Mech. Engrs*, **55** (1933), 39–44, discusses spherical inclusions, and Edwards, *J. Appl. Mech.*, **18** (1951), 19–30, studies spheroidal inclusions.

52. DISPLACEMENTS

Throughout this work, the emphasis has been mainly on the calculation of stresses, largely because of their importance in connexion with failure. Nevertheless, direct measurement of stress is difficult, so that in practice stresses are determined from the displacements associated with them, and moduli of elasticity are calculated by measuring the displacements caused by a known applied stress.

In some problems, such as § 36 (i), the displacements are found in the course of the solution. More frequently, as in § 36 (iii), the stresses are calculated first, the strains are then found from stress-strain relations such as § 13 (23), and integration, together with a careful discussion of the arbitrary functions introduced, gives the displacements. If the complex variable is used, displacements are given by § 51 (9) which may be generalized to

$$2G(u+iv) = \kappa\phi(z) - z\overline{\phi}'(\bar{z}) - \bar{\chi}'(\bar{z}), \qquad . \qquad . \qquad (1)$$

where
$$\begin{array}{l} \kappa = 3 - 4\nu, \text{ for plane strain,} \\ \kappa = (3-\nu)/(1+\nu), \text{ for plane stress.} \end{array} \Bigg\} \qquad . \qquad (2)$$

The formula for rotation of axes is also needed. It follows from § 7 (5) that if u', v' are displacements referred to axes inclined at θ to those for u, v, then

$$u'+iv' = (u+iv)e^{-i\theta} \qquad . \qquad . \qquad . \qquad (3)$$

Some examples of practical importance will now be given.

(i) The Hollow Cylinder $a<r<b$ with Surface Pressures p_1 and p_2

For the case of plane strain, the displacement u radially inwards (the positive sense of this chapter) follows immediately from § 36 (4). It is

$$u = \frac{(b^2p_2 - a^2p_1)r}{2(\lambda+G)(b^2-a^2)} + \frac{(p_2-p_1)a^2b^2}{2G(b^2-a^2)r}. \qquad . \qquad (4)$$

If $b \to \infty$ and $p_2 = 0$, the displacement at $r=a$ is $-ap_1/2G$. This provides a method for measuring G in situ, cf. Talobre, loc. cit.

If $p_1 = 0$, the displacement at $r=a$ is

$$ab^2p_2(\lambda+2G)/2G(\lambda+G)(b^2-a^2). \qquad . \qquad (5)$$

If the solution of a problem in plane strain is known, that of the corresponding problem in plane stress may be obtained by replacing λ by $2\lambda G/(\lambda+2G)$. This statement, which is equivalent to (2), follows from the fact that if this substitution is made in the equations § 14 (4) for plane strain they take the form corresponding to § 14 (2) for plane stress. Using this result and § 13 (18) in (5), the displacement at $r=a$ for the case of plane stress is found to be

$$2ab^2p_2/E(b^2-a^2). \qquad . \qquad . \qquad . \qquad (6)$$

(6) has been used for laboratory measurements of E on hollow cylindrical cores.

(ii) *Plane Strain or Stress in the Region around the Circular Hole $r=a$ with Principal Stresses p_1, p_2 along the x, y Axes at Infinity.*

The stresses in polar coordinates are given by § 50 (3)–(5), the strains can then be calculated, and the radial and transverse displacements u_r and u_θ obtained by integration. However, it is simpler to insert the values of $\phi(z)$ and $\chi'(z)$ from § 51 (14) into (1), using (3) to convert from displacements u, v in the directions of p_1 and p_2 to the more useful radial and transverse displacements u_r, u_θ in polar coordinates. This gives

$$u_r = (p_1+p_2)\left\{\frac{(\kappa-1)r}{8G}+\frac{a^2}{4Gr}\right\}$$
$$+(p_1-p_2)\left\{\frac{r}{4G}+\frac{(\kappa+1)a^2}{4Gr}-\frac{a^4}{4r^3G}\right\}\cos 2\theta, \quad . \quad . \quad (7)$$

$$u_\theta = (p_2-p_1)\left\{\frac{r}{4G}-\frac{(1-\kappa)a^2}{4Gr}+\frac{a^4}{8Gr^3}\right\}\sin 2\theta, \quad . \quad . \quad . \quad (8)$$

where κ is defined in (2)

The terms proportional to r in (7) and (8) are the displacements which would be produced in an infinite solid by the stresses p_1, p_2 at infinity. The terms in r^{-1} and r^{-3} are the additional displacement caused by the existence of the hole.

These results may easily be generalized to the important case in which there is an additional constant axial strain along the hole and conditions in the perpendicular direction are those of plane strain. In this case, using (2), (7) is replaced by

$$u_r = (p_1+p_2)\left\{\frac{(1-2\nu)r}{4G}+\frac{a^2}{4Gr}\right\}$$
$$+(p_1-p_2)\left\{\frac{r}{4G}+\left(4-4\nu-\frac{a^2}{r^2}\right)\frac{a^2}{4Gr}\right\}\cos 2\theta - \nu\epsilon r. \quad (9)$$

(iii) *The Region Outside the Circular Hole $r=a$ with Pressure p Applied over the Arcs $-\alpha<\theta<\alpha$ and $\pi-\alpha<\theta<\pi+\alpha$ of the surface*

This is an example of the theory of § 51 (iii). The solution is determined from the functions

$$\phi'(z) = \frac{p}{\pi}\sum_{m=1}^{\infty}\frac{\sin 2m\alpha}{m}\left(\frac{a}{z}\right)^{2m}, \quad \chi''(z) = -\frac{2\alpha pa^2}{\pi z^2}+\frac{2p}{\pi}\sum_{m=1}^{\infty}\left(\frac{a}{z}\right)^{2m+2}\sin 2m\alpha. \quad (10)$$

The tangential stress σ_θ in the surface $r=a$ is found to be $p-(4p\alpha/\pi)$ in the loaded regions and $(-4p\alpha/\pi)$ outside them.

The radial displacement u_r at $r=a$ is given by

$$\frac{2\pi Gu_r}{ap} = -2\alpha - \sum_{m=1}^{\infty}\frac{1}{m}\left\{\frac{\kappa}{2m-1}+\frac{1}{2m+1}\right\}\sin 2m\alpha \cos 2m\theta. \quad . \quad (11)$$

The series in (11) can be summed if $\theta=0$ or $\theta=\frac{1}{2}\pi$, and if $\theta=\frac{1}{2}\pi$ and α is small the displacement is

$$(\kappa-1)\alpha pa/4G. . \quad . \quad . \quad . \quad (12)$$

Either (11) or (12) may be used to determine G if κ is assumed to be known.

(iv) *The Solid Cylinder of Radius a with Pressure p Applied over the Arcs* $-\alpha<\theta<\alpha$ *and* $\pi-\alpha<\theta<\pi+\alpha$ *of its Surface*

The displacements follow from (1) and § 51 (49). The radial displacement at $r=a$ is given by

$$\frac{2\pi Gu_r}{ap}=\alpha(\kappa-1)+\sum_{m=1}^{\infty}\frac{1}{m}\left\{\frac{\kappa}{2m+1}+\frac{1}{2m-1}\right\}\cos 2m\theta \sin 2m\alpha. \quad . \quad (13)$$

If α is small, the displacement at $\theta=\frac{1}{2}\pi$ is

$$-[2(\kappa+1)-\pi(\kappa-1)]\alpha pa/4\pi G. \quad . \quad . \quad (14)$$

(v) *Pressure p in a Crack of Width 2c in an Infinite Solid*

This has been discussed by Anderson, *loc. cit.* The solution can be obtained by the methods of § 51 by adding the results $\phi(z)=\frac{1}{2}pz$, $\chi(z)=0$, for uniform hydrostatic pressure p to the values of $\phi(z)$ and $\chi(z)$ deduced from § 51 (26) and (27) for an all-round tension, $-p$, at infinity. This gives

$$\phi(z)=\frac{1}{2}pce^{-\zeta}, \quad \chi(z)=\frac{1}{2}pc^2\zeta. \quad . \quad . \quad (15)$$

The displacements u_ξ and u_η in elliptic coordinates, § 51 (23), are by (1) and (3)

$$u_\xi+iu_\eta=(u+iv)e^{-i\delta}$$
$$=\{\kappa\phi(z)-z\bar{\phi}'(\bar{z})-\bar{\chi}'(\bar{z})\}\{\sinh \zeta \operatorname{cosech} \zeta\}^{\frac{1}{2}}/2G, \quad . \quad . \quad (16)$$

where δ is defined in Fig. 75, and its value § 51 (19) has been used. It follows that, using the notation § 51 (33),

$$u_\xi=(pc/8G)(2\alpha)^{\frac{1}{2}}\{(1-\kappa)e^{-2\xi}+(1+\kappa)\cos 2\eta-2\}, \quad . \quad . \quad (17)$$
$$u_\eta=(pc/8G)(2\alpha)^{\frac{1}{2}}(1-\kappa) \sin 2\eta. \quad . \quad . \quad . \quad (18)$$

If $\eta=\frac{1}{2}\pi$, that is, along the y-axis perpendicular to the crack,

$$u_y=u_\xi=(pc/4G)(2\cosh 2\xi+2)^{-\frac{1}{2}}\{(1-\kappa)e^{-2\xi}-\kappa-3\}, \quad . \quad . \quad (19)$$

where

$$\sinh \xi=y/c. \quad . \quad . \quad . \quad . \quad (20)$$

For the case of plane stress in which $\kappa=(3-\nu)/(1+\nu)$ this may be put in the form

$$u_y=-pc\{(1-\nu)[(1+Y^2)^{\frac{1}{2}}-Y]+(1+\nu)(1+Y^2)^{-\frac{1}{2}}\}/E, \quad . \quad (21)$$

where

$$Y=y/c. \quad . \quad . \quad . \quad . \quad (22)$$

The displacement caused by uniaxial stress p in a direction normal to a flat crack may be found by subtracting (21) from the displacement yp/E in the absence of the crack, so that it is

$$u_y=pc\{\nu Y+(1-\nu)(1+Y^2)^{\frac{1}{2}}+(1+\nu)(1+Y^2)^{-\frac{1}{2}}\}/E. \quad . \quad (23)$$

When $Y\to 0$, $u_y\to 2pcE$ and the crack will close when this is equal to the small length $c\xi_0$ of its minor axis. Thus, the normal stress p necessary to close a flat crack of aspect ratio ξ_0 under conditions of plane stress is

$$p=\frac{1}{2}E\xi_0. \quad . \quad . \quad . \quad . \quad (24)$$

This is not affected by a component of stress parallel to the crack.

(vi) *The Slab* $-\infty < x < \infty$, $0 < y < h$ *with Sinusoidal Displacements*

It is easy to verify that

$$\phi(z) = Ae^{i\omega z} + Be^{-i\omega z}, \qquad . \qquad . \qquad . \qquad (25)$$

$$\chi'(z) = (C - i\omega z A)e^{i\omega z} + (D + i\omega z B)e^{-i\omega z}, \qquad . \qquad (26)$$

where A, B, C, D are constants, leads to displacements of type $u = f(y) \cos \omega x$, $v = g(y) \sin \omega x$. Using these, various problems in which the surface $y = 0$ is free and displacements at $y = h$ are sinusoidal, or of any more general form, may be solved. Such problems correspond to uplift of an elastic region and have been studied in detail by Sanford.[1]

(viii) *A Line Load, P per Unit Length, is Applied to the Surface of the Semi-infinite Solid $x > 0$ at the Origin in a Direction Making an Angle β with the Normal to the Surface.*

The solution is obtained from

$$\phi(z) = (P/2\pi)e^{i\beta} \ln z, \quad \chi'(z) = -(P/2\pi)e^{-i\beta} \ln z. \qquad . \qquad (27)$$

If $\beta = 0$, the previous results, § 36 (10), (11), (12) follow from (27) using § 51 (17), (18), and the displacement is given by

$$2G(u + iv) = (P/2\pi)\{(\kappa + 1)\ln r - \cos 2\theta + i[(\kappa - 1)\theta - \sin 2\theta]\} \qquad . \qquad (28)$$

The displacement normal to the surface is

$$2Gu = (P/2\pi)\{(\kappa + 1)\ln r - (x^2 - y^2)r^{-2}\} . \qquad . \qquad . \qquad (29)$$

in the coordinates of Fig. 45. For a distributed load $p(y)$ on the surface, the displacement is

$$4\pi Gu = \int_{-\infty}^{\infty} \{\tfrac{1}{2}(\kappa + 1) \ln [x^2 + (y - \eta)^2] - [x^2 - (y - \eta)^2]$$
$$[x^2 + (y - \eta^2)^{-1}\}p(\eta)\, d\eta. \qquad . \qquad (30)$$

The displacement in the plane $x = 0$ is

$$4\pi G[u]_{x=0} = (\kappa + 1)\int_{-\infty}^{\infty} \ln (y - \eta)p(\eta)\, d\eta. \qquad . \qquad . \qquad (31)$$

Now consider the function

$$U = \frac{(\kappa + 1)}{4\pi G} \int_{-\infty}^{\infty} \ln[x^2 + (y - \eta)^2]^{\frac{1}{2}}p(\eta)\, d\eta. \qquad . \qquad . \qquad (32)$$

which is the logarithmic potential of a distribution $(\kappa + 1)p(\eta)/4\pi G$ on the plane $x = 0$, so that[2]

$$\nabla^2 U = 0, \qquad . \qquad . \qquad . \qquad . \qquad . \qquad (33)$$

and

$$\left[\frac{\partial U}{\partial x}\right]_{x=0} = \frac{(\kappa + 1)}{4G}p(y) \qquad . \qquad . \qquad . \qquad (34)$$

---

[1] A. R. Sanford, *Bull. Geol. Soc. Amer.*, **70** (1959), 19–51.

[2] A. G. Webster, *Partial Differential Equations of Mathematical Physics*, p. 200 (Teubner, 1927).

Since $[u]_{x=0}=[U]_{x=0}$ it follows that the value of u in the plane $x=0$ is known if U can be found, and since U is harmonic (although u is not) this is easily done by numerical or analogue methods if U or $\partial U/\partial x$ in the plane $x=0$ is known. A similar result holds in three dimensions. This method has been extensively used for studying surface displacements in extensive plane ('tabular' excavations: such as occur in coal and some gold mines). The effect of mining is to induce changes in normal stress over this surface and their effects can be calculated by the methods outlined above.[1]

53. UNDERGROUND MEASUREMENTS AND THEIR RESULTS

The object of this section is to indicate briefly the way in which formulae which have previously been deduced apply in underground measurements, particularly of stresses. Fuller descriptions of the methods are given by various authors.[2]

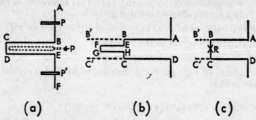

FIG. 78 (a) Flat-jack method
(b) Borehole deformation method
(c) Strain gauges on the flat end of a borehole

A knowledge of the state of stress underground is of considerable geophysical interest and is essential for the design of underground structures. Three different quantities may be measured or deduced from one another. These are: (a) *Virgin rock stresses* which are the stresses in a region in the absence of all excavation, (b) *Field stresses* which are the virgin rock stresses in a region as modified by all excavations in its vicinity, and (c) *Practical stresses*, which are those in or close to the wall of an excavation. If, for example, the stresses (c) are measured, a correction for the stress-concentration around the excavation, derived theoretically, as in

[1] Jaeger and Cook, *loc. cit.*
[2] J. C. Jaeger and N. G. W. Cook, *loc. cit.*; L. Obert and W. I. Duvall, *Rock Mechanics and the Design of Structures in Rock* (Wiley, 1967); E. R. Leeman, *J. S. Afr. Inst. Min. Metall.*, **65** (1964), 45–114, 254–84.

§ 50, or photoelastically, § 49, is made to deduce the stresses (*a*) or (*b*). Various methods of measurement are in use:

(i) The Flat-jack Method

This measures the stress in any direction parallel to a plane face *AF* of an excavation, Fig. 78 (*a*). In it, two measuring pins *P*, *P'* are cemented into the face and the distance between them is measured. A slot *BCDE*, usually about one foot square, is cut into the face in a plane perpendicular to the line *PP'* and the new distance between the pins *P*, *P'* is measured. From the change in length of *PP'*, Young's modulus for the rock can be found from § 52 (23). A flat hydraulic cell, shown dotted in Fig. 78 (*a*), is then cemented into the slot and pumped up. The pressure *p* in the cell at which the pins *P*, *P'* have returned to their original distance apart gives the normal stress in the rock in a direction perpendicular to the line *PP'*. The method is thus an absolute one, and its similarity to the definition of stress, § 2, is noteworthy. Measurements with jacks in three perpendicular directions give the components of normal stress in these directions. In practice, minor corrections have to be made; in particular, creep occurs and is usually allowed for by assuming a logarithmic law. As remarked earlier, this method only gives the stresses in the surface of an excavation and field or virgin rock stresses can only be deduced by allowing for the stress-concentration around the excavation.

(ii) Overcoring Methods, Fig. 78 (b)

In these, a borehole *ABCD* is drilled with diameter *BC* from a face *AD* and is continued centrally at *EFGH* in smaller diameter. Usually *BC* is of the order of six inches and *FG* of the order of one inch. In the borehole deformation methods, the diameter of the hole *EFGH* is measured in three or more directions by a sensitive, remote-reading device. Drilling at diameter *BC* is now continued to *B'C'* so that the region containing the hole *EFGH* is 'overcored' and the stress in it is relieved. The changes in diameter are given by § 52 (7) or (9), and from their values in three directions the magnitudes and directions of the subsidiary principal stresses in the plane perpendicular to the borehole can be found by the methods of § 10. The elastic properties of the material are found from measurements on the core. Measurements in three inclined boreholes give the complete state of stress. In variants of the method a stress-measuring device can be installed in the hole $EFGH$ or a plug containing a number of strain gauges can be cemented into it. These methods can be used to distances of some tens of feet from the face AD.

(iii) *Measurements at the End of a Borehole*

A simple method which has been much used consists of drilling a hole $ABCD$, Fig. 78 (c), with a flat end and attaching a rosette of strain gauges R to this end. This is then overcored at the original diameter along BB', CC' so that the stresses on R are relieved. As an alternative to the strain gauges a photoelastic disc may be attached to the end of the hole and observed optically. The difficulty with this method is that stress-concentrations exist at the end of the borehole $ABCD$ and that the values of these are not well known. Galle and Wilhoit[1] by photoelastic methods found the stress-concentration factors to be approximately 1·5 times the stresses perpendicular to the hole and −1·0 times the stress parallel to it but there is not yet general agreement on the values to be used. These methods may be used in holes of the order of 100 feet in length.

(iv) *Hydraulic Fracturing*

The mechanical methods described above can only be used for limited distances from an excavation. The method of hydraulic fracturing gives less information but is available at all distances. In it, portion of a borehole is sealed off by packers and fluid pressure in this region is increased until fracture takes place, as indicated by the fact that fluid can be forced into the hole. For radial fracture, this pressure is $3p_2 - p_1 + T_0$ by § 50 (9) where T_0 is the tensile strength of the rock. The direction of fracture, which may be observed with a borehole camera, is that of the major principal stress p_1.

(v) *Inclusion Stress-meters*

In these, a plug of material containing stress-measuring elements is inserted, with or without some pre-stressing, into the

[1] E. M. Galle and J. C. Wilhoit, Jr, *J. Soc. Petrol. Engrs*, **225** (1962), 145–60.

end of a borehole. The stress in the inclusion is related to the external stress by formulae such as § 51 (56). Inclusion stress-meters can be made absolute but are more usually used for monitoring changes of stress.

(vi) *Measuring Bolts*

These are rock bolts anchored at some distance in the rock and otherwise free so that the relative movement between the anchor and the surface or other points of the rock can be measured. If such bolts are installed radially at a plane end of a circular tunnel and the tunnel is then extended, the principal stresses can be inferred from the changes in displacement by § 52 (7).

(vii) *Measurement of Rock Properties* in situ

Laboratory measurements on selected samples are not always a good guide to the behaviour of rock in the mass. Measurements of rock properties can frequently be made in conjunction with underground stress measurements. For example, hydrostatic pressure in circular holes gives G by § 52 (4) and directed stress may also be used, § 52 (12). Sonic measurements, § 38, give useful information. Displacement across a flat-jack on slot-cutting gives E by § 52 (23), or on pumping up by § 52 (21). The method most used is the plate bearing test, § 43 (ii), and large direct shear tests are also frequently made.

(viii) *Results of Underground Measurements*

Much of the work done on stress measurement has been developmental so that sufficient measurements are not yet available to distinguish between the two simple formulae § 47 (1) and (5). A number of measurements favour the latter, and a rather lesser number, the former. However, a great many 'anomalous' cases have been found in most of which horizontal stresses are up to twice the vertical stresses, but occasionally vertical stresses considerably greater than the overburden pressure occur. A variety of causes has been suggested for these. First, they may be the effects of gravity in an irregular terrain. Secondly, there may be horizontal tectonic stresses whose effects would be enhanced by the stress-concentrations caused by surface irregularities. Other tectonic effects are possible; for example, high horizontal stresses have been measured in regions known to be undergoing uplift, notably Scandinavia. Finally, in rheological materials undergoing erosion, there is a possibility of residual stresses 'remembered' from a time when stresses were higher.

54. MEASUREMENT OF ROCK PROPERTIES

The measurement of uniaxial compressive strength and the triaxial test which determines σ_1 as a function of $\sigma_2=\sigma_3$ at failure remain the most important measurements made of rock properties. Young's modulus and Poisson's ratio are most frequently measured during tests of these types, though less direct methods, e.g. those based on § 52 (4), (6), (12), (21), (23), § 36 (30), § 43 (2), etc., may be used. In general, it is found that Young's modulus when measured in tension is less than the value obtained under compressive conditions. Elastic moduli may also be measured by sonic methods: P waves, § 38 (7), give $\lambda+2G$; S waves, § 38 (8), give G; and longitudinal waves in a thin rod give E. All these waves may be excited and detected by suitable transducers. It has been known for some time that values of elastic moduli measured by sonic methods are higher (of the order of 20 per cent) than those measured by static methods. This effect is attributed to minute cracks in the material, cf. § 56, and disappears at high confining pressures.

Direct measurement of the uniaxial tensile strength is not easy because of the difficulty of ensuring true axial loading. Extension failures are frequently studied by using shaped specimens in a triaxial apparatus so that the stress condition is $\sigma_1=\sigma_2>\sigma_3$. This does not give a true uniaxial value since $\sigma_3>0$. The so-called Brazilian or diametral compression test in which a circular cylinder is compressed along a diameter is also very commonly used. The tensile strength is calculated from the formula $W/\pi a$, § 51 (55), but since there is also a compressive stress in the perpendicular direction this does not give a true uniaxial value. However, tensile strengths measured in this way are in reasonable agreement with directly measured uniaxial values. This is not the case with the results of diametral compression of hollow cylinders or of experiments on bending, both of which give values of the tensile strength which are too high by a factor of two or more.[1] In these cases, the stresses are inhomogeneous and

---

[1] The various methods of measuring tensile strength are compared by

the discrepancy may be due to the effect of stress gradients on failure (cf. § 55) or to the difference between Young's modulus in tension and compression, or to a combination of these effects.

Measurements of the above types give no information about the effect of the intermediate principal stress, σ_2, on failure, and in view of the common occurrence in practice of *polyaxial stress systems* in which $\sigma_1 > \sigma_2 > \sigma_3$ it is desirable that this question be clarified. If σ_2 and σ_3 are fixed and σ_1 is increased until failure occurs, its value would define a surface.

$$\sigma_1 = f(\sigma_2, \sigma_3) \quad . \quad . \quad . \quad . \quad (1)$$

which will be called the *failure surface*. On the Mohr theory, § 22, in which the magnitude of σ_2 has no effect, this reduces to

$$\sigma_1 = F(\sigma_3), \quad . \quad . \quad . \quad . \quad (2)$$

and on the Coulomb–Navier theory, § 21, it becomes the plane

$$\sigma_1 = C_0 + k\sigma_3, \quad . \quad . \quad . \quad . \quad (3)$$

where C_0 is the uniaxial compressive strength, and $k = \tan^2(\frac{1}{4}\pi + \frac{1}{2}\phi)$, § 44 (9).

A hypothetical failure surface is shown in Fig. 79: the information readily available about it is the points C_0 and T_0 corresponding to uniaxial compression and tension, and the curve $C_0 T$ corresponding to triaxial compression. On the basis of (3) or the modified Griffith theory, § 46 (iii), $C_0 T$ would be a straight line: in fact, it is usually concave downwards and probably better represented by a power law. Failure under biaxial stresses on the basis of (1) should give a curve $C_0 B$, and, in general, the surface can be mapped experimentally. However, it is difficult to work with homogeneous polyaxial stresses because of friction at platens but such experiments[1] indicate an effect of σ_2.

By using thick-walled hollow cylinders with axial load and internal or external pressure a wide variety of stress-conditions

R. Berenbaum and I. Brodie, *Brit. J. Appl. Phys.*, **10** (1959), 281–6, and J. C. Jaeger and E. R. Hoskins, *ibid.*, **17** (1966), 685–92.

[1] G. A. Wiebols, J. C. Jaeger and N. G. W. Cook, *Tenth Rock Mechs. Symp. Houston* (1968) have minimized friction by applying σ_2 and σ_3 by flat-jacks. J. Handin, H. C. Heard and J. N. Magourk, *J. Geophys. Res.* **72** (1967), 611–40, obtain approximately homogeneous stresses by using thin-walled hollow cylinders as in the classical experiments on metals, § 27.

may be obtained and the failure surface mapped.[1] These experiments show an important influence of σ_2, but since the stresses are inhomogeneous their results may also include the effects of stress gradients.

The type of behaviour to be expected under polyaxial systems of stress may be seen most easily from an empirical generalization of Griffith theory due to Murrell (*loc. cit.*) in which the parabola

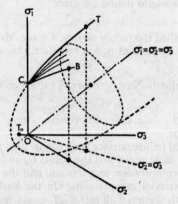

FIG. 79. Portion TC_0B of the failure surface under compressive conditions on Murrell's paraboloidal assumption

§ 24 (5) with axis along $\sigma_1=\sigma_2$ is replaced by a paraboloid with axis along $\sigma_1=\sigma_2=\sigma_3$, Fig. 79. The equation of the failure surface in this case under compressive conditions becomes

$$(\sigma_2-\sigma_3)^2+(\sigma_3-\sigma_1)^2+(\sigma_1-\sigma_2)^2=24T_0(\sigma_1+\sigma_2+\sigma_3), \qquad (4)$$

where T_0 is the uniaxial compressive strength. It follows from (4) that the uniaxial compressive strength $C_0=12T_0$. For biaxial stress, $\sigma_3=0$, (4) becomes

$$\sigma_1{}^2-\sigma_1\sigma_2+\sigma_2{}^2=C_0(\sigma_1+\sigma_2) \qquad . \qquad . \qquad (5)$$

[1] J. C. Jaeger and N. G. W. Cook, *loc. cit.*; J. C. Jaeger, *Proc. Eighth Symp. Rock Mechs. Minnesota* (1967), 1–57; S. A. F. Murrell, *Proc. Fifth Rock Mechs. Symp. Minnesota* (1963), 563–77; J. C. Jaeger and E. R. Hoskins, *J. Geophys. Res.*, **71** (1966), 2651.

55. EFFECTS OF FLAWS, SIZE AND STRESS GRADIENT

As remarked in § 52, the various methods of measuring tensile strength lead to different values, and this has been attributed to the statistical effect of flaws in the material. The following simple argument shows the sort of effects to be expected. Suppose that $P_0(\sigma)$ is the probability that a specimen of unit volume will fail under tensile stress σ so that $1 - P_0(\sigma)$ is the probability that it will not fail. If m such specimens are arranged in series, the probability $1 - P(\sigma)$ that none of them will fail under stress σ is given by

$$1 - P(\sigma) = [1 - P_0(\sigma)]^m = [1 - P_0(\sigma)]^V = \exp \{V \ln (1 - P_0(\sigma))\}, \quad . \quad (1)$$

where V is the total volume of the specimen. Since $1 - P(\sigma) < 1$ we may write

$$\ln [1 - P_0(\sigma)] = -n(\sigma), \quad . \quad . \quad . \quad (2)$$

and (1) becomes $P(\sigma) = 1 - \exp (-V n(\sigma))$ which may be generalized to

$$P(\sigma) = 1 - \exp \{- \int n(\sigma) \, dv\}, \quad . \quad . \quad . \quad (3)$$

if the stress varies over the volume V of the specimen and the integral is taken over this volume. The mean stress at failure is then

$$\bar{\sigma} = \int_0^1 \sigma \, dP = - \int_0^\infty \sigma \frac{d(1-P)}{d\sigma} d\sigma = \left[-\sigma(1-P) \right]_0^\infty + \int_0^\infty (1-P) \, d\sigma$$

$$= \int_0^\infty \exp \{- \int n(\sigma) \, dv\} \, d\sigma. \quad . \quad . \quad . \quad (4)$$

Weibull[1] makes the simple assumption

$$n(\sigma) = k\sigma^m, \quad . \quad . \quad . \quad . \quad (5)$$

where k and m are constants. This assumption leads to integrals which are easy to evaluate and gives generally good agreement with observation.

Using (5) in (4) gives for uniform stress σ

$$\bar{\sigma} = \int_0^\infty \exp \{-kV\sigma^m\} \, d\sigma = (kV)^{-1/m} I_m, \quad . \quad . \quad (6)$$

where

$$I_m = \int_0^\infty \exp (-z^m) \, dz \quad . \quad . \quad . \quad . \quad (7)$$

The value of I_m ranges from $\frac{1}{2}\pi^{\frac{1}{2}} = 0.886$ when $m = 2$ to 0.963 when $m = 16$, so that it is always near unity and its variation is not important. The important conclusion from (6) is that for homogeneous tensile stress σ, the mean stress at failure decreases with specimen volume according to the power law $V^{-1/m}$.

---

[1] W. Weibull, *Ingvetensk. Akad. Handl.*, No. 151 (1939).

The effect of inhomogeneous stresses may be illustrated by considering the simple case of a beam bent by couples M (four-point bending). If the depth of the beam is $2b$ and σ_f is the extreme fibre stress when $y=b$, it follows from § 36 (22) (23) that the stress σ_x at depth y is

$$\sigma_x=(y/b)\sigma_f. \qquad \qquad (8)$$

Here the stress is tensile (positive with the convention of § 32) and if $y<0$ the stresses are compressive and assumed to have no effect. Using (8) and (5) in (3) it follows that for a beam of width a and length l and (5)

$$P(\sigma) = 1-\exp\left\{ -kal(\sigma_f)^m \int_0^b (y/b)^m \, dy\right\}$$
$$= 1-\exp\{-kV\sigma_f{}^m/(2m+2)\}, \qquad \qquad (9)$$

where V is the volume of the beam.

Using (9) in (4) it follows that the mean value $\bar{\sigma}_f$ of the extreme fibre stress is

$$\left. \begin{aligned} \bar{\sigma}_f &= \int_0^\infty \exp\{-kV\sigma_f{}^m/(2m+2)\}\,\mathrm{d}\sigma_f \\ &= [kV/(2m+2)]^{-1/m}I_m = (2m+2)^{1/m}\bar{\sigma}, \end{aligned} \right\} \qquad (10)$$

using (6), where $\bar{\sigma}$ is the mean failure stress for the same volume in pure tension. The numerical factor is $1\cdot78$ for $m=4$ and $1\cdot44$ for $m=8$. Other cases of inhomogeneous stress may be studied in the same way. For $m=8$ the ratio of the mean value of the extreme stress to the mean value in pure tension is $1\cdot89$ for three-point bending of a rectangular beam, $1\cdot41$ for internal pressure in a $2:1$ hollow cylinder, and $1\cdot28$ in torsion. Results of this type provide a possible explanation for the difference between values of tensile strength measured by different methods using inhomogeneous stresses. Durelli and Parks[1] interpreted their results in terms of the volume V_{95} of the specimen subjected to 95 per cent of the maximum stress and showed that if experimental values of the stress at failure are plotted against $\ln(V_{95})$ a good straight line covering the results of all experimental systems is obtained.

The simplified discussion above refers specifically to tensile conditions. It is known experimentally that similar results hold under compressive conditions. For example, it is found for coal[2] that the crushing strength σ_c of cubes of side a is given by

$$\sigma_c = pa^{-\alpha} \qquad \qquad (11)$$

where p and α are constants and α varies between $0\cdot2$ and $0\cdot5$. For a specimen of height a and least diameter d this is generalized to

$$\sigma_c = qa^{-\beta}d^\gamma, \qquad \qquad (12)$$

where q, β and γ are constants. Relations of this sort are of great importance in the design of pillars in mines.

[1] A. J. Durelli and V. Parks, *Proc. Fourth U.S. Cong. Appl. Math.* (1962), 931–8.

[2] I. Evans and C. D. Pomeroy, in *Mechanical Properties of Non-metallic and Brittle Materials* (Butterworths, London, 1958), 5–28.

An alternative approach due to Protodiakonov[1] leads to the formula

$$\sigma_d/\sigma_r = 1 + C/[(d/b)+1], \quad . \quad . \quad . \quad (13)$$

where σ_r is the crushing strength of the rock mass as a whole, σ_d is the crushing strength of a cylindrical specimen of diameter d, b is the average spacing between flaws in the rock, and C is a parameter depending on the nature of the rock. This formula is in good agreement with observations on coal.

56. THE COMPLETE STRESS-STRAIN CURVE

In § 12, it was stated that when brittle materials such as rocks are tested in uniaxial compression they show the behaviour of Fig. 19 (c) and fail suddenly with complete loss of cohesion. It has only recently been appreciated that such catastrophic failure is caused by instability of the whole system consisting of the specimen and the testing machine. When rock is stressed in a

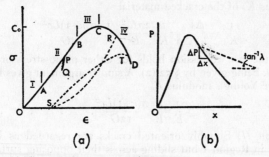

FIG. 80 (a) The complete stress-strain curve
       (b) Load-displacement curve showing conditions for instability

sufficiently stiff testing machine, sudden failure may not occur and rock which will be described as having failed can still sustain considerable load. This is of great practical importance.

The stress-strain curve measured in a stiff testing machine is known as the *complete stress-strain curve* and its details give important information about the mechanism of failure. The curve, Fig. 80 (a), divides essentially into four regions: I, *OA*, in which it is concave upwards; II, an approximately linear region, *AB*;

[1] M. N. Protodiakonov, *Fourth Int. Conf. Strata Control and Rock Mechs.* (1964).

III, a region BC in which it is concave downwards reaching a maximum at C; IV, a falling region CD. The maximum ordinate of the curve at C is the uniaxial compressive strength C_0 and the rock will be described as having failed at this point. The processes involved in the four regions will now be discussed in detail.[1]

Region I. This region is associated with the closing of open cracks, cf. § 43. The effect of open cracks is to decrease the elastic moduli of the body. This may be seen most easily for the bulk modulus. Suppose that volume V_0 of the body contains length LV_0 of cracks which will be taken to be in plane stress so that the previous formula § 52 (23) can be used. This shows that an increase Δp in hydrostatic pressure, which gives an increase Δp in normal stress across the cracks, causes a decrease in volume $2\pi c^2 L V_0 \Delta p / E$ of the cracks and a decrease in volume $V_0 \Delta p / K$ of the solid material. Adding these gives for the effective bulk modulus K_c of the cracked material

$$\frac{1}{K_c} = -\frac{\Delta V_0}{V_0 \Delta p} = \frac{1}{K} + \frac{2\pi L c^2}{E} = \frac{1}{K} + \frac{\pi(\kappa+1)Lc^2}{4G}, \qquad (1)$$

where the last expression holds for either plane stress or plane strain, κ being given by § 52 (2). A similar argument gives for the effective Young's modulus E_c

$$\frac{1}{E_c} = \frac{1}{E} + \frac{\pi(\kappa+1)Lc^2}{12G}. \qquad (2)$$

Region II. Suitably oriented cracks are regarded as having closed[2] in Region I but sliding across their opposing surfaces is assumed to occur as in § 46 (iii). It follows that in this region Young's modulus is less than its value for the uncracked material. However, if the stress is lowered at any point P, reverse sliding

---

[1] The complete stress-strain curve for concrete and the effects associated with it was discussed very fully by P. R. Barnard, *Mag. Concr. Res.*, **16** (1964), 203. The study of rock properties in stiff machines is discussed by G. A. Wiebols, J. C. Jaeger and N. G. W. Cook, *loc. cit.*

[2] W. F. Brace, *J. Geophys. Res.*, **70** (1965), 391–8, and J. B. Walsh, *ibid.*, **70** (1965), 399–411, **70** (1965), 5249–57, **71** (1966), 2591–9, have discussed in detail the effect of cracks on the elastic properties of rock. W. F. Brace, A. S. Orange and T. R. Madden, *J. Geophys. Res.*, **70** (1965), 5669–78, have shown that changes in the electrical conductivity of rocks (determined largely by fluid in cracks) may be related to the closing of cracks.

will not begin immediately so that the slope of the unloading curve PQ should give E for the uncracked material.

Region III. In this region it is believed that existing cracks begin to propagate stably so that the stress corresponding to the point B would correspond to criteria of the Griffith type which indicate when an existing crack would begin to grow. As the stress is increased, the network of cracks increases irreversibly and at C the material is regarded as having failed.

Region IV. The failed material can still support considerable stress and if the sample is unloaded and reloaded as at RST there is permanent set OS and a maximum stress is attained at T.

The way in which the stress-strain curve is affected by the stiffness of the testing machine will now be discussed. It is a little more convenient to work in terms of the load-displacement curve, Fig. 80 (*b*) in which P is the load applied to the specimen and x the relative displacement of its ends. Let the stiffness (force per unit displacement) of the testing machine be λ. In the falling region of the stress-strain curve, an increase of displacement Δx leads to a fall ΔP in the load which the specimen can support, and for the system to be stable this must be less than the fall $\lambda \Delta x$ in the load applied by the machine. That is, the condition for stability is

$$\left| \frac{dP}{dx} \right| < \lambda. \qquad . \qquad . \qquad . \qquad (3)$$

If this condition is not satisfied, sudden failure, usually very near the point C, results, the load-displacement curve following a path determined by the stiffness of the machine, which for many machines is of the order 10^6 lb./in.

The behaviour described above is for uniaxial compression. Similar behaviour occurs for triaxial compression except that the curve CD tends asymptotically to a fixed value (the *residual strength*) corresponding to sliding across a plane of shear failure. For soft machines there is unstable failure, AB of Fig. 60, at the maximum stress.

The fact that 'failed' material in the region CD can support considerable load is of the greatest practical importance: it implies that failed material can be useful, and that what has to be avoided is unstable failure. For example, failed pillars, or the ring of failed rock around a tunnel, may support considerable load.

The conditions for stable failure in the latter case may be found as follows. Suppose that there is a thin layer of failed rock of thickness t on the inside of a circular tunnel of radius a. Let σ_r and u_r be the radial stress and displacement inwards of the annulus at the boundary. The stiffness of the solid material which is stressing the annulus is $2G/a$, by § 52 (4) so that, as in (3), the criterion for stability of the annulus is

$$\left|\frac{d\sigma_r}{du_r}\right| < \frac{2G}{a}. \qquad . \qquad . \qquad . \qquad (4)$$

Let σ and ε be the tangential displacement and strain in the annulus: these are the quantities which appear in its stress-strain curve. From statical considerations they are related to σ_r and u_r by

$$t\sigma = a\sigma_r, \quad \text{and} \quad \varepsilon = u_r/a. \qquad . \qquad . \qquad (5)$$

Using (5) in (4), the criterion for stability becomes

$$\left|\frac{d\sigma}{d\varepsilon}\right| < \frac{2aG}{t}. \qquad . \qquad . \qquad . \qquad (6)$$

The theory of § 50 (iii) may be extended to the case of solid material outside a region of fractured material whose complete stress-strain curve is known.

CHAPTER V

APPLICATIONS TO STRUCTURAL GEOLOGY

57. INTRODUCTORY

THE theory of finite strain developed in §§ 6–9 is fundamental for structural geology. In particular, the theory of finite homogeneous strain provides a means of describing large strains and following the processes involved: it is still extensively used.[1] While the strains occurring in geology are far from being homogeneous, sometimes even in quite small regions, it is impossible to treat practical types of inhomogeneous strain except by numerical or analogue methods[2] so that for a mathematical description it is essential to use simple types of finite homogeneous strain. Because of the importance of the subject, the object of this chapter is to extend the theory given in Chapter I with specifically geological examples and also to indicate applications of some of the theory of Chapters II and III to geological problems.[3] Because this chapter is essentially a sequel to Chapter I, the convention of that chapter will be used; in particular, strains are reckoned positive when they are extensions.

58. COMBINATION OF STRAINS

The whole of the discussion of § 7 referred to a single finite strain, but it is only rarely that a single strain is in question, and

[1] The study of finite homogeneous strain in geology derives from Becker's work (*loc. cit.*) which was made fundamental by B. Sander in his *Gefügekunde der Gesteine* (Springer, 1930). However, many recent works give elementary discussions *ab initio* similar to those of Becker, e.g. H. Ramberg, *Norsk Geol. Tids.*, **39** (1959), 99–151, and D. Flinn, *Quart. J. Geol. Soc. Lond.*, **118** (1962), 385–433. The theory is made fundamental by J. G. Ramsay, *Folding and Fracturing of Rocks* (McGraw-Hill, 1967).
[2] For example, E. S. O'Driscoll, *J. Alberta Soc. Petrol. Geol.*, **10** (1962), 145–67, and *Econ. Geol.*, **59** (1964), 1061–93 uses card models.
[3] For structural geology in general, see L. U. de Sitter, *Structural Geology*, Ed. 2 (McGraw-Hill, 1964) F. J. Turner and L. E. Weiss, *Structural Analysis of Metamorphic Tectonites* (McGraw-Hill, 1963).

in general a number of strains, finite or infinitesimal, are applied to the system successively. The combination of such strains be best handled in matrix notation.

A matrix of m rows and n columns, which may be written symbolically (A) or $(A_{m,n})$, consists of the array of numbers

$$(A_{m,n}) = \begin{pmatrix} a_{11} & a_{12} & \cdots & a_{1n} \\ a_{21} & a_{22} & \cdots & a_{2n} \\ \cdots\cdots\cdots\cdots\cdots \\ a_{m1} & a_{m2} & \cdots & a_{mn} \end{pmatrix}. \qquad (1)$$

If $m=n$, the matrix is called *square*. In a square matrix, if $a_{rs}=a_{sr}$ for all r and s, the matrix is *symmetrical*; if $a_{rs}=-a_{sr}$ and so $a_{rr}=0$, the matrix is *anti-symmetrical*; if $a_{rs}=0$ if $r \neq s$, it is *diagonal*; and if it is diagonal and all $a_{rr}=1$ it is the *unit matrix* (1). Two matrices of the same number of rows and columns may be added or subtracted by adding or subtracting the corresponding elements.

The simplification introduced by the use of matrices in the present context arises from the law of multiplication which states that the product $(A_{m,n}) \times (B_{n,p})$ of a matrix $(A_{m,n})$ of m rows and n columns with a matrix $(B_{n,p})$ of n rows and p columns is a matrix $(C_{m,p})$ of m rows and p columns, whose r,s-th element $c_{r,s}$ is given by

$$c_{rs} = \sum_{t=1}^{n} a_{rt}b_{ts} = a_{r1}b_{1s} + a_{r2}b_{2s} + \ldots + a_{rn}b_{ns}, . \qquad (2)$$

and so is found by multiplying the elements of the r-th row of $(A_{m,n})$ in order by those of the s-th column of $(B_{n,p})$ and adding. It has to be noted that in general matrix multiplication is not commutative, that is $(A) \times (B) \neq (B) \times (A)$ and in the present context this implies that in general, a finite strain (B) followed by a finite strain (A) gives a different result to a finite strain (A) followed by a finite strain (B).

After these preliminaries, the results of § 7 may be set out in matrix notation; § 7 (7) becomes

$$\begin{pmatrix} x' \\ y' \end{pmatrix} = \begin{pmatrix} a & b \\ c & d \end{pmatrix} \begin{pmatrix} x \\ y \end{pmatrix}, \qquad (3)$$

and the equations for rotation of axes, §7 (5) (6), become[1]

$$\begin{pmatrix} x' \\ y' \end{pmatrix} = \begin{pmatrix} \cos\theta & \sin\theta \\ -\sin\theta & \cos\theta \end{pmatrix} \begin{pmatrix} x \\ y \end{pmatrix}, \quad \begin{pmatrix} x \\ y \end{pmatrix} = \begin{pmatrix} \cos\theta & -\sin\theta \\ \sin\theta & \cos\theta \end{pmatrix} \begin{pmatrix} x' \\ y' \end{pmatrix}. \quad (4)$$

The two square matrices in (4) are in fact inverses, the inverse $(A)^{-1}$ of a matrix (A) being defined by

$$(A)\times(A)^{-1} = (A)^{-1}\times(A) = (\mathbf{I}). \qquad \cdot \qquad \cdot \qquad (5)$$

The solution of a set of linear equations is equivalent to finding the inverse of a matrix and this, as well as all operations involving matrices, is very easily done on a computer.

Finite strains may now be combined by using matrix multiplication, for example if

$$\begin{pmatrix} x'' \\ y'' \end{pmatrix} = \begin{pmatrix} a_1 & b_1 \\ c_1 & d_1 \end{pmatrix} \begin{pmatrix} x' \\ y' \end{pmatrix}, \quad \begin{pmatrix} x' \\ y' \end{pmatrix} = \begin{pmatrix} a & b \\ c & d \end{pmatrix} \begin{pmatrix} x \\ y \end{pmatrix}$$

it follows that

$$\begin{pmatrix} x'' \\ y'' \end{pmatrix} = \begin{pmatrix} a_1 a + b_1 c & a_1 b + b_1 d \\ c_1 a + d_1 c & c_1 b + d_1 d \end{pmatrix} \begin{pmatrix} x \\ y \end{pmatrix}. \qquad \cdot \qquad \cdot \qquad (6)$$

As a special case, if a_1, b_1, c_1, d_1 is an infinitesimal strain so that by § 10 (5) (6) the first of equations (6) is

$$\begin{pmatrix} x'' \\ y'' \end{pmatrix} = \begin{pmatrix} 1+\varepsilon_1 & \tfrac{1}{2}\gamma-\omega \\ \tfrac{1}{2}\gamma+\omega & 1+\varepsilon_2 \end{pmatrix} \begin{pmatrix} x' \\ y' \end{pmatrix}, \qquad \cdot \qquad \cdot \qquad (7)$$

(6) becomes

$$\begin{pmatrix} x'' \\ y'' \end{pmatrix} = \begin{pmatrix} a(1+\varepsilon_1)+c(\tfrac{1}{2}\gamma-\omega) & b(1+\varepsilon_1)+d(\tfrac{1}{2}\gamma-\omega) \\ a(\tfrac{1}{2}\gamma+\omega)+c(1+\varepsilon_2) & b(\tfrac{1}{2}\gamma+\omega)+d(1+\varepsilon_2) \end{pmatrix} \begin{pmatrix} x \\ y \end{pmatrix} \qquad (8)$$

The theory of § 7 was set out in what are now regarded as the components a, b, c, d of the transformation matrix (3) and, because of the importance of matrix theory in connection with the superposition of strains, this will continue to be the most important representation. However, for geological purposes the position and axes of the strain ellipse and the rotation are the

[1] These equations arise in two different contexts and should always be interpreted by reference to Fig. 10 (a). As set out in (4) and § 7 (5) (6) they refer to a change of axes from Oxy to $Ox'y'$ inclined at θ to them, and they are frequently used for this purpose, e.g. in (28) below. Alternatively, the effect of a finite rotation of the axes Oxy, carrying the point x, y with them, is often needed, and this is found by replacing x, y by x', y' in (4), or, what amounts to the same thing as may be seen from Fig. 10 (a), by replacing θ by $-\theta$ in (4).

most obvious quantities, and it is useful to develop relations between all the quantities in use.

The quadratic elongation λ was defined in §§ 7 (40), 9 (3), and the principal quadratic elongations λ_1 and λ_2 are just the squares of the semi-major and minor axes A and B, § 7 (26)–(29), of the strain ellipse, so that

$$\lambda_1^{\frac{1}{2}}=A, \quad \lambda_2^{\frac{1}{2}}=B, \qquad . \qquad . \qquad . \quad (9)$$

where, as usual, $\lambda_1 \geq \lambda_2$.

Using these and § 7 (14), equation § 7 (40) for the quadratic elongation λ becomes[1]

$$\lambda=\tfrac{1}{2}(\lambda_1+\lambda_2)+\tfrac{1}{2}(\lambda_1-\lambda_2)\cos 2(\theta-\alpha), \qquad . \qquad . \quad (10)$$

and § 7 (13) for the shear strain $\gamma=\tan\psi$ becomes

$$\gamma=-\tfrac{1}{2}(\lambda_1-\lambda_2)(\lambda_1\lambda_2)^{-\frac{1}{2}}\sin 2(\theta-\alpha) \qquad . \qquad . \quad (11)$$

$$=-\tfrac{1}{2}\left(\frac{\lambda_1}{\lambda_2}+\frac{\lambda_2}{\lambda_1}-2\right)^{\frac{1}{2}}\sin 2(\theta-\alpha), \qquad . \qquad . \quad (12)$$

where α is given by § 7 (14). The form (12) shows that γ involves only the ratio λ_1/λ_2.

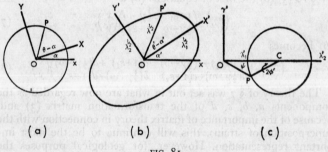

FIG. 81

The situation is shown in Fig. 81 (a) (b). Here OX, OY are the initial positions of the principal axes of strain with OX inclined at α to the reference direction Ox. OX' and OY' are the final positions of the principal axes of strain with OX' inclined at

[1] It is assumed, as usual, that $\lambda_1 \geq \lambda_2$ and that λ_1 is associated with the direction α and λ_2 with $\alpha+\tfrac{1}{2}\pi$. Ambiguities in sign can be settled by considering the special case $b=c=0$.

α' to the reference direction. λ and γ given by (10) and (11) refer to a direction inclined at $\theta-\alpha$ to OX corresponding to the point P on a unit circle. This transforms into a point P' on the strain ellipse in a direction inclined at $\theta'-\alpha'$ to OX', and the axes of the strain ellipse are $\lambda_1^{\frac{1}{2}}$ and $\lambda_2^{\frac{1}{2}}$. Relative to axes OX, OY, the point P has coordinates $\cos(\theta-\alpha)$, $\sin(\theta-\alpha)$ and this transforms to the point $\lambda_1^{\frac{1}{2}}\cos(\theta-\alpha)$, $\lambda_2^{\frac{1}{2}}\sin(\theta-\alpha)$ relative to axes OX', OY'; but this point is also, from Fig. 81 (b), $\lambda^{\frac{1}{2}}\cos(\theta'-\alpha')$, $\lambda^{\frac{1}{2}}\sin(\theta'-\alpha')$, and therefore

$$\lambda_1^{\frac{1}{2}}\cos(\theta-\alpha)=\lambda^{\frac{1}{2}}\cos(\theta'-\alpha'), \qquad . \qquad . \quad (13)$$

$$\lambda_2^{\frac{1}{2}}\sin(\theta-\alpha)=\lambda^{\frac{1}{2}}\sin(\theta'-\alpha'). \qquad . \qquad . \quad (14)$$

It follows from (13) and (14) that

$$(\lambda_1\lambda_2)^{\frac{1}{2}}\sin 2(\theta-\alpha)=\lambda\sin 2(\theta'-\alpha'), \qquad . \qquad . \quad (15)$$

and $\quad \lambda^{-1}=\lambda_1^{-1}\cos^2(\theta'-\alpha')+\lambda_2^{-1}\sin^2(\theta'-\alpha')$

$$=\tfrac{1}{2}(\lambda_1^{-1}+\lambda_2^{-1})+\tfrac{1}{2}(\lambda_1^{-1}-\lambda_2^{-1})\cos 2(\theta'-\alpha'). \quad . \quad (16)$$

Using (15) in (11) gives

$$\gamma\lambda^{-1}=-\tfrac{1}{2}(\lambda_2^{-1}-\lambda_1^{-1})\sin 2(\theta'-\alpha'). \qquad . \qquad . \quad (17)$$

(16) and (17) give the quadratic elongation and shear strain in terms of the final position of the point concerned and thus are rather more useful than (10) and (11) which involve their initial positions. λ^{-1} is the *reciprocal quadratic elongation* and because of the common occurrence of this quantity it is convenient to adopt a special notation, namely

$$\lambda^{-1}=\lambda', \quad \lambda_1^{-1}=\lambda_1', \quad \lambda_2^{-1}=\lambda_2', \quad \gamma\lambda^{-1}=\gamma'. \qquad . \quad (18)$$

With this notation, and writing $\phi'=\theta'-\alpha'$, (16) and (17) become

$$\lambda'=\lambda_1'\cos^2\phi'+\lambda_2'\sin^2\phi'=\tfrac{1}{2}(\lambda_1'+\lambda_2')-\tfrac{1}{2}(\lambda_2'-\lambda_1')\cos 2\phi', \quad (19)$$

$$\gamma'=-\tfrac{1}{2}(\lambda_2'-\lambda_1')\sin 2\phi', \quad . \qquad . \qquad . \qquad . \qquad . \quad (20)$$

here, since $\lambda_1\geq\lambda_2$, $\lambda_2'\geq\lambda_1'$.

The variation of λ' and γ' with ϕ' is shown in Fig. 81 (c); it is similar to the Mohr circle construction of Fig. 4 and many methods based on the use of this construction are available, cf. Ramsay, *loc. cit.*; Brace, *loc. cit.* Since, by definition,

$$\gamma'=\lambda'\gamma=\lambda'\tan\psi$$

the angle POC, Fig. 81 (c), is the angle ψ of the shear.

Formulae for change of axes follow from (19) and (20). Suppose that axes $O\xi$, $O\eta$ make angles ϕ' and $\phi' + \frac{1}{2}\pi$ with the principal direction OX', then if λ_ξ', λ_η', γ_ξ' refer to these,

$$\left.\begin{aligned} \lambda_\xi' &= \lambda_1' \cos^2 \phi' + \lambda_2' \sin^2 \phi, \\ \lambda_\eta' &= \lambda_1' \sin^2 \phi' + \lambda_2' \cos^2 \phi', \end{aligned}\right\} \qquad (21)$$

$$\gamma_\xi' = -\tfrac{1}{2}(\lambda_2' - \lambda_1') \sin 2\phi' \qquad . \qquad . \qquad . \qquad (22)$$

It should be emphasized that these refer to two directions which are perpendicular in the final state but will not be so in the initial state.

It follows from (21) and (22) that

$$\left.\begin{aligned} \lambda_\xi' + \lambda_\eta' &= \lambda_1' + \lambda_2' = j_1, \text{ constant,} \\ \lambda_\xi' \lambda_\eta' - \gamma_\xi'^2 &= \lambda_1' \lambda_2' = j_2, \end{aligned}\right\} \qquad . \qquad . \qquad (23)$$

and

so that these are *invariants of finite strain*. Also by (23), λ_1' and λ_2', are the roots of the quadratic

$$\lambda'^2 - j_1\lambda' + j_2 = 0, \qquad . \qquad . \qquad . \qquad (24)$$

or

$$\begin{vmatrix} \lambda_\xi' - \lambda & \gamma_\xi' \\ \gamma_\xi' & \lambda_\eta' - \lambda \end{vmatrix} = 0.$$

The equation of the strain ellipse referred to its principal axes OX', OY' is

$$\lambda_1^{-1}x_1^2 + \lambda_2^{-1}y_1^2 = \lambda_1'x_1^2 + \lambda_2'y_1^2 = 1, \qquad . \qquad . \qquad (25)$$

and referred to axes $O\zeta$, $O\eta$ inclined at ϕ' to these it is, using § 7 (6)

$$\lambda_\xi'\xi^2 - 2\gamma_\xi'\xi\eta + \lambda_\eta'\eta^2 = 1, \qquad . \qquad . \qquad (26)$$

where λ_ξ' and γ_ξ' are defined in (21) and (22).

The above treatment, like that of § 7, has proceeded from the transformation matrix a, b, c, d to parameters such as λ_1, λ_2, etc., describing the strain. It is also of interest to deduce the transformation matrix from parameters describing the strain. Consider first an irrotational (pure) strain whose principal quadratic elongations are λ_1 and λ_2 and whose principal axes are inclined at α and $\alpha + \frac{1}{2}\pi$ to Ox. Relative to principal axes the strain is

$$\begin{pmatrix} x_1' \\ y_1' \end{pmatrix} = \begin{pmatrix} \lambda_1^{\frac{1}{2}} & 0 \\ 0 & \lambda_2^{\frac{1}{2}} \end{pmatrix} \begin{pmatrix} x_1 \\ y_1 \end{pmatrix}, \qquad . \qquad . \qquad (27)$$

and referred to axes Oxy it becomes by (4)

$$\begin{aligned} \begin{pmatrix} x' \\ y' \end{pmatrix} &= \begin{pmatrix} \cos \alpha & -\sin \alpha \\ \sin \alpha & \cos \alpha \end{pmatrix} \begin{pmatrix} \lambda_1^{\frac{1}{2}} & 0 \\ 0 & \lambda_2^{\frac{1}{2}} \end{pmatrix} \begin{pmatrix} \cos \alpha & \sin \alpha \\ -\sin \alpha & \cos \alpha \end{pmatrix} \begin{pmatrix} x \\ y \end{pmatrix} \\ &= \begin{pmatrix} \lambda_1^{\frac{1}{2}} \cos^2 \alpha + \lambda_2^{\frac{1}{2}} \sin^2\alpha & (\lambda_1^{\frac{1}{2}} - \lambda_2^{\frac{1}{2}}) \sin \alpha \cos \alpha \\ (\lambda_1^{\frac{1}{2}} - \lambda_2^{\frac{1}{2}}) \sin \alpha \cos\alpha & \lambda_1^{\frac{1}{2}} \sin^2 \alpha + \lambda_2^{\frac{1}{2}} \cos^2 \alpha \end{pmatrix} \begin{pmatrix} x \\ y \end{pmatrix} \qquad . \qquad 28) \end{aligned}$$

which has the form (3) with

$$a=\lambda_1^{\frac{1}{2}}\cos^2\alpha+\lambda_2^{\frac{1}{2}}\sin^2\alpha, \quad d=\lambda_1^{\frac{1}{2}}\sin^2\alpha+\lambda_2^{\frac{1}{2}}\cos^2\alpha,$$
$$b=c=(\lambda_1^{\frac{1}{2}}-\lambda_2^{\frac{1}{2}})\sin\alpha\cos\alpha. \qquad \qquad \qquad (29)$$

Using these values in § 7 (21) gives the form (26) of the strain ellipse. Also, it follows from (29) that $\lambda_1^{\frac{1}{2}}+\lambda_2^{\frac{1}{2}}=a+d$, and $\lambda_1^{\frac{1}{2}}\lambda_2^{\frac{1}{2}}=ad-b^2$ so that λ_1 and λ_2 may be determined from a, b, d by a calculation similar to (24).

As remarked in § 7, a general homogeneous strain may be regarded as a pure strain, specified as above by λ_1, λ_2, α or a, b, d followed by a finite rotation ω. Using (4), the combined effect of these is,

$$\begin{pmatrix} x' \\ y' \end{pmatrix} = \begin{pmatrix} \cos\omega & -\sin\omega \\ \sin\omega & \cos\omega \end{pmatrix}\begin{pmatrix} a & b \\ b & d \end{pmatrix}\begin{pmatrix} x \\ y \end{pmatrix}$$
$$= \begin{pmatrix} a\cos\omega-b\sin\omega & b\cos\omega-d\sin\omega \\ a\sin\omega+b\cos\omega & b\sin\omega+d\cos\omega \end{pmatrix}\begin{pmatrix} x \\ y \end{pmatrix}. \qquad (30)$$

which has the general form (3) so that the elements of the matrix are known if λ_1, λ_2, α, ω are given.

Similar results hold in three dimensions. Suppose that λ_1, λ_2, λ_3 are the principal quadratic elongations and that their direction cosines are l_1, m_1, n_1; l_2, m_2, n_2; l_3, m_3, n_3, relative to axes $Oxyz$.

In three dimensions, the formulae for transformation from a set of rectangular axes Ox, Oy, Oz to another set $O\xi$, $O\eta$, $O\zeta$, whose direction cosines relative to $Oxyz$ are (l_1, m_1, n_1), (l_2, m_2, n_2), (l_3, m_3, n_3) respectively, are[1]

$$\begin{pmatrix} \xi \\ \eta \\ \zeta \end{pmatrix} = \begin{pmatrix} l_1 & m_1 & n_1 \\ l_2 & m_2 & n_2 \\ l_3 & m_3 & n_3 \end{pmatrix}\begin{pmatrix} x \\ y \\ z \end{pmatrix}, \quad \begin{pmatrix} x \\ y \\ z \end{pmatrix} = \begin{pmatrix} l_1 & l_2 & l_3 \\ m_1 & m_2 & m_3 \\ n_1 & n_2 & n_3 \end{pmatrix}\begin{pmatrix} \xi \\ \eta \\ \zeta \end{pmatrix} \quad . \quad (31)$$

The two square matrices in (31) are inverses since a number of relations of type

$$\left. \begin{array}{l} l_1^2+m_1^2+n_1^2=1,\; l_1^2+l_2^2+l_3^2=1, \\ l_1l_2+m_1m_2+n_1n_2=0,\quad l_1m_1+l_2m_2+l_3m_3=0,\text{ etc.} \end{array} \right\} \quad . \quad (32)$$

hold between the direction cosines of two sets of mutually perpendicular lines.

Using (31), a pure strain with principal quadratic elongations λ_1, λ_2, λ_3 along the axes $O\xi$, $O\eta$, $O\zeta$ becomes when referred to axes $Oxyz$

$$\begin{pmatrix} x' \\ y' \\ z' \end{pmatrix} = \begin{pmatrix} l_1 & l_2 & l_3 \\ m_1 & m_2 & m_3 \\ n_1 & n_2 & n_3 \end{pmatrix}\begin{pmatrix} \lambda_1^{\frac{1}{2}} & 0 & 0 \\ 0 & \lambda_2^{\frac{1}{2}} & 0 \\ 0 & 0 & \lambda_3^{\frac{1}{2}} \end{pmatrix}\begin{pmatrix} l_1 & m_1 & n_1 \\ l_2 & m_2 & n_2 \\ l_3 & m_3 & n_3 \end{pmatrix}\begin{pmatrix} x \\ y \\ z \end{pmatrix}$$
$$= \begin{pmatrix} a_1 & b_1 & c_1 \\ b_1 & b_2 & c_2 \\ c_1 & c_2 & c_3 \end{pmatrix}\begin{pmatrix} x \\ y \\ z \end{pmatrix}, \qquad \qquad . \qquad (33)$$

where (33) is a symmetrical matrix in which

$$\left. \begin{array}{ll} a_1=\lambda_1^{\frac{1}{2}}l_1^2\;\;+\lambda_2^{\frac{1}{2}}l_2^2\;\;+\lambda_3^{\frac{1}{2}}l_3^2, & b_1=\lambda_1^{\frac{1}{2}}l_1m_1+\lambda_2^{\frac{1}{2}}l_2m_2+\lambda_3^{\frac{1}{2}}l_3m_3 \\ c_1=\lambda_1^{\frac{1}{2}}l_1n_1+\lambda_2^{\frac{1}{2}}l_2n_2+\lambda_3^{\frac{1}{2}}l_3n_3, & b_2=\lambda_1^{\frac{1}{2}}m_1^2+\lambda_2^{\frac{1}{2}}m_2^2+\lambda_3^{\frac{1}{2}}m_3^2 \\ c_2=\lambda_1^{\frac{1}{2}}m_1n_1+\lambda_2^{\frac{1}{2}}m_2n_2+\lambda_3^{\frac{1}{2}}m_3n_3, & c_3=\lambda_1^{\frac{1}{2}}n_1^2\;\;+\lambda_2^{\frac{1}{2}}n_2^2+\lambda_3^{\frac{1}{2}}n_3^2 \end{array} \right\} \quad (34)$$

---

[1] R. J. T. Bell, *Coordinate Geometry of Three Dimensions*, Chap. IV (Macmillan, 1920).

It follows that a general pure strain in three dimensions corresponds to the symmetrical matrix (33) and the most general finite homogeneous strain is obtained by superimposing a finite rotation on (33) by matrix multiplication using (31).

59. DETERMINATION OF FINITE STRAIN FROM DEFORMED OBJECTS

During geological deformation of a rock matrix, objects such as pebbles, fossils and ooids embedded in it will be deformed and measurements of their final shapes can be used to give an indication of the finite strain in the rock.[1] Details of procedure differ according to whether the undeformed objects are spherical or non-spherical and to whether their mechanical properties are the same as, or different from, those of the matrix. A necessary preliminary in all cases is the determination of the directions and lengths of the principal axes of an ellipsoid from three perpendicular non-central sections.

(i) Determination of the Principal Axes and Direction of an Ellipse

Suppose that the equation of the ellipse is

$$p_1 x^2 + 2p_{12}xy + p_2 y^2 = 1. \qquad . \qquad . \qquad . \qquad (1)$$

Two methods have already been used for solving this problem: (i) finding the directions in which the radius vector is a maximum or a minimum, so that the lengths of the radius vector in these directions will be the semi-axes; (ii) studying the intersection of (1) with a circle of radius R as in § 7 (23), which gives an equation for the lengths of the semi-axes. Also, since any ellipse may be regarded as the strain ellipse of some strain, finding the principal axes and elongations of this strain as in § 58 (24) is an equivalent problem. A similar treatment, set out in purely geometrical terms, will be followed here.

Suppose that the principal axes Ox_1, Oy_1 of (1) are inclined at θ and $\theta + \frac{1}{2}\pi$ to Ox, and that relative to them its equation is

$$q_1 x_1{}^2 + q_2 x_2{}^2 = 1. \qquad . \qquad . \qquad . \qquad (2)$$

When referred to axes Oxy, (2) becomes by § 7 (5)

$$q_1(x \cos \theta + y \sin \theta)^2 + q_2(x \sin \theta - y \cos \theta)^2 = 1. \qquad . \qquad (3)$$

---

[1] J. G. Ramsay, loc. cit., gives a full discussion and references. Critical discussions are given by W. F. Brace, Bull. Geol. Soc. Amer., **72** (1961), 1059–80, and B. E. Hobbs and J. L. Talbot, J. Geol., **74** (1966) 500–13. See also E. Cloos, Bull. Geol. Soc. Amer., **58** (1947), 843–918.

Comparing coefficients between (1) and (3) gives

$$p_1 = q_1 \cos^2 \theta + q_2 \sin^2 \theta, \quad p_2 = q_1 \sin^2 \theta + q_2 \cos^2 \theta, \quad (4)$$

$$p_{12} = \tfrac{1}{2}(q_1 - q_2) \sin 2\theta. \quad\quad\quad\quad (5)$$

It follows that

$$p_1 + p_2 = q_1 + q_2 = j_1, \quad p_1 p_2 - p_{12}{}^2 = q_1 q_2 = j_2, \quad\quad (6)$$

where the quantities j_1 and j_2, being independent of θ, are invariants. It follows from (6) that

$$q_1 - q_2 = \pm(j_1{}^2 - 4j_2)^{\frac{1}{2}}, \quad\quad\quad (7)$$

and q_1 and q_2 are found from (6) and (7). Also by (6) they are the roots of the equation in q

$$\begin{vmatrix} p_1 - q & p_{12} \\ p_{12} & p_2 - q \end{vmatrix} = 0. \quad\quad\quad (8)$$

The ambiguity of sign in (7) must be noted and it is usually necessary to return to (4) and (5) to see which semi-axis is associated with a given principal direction.

It follows from (4) that

$$\sin^2 \theta = (p_1 - q_1)/(q_2 - q_1) \quad\quad\quad (9)$$

Alternatively from (4)

$$p_1 - p_2 = (q_1 - q_2) \cos 2\theta, \quad\quad\quad (10)$$

and so from (10) and (5)

$$\tan 2\theta = 2p_{12}/(p_1 - p_2). \quad\quad\quad (11)$$

(ii) *Determination of the Lengths and Directions of the Principal Axes of an Ellipsoid*

Here, again, many methods may be used and the one given here is similar to that used in § 4 for the determination of principal stresses. Suppose the equation of the ellipsoid is

$$p_1 x^2 + p_2 y^2 + p_3 z^2 + 2p_{23} yz + 2p_{31} zx + 2p_{12} xy = 1. \quad\quad (12)$$

Let R be the radius vector in the direction l, m, n, so that $x = lR$, $y = mR$, $z = nR$. Inserting this in (12) and writing $\rho = R^{-2}$ for shortness gives,

$$p_1 l^2 + p_2 m^2 + p_3 n^2 + 2p_{23} mn + 2p_{31} nl + 2p_{12} lm = R^{-2} = \rho. \quad (13)$$

The conditions for R or ρ to be stationary are as in § 4 (9) (10)

$$\frac{\partial \rho}{\partial l} = 0, \quad \frac{\partial \rho}{\partial m} = 0, \quad\quad\quad (14)$$

with

$$l + n\frac{\partial n}{\partial l} = 0, \quad m + n\frac{\partial n}{\partial m} = 0. \quad\quad\quad (15)$$

Using (14) in (13) gives

$$p_1 l + p_{12} m + p_{31} n + (p_{31} l + p_{23} m + p_3 n)(\partial n / \partial l) = 0, \qquad . \qquad . \quad (16)$$

$$p_{12} l + p_2 m + p_{23} n + (p_{31} l + p_{23} m + p_3 n)(\partial n / \partial m) = 0, \qquad . \qquad . \quad (17)$$

and using (15) these give

$$(p_1 l + p_{12} m + p_{31} n)/l = (p_{12} l + p_2 m + p_{23} n)/m = (p_{31} l + p_{23} m + p_3 n)/n = k, \qquad . \quad (18)$$

where k is unknown. Multiplying the three equations (18) by l^2, m^2, n^2, respectively, adding, and using (13) and $l^2 + m^2 + n^2 = 1$ gives $k = \rho$ so that the three equations (18) become

$$\left. \begin{array}{c} (p_1 - \rho) l + p_{12} m + p_{31} n = 0 \\ p_{12} l + (p_2 - \rho) m + p_{23} n = 0 \\ p_{31} l + p_{23} m + (p_3 - \rho) n = 0 \end{array} \right\} \qquad . \qquad . \quad (19)$$

which are of the same form as § 4 (14). They have a non-zero solution only if ρ is a root of

$$\begin{vmatrix} p_1 - \rho & p_{12} & p_{31} \\ p_{12} & p_2 - \rho & p_{23} \\ p_{31} & p_{23} & p_3 - \rho \end{vmatrix} = 0. \qquad . \qquad . \quad (20)$$

It is known that the cubic (20) has three real roots and these will be A^{-2}, B^{-2}, C^{-2}, where A, B, C, are the semiaxes of the ellipsoid. For each value of ρ, solving any two of (19) gives the corresponding direction of a principal axis, and it can be shown that these directions are orthogonal. As in § 4 (17)–(20) the determinant in (20) can be expanded so that (20) takes the form

$$\rho^3 - j_1 \rho^2 - j_2 \rho - j_3 = 0, \qquad . \qquad . \qquad . \quad (21)$$

where j_1, j_2, j_3 are invariants. This cubic is readily solved graphically.

(iii) Determination of an Ellipsoid from Three Orthogonal Non-central Sections

In the geological context an ellipsoidal object, such as a pebble contained in a matrix, may readily be sawn across three mutually perpendicular planes: it is desired to find the equation of the ellipsoid from a knowledge of these sections. Suppose the planes are perpendicular to rectangular axes $Oxyz$ and that relative to these the equation of the ellipsoid is (12). The section of this by the plane $z = z_0$ is

$$p_1 x^2 + p_2 y^2 + 2 p_{12} xy + 2 p_{23} y z_0 + 2 p_{31} x z_0 + p_3 z_0^2 = 1, \qquad . \qquad . \quad (22)$$

which may be written in the form

$$p_1 (x - \alpha)^2 + p_2 (y - \beta)^2 + 2 p_{12} (x - \alpha)(y - \beta) = \gamma, \qquad . \qquad . \quad (23)$$

where α, β, γ can be expressed in terms of $p_1, p_{23}, \ldots, z_0$.

This is an ellipse with centre α, β which is similar and similarly situated to the section of (12) by the plane $z = 0$ which is

$$p_1 x^2 + p_2 y^2 + 2 p_{12} xy = 1. \qquad . \qquad . \qquad . \quad (24)$$

It follows that p_1, p_2 and p_{12} are determined from measurements of the section (23) except for a constant factor k_1, that is,

$$p_1 = k_1 C_1, \quad p_2 = k_1 C_2, \quad p_{12} = k_1 C_3, \qquad . \qquad . \quad (25)$$

where C_1, C_2, C_3 are known and k_1 is unknown. Similarly from sections perpendicular to the y- and x-axes it follows that

$$\left.\begin{array}{llll} p_1=k_2C_4\,, & p_3=k_2C_5\,, & p_{31}=k_2C_6\,, \\ p_2=k_3C_7\,, & p_3=k_3C_8\,, & p_{23}=k_3C_9\,, \end{array}\right\} \qquad . \qquad . \quad (26)$$

where $C_4\,,\ldots,\,C_9$ are known and k_2 and k_3 are unknown.

These equations are not all independent and, in fact,

$$C_1C_5C_7=C_2C_4C_8\,.$$

All of $p_1\,,\ldots,\,p_{31}$ can be determined from them except for a constant factor, say, k_3. If this is to be found, an additional measurement is necessary however, in the present context this is usually unimportant, and, neglecting it, the equation of the ellipsoid is found in the form (12). The case of three general sections is treated by Ramsay, *loc. cit.*

(iv) *Deformation of Initially Spherical Objects*

Examples of this case are ooids, spherulites and pisolites. If it is assumed that they deform homogeneously with the matrix in which they are embedded, their final shape corresponds to the strain ellipsoid for the deformation. A sample, oriented with respect to the bedding or cleavage of the rock, is then cut in three perpendicular directions. Each of these cuts will intersect many deformed objects. For each cut, mean values of the axial ratios of the objects intersected and the directions of the axes of the elliptical sections may be calculated. From these, the equation of the strain ellipsoid and the principal strains may be found by the methods of (iii) and (ii) above.

(v) *Deformation of Non-spherical Objects*

In this case, the situation is more complicated since the objects are both rotated and deformed. For simplicity, only the two-dimensional case will be considered. Suppose that an elliptical object whose equation is (1) is deformed by a pure strain with principal quadratic elongations λ_1 and λ_2 along the x- and y-axes. Then the equation of the deformed ellipse will be

$$\lambda_1^{-1}p_1x^2+2(\lambda_1\lambda_2)^{-\frac{1}{2}}p_{12}xy+\lambda_2^{-1}p_2y^2=1, \qquad . \qquad . \quad (27)$$

and by (11) its major axis is inclined at an angle ϕ to Ox given by

$$\tan 2\phi=\frac{2(\lambda_1\lambda_2)^{-\frac{1}{2}}p_{12}}{\lambda_1^{-1}p_1-\lambda_2^{-1}p_2} \qquad . \qquad . \qquad . \qquad . \quad (28)$$

$$=\frac{2(q_1-q_2)(\lambda_1\lambda_2)^{-\frac{1}{2}}\sin 2\theta}{(\lambda_1^{-1}-\lambda_2^{-1})(q_1+q_2)+(\lambda_1^{-1}+\lambda_2^{-1})(q_1-q_2)\cos 2\theta} \quad (29)$$

using (4) and (5). This gives the direction of the axis of the deformed ellipse in terms of the parameters λ_1, λ_2 of the strain and q_1, q_2, θ. These formulae are most conveniently expressed in terms of R_s, the square of the axial ratio of the strain ellipse, and R_0 and R_f of the initial and deformed shapes of the pebble so that

$$R_0 = q_2/q_1, \quad R_s = \lambda_1/\lambda_2 \quad . \quad . \quad . \quad (30)$$

In terms of these, (29) becomes

$$\tan 2\phi = \frac{2(R_0-1)R_s^{\frac{1}{2}} \sin 2\theta}{(R_s-1)(R_0+1)+(R_0-1)(R_s+1) \cos 2\theta} \quad . \quad (31)$$

To find the value of R_f, (4) gives

$$\frac{p_1}{p_2} = \frac{1+R_0 \tan^2 \theta}{R_0+\tan^2 \theta} \quad . \quad . \quad . \quad (32)$$

and from (27) in the same way

$$\frac{\lambda_2 p_1}{\lambda_1 p_2} = \frac{p_1}{R_s p_2} = \frac{1+R_f \tan^2 \phi}{R_f+\tan^2 \phi}. \quad . \quad . \quad (33)$$

Eliminating p_1/p_2 between (32) and (33) gives

$$R_f = \frac{(1+R_0 \tan^2 \theta) \tan^2 \phi-(R_0+\tan^2 \theta)R_s}{R_s(R_0+\tan^2 \theta) \tan^2 \phi-(1+R_0 \tan^2 \theta)}, \quad . \quad (34)$$

where ϕ is given by (29). There is some ambiguity in these formulae since (29) gives two possible values of ϕ. Two special cases are of importance. If $\theta=0$, so that the object is aligned in the direction of greatest elongation, $\phi=0$, $R_f=R_0 R_s$, and this is its maximum value. If $\theta=\frac{1}{2}\pi$ so that the object is aligned in the direction of least elongation, R_f has its least value but two cases arise: if $R_0>R_s$, $\phi=\frac{1}{2}\pi$ and $R_f=R_0/R_s$, while if $R_s>R_0$, $\phi=0$, and $R_f=R_s/R_0$.

The most common non-spherical objects used for the determination of finite strain are pebbles, the shapes of which are approximately ellipsoidal. Here the difficulty arises that neither the initial shape nor orientation of the pebbles is known. The shape factor is sometimes allowed for by measuring undeformed pebbles of the same composition and assuming that pebbles of the same composition will have approximately the same shape. It is usually assumed that the pebbles are randomly oriented. The procedure then is to choose some arbitrary direction in a surface intersecting many pebbles and to measure the inclinations ϕ of the major axes of all pebbles relative to this direction as well as the squares of the axial ratios R_f of all pebbles. R_f is then plotted against ϕ. As shown above, the maximum value of R_f is $R_0 R_s$ and occurs in the direction of the maximum principal strain. From the maximum and minimum values of R_f, both R_0 and R_s can be found and the technique can be extended to pebbles with varying values of R_0, Ramsay, *loc. cit.*

Strains determined from deformed pebbles generally refer to the pebbles themselves and not to the total strain experienced by the rocks containing them. This is because there is usually a difference in competence between the pebble and the surrounding matrix, the pebble being generally stiffer than the matrix and therefore suffering less strain than the surrounding rock. To estimate this effect, Gay[1] assumed a viscous model for both pebble and rock, the ratio of the viscosity of the pebble to that of the rock being R. He finds that if λ_1 and λ_2 are principal quadratic elongations of an irrotational strain for the rock and λ_{1p}, λ_{2p} are those for the pebble,

$$\lambda_{1p}/\lambda_{2p} = [25/(2R+3)^2](\lambda_1/\lambda_2). \qquad . \qquad . \qquad (35)$$

R can be estimated from the viscosities of the pebbles and the matrix and the volume concentration of pebbles. As the latter approaches unity, $R \to 1$, and the importance of the difference in competence diminishes.

(vi) *Determination of Finite Strain from Deformed Fossils*

Fossils are probably the best indicators for the determination of finite strain in rocks because their undeformed shapes are generally known, and because there is usually no difference in competence between them and the surrounding rock so that they reflect the total finite strain experienced by the rock.

Many common fossils may be used for this purpose and the treatment depends to some extent on their shape and symmetry. While the original size of the undeformed fossil is not known, it is usually the case that the ratio of the lengths of certain characteristic lines fixed in the fossil is known. However, many fossils are relatively planar in shape and so will only indicate the strain in one plane. To determine the strain ellipsoid it will be necessary to find deformed fossils in three mutually inclined planes.

[1] N. C. Gay, *Tectonophysics*, **5** (1968), 211–34.

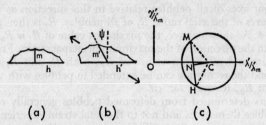

FIG. 82. (a) Brachiopod, showing hinge length h and median length m
(b) Deformed Brachiopod
(c) Mohr construction leading to λ_1/λ_2

As an example, the case of brachiopods will be considered. These are relatively flat objects, and so are well suited for the determination of strain in their plane. Their undistorted shape is sketched in Fig. 82 (a), and the ratio of the length h of the hinge line to the length m of the (perpendicular) median line is known to be a constant K for a given species, so that

$$h/m=K. \qquad \qquad \cdot \qquad \cdot \qquad \cdot \qquad (36)$$

In the deformed fossil, these lengths will have become h' and m' and the median line will have rotated through an angle ψ, Fig. 82 (b), so that the shear strain is $\gamma_m=-\gamma_h=\tan\psi$. The reciprocal quadratic elongations are $\lambda_h'=(h/h')^2$, $\lambda_m'=(m/m')^2$ so that, using (36), all quantities can be scaled in terms of λ_m' with numerical factors involving the known ratio K and the measured ratio $K'=h'/m'$, so that

$$\left.\begin{array}{l}\lambda_h'=(K/K')^2\lambda_m', \quad \gamma_m'=\lambda_m'\tan\psi,\\ \gamma_h'=\lambda_h'\lambda_h=-(K/K')^2\lambda_m'\tan\psi.\end{array}\right\} \qquad \cdot \qquad (37)$$

Knowing these quantities, the ratio λ_1/λ_2 of the principal quadratic elongations and the directions of the principal axes may be found by the Mohr construction of § 58 (19) (20). As an example, suppose $K=2$, $K'=1·87$, $\psi=30°$. Then $\lambda_h'=1·14\lambda_m'$, $\gamma_m'=0·58\lambda_m'$, $\gamma_h'=-0·66\lambda_m'$. Thus two points $H(\lambda_h', \gamma_h')$ and $M(\lambda_m', \gamma_m')$ on the Mohr circle in the λ', γ' plane are known, and its centre C must be the intersection of the perpendicular bisector NC of HM with the λ'-axis. This is shown in Fig. 82 (c) which is scaled in terms of λ_m'. It follows by measurement of the diagram that $\lambda_1'/\lambda_m'=0·71$, $\lambda_2'/\lambda_m'=2·15$ so that $\lambda_1/\lambda_2=3·03$. Also from

§ 58 (20), the angle $OCH = 64°$ is twice the angle between the final position of the hinge line and the direction of maximum elongation. This direction is shown in Fig. 82 (*b*).

Other examples, both of the use of other fossils and of the Mohr diagram, are given by Ramsay, *loc. cit.*, and Brace, *loc. cit.*

(vii) *Determination of Finite Strain from Deformed Sedimentary Structures*

Sedimentary structures which can be used for the determination of finite strain include cross-bedding, worm burrows, mud cracks, and ripple marks. Of these, only ripple marks provide sufficient information for the determination of a cross-section of the strain ellipsoid. Essentially, a ripple mark has an approximately triangular cross-section, two angles α, β of which are changed by the strain of α', β'. Hobbs and Talbot, *loc. cit.*, describe an analysis of strain using ripple marks but conclude that it is not possible to define the initial shape factors sufficiently accurately to allow quantitative determination of strain.

60. PROGRESSIVE DEFORMATION

The theory of finite strain developed in §§ 7–9 and § 58 was concerned only with the geometry of two sets of positions of the particles of the body, described as the initial state and the final state. It did not consider the way in which the particles moved from their initial positions to their final positions or the way in which the parameters describing the strain varied during this movement. This sort of study is fundamental for structural geology.

It is of the greatest importance to be clear that two separate but interacting types of calculation are involved. First, the actual movement of individual material or *marker* points, lines or curves, may be studied: since such lines and curves do commonly occur in geological materials in the form of veins or outlines of fossils, this study is of direct practical significance. Since only homogeneous strain is under consideration here (and in this case parallel lines remain parallel during straining) any line may be used as a marker line for its direction. Secondly, the movement of certain *mathematical* lines or curves may be followed, for example the principal axes of strain or the principal axes of a marker ellipse: these mathematical lines move relatively to the marker points or lines and at every stage are associated with a different set of them.

The types of effect involved may be illustrated by typical examples.

(i) Steadily Increasing Pure Shear

Many of the most important features of progressive deformation are illustrated by this case. Here, by § 7 (3)

$$x'=kx, \quad y'=k^{-1}y, \qquad \qquad (1)$$

where k increases steadily, and the lengths A and B of the semi-major and semi-minor axes at any stage are $A=k$, $B=k^{-1}$. A

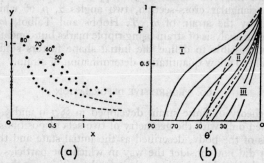

FIG. 83 (a) The movement of lines, initially of unit length and at various angles to Ox, for pure shear, $x'=kx$, $y'=k^{-1}y$. Dots correspond successively to $k=1, 1\cdot2, 1\cdot4, 1\cdot6, \ldots$
(b) The variation of the inclination θ' of a line with the fractional shortening $F=1-k^{-1}$ in the y-direction. I, region of shortening; II, shortening followed by lengthening; III, region of lengthening

point $x=\cos\theta$, $y=\sin\theta$ on a circle of unit radius becomes $x'=k\cos\theta$, $y'=k^{-1}\sin\theta$ on the strain ellipse whose distance r' from the origin is

$$r'^2=k^2\cos^2\theta+k^{-2}\sin^2\theta, \qquad . \qquad . \qquad (2)$$

and whose direction θ' is given by

$$\tan\theta'=y'/x'=k^{-2}\tan\theta. \qquad . \qquad . \qquad (3)$$

(2) and (3) give the movement of marker points under these conditions. The corresponding points for $\theta=90°$, $80°$, $70°$, $60°$,

$50°$ and o, and for regular steps $k=1$, $1\cdot2$, $1\cdot4$, $1\cdot6$, $\ldots$, are shown by the circles in Fig. 83 (*a*). If $\theta=90°$, $\theta'=90°$ and r' decreases steadily. If $90>\theta>45°$, r' falls to a minimum and then increases, so that any lines whose inclinations are in this region are first contracted and subsequently extended: in this region r' as a function of k has a minimum value of $(\sin 2\theta)^{\frac{1}{2}}$ when $\tan \theta=k^2$ so that $\theta'=45°$. If $0<\theta<45°$, r' increases steadily and all lines in this angular region are extended. The fact that the regions of initial contraction and extension are separated by $\theta=45°$ follows from (2) since this gives

$$r'(dr'/dk)=k\cos^2\theta-k^{-3}\sin^2\theta, \qquad . \qquad . \qquad (4)$$

and if $k=1$ this is positive if $\theta<45°$ and negative if $\theta>45°$.

An interesting alternative representation, Fig. 83 (*b*), plots the fractional shortening $1-k^{-1}$ in the *y*-direction against θ' derived from (3). From the previous type of calculation this is found to divide into three regions: I, in which lines are shortened; II, in which lines previously shortened are subsequently lengthened; III, in which lines are lengthened. The boundaries between these are shown by the dotted lines, the boundary between regions II and III is the curve corresponding to $\theta=45°$.

Since from (1)

$$x'y'=xy, \qquad . \qquad . \qquad . \qquad (5)$$

the points of Fig. 83 (*a*) in fact lie on hyperbolae which are shown as broken lines in the figure. These may be compared with the stream lines in viscous flow between parallel planes, Fig. 50, and, in fact, these stream lines, § 40 (16) are approximately hyperbolae in the region $x\ll h$, $y\ll h$, near the origin.

(ii) *Progressive Flattening of a Sphere to an Oblate Spheroid with No Change in Volume*

In this case the transformation is

$$x'=kx, \quad y'=ky, \quad z'=k^{-2}z, \qquad . \qquad . \qquad (6)$$

The point $x=\cos\theta$, $y=0$, $z=\sin\theta$ in a direction inclined at $\frac{1}{2}\pi-\theta$ to the *z*-axis is transformed to $x'=k\cos\theta$, $y'=0$, $z'=k^{-2}\sin\theta$ at distance r' from the origin given by

$$r'^2=k^2\cos^2\theta+k^{-4}\sin^2\theta, . \qquad . \qquad . \qquad (7)$$

so that

$$r'(dr'/dk)=k\cos^2\theta-2k^{-5}\sin^2\theta \qquad . \qquad . \qquad (8)$$

For $k=1$, $(dr'/dk)<0$ if $\tan\theta>2^{-\frac{1}{2}}$ or $90>\theta>35\cdot3°$, so that lines in this cone are initially contracted and subsequently extended. For a given value of θ the minimum value of r' occurs when

$$k^3=2^{\frac{1}{2}}\tan\theta \quad \text{or} \quad \tan\theta'=z'/x'=k^{-3}\tan\theta=2^{-\frac{1}{2}},$$

and this minimum value is $(27/4)^{\frac{1}{2}} \sin^{\frac{1}{2}} \theta \cos^{\frac{3}{2}} \theta$. The paths of the particles in this case are $x'^2 z =$ Constant.

The deformation of a sphere to a prolate spheroid may be treated similarly: in this case lines inclined at angles greater than $\tan^{-1} 2^{\frac{1}{2}} = 54 \cdot 8°$ to the axis of symmetry are initially contracted and subsequently lengthened.

(iii) *Progressive simple shear*

Here by § 7 (4)

$$x' = x + 2sy, \quad y' = y, \qquad . \qquad . \qquad . \qquad (9)$$

and the semi-axes A and B of the strain ellipse are

$$A = (s^2 + 1)^{\frac{1}{2}} + s, \quad B = (s^2 + 1)^{\frac{1}{2}} - s, \qquad . \qquad . \qquad (10)$$

and its major axis makes an angle χ

$$\chi = \tfrac{1}{4}\pi - \tfrac{1}{2}\tan^{-1} s \qquad . \qquad . \qquad . \qquad (11)$$

with Ox, cf. p. 33. The principal quadratic elongations are $\lambda_1 = A^2$, $\lambda_2 = B^2$. Lines $y = x \tan \theta$ are extended if $0 < \theta < 90°$ and are initially shortened and subsequently extended if $90 < \theta < 180°$.

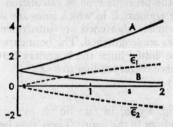

FIG. 84. Progressive simple shear. Variation of A, B, $\bar{\epsilon}_1$ and $\bar{\epsilon}_2$ with s

Suppose, now, that s increases steadily from zero, then (9) shows the way in which the axes of the strain ellipse vary, and their ratio A/B gives a measure of the way in which the shape of the ellipse changes. Alternatively, the logarithmic strains, § 18.(4)

$$\bar{\epsilon}_1 = \ln A = \tfrac{1}{2}\ln \lambda_1, \quad \bar{\epsilon}_2 = \ln B = \tfrac{1}{2}\lambda_2, \qquad . \qquad . \qquad (12)$$

may be studied. These quantities are plotted against s in Fig. 84.

The same results apply to the three-dimensional case $x' = x + 2sz$, $y' = y$, $z' = z$, in which the axes of the strain ellipsoid are A, 1, B.

(iv) *The Representation of the Parameters Specifying Strain*

In two dimensions, strain is specified by the semi-axes $A = \lambda_1^{\frac{1}{2}}$, $B = \lambda_2^{\frac{1}{2}}$ of the strain ellipse and the rotation ω. A and B may be plotted against one another as in Fig. 85 (a). This diagram divides into three regions, OPQ of contraction in which $A < 1$, $B < 1$; SPR of expansion in which $A > 1$, $B > 1$; and $RPQT$ in which $A > 1$, $B < 1$. The hyperbola PT corresponds to the case $AB = 1$ in which areas are unchanged. If rotation, also, is to be considered, a third coordinate axis is needed.

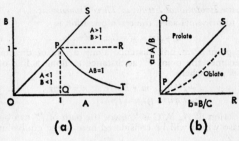

FIG. 85. Representation of the shapes of strain ellipsoids: (a) in two dimensions, (b) in three dimensions

In three dimensions, apart from rotation, three semi-axes $A=\lambda_1^{\frac{1}{2}}$, $B=\lambda_2^{\frac{1}{2}}$, $C=\lambda_3^{\frac{1}{2}}$ have to be represented. The shape of the strain ellipsoid can be specified by the two ratios

$$a=A/B, \quad b=B/C, \quad \quad \quad \quad (13)$$

and in the equivoluminal case in which $ABC=1$, the quantities (13) specify the ellipsoid completely since in this case

$$A=a^{\frac{2}{3}}b^{\frac{1}{3}}, \quad B=a^{-\frac{1}{3}}b^{\frac{1}{3}}, \quad C=a^{-\frac{1}{3}}b^{-\frac{2}{3}}. \quad \quad (14)$$

This case is illustrated in Fig. 85 (b) in which a is plotted against b. The line PS, $a=b$, corresponds to $B=1$. PQ corresponds to a prolate spheroid, $B=C$; and PR to an oblate spheroid $A=B$. The region QPS corresponds to prolate or constriction-type ellipsoids with $A>1>B>C$, and SPQ to oblate or flattening-type ellipsoids with $A>B>1>C$.

Any continuous deformation corresponds to a curve or *deformation path* such as PU in the a, b plane; for example, (6) runs along PR. It should be understood that there is an infinite number of possible deformation paths between a given initial state P and a given final state U: specific assumptions, such as those made above, lead to specific paths. For example, Flinn, *loc. cit.*, defines

$$\kappa=(a-1)/(b-1) \quad \quad \quad \quad (15)$$

and takes deformation paths to be straight lines[1] of constant κ. In this case, taking a as the parameter specifying the strain, (14) becomes

$$A=a^{\frac{2}{3}}[1+(a-1)\kappa^{-1}]^{\frac{1}{3}}, \quad B=a^{-\frac{1}{3}}[1+(a-1)\kappa^{-1}]^{\frac{1}{3}} \atop C=a^{-\frac{1}{3}}[1+(a-1)\kappa^{-1}]^{-\frac{2}{3}}. \quad \bigg\} \quad \quad (16)$$

In (15) and (16), $0\leqslant\kappa<1$ corresponds to a flattening (oblate) deformation; $\kappa=1$ is the case $B=1$; and $1<\kappa<\infty$ corresponds to a prolate (constriction-type) deformation, Fig. 85 (b).

---

[1] This assumption is made because of its mathematical simplicity. D. Flinn in *Controls of Metamorphism* (ed. Pitcher and Flinn, Oliver and Boyd, 1965) and J. G. Ramsay, *Trans. Amer. Geophys. Union*, **45** (1964), 106 remark that the case $\kappa=(\ln a)/(\ln b)$ is probably more meaningful.

(v) *Progressive Irrotational Strain in Three Dimensions*

Referred to principal axes, the transformation is

$$x'=Ax, \quad y'=By, \quad z'=Cz, \qquad \qquad (17)$$

so that the point P at unit distance along a line of direction cosines (l, m, n) becomes the point P' at distance r' along a line of direction cosines (l', m', n') where

$$l'=Al/r', \quad m'=Bm/r', \quad n'=Cn/r', \qquad (18)$$

and

$$r'=(A^2l^2+B^2m^2+C^2n^2)^{\frac{1}{2}} \qquad \qquad (19)$$

If the variation of A, B, C is known, the path of P' can be followed. The only case which will be considered here is the equivoluminal case

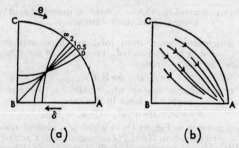

(a)   (b)

FIG. 86. Equivoluminal strain in three dimensions: (a) Regions on the stereographic projection in which lines are all extended (nearest to A) and contracted and subsequently extended (nearest to C). The numbers on the separating lines are values of κ, (b) Changes in direction shown on the stereographic projection of a number of lines as a increases from 1 to 6 for the case $\kappa=1$.

with κ constant in which A, B, C are given by (16) with a as parameter. As in (i) above, lines in some directions are continually extended as deformation proceeds, while lines in other directions are initially contracted and subsequently extended. The boundary between these two regions in the initial state is given by $(dr'/da)_{a=1}=0$, or, using (16) in (19),

$$(2\kappa+1)l^2-(\kappa-1)m^2-(\kappa+2)n^2=0, \qquad (20)$$

which agrees with the results of (ii) for the case $\kappa=0$ and $\kappa=\infty$. Results for other values of κ are conveniently shown on the stereographic projection on the AC plane, Fig. 86 (a).

Changes in length and direction of any line as a increases may be calculated from (18) and (19). As an example, Fig. 86 (b) shows the changes in direction of lines in various initial positions as a increases from 1 to 6 for the case $\kappa=1$. The general movement of the directions towards the direction of maximum extension is very clearly shown. Flinn, *loc. cit.*, discusses problems of this sort in great detail.

(vi) *The General Case*

The examples given above show the way in which parameters such as A and B which specify the strain behave, and the way in which marker lines move, in special cases in which the strain is of a simple specified type and its amount increases steadily. In fact, conditions will be much more complicated and the nature of the strain may change, continuously or discontinuously throughout deformation. At any particular moment of time there will be a completed finite strain and on this an incremental strain will be superimposed. Suppose that the principal axes A, B of the strain ellipse of the finite strain lie along the x- and y-axes and that the incremental strain is the infinitesimal strain § 58 (7). The resultant strain is by § 58 (8).

$$\begin{pmatrix} x' \\ y' \end{pmatrix} = \begin{pmatrix} A(1+\epsilon_1) & B(\tfrac{1}{2}\gamma-\omega) \\ A(\tfrac{1}{2}\gamma+\omega) & B(1+\epsilon_2) \end{pmatrix} \begin{pmatrix} x \\ y \end{pmatrix} \quad . \quad . \quad . \quad (21)$$

It follows from § 7 (28) (29) that the semi-axes A_1, B_1 of the strain ellipse of (21) are

$$A_1 = A(1+\epsilon_1), \quad B_1 = B(1+\epsilon_2), \quad . \quad . \quad . \quad (22)$$

and from § 7 (17) (18) that the angles α, α' specifying the initial and final positions of the principal axes are

$$\alpha = \gamma AB/(A^2-B^2), \quad \alpha' = \omega + \gamma(A^2+B^2)/2(A^2-B^2) \quad . \quad (23)$$

(22) and (23) show the way in which an existing strain is modified by an additional small strain, and if further small strains are progressively superimposed, the parameters describing the strain will vary continuously. Curves describing this variation are called strain paths or deformation paths.

At any stage in the deformation, the strain ellipse for the existing deformation can be divided into regions in which lines have been either lengthened or shortened: these are separated by the directions of zero extension, § 7 (32). Similarly, the strain ellipse for the incremental strain can be divided into regions corresponding to lengthening and shortening. Since the strain ellipse for the incremental strain will not in general coincide with that for the existing finite strain, it should in general be possible to recognize four zones in any state of strain: (i), a zone in which lines, previously shortened, are still contracting; (ii), a zone in which lines, previously shortened, are now being lengthened; (iii), a zone in which lines, previously lengthened are still being lengthened; (iv), a zone in which lines, previously lengthened, are now being shortened. Clearly, even more complicated situations are possible. Fig. 83 illustrates some cases of shortening followed by lengthening. These ideas can be used to explain the occurrence of such diverse structures as ptygmatic folds, boudinage, disrupted folds and folded boudins in a single deformed area; Ramsay, *loc. cit.*, Ramberg, *loc. cit.*

(vii) *A Numerical Example*

To illustrate the effects observed, consider the deformation of an ellipsoidal pebble of semi-axes $X=2$, $Y=1$, $Z=0\cdot5$, embedded in a matrix of the same properties (so that it is a marker ellipsoid in the material).

The applied strain will be taken to consist of pure shear in the xz-plane together with simple extension in the y-direction. This will be assumed to be applied in successive finite increments for each of which $\lambda_1 = 1 \cdot 22$, $\lambda_2 = 1 \cdot 11$, $\lambda_3 = 0 \cdot 82$, or $\bar{\epsilon}_1 = 0 \cdot 1$, $\bar{\epsilon}_2 = 0 \cdot 05$, $\bar{\epsilon}_3 = -0 \cdot 1$. The pebble will be supposed initially to be inclined with its intermediate axis parallel to the y-direction and with its major axis making an angle of $60°$ with the x-direction.

Using § 7 (6), the equation of the pebble in the xz-plane is initially

$$\tfrac{1}{4}(x \cos 60° + z \sin 60°)^2 + 4(-x \sin 60° + z \cos 60°)^2 = 1$$

or

$$3 \cdot 06x^2 - 3 \cdot 25xz + 1 \cdot 19z^2 = 1, \qquad . \qquad . \qquad . \quad (24)$$

which could have been written down from § 59 (3). After the first increment it becomes by § 59 (27)

$$2 \cdot 51x^2 - 3 \cdot 25xz + 1 \cdot 45z^2 = 1 \qquad . \qquad . \qquad . \quad (25)$$

By § 59 (11) the major axis of this is inclined at $\theta = 54°$ to Ox and the new semi-axes are $X = 1 \cdot 92$ and $Z = 0 \cdot 52$, using § 59 (6) (7). An alternative derivation will be given later. The deformation in the y-direction is independent of that in the xz-plane and the new semi-axis of the pebble in this direction after the first increment is $Y = (1 \cdot 11)^{\frac{1}{2}} = 1 \cdot 05$. The effects of subsequent increments may be calculated in the same way and the results are shown in Table I, which gives the changes in the axial lengths and axial ratios of the pebble as well as those of the strain ellipsoid. The direction θ of the major axis of the pebble after each increment is given, together with the direction θ' of the line whose initial position was along the major axis of the pebble; this, of course, does not remain the major axis of the pebble after deformation.

The data in Table VI are plotted in Fig. 87. The table and figure show clearly the effect of the successive increments of strain on the shape of the pebble. During the first two strain increments, the major axis of the pebble is situated in the contracting zone ($\theta < 45°$) of the strain ellipse and its length is reduced by each successive increment. During the third increment, this axis rotates into the zone of extension and subsequently

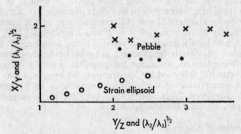

FIG. 87. Strain path, for the strain ellipsoid (circles) and for the pebble (dots) from the data of Table VI. Crosses are the strain path for the pebble with additional rotation as specified in (28)

TABLE VI

Step	X	Y	Z	θ	X/Y	Y/Z	$(\lambda_1/\lambda_2)^{\frac12}$	$(\lambda_2/\lambda_3)^{\frac12}$	$(\lambda_1/\lambda_3)^{\frac12}$	θ'
0	2	1	0·5	60°	2	2	1	1	1	60°
1	1·92	1·05	0·52	54	1·82	2·02	1·05	1·16	1·22	55
2	1·88	1·11	0·53	48	1·70	2·09	1·10	1·35	1·49	49
3	1·89	1·17	0·53	41	1·61	2·21	1·15	1·57	1·82	44
4	1·94	1·23	0·52	34	1·57	2·38	1·21	1·83	2·22	38
5	2·03	1·30	0·49	29	1·56	2·63	1·27	2·13	2·70	33
6	2·15	1·37	0·46	24	1·57	2·94	1·33	2·48	3·30	28

increases steadily, its length being greater than its initial value at the end of the fifth increment. The intermediate axis of the pebble is parallel to the intermediate axis of the strain ellipsoid in which direction the strain is a simple extension and hence the intermediate axis of the pebble increases in length with each increment. The shortest axis of the pebble lies initially in the zone of elongation and its length increases in the first two increments. It then rotates into the zone of contraction and subsequently decreases in length. In Fig. 87, the ratio X/Y for the pebble is plotted against Y/Z in the manner of Fig. 85 (b). The corresponding ratios $(\lambda_1/\lambda_2)^{\frac{1}{2}}$ and $(\lambda_2/\lambda_3)^{\frac{1}{2}}$ for the strain ellipsoid are also plotted. The curves show that initially the pebble follows a strain path markedly different from that of the strain ellipsoid. However, with increasing strain the paths approach each other and the orientation of the pebble moves towards that of the strain ellipsoid.

The preceding calculation was carried out using the elementary methods of § 59. Alternatively, the matrix methods of § 58 might have been used. The initial parameters $X=2$, $Z=0.5$, $\theta=60°$ of the pebble may be regarded as specifying a strain ellipse and by § 58 (29) the transformation matrix for this is

$$\begin{pmatrix} x' \\ y' \end{pmatrix} = \begin{pmatrix} 0.875 & 0.649 \\ 0.649 & 1.625 \end{pmatrix} \begin{pmatrix} x \\ y \end{pmatrix}. \qquad . \qquad . \qquad (26)$$

The first increment of strain gives

$$\begin{pmatrix} x'' \\ y'' \end{pmatrix} = \begin{pmatrix} 1.104 & 0 \\ 0 & 0.906 \end{pmatrix} \begin{pmatrix} 0.875 & 0.649 \\ 0.649 & 1.625 \end{pmatrix} \begin{pmatrix} x \\ y \end{pmatrix}$$

$$= \begin{pmatrix} 0.966 & 0.717 \\ 0.588 & 1.471 \end{pmatrix} \begin{pmatrix} x \\ y \end{pmatrix}. \qquad . \qquad . \qquad . \qquad (27)$$

and, using § 7 (28) (29) (19) the semi-axes and inclination of this are $X=1.92$, $Z=0.52$, $\theta=54°$ as found previously.

This method becomes more convenient as the transformation becomes more complicated; for example, if rotation occurs as it frequently does. Suppose, for example, that each increment consists of a pure strain as specified above together with a clockwise rotation of $20°$. Then, using (27) as in § 58 (30) the transformation corresponding to the first increment is

$$\begin{pmatrix} x'' \\ y'' \end{pmatrix} = \begin{pmatrix} 0.940 & 0.342 \\ -0.342 & 0.940 \end{pmatrix} \begin{pmatrix} 0.966 & 0.717 \\ 0.588 & 1.471 \end{pmatrix} \begin{pmatrix} x \\ y \end{pmatrix}$$

$$= \begin{pmatrix} 1.109 & 1.177 \\ 0.222 & 1.137 \end{pmatrix} \begin{pmatrix} x \\ y \end{pmatrix}, \qquad . \qquad . \qquad . \qquad (28)$$

leading to $X=1.92$, $Z=0.52$, $\theta=34°$. The strain path corresponding to further increments is shown by crosses in Fig. 87.

(viii) *The Methods of Structural Geology*

Structural geology has an approach of its own to the deformation of rocks, which is based on observation and simple deductions from the theory of finite homogeneous strain.

Many rocks contain structures which give an indication of the strains they have undergone. For example, tension cracks form in planes perpendicular to the direction of greatest extension, and, if they are curved, may give an indication of the lack of homogeneity of the strain. Again, slaty cleavage forms in planes perpendicular to the direction of maximum contraction. These observations can be verified from markers in the rocks such as deformed fossils or ooids.

More precise indications of the deformation history of the rock can be obtained if it contains layers of more competent[1] material. If these lie near the direction of the greatest extension, they are pulled apart into fragments (boudinage) and possibly the interstices are filled. If they lie near the direction of maximum shortening, they are crumpled (ptygmatic folding). If, as in (i) and (ii) above, they are first shortened and then lengthened, the folds first formed may be disrupted: if they are first lengthened and subsequently shortened, the boudins first formed may be pushed together or folded. Such effects are greatly dependent on the orientation of the layers and the relative competence of them and the matrix. All these effects may be reproduced in model experiments, cf. Ramberg (*loc. cit.*), also many of them may be produced on actual rocks at high confining pressures, Griggs and Handin,[2] Paterson and Weiss.[3]

These observations are made on strain only and give information about the strain-history of the rock completely independent of its mechanical condition and the stresses operating. Attempts may be made to deduce from them information about the stresses operating or the mechanical properties of the rocks, but these present much greater difficulties.

61. ANALYSIS OF STRAIN IN FOLDING

Here, only the most common type of folding, cylindrical folding, will be considered. Cylindrical folds are generated by parallel lines and so can be represented by their sections by a plane perpendicular to these lines and treated two-dimensionally, Fig. 88. The line through the point H', Fig. 88 (a), at which the curvature of the section is greatest, is called the *hinge line*, and the plane $H'K'$ through this line and the centre of curvature is the *axial plane*. The region near the hinge line H' is called the *hinge zone*, and the regions C', D', Fig. 88 (a), remote from this at which the curvature is least are called the *limbs*.

In the simplest type of folding, parallel marker beds such as AB, CD, Fig. 88 (b), are deformed by inhomogeneous plane strain into the folded form, $A'B'$, $C'D'$. In practice, the nature of the strain may be specified by measuring (i) the distance between

---

[1] In structural geology, competence is used in a qualitative sense to describe the degree of ductility. Thus competent layers are relatively difficult to deform, while incompetent layers deform readily.

[2] D. Griggs and J. Handin, *Geol. Soc. Amer. Mem.*, **79** (1960), 347–64.

[3] M. S. Paterson and L. E. Weiss, *Bull. Geol. Soc. Amer.*, **79** (1968), 795–812.

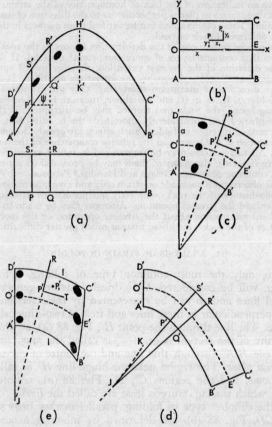

FIG. 88. Basic types of folding of the region *ABCD* shown in (*b*). (*a*) Similar folding; (*c*) simple concentric folding; (*d*) parallel folding; (*e*) simple concentric shear

two surfaces in a direction parallel to the axial plane, or (ii) the distance between the tangents to the surfaces in specified directions, or (iii) by drawing dip isogons which are curves joining points on the surfaces at which the dip is the same, Ramsay, *loc. cit.* However, particularly in the older literature, a great deal of attention has been paid to simple idealized types of folding in which a rectangle *ABCD*, Fig. 88 (*b*), is deformed by inhomogeneous strain into other shapes. Although the strain is inhomogeneous, it is approximately homogeneous in smaller regions and may be represented by strain ellipses in these. The variation in shape and orientation of these strain ellipses gives an indication of the inhomogeneity of the strain. The strain as defined by the initial and final states will be described first: effects of strain paths will be considered later.

(i) *Similar Folding*

In this case, the transformation is

$$y'=y+f(x), \quad x'=x, \qquad . \qquad . \qquad . \qquad (1)$$

where $f(x)$ is any prescribed function. A layer *PS* parallel to *Oy* is displaced by $f(x)$, and a thin rectangle *PQRS* is transformed by simple shear into the parallelogram *P'Q'R'S'*, Fig. 88 (*a*). This simple shear may be written

$$y'=y+2sx, \quad x'=x, \quad \text{where } 2s=\tan \psi=f'(x), \qquad . \qquad (2)$$

and the strain ellipse can be found from § 7 (17)–(29), remembering that x and y are interchanged in the present notation. Fig. 87 (*a*) is drawn for $f(x)=\frac{1}{2}l \sin \pi x/l$, and the variation of the shape and orientation of the strain ellipse along the fold is shown.

Similar folding may be represented by displacement of a pack of cards, and consecutive episodes of similar folding about different axes may be studied by the use of card models (O'Driscoll, *loc. cit.*)

In the present case, all strain ellipses have a direction of no finite elongation ($\lambda=1$) parallel to the y-axis, corresponding to the fact that the distance between two surfaces in the y-direction is unchanged by the strain. This latter effect, which is all that can be observed in the final state, also occurs if the material is subjected to a homogeneous pure strain with principal axes parallel to the x- and y-directions before the inhomogeneous simple shear.

Similar-type folds on all scales occur very frequently. Whether they are formed by the obvious mechanisms of progressive shear or flow across the beds is a matter of argument. Some writers[1]

[1] S. W. Carey, *J. Alberta Soc. Petrol. Geol.*, **10** (1962), 95–144.

suggest that they are. An alternative mechanism is an initial buckling of the layers, of the type described in § 62, followed by a homogeneous pure strain.[1]

(ii) Simple Concentric Folding

A great deal of attention has been paid to models in which a rectangular region $ABCD$, Fig. 88 (b), is deformed in such a way that parallel beds AB, OE, DC, Fig. 88 (b), become arcs of concentric circles. Such structures are very common in nature.

In the simplest deformation of this type, it is assumed that straight lines AD, BC, parallel to the y-axis remain straight lines of unchanged length and that straight lines parallel to Ox become arcs of concentric circles, Fig. 88 (c). If the rectangle $ABCD$, $0 < x < l$, $-a < y < a$ is deformed in this way so that the length $OE = l = O'E'$ is unchanged and $O'E'$ is a circle of radius R, the final configuration is shown in Fig. 88 (c). The line $O'E'$ of unchanged length is called the neutral line. The region $a > y > 0$ undergoes extension and $0 > y > -a$ undergoes contraction. The total area $ABCD = 2al$ is equal to the area $A'B'C'D'$.

The point $P(x,y)$ becomes P' whose polar coordinates r, θ are

$$r = R + y, \quad \theta = x/R. \qquad . \qquad . \qquad (3)$$

The neighbouring point $P_1(x+x_1, y+y_1)$, Fig. 88 (b), becomes P_1' whose polar coordinates are $r_1 = R+y+y_1$, $\theta_1 = (x+x_1)/R$, so that the projections x_1', y_1' of $P'P_1'$ on the tangential and radial directions $P'T$, $P'R$, Fig. 88 (c), are

$$x_1' = (R+y+y_1)x_1/R = x_1(1+y/R), \quad y_1' = y_1, \qquad . \qquad (4)$$

neglecting the small quantity $x_1 y_1$. Thus the parameters § 7 (7) of the strain are

$$a = 1 + y/R, \quad b = 0, \quad c = 0, \quad d = 1. \qquad . \qquad . \qquad (5)$$

It follows from § 7 (28) (29) that the semi-axes of the strain ellipse are $A = (1+y/R)$, $B = 1$ and the principal directions are radial and tangential. These results hold for all values of x. The strain ellipses are shown in Fig. 88 (c).

This geometry is by no means the only simple one which can be postulated. Alternatively, instead of assuming that distances measured in the y-direction are unchanged, it might be assumed that areas are unchanged. Suppose that $y = 0$ is the neutral line whose length is unaltered,

[1] D. Flinn, *loc. cit.*; J. G. Ramsay, *J. Geol.* **70** (1962), 309–27.

then for the area between this line and the line of ordinate y to be unchanged we need

$$ly = \tfrac{1}{2}[(y'+R)^2 - R^2]l/R = \tfrac{1}{2}[y'^2 + 2Ry']l/R,$$

so that

$$y' = (R^2 + 2Ry)^{\frac{1}{2}} - R, \quad . \qquad . \qquad . \qquad . \qquad (6)$$

and this formula holds for both signs of y. The point $P(x, y)$ then becomes P' whose polar coordinates are $(R^2 + 2Ry)^{\frac{1}{2}}$, x/R in place of (3). The neutral line is not now in the middle of the deformed region. Proceeding as before, the axes of the strain ellipse for the point (x, y) are

$$A = (R^2 + 2Ry)^{\frac{1}{2}}/R, \quad B = (R^2 + 2Ry)^{-\frac{1}{2}}R \qquad . \qquad . \qquad (7)$$

Elastic materials show approximately the behaviour described by (5) and perfectly ductile material that described by (7). Clearly, all possible intermediate types of behaviour may be expected, depending on the ductility of the material, Ramsay, *loc. cit.*

During the growth of folds of this type, tensional features such as radial cracks may form on the outer arc and thin competent layers may be boudinaged, cf. § 60 (viii). On the inner arc, compressive features such as crumpling of the layers and conjugate shears may develop: if the material is relatively incompetent, slaty cleavage may develop parallel to the axial plane of the fold. Finally, during the growth of a fold, it is possible for the neutral surface to change its position and so it is possible for early compressive structures to be modified by later elongation and vice versa.

(iii) *Parallel Folding*

Two curves are said to be parallel if the distance between them, measured along a common normal, is constant. The situation is shown in Fig. 88 (*d*). The normal to the curve $A'P'B'$ has also to be a normal to the curve $D'S'C'$ and the distance $S'P'$ is constant and equal to $2a$. The normal $Q'R'$ at a neighbouring point Q' will intersect $P'S'$ in $\mathcal{J}$, the centre of curvature at the point P'. It is assumed that the curvature varies continuously and the locus $K\mathcal{J}$ of the centre of curvature is the evolute of the curve $A'P'B'$. All parallel curves such as $A'P'B'$, $D'S'C'$, are involutes of the curve $K\mathcal{J}$ and they may be constructed and their properties studied from this relationship.[1]

---

[1] H. Lamb, *Infinitesimal Calculus* (Cambridge, 1913). J. B. Mertie, Jr, *Bull. Geol. Soc. Amer.*, **58** (1947), 779–802.

If the rectangle $ABCD$, Fig. 88 (b), is folded to lie between the parallel curves $A'B'C'D'$ of Fig. 88 (d) the previous theory and (3)–(5) still apply to any small region $P'Q'R'S'$ so that the axes of the strain ellipses will be aligned normal and tangential to the curve $A'P'B'$ and their lengths will vary continuously with position according to (5).

Concentric folding as described in (ii) is, of course, a special case of parallel folding, and parallel folds may tend to develop by maintaining a constant curvature at the hinge and increasing the curvature at the limbs so that they become more nearly concentric. The maximum shortening obtainable in this way (corresponding to deformation into a semicircle) is in the ratio $2/\pi$ or 36 per cent.

(iv) Simple Concentric Shear

A completely alternative model to that of (ii) for straining into a circular fold involves tangential shear such as would occur in wrapping a pile of paper around a circular cylinder. Suppose that the region $ABCD$ of Fig. 88 (b) is folded around a circle $A'B'$ of radius $R-a$ in such a way that $A'D'$ remains a radial direction, thicknesses in the radial direction are preserved, and distances along the arcs of all concentric circles are unchanged, Fig. 87 (e). Then the point $P(x, y)$ becomes P' whose polar coordinates are $r=R+y$, $\theta=x/(R+y)$. The neighbouring point $P_1(x+x_1, y+y_1)$ becomes P_1' whose polar coordinates are $R+y+y_1$ and $(x+x_1)/(R+y+y_1)$.

The projections x_1', y_1' of $P'P_1'$ on $P'T$ and $P'R$ are

$$x_1' = \left[\frac{x+x_1}{R+y+y_1} - \frac{x}{R+y}\right](R+y+y_1) = x_1 - xy_1/(R+y), \quad y_1'=y_1 \quad (8)$$

This is a simple shear with

$$\tan\psi = 2s = -x/(R+y) = -\theta, \qquad . \qquad . \qquad (9)$$

where θ, Fig. 88 (e) is the dip of the beds. The value of this varies from zero when $x=0$ to $-l/(R+y)$ when $x=l$. The variation of the strain ellipse with position is shown in Fig. 88 (e). Clearly, the model can be generalized to parallel slip folding in which the region $ABCD$ is wrapped around a curve whose curvature varies continuously.

Geological examples of this type occur very frequently: if the shear is uniformly distributed over the cross-section, as above, they are described as flexural flow folds, Ramsay, *loc. cit.* However, in many cases the shear is inhomogeneously distributed, being much greater near the boundaries of the region and such folds are known as flexural slip folds.[1]

(v) More General Cases

It is clear that natural folds as well as many sketched as illustrations in textbooks do not conform to those simple types and show mismatches in either geometry or the strain parameters. The simplest example of this is a sudden change of curvature in parallel folding at which a sudden change in the parameters of the strain ellipse will occur. These more general cases may be handled by postulating more general types of strain which are essentially combinations of the basic types discussed above.

62. INSTABILITY THEORY: FOLDING AND KINKING

A number of problems arise in which a long thin sheet or fibre is stressed in the direction of its length. Taking $x=0$ as the direction of the sheet and stress, the undeflected state $x=0$ is always a possible state, but if it is disturbed slightly this disturbance may grow so that the solution $x=0$ becomes unstable. Examples of this are the buckling of plates and columns in engineering theory and folding and kinking in structural geology.

Folding

The simplest case of instability related to folding follows by an extension of the theory of bending of beams given in § 36.

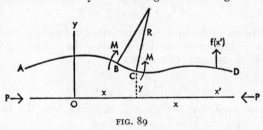

FIG. 89

[1] F. A. Donath, *Trans. N.Y. Acad. Sci.* (2), **24** (1962), 236–49.

Suppose that a long sheet, of unit length perpendicular to the plane of the paper and thickness $2b$, which was initially straight and along the x-axis is deflected into the position $ABCD$ of Fig. 89. If R is the radius of curvature of the small element BC at x, y, and M is the couple applied to it by the rest of the beam, it follows from § 36 (30) that $R=EI/M$, where $I=2b^3/3$ is a constant determined by the cross-section of the sheet and known as the moment of inertia of the cross-section. If the slope dy/dx of the sheet is small, the radius of curvature is given by

$$\frac{1}{R}=\frac{d^2y}{dx^2}=\frac{M}{EI}. \qquad . \qquad . \qquad (1)$$

This is a differential equation for the deflection of the sheet which can be solved if M is known. M can be found by taking moments about C. If there are forces $f(x')$ at x' in the direction Oy, the contribution M_1 of these to the value of M at x is

$$M_1 = \int_x^\infty f(x')(x'-x)\,dx', \qquad . \qquad . \qquad (2)$$

so that

$$\frac{dM_1}{dx}=-\int_x^\infty f(x')\,dx', \qquad \frac{d^2M_1}{dx^2}=f(x). \qquad . \qquad . \qquad (3)$$

The moment about C of the axial force P along Ox is just $-Py$. Thus (1) gives

$$EI\frac{d^2y}{dx^2}=M_1-Py, \qquad . \qquad . \qquad . \qquad (4)$$

or, using (3),

$$EI\frac{d^4y}{dx^4}+P\frac{d^2y}{dx^2}-f(x)=0. \qquad . \qquad . \qquad (5)$$

Now suppose that the sheet is immersed in a viscous fluid which provides resistance to motion η times the velocity $\dot{y}$ so that $f(x)$ is (5) is $-\eta\dot{y}$ and (5) becomes

$$\eta\frac{dy}{dt}+P\frac{d^2y}{dx^2}+EI\frac{d^4y}{dx^4}=0. \qquad . \qquad . \qquad (6)$$

Suppose now that the sheet is deflected into the harmonic form of amplitude Y and wave length λ,

$$y=Y\sin(2\pi x/\lambda). \qquad . \qquad . \qquad (7)$$

Substituting (7) in (6) gives

$$\eta\frac{dY}{dt}=\frac{4\pi^2}{\lambda^2}\left\{P-\frac{4\pi^2EI}{\lambda^2}\right\}Y. \qquad . \qquad . \qquad . \qquad (8)$$

The solution of this is

$$Y=Y_0\exp\left\{\frac{4\pi^2}{\lambda^2\eta}\left(P-\frac{4\pi^2EI}{\lambda^2}\right)t\right\}, \qquad . \qquad . \qquad (9)$$

where Y_0 is the value of Y when $t=0$, that is, the amplitude of the initial disturbance. If $P<4\pi^2EI/\lambda^2$, Y dies away exponentially; but if $P>4\pi^2EI/\lambda^2$ the system is unstable, and Y increases exponentially. The rate of increase is a maximum if

$$\frac{d}{d\lambda}\left\{\frac{P}{\lambda^2}-\frac{4\pi^2EI}{\lambda^4}\right\}=0,$$

that is if $\lambda=2\pi(2EI/P)^{\frac{1}{2}}$. This is called the *dominant wave length*, and if the initial deflection consists of a sum of terms of type (7), those of the dominant wave length will increase most rapidly and thus determine the final shape of the sheet.

This elementary theory was given by Biot[1] and corresponds approximately to the case of a layer of competent rock in viscous material. He also considers the case of a plane sheet of viscous material of thickness h and viscosity η immersed in a viscous material of viscosity η_1. In this case, the dominant wave length is found to be

$$\lambda=2\pi h(\eta/6\eta_1)^{\frac{1}{3}}. \qquad . \qquad . \qquad . \qquad (10)$$

This theory applies only to the case $\eta/\eta_1\gg1$, as may be seen from the fact that (10) gives a definite value of $\lambda/h=3\cdot46$ for the case of no contrast in viscosity, $\eta=\eta_1$, when no folding would be expected. The theory has been verified experimentally by Biot, Ode and Roever.[2]

It is clear that on the theory leading to (10) the dominant wave length is directly proportional to the thickness of the folded layer. This relationship is easily recognized in natural fold systems, and Currie, Patnode and Trump[3] have shown that it holds for folds ranging in wave length from one inch to nearly one hundred thousand feet. Fig. 90 shows their results. From this graph, it is found that the average ratio of wave length to thickness for the folds is $\lambda/h=27$. Currie *et al.* derive an equation very similar to Biot's for the buckling of one elastic layer embedded in a less

[1] M. A. Biot, *Bull. Geol. Soc. Amer.*, **72** (1961), 1595.
[2] M. A. Biot, H. Odé and W. J. Roever, *ibid.*, **72** (1961), 1621.
[3] J. B. Currie, H. W. Patnode and R. P. Trump, *ibid.*, **73** (1962), 655.

competent, but still elastic, medium and the observed value for λ/h suggests that the ratio of these elastic moduli is about $500:1$ during folding. This result is similar to Biot's conclusion that for well-defined folding to develop by viscous buckling, the viscosity ratio should lie in the range $100 < \eta/\eta_1 < 1,000$.

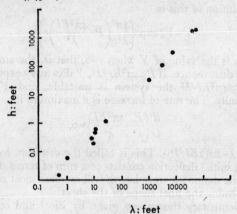

FIG. 90. Variation of dominant wave length λ with thickness h of beds for natural folds on all scales

For values of $\eta/\eta_1 < 100$ the amplitude of folds generated by buckling is very small until a significant amount of shortening of the layer by homogeneous compressive strain has occurred. Ramberg[1] has discussed in detail the effect of layer shortening by simultaneous buckling and homogeneous strain. He derived the following equation which relates the rate of buckling to the rate of layer shortening:

$$\dot\lambda/\lambda = (4/3)\pi^2[6(\eta/\eta_1)^2]^{\frac{1}{3}}(A/\lambda)^2\dot\epsilon, \quad . \quad . \quad . \quad (11)$$

where $\dot\epsilon$ is the rate of strain in layer shortening, $\dot\lambda$ is the rate of change of wave length (that is, the rate of shortening by buckling) and A is the amplitude of the fold at a particular time. From this equation it follows that the rate of shortening by buckling relative to the rate of layer shortening increases with η/η_1 and also as the amplitude of the fold grows. Thus in a rock made up of layers of varying competence, the least competent materials will deform mainly by homogeneous strain while the more competent layers will buckle.

Sherwin and Chapple[2] recently measured several hundred folded quartz veins in slate and phyllite to test Biot's equation and found that

[1] H. Ramberg, *Tectonophysics*, **1** (1964), 307–41.
[2] Jo-Ann Sherwin and W. M. Chapple, *Amer. J. Sci.*, **266** (1968), 167–79.

the mean values of λ/h fell in the range $4\cdot0-6\cdot8$, indicating very small viscosity ratios in the range $2<\eta/\eta_1<8$. They therefore modified Biot's theory to allow for uniform layer shortening accompanying the folding and found for the dominant wave length

$$\lambda=\pi h[2\eta(T+1)/3\eta_1 T^2]^{\frac{1}{3}}, \quad . \quad . \quad . \quad . \quad (12)$$

where T is the final value of the quadratic elongation associated with the shortening. Applying this modified theory to the measured folds gave viscosity ratios in the range $14<\eta/\eta_1<30$ and values of T in the range $2\cdot7<T<5\cdot7$.

Recently, Biot[1] has extended his analysis to the internal buckling of a multilayered medium consisting of alternate layers of competent and incompetent material of viscosities η_1 and η_2. If η_1/η_2 is large, he finds for the dominant wave length

$$\lambda=1\cdot66h(H/h)^{\frac{1}{2}}(\eta_1/\eta_2)^{\frac{1}{4}}, \quad . \quad . \quad . \quad . \quad (13)$$

where h is the thickness of the individual competent layers and H is the total thickness of the material. For smaller values of η_1/η_2 the result tends to

$$\lambda=1\cdot90(hH)^{\frac{1}{2}}. \quad . \quad . \quad . \quad . \quad . \quad (14)$$

Kinking

In its simplest form this is a mode of instability failure of fibrous materials such as wood, and of strongly laminated rocks, in which axial load causes initially straight fibres to be deformed into the ramp shape $ABCD$ of Fig. 91. The deformation occurs

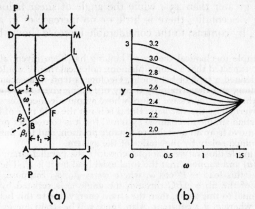

FIG. 91. (a) Geometry of kinking; (b) the function $y=\omega^2+a\cos\omega$. Numbers on the curves are values of a

[1] M. A. Biot, *Bull. Geol. Soc. Amer.*, **75** (1964), 563-8.

sharply at the edges of a parallelogram $BCLK$ known as a kink band. Such a kink band requires three parameters to specify it, namely the angles β_1, β_2 and the length $BC=l$, Fig. 91 (a).

The morphology of kink bands has been extensively studied on both natural and artificially deformed rocks.[1] Observed values of β_1 and β_2 vary widely, but their mean values are both between $55°$ and $65°$ with β_1 usually less than β_2. The normal thicknesses t_2 of the kink band and t_1 of the undisturbed fibres are related by

$$t_1 \operatorname{cosec} \beta_1 = BF = t_2 \operatorname{cosec} \beta_2 \qquad . \qquad . \quad (15)$$

so that there will be a dilatation

$$\Delta = (t_2 - t_1)/t_1 = \sin \beta_2 \operatorname{cosec} \beta_1 - 1 \qquad . \qquad . \quad (16)$$

which is positive if $\beta_2 > \beta_1$ as is usually the case. In natural kinks, open fissures formed during this dilatation are frequently filled with segregation veins. If $\beta_1 = \beta_2$ the transformation of the parallelogram $BCGF$ from its initial state to its final state is one of simple shear although the deformation path may be very different.

Wood commonly fails by kinking and its behaviour in the triaxial test is of a completely different type to that of rocks as described in §§ 20, 21. Firstly, the angle β_1 of failure in the kink band is greater than $45°$, while the angle of shear failure is less than $45°$. Secondly, there is little or no increase of σ_1 at failure with σ_3, by contrast to the considerable increase shown by rocks.

No simple mechanical theory of kinking has been given, although it might be expected that a simple phenomenological theory would exist for so well defined a type of behaviour. Geologists tend to associate kinking with folding, and the instability theory of folding given above essentially regards this as a progressive failure whose amplitude increases steadily at a rate governed by the viscosity. But this is not the only type of behaviour open to such simple mechanical systems: for it is sometimes possible for them to move from an unstable to a stable position, and this final position is determined solely by the statics of the system.

As a simple illustrative example, consider the parallelogram $BFGC$ of Fig. 91 (a) and suppose that the total axial load on it is P. The potential energy of this load is $Pl \cos \omega$, where $\omega = \pi - \beta_1 - \beta_2$. Suppose, also, that bending of the fibre ABC through the angle ω is resisted by a couple proportional to this angle, then the strain energy due to this bending will be $k_1 \omega^2$, where k_1 is a constant. Also, there will be strain energy of distortion of the parallelogram $CGFB$; this would be difficult to estimate

[1] T. B. Anderson, Nature, 202 (1964), 272–4. M. S. Paterson and L. E. Weiss, Bull. Geol. Soc. Amer., 77 (1966), 343–74.

because it undergoes a complicated finite strain, but for simplicity suppose that the strain energy is proportional to the square of the displacement of C from its initial position resolved in the direction BFK as it would be in the case of infinitesimal strain. This component of strain energy would then be

$$k_2 l^2 [\cos \beta_1 + \cos \beta_2]^2 = 4 k_2 l^2 \cos^2 \tfrac{1}{2}(\beta_1 + \beta_2) \cos^2 \tfrac{1}{2}(\beta_1 - \beta_2), \quad . \quad (17)$$

where k_2 is a constant.

The total potential energy V is given by

$$V = Pl \cos \omega + k_1 \omega^2 + 4 k_2 l^2 \sin^2 \tfrac{1}{2}\omega \sin^2 (\beta_1 + \tfrac{1}{2}\omega) \quad . \quad . \quad (18)$$

For equilibrium it is necessary that

$$\partial V / \partial \omega = 0 = \partial V / \partial \beta_1, \quad . \quad . \quad . \quad (19)$$

and the second of these gives $\omega = 0$ or

$$\sin (2\beta_1 + \omega) = 0. \quad . \quad . \quad . \quad (20)$$

That is,

$$\omega = \pi - 2\beta_1 \quad . \quad . \quad . \quad . \quad (21)$$

or $\beta_2 = \beta_1$ which is, approximately, the relation observed in practice. With this value of β_1, (18) becomes

$$V = Pl \cos \omega + k_1 \omega^2 + 4 k_2 l^2 \sin^2 \tfrac{1}{2}\omega$$

$$= (Pl - 2 k_2 l^2) \cos \omega + 2 k_2 l^2 + k_1 \omega^2 \quad . \quad . \quad (22)$$

$$= [a \cos \omega + \omega^2 + b] k_1, \quad . \quad . \quad . \quad (23)$$

where $a = (Pl - 2 k_2 l^2)/k_1$ and $b = 2 k_2 l^2 / k$.

For the system to be in stable equilibrium, the value of V given by (23) must be a minimum. Fig. 91 (b) shows its behaviour for the relevant values of a. If $a < 2$, V has a minimum at $\omega = 0$ so that the undeflected position is stable. If $2 < a < \pi$, V has a maximum at $\omega = 0$ so that this position is unstable, and it has a minimum at some value of ω between 0 and $\pi/2$ giving a stable inclined position. If $a \geqslant \pi$ there is no stable position. It appears then, that for small values of P the straight position is stable: if P is increased sufficiently this becomes unstable and a kinked position becomes stable. It should be emphasized that this discussion is illustrative only.

Both in the field and laboratory experiments,[1] further deformation involves the production of additional, intersecting kink bands and it is an open question whether some types of fold are produced by the buckling mechanism described earlier or by progressive development of kink bands.

63. DEVELOPMENT OF PREFERRED ORIENTATIONS OF ELLIPSOIDAL PARTICLES

Particles which are immersed in a matrix of viscous fluid generally change their position, and, if they are not rigid, their shape, during

---

[1] Paterson and Weiss, *loc. cit.* L. E. Weiss, *Geol. Survey Canada* (in press, 1968).

deformation of the particle-fluid system. These changes in position and shape can be related to, and used to determine, the total finite strain experienced by the system. Moreover, with increasing deformation, the particles tend to move to stable positions, and, in this way, preferred orientations of the particles are set up. The development of preferred orientations under stress during metamorphism is of great geological interest. The motion of small particles in a viscous fluid has been extensively studied in physics, biology and rheology. Much of this work is based on a fundamental paper by Jeffery,[1] who considers the slow motion of a small, rigid ellipsoidal particle of semi-axes A, B, C immersed in fluid of viscosity η.

Let x, y, z be rectangular axes, chosen along the principal axes of the ellipsoid and moving with it, so that its equation is

$$x^2/A^2+y^2/B^2+z^2/C^2=1. \qquad . \qquad . \qquad (1)$$

Let $\dot{u}$, $\dot{v}$, $\dot{w}$ be the components of velocity in the undisturbed motion of the fluid in the neighbourhood of the particle referred to the x, y, z-axes so that as in § 11 (7)–(9)

$$\left.\begin{aligned} \dot{u}&=ax+hy+gz+qz-ry \\ \dot{v}&=hx+by+fz+rx-pz \\ \dot{w}&=gx+fy+cz+py-qx \end{aligned}\right\}, \qquad . \qquad . \qquad (2)$$

where, for shortness, a, b, c, f, g, h are written for the components of rate of strain, and p, q, r for the components of rate of rotation, in the fluid motion. The Navier–Stokes equations for slow viscous motion (the equivalent of § 40 (2), (3) in three dimensions) are

$$\eta\Delta^2\dot{u}=\partial p/\partial x, \quad \eta\nabla^2\dot{v}=\partial p/\partial y, \quad \eta\nabla^2\dot{w}=\partial p/\partial z, \qquad . \qquad (3)$$

together with the equation of continuity § 19 (14).

Now suppose that the angular velocities of the ellipsoid about the x, y, z-axes are ω_1, ω_2, ω_3, then we have to find a solution of (3) which tends to (2) at large distances and is such that there is no slip at the surface of the particle, that is, that the boundary conditions there are

$$\dot{u}=\omega_2 z-\omega_3 y, \quad \dot{v}=\omega_3 x-\omega_1 z, \quad \dot{w}=\omega_1 y-\omega_2 x. \qquad . \qquad (4)$$

When this solution has been found, the resultant couple on the particle due to the fluid can be calculated, and the condition that this should be zero gives the equations of motion of the particle. Jeffery (*loc. cit.*) carries out this calculation and finds the equations of motion to be

$$\left.\begin{aligned} (B^2+C^2)\omega_1&=B^2(p+f)+C^2(p-f) \\ (C^2+A^2)\omega_2&=C^2(q+g)+A^2(q-g) \\ (A^2+B^2)\omega_3&=A^2(r+h)+B^2(r-h) \end{aligned}\right\}. \qquad . \qquad (5)$$

These equations are referred to x, y, z-axes which move with the particle, and to specify the undisturbed motion of the fluid a new set of axes x', y', z', fixed in space, is needed. Let the direction cosines of the x, y, z-axes relative to the x', y', z' system be (l_1, m_1, n_1), (l_2, m_2, n_2), (l_3, m_3, n_3), respectively. The transformation between the two sets of axes is § 58 (31), namely

$$x=l_1 x'+m_1 y'+n_1 z', \quad x'=l_1 x+l_2 y+l_3 z, \text{ etc.}, \qquad . \qquad (6)$$

and velocities transform according to the same law.

---

[1] G. B. Jeffery, *Proc. Roy. Soc.*, A, **102** (1922), 161–79.

Equations (5) may now be solved in simple special cases. Jeffery (*loc. cit.*) considers the case of simple shear in the $y'z'$ plane for which

$$u'=0, \quad v'=0, \quad w'=\dot{\gamma}y', \qquad \qquad (7)$$

where $\dot{\gamma}$ is the rate of shear. Using (6) for velocities gives

$$\begin{aligned} \dot{u} &= l_1 u' + m_1 v' + n_1 w' \\ &= \dot{\gamma} n_1 y' \\ &= \dot{\gamma} n_1 (m_1 x + m_2 y + m_3 z), \qquad \qquad (8) \end{aligned}$$

using (7) and (6). Comparing coefficients between (8) and (2) gives

$$a = \dot{\gamma} m_1 n_1, \quad (h-r) = \dot{\gamma} n_1 m_2, \quad (g+q) = \dot{\gamma} n_1 m_3 \qquad (9)$$

Similarly, from the equations for $\dot{\omega}$ and $\dot{w}$,

$$(h+r) = \dot{\gamma} m_1 n_2, \quad b = \dot{\gamma} m_2 n_2, \quad f-p = \dot{\gamma} n_2 m_3, \qquad (10)$$

$$(g-q) = \dot{\gamma} m_1 n_3, \quad f+p = \dot{\gamma} m_2 n_3, \quad c = \dot{\gamma} m_3 n_3 \qquad (11)$$

Using the values (9)–(11) in (5) gives for the equations of motion of the particle corresponding to simple shear motion of the fluid

$$(B^2+C^2)\omega_1 = \dot{\gamma}(B^2 m_2 n_3 - C^2 n_2 m_3), \qquad \qquad (12)$$

$$(C^2+A^2)\omega_2 = \dot{\gamma}(C^2 n_1 m_3 - A^2 m_1 n_3), \qquad \qquad (13)$$

$$(A^2+B^2)\omega_3 = \dot{\gamma}(A^2 m_1 n_2 - B^2 n_1 m_2). \qquad \qquad (14)$$

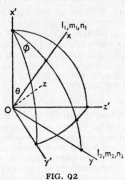

FIG. 92

These equations can easily be integrated for the case of an ellipsoid of revolution, $B=C$. In this case, the position of the ellipsoid can be specified by the Eulerian angles θ, ϕ of its axis of symmetry, where θ is the angle $x'Ox$ and ϕ is the angle between the planes $x'Oy'$ and $x'Ox$, Fig. 92. Oy is chosen in the plane $x'Ox$. The direction cosines of the axes $Oxyz$ are seen to be

$$l_1 = \cos\theta, \quad m_1 = \sin\theta\cos\phi, \quad n_1 = \sin\theta\sin\phi, \qquad (15)$$

$$l_2 = -\sin\theta, \quad m_2 = \cos\theta\cos\phi, \quad n_2 = \cos\theta\sin\phi, \qquad (16)$$

$$l_3 = 0, \quad m_3 = -\sin\phi, \quad n_3 = \cos\phi. \qquad \qquad (17)$$

Also, the angular velocities required are

$$\omega_2 = -\dot{\phi} \sin \theta, \quad \omega_3 = \dot{\theta}. \qquad . \qquad . \qquad . \qquad (18)$$

Using (15)–(18) in (13) and (14) gives

$$(A^2 + C^2)\dot{\phi} = \dot{\gamma}(A^2 \cos^2 \phi + C^2 \sin^2 \phi), \qquad . \qquad (19)$$

$$(A^2 + C^2)\dot{\theta} = \tfrac{1}{4}\dot{\gamma}(A^2 - C^2) \sin 2\theta \sin 2\phi. \qquad . \qquad (20)$$

Integrating (19) gives

$$\tan \phi = (A/C) \tan [\gamma AC/(A^2 + C^2)] \qquad . \qquad . \qquad (21)$$

for the case in which $\phi = 0$ when $\gamma = 0$. Also dividing (19) by (20) and integrating gives

$$(A^2 \cos^2 \phi + C^2 \sin^2 \phi) \tan^2 \theta = k^2 A^2 C^2, \qquad . \qquad (22)$$

where k is a constant. Thus the axis of symmetry of the particle describes a cone about the x'-axis (which is normal to the $y'z'$-plane of deformation) and the angle of this cone varies from $\tan^{-1}(kC)$ when $\phi = 0$ to $\tan^{-1}(kA)$ when $\phi = \tfrac{1}{2}\pi$.

The above theory applies to both prolate and oblate ellipsoids. In the latter case, $A < C$, if e is the eccentricity so that $e^2 = (C^2 - A^2)/C^2$, (22) may be written

$$(1 - e^2 \cos^2 \phi) \tan^2 \theta = \tan^2 \theta_i, \qquad . \qquad . \qquad (23)$$

where θ_i is the value of θ when $\phi = \tfrac{1}{2}\pi$. This shows that the angle θ between the axis of symmetry and the normal to the $y'z'$ plane of deformation oscillates between a minimum value of θ_i and a maximum when $\phi = 0$. This maximum increases towards $\tfrac{1}{2}\pi$ as the eccentricity e increases towards 1, that is, the ellipsoid tends to set itself parallel to the planes of shearing.

Gay[1] has developed similar theory for the case of pure shear in the $x'y'$-plane so that (7) is replaced by

$$\dot{u}' = \dot{\epsilon}x', \quad \dot{v}' = -\dot{\epsilon}y', \quad \dot{w}' = 0, \qquad . \qquad . \qquad (24)$$

where $\dot{\epsilon}$ is the rate of natural strain. He shows that any ellipsoid oriented with its axes aligned parallel to any of the strain axes will retain this orientation throughout the deformation. However, for inclined positions, the axis of a prolate ellipsoid will rotate towards the direction of maximum elongation and the axis of an oblate ellipsoid will rotate towards the direction of maximum shortening, these rates of rotation increasing with increasing eccentricity of the elliptic cross-section.

The theory given above applies only to rigid particles immersed in a viscous fluid. If the particles are not rigid, they experience both a rigid-body rotation and a change of shape during the deformation of the fluid. Several workers[2] have discussed the behaviour of small, initially spherical, viscous particles immersed in a viscous fluid during pure

[1] N. C. Gay, *Tectonophysics*, **5** (1968), 81–8.

[2] G. I. Taylor, *Proc. Roy. Soc.*, A, **138** (1932), 41–8; **146** (1934), 501–23; W. Bartok and S. G. Mason, *J. Colloid Sci.*, **13** (1958), 293–307; F. D. Rumscheidt and S. G. Mason, *J. Colloid Sci.*, **16** (1961), 210–37; R. Cerf, *J. Chim. Phys.*, **49** (1951), 59–105.

shear and simple shear, and recently Gay[1] has analysed, numerically, the behaviour of two-dimensional circular and elliptical particles in a viscous fluid during shear deformation of the fluid. During a pure shear deformation, a particle initially inclined with its major axis at an angle ψ of less than $45°$ to the direction of shortening becomes less eccentric in shape and rotates towards the direction of elongation. However, once the particle has passed through the angle $\psi = 45°$ it enters the field of elongation and becomes more eccentric as its major axis moves towards the direction of maximum elongation. The rate of rotation and change in shape decrease rapidly with increasing viscosity contrast between the particle and the surrounding fluid. During simple shear, an elliptical particle both deforms and rotates towards the shearing direction. The rate of change of shape of the particle as its major axis rotates towards the shearing direction depends greatly on the ratio of the viscosities of the particle and fluid, being high for a low viscosity ratio and small for a high ratio.

This single-particle theory may be extended to cover the development of preferred orientations in multi-particle systems by the use of statistical considerations. Thus in pure shear of a multi-particle system, particles will tend to lie with their major axes oriented parallel to the direction of maximum elongation in the deformation plane. For simple shear, all particles again tend towards the deformation plane.

[1] N. C. Gay, *Tectonophysics*, **5** (1968), 211–34. Two-dimensional effects may conveniently be illustrated by model experiments, E. S. O'Driscoll, *Nature*, **203** (1964), 832–5.

NOTATION

SOME symbols which are frequently used are listed below, together with the pages on which they are defined.

A, B, C	semi-axes of strain ellipsoid, 34	
E	Young's Modulus, 57	
e_x, etc.	Strain deviation, 90	
G	Modulus of rigidity, 56	
g	Acceleration of gravity	
$I_1, I_2, \ldots$	Invariants of stress, 14	
$\mathcal{J}_1, \mathcal{J}_2, \ldots$	Invariants of stress deviation, 92	
K	Bulk modulus, 56	
l, m, n	Direction cosines, 11	
s_x, etc.	Stress deviation, 90	
S_0	Shear strength, 76	
T_0	Tensile strength, 77, 85	
u, v, w	Displacements, 45	
X, Y, Z	Body forces, 115	
γ	Shear strain, 22	
γ_{yz}, etc.	Shear strain components, 46	
Δ	Dilatation, 47	
ϵ_x, etc.	Normal strain components, 46	
$\epsilon_1, \epsilon_2, \epsilon_3$	Principal strains, 47	
η	Viscosity, 71	
λ, G	Lamé's parameters, 56	
λ	Quadratic elongation, 30, 224	
$\lambda_1, \lambda_2, \lambda_3$	Principal quadratic elongations, 35, 224	
λ'	Reciprocal quadratic elongation 37, 225	
$\lambda_1', \lambda_2', \lambda_3'$	Principal reciprocal quadratic elongations, 37, 225	
$\gamma' = \lambda'\gamma$	37, 225	
μ	Coefficient of internal friction, 76, 160	
ν	Poisson's ratio, 57	
ρ	Density, 116	
σ_x, etc.	Normal stress components, 3, 150	
$\sigma_1 > \sigma_2 > \sigma_3$	Principal stresses, 13, 151	
τ_{yz}, etc.	Shear stress components, 3	
$\phi = \tan^{-1}\mu$	Angle of (internal) friction, 83, 160	
ω_z, etc.	Components of rotation, 46	

NOTE: Stresses and strains are reckoned positive when **compressive** in Chapter IV and when tensile in the other chapters.

AUTHOR INDEX

263

SUBJECT INDEX

265